19,80

8 €

Wirtschaftsenglisch
Grund- und Aufbauwortschatz

von Erich Weis und Eva Haberfellner

Ernst Klett Stuttgart

1. Auflage   1 ⁴ 3 2 1 | 1979 78 77 76

Die letzte Zahl bezeichnet das Jahr dieses Druckes.
© Ernst Klett Verlag, Stuttgart 1976. Alle Rechte vorbehalten.
Druck: Ernst Klett, 7 Stuttgart, Rotebühlstraße 77.
Printed in Germany.
ISBN 3-12-518600-5

Inhalt

Vorwort	5
Abkürzungen	7
Grundwortschatz	9
Aufbauwortschatz	116

I. Retail and Wholesale Trade — Einzel- und Großhandel
1. Retail Trade — Einzelhandel ... 116
2. Large-scale Trading — Einzelhandel im großen ... 120
3. Wholesale Trade — Großhandel ... 122

II. Import and Export Trade — Einfuhr- und Ausfuhrhandel
1. Import Trade — Einfuhrhandel ... 123
2. Export Trade — Ausfuhrhandel ... 125

III. Markets, Fairs and Exhibitions — Märkte, Messen und Ausstellungen
1. Markets — Märkte ... 127
2. Fairs and Exhibitions — Messen und Ausstellungen ... 128

IV. Commercial Practice — Kaufmännische Praxis
1. Business Correspondence — Handelskorrespondenz ... 130
2. Sales Contract — Kaufvertrag ... 133
3. Invoicing and Payment — Fakturierung und Bezahlung ... 134
4. Packing and Delivery — Verpackung und Lieferung ... 137
5. Complaints and Adjustments, Apologies — Beschwerden und deren Erledigung, Entschuldigungen ... 140

V. Banking — Bankwesen
1. General Terms — Allgemeine Begriffe ... 142
2. Merchant Bank — Merchantbank ... 144
3. The Bank of England — Die Bank von England ... 145
4. Discount Market — Diskontmarkt ... 147
5. Accounts — Konten ... 148
6. Cheque — Scheck ... 150
7. Bill of Exchange (B/E) — Wechsel ... 152

VI. Stock Exchange — Börse
1. General Terms — Allgemeine Begriffe ... 155
2. Persons Involved — Beteiligte ... 156
3. Types of Securities — Effektenarten ... 156

VII. Insurance — Versicherungswesen
1. General Terms — Allgemeine Begriffe 160
2. Persons Involved — Beteiligte 160
3. Documents — Dokumente 161
4. Types of Insurance — Versicherungsarten 161

VIII. Customs — Zollwesen
1. Tariffs and Duties — Zölle und Abgaben 164
2. Types of Tariffs — Zollarten 165

IX. Transport — Transportwesen
1. General Terms — Allgemeine Begriffe 168
2. Motor Transport — Kraftfahrzeugverkehr 170
3. Rail Transport — Eisenbahnverkehr 173
4. Air Transport — Luftverkehr 178
5. Water Transport — Transport zu Wasser 184
6. Other Means of Transport — Andere Transportmittel ... 191

X. Business Enterprise — Unternehmen
1. General Terms — Allgemeine Begriffe 191
2. Partnerships — Personengesellschaften ... 192
3. Companies and Corporations — Kapitalgesellschaften 193
4. Business Combinations — Unternehmenszusammenschlüsse 195
5. Management — Betriebs-, Geschäftsführung 195
6. Financing — Finanzierung, Kapitalbeschaffung 196

XI. Advertising — Werbung

XII. Communications — Nachrichtenverkehr
1. Postal Service — Postdienst 206
2. Postal Cheque/*Am* Check Office — Postscheckamt 212
3. Mass Communication Media — Massenkommunikationsmittel 215

Englisches Register zum Aufbauwortschatz 226

Deutsches Register zum Aufbauwortschatz 259

Vorwort

In der Spracherlernung hat die Wortschatzarbeit selbst im Zeichen der Linguistik noch keineswegs den ihr zukommenden Platz gefunden. Diese Feststellung gilt auch für die Forschung. Das ist umso verwunderlicher als der Umfang des Wortschatzes einer Sprache und die Vielfalt der Wortinhalte den Umfang ihrer Grammatik bei weitem übertrifft.

Wörterbücher und Wortzusammenstellungen sind keine Friedhöfe, in denen sich durch eine scheinbare Ordnung – das Alphabet – Ungeordnetes sammelt. Denken und sprachlicher Kode sind durch einen dynamischen Prozeß aufs engste miteinander verbunden. Die Vorstellung, bei der Spracherlernung genüge es, eine mehr oder weniger große Anzahl Wörter wie Baukastenelemente zusammenzustellen und sie entsprechend der Struktur der Sprache miteinander zu verbinden, ist ein Irrtum und führt zu Mißverständnissen. Wörter haben ihren eigenen Stellenwert und sind keineswegs geneigt, sich in jede beliebige Umgebung einzupassen. Nur dem Dichter steht es zu, von einem »klirrenden Gedicht« zu reden. Die Wortwahl im Rahmen eines sprachlichen Systems ist das Ergebnis eines schöpferischen, auf Erkenntnis gerichteten Aktes.

Das allein dürfte genügen, sich mit dem Wortschatz einer Sprache als eigenständigem Element eingehend zu befassen und sich zu überlegen, welche Gesichtspunkte beachtet werden müssen, um die Beschäftigung mit dem Wortschatz im Rahmen des Lernprozesses sinnvoll zu gestalten.

Bei Fachsprachen fällt der Einstieg leichter. Ihre lexikalisch-semantischen Kategorien haben einen unmittelbaren Bezug zur greifbaren Welt. Sie erfassen das Tun der Menschen, ihr Verhalten und ihre Beziehungen zueinander und zu ihrer Umwelt. Einem Sachverhalt oder einem Gegenstand wird ein Terminus zugeordnet, der, wie im Bereich der Technik, sogar genormt sein kann.

Im wirtschaftlichen Bereich ist die Zuordnung das Ergebnis einer Entwicklung, die heute vorwiegend von der Theoriesprache ausgeht und in der Auseinandersetzung mit der Praxis die endgültige Gestalt und den endgültigen Inhalt findet. Die Fachsprache Wirtschaft gibt auf die Wirtschaft bezogene Informationen weiter. Für den Lernenden jedoch ist sie damit zugleich das Mittel zur Erkenntnis und zum Kennenlernen der wirtschaftlichen Sachverhalte.

Da die Wirtschaft international ist, müssen dieselben Sachverhalte in allen Sprachen benannt und die wirtschaftsorientierten Inhalte der verschiedenen Zeichen in allen Sprachen zur Deckung gebracht werden, wenn eine ungehinderte Kommunikation möglich sein soll. Infolgedessen herrscht weitgehender Konsens darüber, welcher Fachwortschatz in den einzelnen Bereichen der Wirtschaft relevant ist.

Vorwort

Die moderne Entwicklung hat es mit sich gebracht, daß eine beträchtliche Anzahl wirtschaftlicher Schlüsselwörter durch die Massenmedien in die Gemeinsprache eingedrungen sind und im Alltag zur Darstellung wirtschaftlicher Gegebenheiten und zur Beschreibung neuer im wirtschaftlich-technischen Bereich entstandener Sachverhalte benutzt werden.

Eine Beschränkung des Lernvorgangs auf die Gemeinsprache ist deshalb heute nicht mehr möglich. Auch gute Beherrschung der Gemeinsprache führt nicht zu ausreichenden Kommunikationsmöglichkeiten, selbst in einfachen fachsprachlichen Bereichen. Eine frühzeitige Ausrichtung des Lernziels auf fachsprachliche Bereiche ist heutzutage ein unabdingbares Erfordernis, zumal noch immer die Fachsprachen, ohne Rücksicht auf die uns im Alltag umgebende Wirklichkeit, bei der Spracherlernung in unzulässiger Weise zugunsten traditioneller Vorstellungen vernachlässigt werden.

Der vorliegende *Grund- und Aufbauwortschatz* erweitert die Sprachwelt des Benutzers, der sich im angelsächsischen Raum in seiner vielfältigen Ausprägung zurechtfinden und aktiv daran teilnehmen will. Damit wurde ein Werk geschaffen, das für Anfänger und Fortgeschrittene den Einstieg in die Fachsprache Wirtschaft ermöglichen und erleichtern soll.

Der *Grundwortschatz* umfaßt den allgemeinen wirtschaftssprachlichen Wortschatz von ca. 2000 lexikalischen Einheiten, die erweitert und semantisiert werden durch eine Vielzahl authentischer Anwendungsbeispiele, typischer Redewendungen und gebräuchlicher Komposita.

Der *Aufbauwortschatz* soll durch seine Aufgliederung in Sachgebiete und die Auswahl der Wörter mit hohem Gebrauchswert in den jeweiligen Sachbereich vom Wort her auch inhaltlich einführen. Großer Wert wurde dabei auf die Kollokationen gelegt, um den semantischen Zusammenhang zu verdeutlichen und die Ausdrucksmöglichkeiten im Rahmen der Wirtschaftssprache sichtbar zu machen. Die Beispielsätze und Wendungen wurden gleichfalls unter diesem Gesichtspunkt ausgewählt; darüber hinaus sollen sie signifikante Situationen des Wirtschaftslebens sprachlich erfassen.

So weit wie möglich wurde ferner als ordnendes Prinzip das Bezugsfeld verwendet, das gestattet, kleinere Fachbereiche in ihrem inneren sachlichen Zusammenhang aufzuzeigen und dadurch den speziellen Wortinhalt faßbar zu machen. Die Schwierigkeiten der Polysemie werden auf diese Weise im wirtschaftlichen Raum tunlichst vermieden. Diese Grundsätze sollen außerdem dazu beitragen, die Trennung von Lexik und Grammatik zu überwinden. Begreiflicherweise ist es möglich, daß in den verschiedenen behandelten Bereichen ein Wort oder Ausdruck fehlt, die dem Fachmann wesentlich erscheinen. Die Verfasser bitten deshalb die Benutzer um Anregungen und Vorschläge, um das Werk für den praktischen Gebrauch stets aktuell zu erhalten.

Abkürzungen

a	Adjektiv, Eigenschaftswort	*adjective*
Abk.	Abkürzung	*abbreviation*
adv	Adverb, Umstandswort	*adverb*
Am	amerikanisch	*American*
Br	britisch	*British*
etw	etwas	*something*
f	weiblich	*feminine*
fam	familiär	*colloquial*
itr	intransitiv	*intransitive*
jdm	jemandem	*to someone*
jdn	jemanden	*someone*
m	männlich	*masculine*
n	sächlich	*neuter*
o.'s	sein	*one's*
pl	Plural, Mehrzahl	*plural*
pred	Prädikat	*predicate*
prp	Präposition	*preposition*
s	Substantiv, Hauptwort	*substantive*
sing	Singular, Einzahl	*singular*
s.o.	jemand	*someone*
s.o.'s	jemandes	*someone's*
s.th.	etwas	*something*
tr	transitiv	*transitive*
u.	und	*and*
v	Verb, Zeitwort	*verb*

Grundwortschatz

A

to abandon [əˈbændən]	aufgeben, preisgeben
to abandon a claim	von einer Forderung Abstand nehmen
acceptance [əkˈseptəns]	Annahme(vermerk m) f, Akzept n
against acceptance	gegen Annahme
upon acceptance	nach Annahme
for non-acceptance	mangels Annahme
to present a bill for acceptance	einen Wechsel zur Annahme vorlegen
accommodation(s pl**)** [əˌkɔməˈdeiʃən(z)]	Unterkunft f
hotel accommodation	Unterbringung f in einem Hotel
account [əˈkaunt]	Konto n
accounts pl	1. Rechnungs-, Jahresabschluß m; 2. Geschäftsbücher n pl
bank account	Bankkonto n
current account, account current	Kontokorrent n, laufende Rechnung f
as per account	laut Rechnung
for account and risk	auf Rechnung und Gefahr
to open an account with a bank	ein Konto bei einer Bank eröffnen
accountancy [əˈkauntənsi]	Buchhaltung f, -führung f; Rechnungswesen n
accountant [əˈkauntənt]	Buchhalter m
chartered accountant	Wirtschaftsprüfer m
accounting [əˈkauntiŋ]	Buchführung f; Rechnungswesen n
factory accounting	Betriebsbuchhaltung f
to accrue [əˈkruː]	auflaufen; an-, zuwachsen
accrued interest	aufgelaufene Zinsen m pl
to acknowledge [əkˈnɔlidʒ]	anerkennen; zugestehen, einräumen
to acknowledge receipt of a letter	den Empfang eines Briefes bestätigen
acknowledgement [əkˈnɔlidʒmənt]	(Empfangs-) Bestätigung f; Anerkennung f
acknowledgement of a debt	Schuldanerkenntnis f
act [ækt]	Handlung f; Urkunde f, Dokument n, Gesetz n, Verordnung f
by act of law	kraft Gesetzes
Act of Parliament	Parlamentsbeschluß m, Gesetz n
adding machine [ˈædiŋ məˈʃiːn]	Addiermaschine f
address [əˈdres]	Anschrift f, Adresse f
envelope address	Anschrift des Empfängers (auf dem Briefumschlag)
inside address	Anschrift des Empfängers (Brief)

— return address	Anschrift des Absenders (auf dem Briefumschlag)
addressee [ˌædreˈsiː]	Empfänger m, Adressat m
— special directions pertaining to the addressee	besondere Hinweise für den Empfänger
to adjust [əˈdʒʌst]	anpassen, angleichen
— to adjust accounts	Konten abstimmen
— to adjust an entry	eine Buchung berichtigen
administration [ədˌminisˈtreiʃən]	(Geschäfts-, Staats-) Verwaltung f; Regierung f
advance [ədˈvɑːns]	Vorschuß m; Kredit m; Darlehen n; Steigerung f, Erhöhung f
cash advance	Barvorschuß m
advance payment	Vorauszahlung f
— advance on salary	Gehaltsvorschuß m
to book in advance	vorausbestellen
advertising [ˈædvətaiziŋ]	Werbung f, Reklame f
radio advertising	Rundfunkwerbung f; Werbefunk m
television advertising	Fernsehwerbung f
advertising agency	Werbe-, Reklamebüro n
advice [ədˈvais]	Anzeige f; Nachricht f, Mitteilung f, Benachrichtigung f; Avis m, n; Bericht m
as per advice	laut Aufgabe, laut Bericht
no advice	mangels Berichts
— credit advice	Gutschriftanzeige f
adviser [ədˈvaizə]	Berater m, Ratgeber m
legal adviser	Rechtsberater m
technical adviser	technischer Berater m
advisory [ədˈvaizəri]	beratend
— in an advisory capacity	in beratender Eigenschaft
⊣ advisory committee	Beirat m
— advisory opinion	Gutachten n
to affect [əˈfekt]	sich auswirken auf, beeinflussen
This did not affect the result.	Es hatte keinen Einfluß auf das Ergebnis.
agency [ˈeidʒənsi]	Vertretung f, Agentur f; Verkaufsbüro n, Lieferstelle f
— head agency	Generalvertretung f
travel agency	Reisebüro n
agenda [əˈdʒendə]	Tagesordnung f
to adopt the agenda	die Tagesordnung annehmen
to be on the agenda	auf der Tagesordnung stehen
agent [ˈeidʒənt]	Vertreter m, Agent m, Vermittler m; Makler m; (Handlungs-) Reisender m
— forwarding agent	Spediteur m
insurance agent	Versicherungsvertreter m
local agent	lokaler Vertreter m/Repräsentant m
sole agent	Alleinvertreter m

agreement [ə'gri:mənt] — Vereinbarung f, Absprache f; Verständigung f
  according to agreement — laut Absprache
  by mutual agreement — durch beiderseitiges Abkommen
  agreement in writing — schriftliche Vereinbarung
  to come to an agreement — zu einem Abschluß/zu einer Vereinbarung kommen
aid [eid] — Hilfe f, Unterstützung f, Beistand m, Beihilfe f
  to administer first aid — Erste Hilfe leisten
  economic aid — Wirtschaftshilfe f
aircraft ['ɛəkrɑ:ft] — Flugzeug n
  aircraft industry — Flugzeugindustrie f
airline ['ɛəlain] — Fluglinie f; Luftverkehrsgesellschaft f
airliner ['ɛəˌlainə] — Passagierflugzeug n
air mail ['ɛə meil] — Luftpost f
  by air mail — mit Luftpost
airport ['ɛəpɔ:t] — Flughafen m
  The aircraft left London Airport this morning. — Das Flugzeug flog heute früh vom Londoner Flughafen ab.
air terminal ['ɛə ˌtə:minl] — Air Terminal m, n (Abfertigungsgebäude im Stadtzentrum)
air traffic ['ɛə ˌtræfik] — Flugverkehr m
to allocate ['æləukeit] — zuteilen, zuweisen; kontingentieren, bewirtschaften
  to allocate shares — Aktien zuteilen
  to allocate expenses — Unkosten verteilen
allocation [ˌæləu'keiʃən] — Zu-, Verteilung f; Kontingentierung f, Bewirtschaftung f
  allocation of seats — Sitzverteilung f
  allocation of shares — Aktienzuteilung f
allowance [ə'lauəns] — Zuschuß m, Beihilfe f; Entschädigung f, Vergütung f; Nachlaß m, Rabatt m
  expense allowance — Aufwandsentschädigung f
  family allowance — Familienzulage f
  mileage allowance — Kilometergeld n
  daily/per diem allowance — Tagegeld n
  tax allowance — Steuerfreibetrag m
  travelling allowance — Reisekostenentschädigung f
  He made allowance for her inexperience. — Er berücksichtigte ihre mangelnde Erfahrung.
to alter ['ɔ:ltə] — ab-, umändern
  to alter the arrangements — die Maßnahmen ändern
alternative [ɔ:l'tə:nətiv] — Alternative f, Wahl(möglichkeit) f
  He has no other alternative. — Er hat keine andere Wahl.
amortization [əˌmɔ:ti'zeiʃən] — (Schulden-) Tilgung f, Amortisation f
to analyse ['ænəlaiz] — analysieren
analysis, pl -ses [ə'næləsis, -i:z] — Analyse f, Auswertung f, gründliche Untersuchung f

in the last analysis — *letzten Endes*
analysis of expenses — *Kostenanalyse f*
anchorage [ˈæŋkərɪdʒ] — Ankerplatz *m*, Anlegestelle *f*
anchorage-dues pl — *Hafengebühren f pl*
to announce [əˈnauns] — ankündigen, anzeigen, bekanntmachen
to announce on the radio — *im Radio ankündigen*
announcement [əˈnaunsmənt] — Ankündigung *f*, Anzeige *f;* Durchsage *f*
announcement of sale — *Verkaufsangebot n,*
Verkaufsanzeige f

announcer [əˈnaunsə] — Ansager *m*, Sprecher *m*
The announcer on the radio — *Der Rundfunksprecher gab die*
read out the news. — *Nachrichten durch.*
annual [ˈænjuəl] — jährlich
annual general meeting — *Jahreshauptversammlung f*
annual report — *Jahresbericht m*
to anticipate [ænˈtɪsɪpeɪt] — vorwegnehmen; im voraus bezahlen
to anticipate payment — *vor Verfallszeit Zahlung leisten*
The amount was larger than — *Der Betrag war größer, als ich*
I had anticipated. — *erwartet hatte.*
to apologize [əˈpɒlədʒaɪz] — sich entschuldigen, um Entschuldigung bitten

We apologize for the delay. — *Wir bitten wegen der Verspätung um Entschuldigung.*

apology [əˈpɒlədʒɪ] — Entschuldigung *f*
Please accept our apologies. — *Wir bitten um Entschuldigung.*
apparatus [ˌæpəˈreɪtəs] — Apparat *m*, Gerät *n*
apparent [əˈpærənt] — sichtbar; offensichtlich, augenscheinlich
apparent damage — *offensichtlicher Schaden*
The engine was apparently — *Allem Anschein nach war der Motor*
undamaged. — *nicht beschädigt.*
to appeal [əˈpiːl] — 1. Einspruch erheben; Beschwerde/
Berufung einlegen;
2. appellieren/sich wenden an;
3. Anklang/Gefallen finden
to appeal to a higher court — *eine höhere Instanz anrufen*
The article appeals to the — *Der Artikel findet bei der Kundschaft*
customers. — *Anklang.*
appliance [əˈplaɪəns] — Gerät *n*, Vorrichtung *f*
applicant [ˈæplɪkənt] — Bewerber *m*, Antragsteller *m*
applicant for a job — *Bewerber m (um eine Stelle)*
application (form) — Antrag(sformular *n*) *m*
[ˌæplɪˈkeɪʃən fɔːm]
to appreciate [əˈpriːʃɪeɪt] — zu schätzen wissen; dankbar anerkennen;
verstehen, einsehen; den Wert/den Preis erhöhen

I would appreciate it, if… — *Ich wäre sehr dankbar, wenn…*
He appreciates the fact that — *Er sieht ein, daß die Arbeit nicht*
the work cannot be done — *sofort erledigt werden kann.*
immediately.

appreciation [əˌpriːʃiˈeiʃən]
    to show an appreciation
    He does not expect any
    appreciation.
apprentice [əˈprentis]
approach [əˈprəutʃ]

    approach to a subject
    He is using the right
    approach.

appropriate [əˈprəupriit]
    if appropriate
    at the appropriate time
to appropriate [əˈprəuprieit]
    Congress appropriates
    money for...
    He appropriated all the
    books.
approval [əˈpruːvəl]
    on approval
    His remark met with great
    approval.
approximate [əˈprɔksimit]
    approximate value
    approximately three months
area [ˈɛəriə]
    parking area
    shopping area
    trading area
    area code Am
argument [ˈɑːgjumənt]

    They had a violent
    argument.
ashore [əˈʃɔː]
    The passengers went
    ashore.
aspect [ˈæspekt]
    They studied every aspect of
    the question.
to assemble [əˈsembl]

    to assemble data
    They assembled in the hall.
    to assemble an engine

---

1. Wertsteigerung *f*, Wertzuwachs *m*;
2. Wertschätzung *f*, Anerkennung *f*, Verständnis *n*
    im Wert gestiegen sein
    Er erwartet keinen Dank.

Auszubildender *m*, Lehrling *m*
Zugang *m*, Annäherung *f*; Einführung *f*; Auffassung *f*, Betrachtungsweise *f*
    Behandlung f eines Themas
    Er hat den richtigen Weg
    eingeschlagen/verwendet die richtige
    Methode.
geeignet, passend, zweckmäßig
    gegebenenfalls
    zu gegebener Zeit
bewilligen, zuweisen; sich aneignen
    Der Kongreß bewilligt Geld für...

    Er nahm alle Bücher in Beschlag.

Bewilligung *f*, Genehmigung *f*
    zur Ansicht
    Seine Bemerkung fand großen Beifall.

annähernd, ungefähr
    Annäherungswert m
    ungefähr drei Monate
Fläche *f*; Gebiet *n*, Gegend *f*
    Parkplatz m
    Einkaufszentrum n
    Wirtschaftsraum m
    Vorwahl(nummer) f
Einwand *m*; Erörterung *f*; Auseinandersetzung *f*
    Sie hatten eine lebhafte
    Auseinandersetzung.
ans/am Ufer
    Die Passagiere gingen an Land.

Gestalt *f*; Gesichts-, Blickpunkt *m*
    Sie prüften alle Seiten des Problems.

1. versammeln, zusammenrufen;
2. zusammenbauen, -setzen, montieren;
3. sich versammeln, zusammentreffen
    Unterlagen zusammenstellen
    Sie versammelten sich in der Halle.
    einen Motor zusammensetzen

assembly - attention

assembly [ə'sembli]   1. Versammlung f, Zusammenkunft f;
2. Montage f
assembly hall   Versammlungshalle f
assembly line   Fließband n
assembly plant   Montagewerk n
assent [ə'sent]   Einwilligung f, Zustimmung f
He gave his assent.   Er gab seine Zustimmung.
to assert [ə'sə:t]   behaupten; geltend machen; bestehen auf
to assert a claim   einen Anspruch geltend machen
to assess [ə'ses]   einschätzen, bewerten; *(Kosten)* festsetzen
to assess the amount of damage   den Umfang des Schadens festlegen
assets *pl* ['æsets]   Aktiva *n pl*, Betriebsvermögen *n*
fixed assets   Anlagevermögen n
assets and liabilities   Aktiva und Passiva
to assist [ə'sist]   helfen, unterstützen, fördern
assistance [ə'sistəns]   Hilfe f, Unterstützung f
Can I be of any assistance to you?   Kann ich Ihnen irgendwie helfen?
national assistance   (öffentliche) Fürsorge f/ Wohlfahrt f
assistant [ə'sistənt]   Assistent *m*, Gehilfe *m*, Mitarbeiter *m*
shop assistant   Ladengehilfe m, Verkäufer m
assistant manager   stellvertretender Direktor m
to assume [ə'sju:m]   1. annehmen, unterstellen; voraussetzen;
2. übernehmen, auf sich nehmen
Let us assume that...   Nehmen wir an, daß...
He assumed new duties.   Er übernahm neue Pflichten.
assumption [ə'sʌmpʃən]   Annahme f, Vermutung f; Voraussetzung f
on the assumption that...   unter der Voraussetzung, daß...
assurance [ə'ʃuərəns]   Zusicherung f, Versprechen n; (Lebens-) Versicherung f; Garantie f
He gave me his assurance that he would be here.   Er versicherte mir, er würde hier sein.
to assure [ə'ʃuə]   1. zusichern, garantieren;
2. *(Leben)* versichern
That's not so, I assure you.   Ich versichere dir, dem ist nicht so.
attendance [ə'tendəns]   Anwesenheit f; Beteiligung f, Zuhörerschaft f
We had a good attendance at the meeting.   Unsere Versammlung war gut besucht.
attendant [ə'tendənt]   Wärter *m*, Aufseher *m*
attention [ə'tenʃən]   1. Beachtung f, Erledigung f;
2. Wartung f, Bedienung f
attention: Mr. John Heely   z. H. von Herrn John Heely
for your kind attention   zur gefälligen Kenntnisnahme
for immediate attention   zur sofortigen Erledigung

attitude [ˈætitjuːd] | Haltung *f;* Standpunkt *m*
You have the wrong attitude towards your work. | *Sie haben eine falsche Einstellung zu Ihrer Arbeit.*
He adopted a negative attitude. | *Er verhielt sich ablehnend.*

attractive [əˈtræktiv] | anziehend, reizvoll
an attractive offer | *ein reizvolles Angebot*

auction [ˈɔːkʃən] | Auktion *f,* Versteigerung *f*
to sell by (Am at) auction | *versteigern*

audience [ˈɔːdjəns] | Zuhörer *m pl,* Zuschauer *m pl,* Besucher *m pl*
The audience applauded loudly. | *Das Publikum klatschte laut Beifall.*

audit [ˈɔːdit] | Rechnungs-, Buchprüfung *f*
to make an audit | *eine Prüfung durchführen*
annual audit | *Jahresabschlußprüfung f*

auditor [ˈɔːditə] | Buch-, Rechnungs-, Wirtschaftsprüfer *m*

authority [ɔːˈθɔriti] | Vollmacht *f,* Befugnis *f;* Autorität *f*
He has full authority to act. | *Er hat unbeschränkte Handlungsvollmacht.*
by authority | *mit amtlicher Genehmigung*
the authorities pl | *die Behörden f pl*

to authorize [ˈɔːθəraiz] | ermächtigen, beauftragen; genehmigen
to be authorized to sign | *zeichnungsberechtigt sein*
through authorized channels | *auf dem Dienstweg*

automatic [ˌɔːtəˈmætik] | automatisch

automobile (bes. *Am*) [ˈɔːtəməbiːl] | Kraftfahrzeug *n*
automobile insurance | *Kraftfahrzeugversicherung f*

automation [ˌɔːtəˈmeiʃən] | Automation *f*

aviation [ˌeiviˈeiʃən] | Luftfahrt *f*
civil aviation | *zivile Luftfahrt f*

to await [əˈweit] | erwarten, warten auf
to await instructions | *Anweisungen abwarten*

award [əˈwɔːd] | Schiedsspruch *m;* Zuerkennung *f;* Preis *m,* Prämie *f*

B

background [ˈbækgraund] | Hintergrund *m;* Werdegang *m,* Vorgeschichte *f*
He stayed in the background. | *Er hielt sich im Hintergrund.*
He has a very good background. | *Er kommt aus einem sehr guten Hause.*

backing - bargain

educational background	Vorbildung f, Bildungsgang m
financial background	finanzieller Rückhalt m
backing ['bækiŋ]	Unterstützung f, Hilfe f; Stützungskäufe m pl; (Banknoten) Deckung f
currency backing	Stützung f der Währung
backlog ['bæklɔg]	Rückstand m; Überhang m; Reserve f
backlog of orders	Auftragsrückstand m, -überhang m
backlog demand	Nachholbedarf m
bail [beil]	Bürgschaft f, Sicherheitsleistung f
to go/to stand bail for s.o.	für jdn Sicherheit leisten/ Kaution stellen
balance ['bæləns]	Bilanz f, Rechnungsabschluß m; Überschuß m
to strike a balance	die Bilanz ziehen
balance brought forward	Saldovortrag m
balance at the bank	Bankguthaben n
balance on/in hand	Kassenbestand m
balance of payments	Zahlungsbilanz f
balance of trade	Handelsbilanz f
balance sheet	Rechnungsabschluß m, Bilanzbogen m
to balance ['bæləns]	ausgleichen, abschließen, saldieren
to balance our account	zum Ausgleich unseres Kontos
to balance the books	die Bücher abschließen, saldieren
bale [beil]	Ballen m
bank [bæŋk]	Bank(haus n) f
bank of issue	Notenbank f
savings bank	Sparkasse f
bank account	Bankkonto n, -guthaben n
bank discount	Bankdiskont m
bank note	Banknote f
bank rate	Diskontsatz m
banker ['bæŋkə]	Bankier m; Bankverbindung f
banking ['bæŋkiŋ]	Bankwesen n, -betrieb m
banking account	Bankkonto n, -guthaben n
banking hours pl	Schalterstunden f pl
bankrupt ['bæŋkrʌpt]	bankrott, zahlungsunfähig
to go bankrupt	in Konkurs geraten, Bankrott machen
bankruptcy ['bæŋkrəp(t)si]	Zahlungseinstellung f, Bankrott m, Insolvenz f
bar [bɑ:]	Anwaltsberuf m, Anwaltschaft f
to practise at the bar	den Anwaltsberuf ausüben
to bargain ['bɑ:gin]	handeln; verhandeln, vereinbaren
We had to bargain for everything.	Wir mußten um alles handeln/feilschen.
collective bargaining	Tarifverhandlungen f pl
bargaining point	Verhandlungspunkt m
bargaining position/power	Verhandlungsposition f

barge [bɑːdʒ] — Lastkahn *m*, Leichter *m*
barrister [ˈbærɪstə] — plädierender Anwalt *m*
barter [ˈbɑːtə] — Tauschhandel *m*
to base on [beɪs] — stützen/gründen auf
  His statements are based on facts. — *Seine Behauptungen beruhen auf Tatsachen.*
basic [ˈbeɪsɪk] — grundlegend
  basic fact — *grundlegende Tatsache* f
  basic industry — *Grundstoffindustrie* f
  basic requirements pl — *Grundvoraussetzungen* f pl
  basic training — *Grundausbildung* f
  basically — *grundsätzlich, im wesentlichen*
basis, *pl* **-ses** [ˈbeɪsɪs, -iːz] — Grundlage *f*, Ausgangspunkt *m*; Grundstock *m*
  on the basis of facts — *auf Grund von Tatsachen*
  to form/to lay the basis of s.th. — *die Grundlage für etwas schaffen*
  basis of discussion — *Diskussionsgrundlage* f
bearer [ˈbɛərə] — Überbringer *m*; (Scheck) Inhaber *m*
  payable to bearer — *zahlbar an Überbringer/auf den Inhaber lautend*
  cheque to bearer — *Inhaberscheck* m
benefit [ˈbenɪfɪt] — Zuwendung *f*, Beihilfe *f*; Leistung *f*; Vorteil *m*, Nutzen *m*
  for the benefit of a third party — *zugunsten eines Dritten*
  social/insurance benefit — *Sozial-/Versicherungsleistung* f
  sickness benefit — *Krankengeld* n
  unemployment benefit — *Arbeitslosengeld* n
berth [bəːθ] — Ankerplatz *m*; Schlafwagenbett *n*
bid [bɪd] — Offerte *f*, Angebot *n*; (Versteigerung) Gebot *n*
  highest/lowest bid — *Meist-/Mindestangebot* n
  call for bids — *Ausschreibung* f
to bid (bid, bid [den]) [bɪd] — bieten
  He bid a fair price. — *Er bot einen angemessenen Preis.*
bidder [ˈbɪdə] — Bietender *m*; Bewerber *m*
  highest bidder — *Meistbietender* m
  no bidders — *keine (Kauf-) Interessenten*
bill [bɪl] — Rechnung *f*; Wechsel *m*; Bescheinigung *f*; Am Banknote *f*
  bill of exchange — *Wechsel* m
  bills payable — *Wechselschulden* f pl
  bill of lading — *Seefrachtbrief* m, *Konnossement* n
  bill of health — *Gesundheitsattest* n
  He paid the bill. — *Er löste den Wechsel ein/bezahlte die Rechnung.*
bill-board [ˈbɪlbɔːd] — Anschlagbrett *n*; Reklamefläche *f*

billion ['biljən] | Billion f; Am Milliarde f
blank [blæŋk] | unbeschriebenes Blatt n; Lücke f (in einem Text); Am Formular n, Vordruck m

  He filled in the blank. Am | Er füllte das Formular aus.
  to leave a blank | unausgefüllt lassen
  a blank sheet of paper | ein leeres/unbedrucktes Blatt Papier
board [bɔ:d] | Ausschuß m, Komitee n; Ministerium n
  board meeting | Vorstands-, Aufsichtsratsitzung f
  board of directors | Direktorium n
  Board of Trade | Handelsministerium n; Am Handelskammer f
  on board (a) ship | an Bord eines Schiffes
bond [bɔnd] | Schuldurkunde f, Obligation f; Zollverschluß m
  in bond | unter Zollverschluß
  investment bonds pl | Anlagepapiere n pl
  bonded warehouse | Zollspeicher m
bonus ['bəunəs] | Zulage f, Gratifikation f; Extradividende f, Bonus m
  cost-of-living bonus | Teuerungszulage f
  incentive bonus | Leistungszulage f
to book [buk] | (ver)buchen; eintragen, aufschreiben, notieren
  all booked up | ausverkauft
  He booked in advance. | Er bestellte im voraus.
  to book an order | einen Auftrag annehmen
  to book a room | ein Zimmer bestellen
  to book a ticket | eine Fahr-/Flugkarte lösen
bookkeeper ['bukıki:pə] | Buchhalter m
bookkeeping ['bukıki:piŋ] | Buchhaltung f, -führung f
boom [bu:m] | wirtschaftlicher Aufschwung m, Hochkonjunktur f; Hausse f
  building boom | Hochkonjunktur f im Bauwesen
to boost [bu:st] | in die Höhe treiben; die Werbetrommel rühren
  to boost business | die Wirtschaft ankurbeln
  to boost prices | die Preise in die Höhe treiben
booth [bu:ð] | (Fernsprech-) Zelle f; (Messe-) Stand m
borrower ['bɔrəuə] | Entleiher m; Kreditnehmer m
borrowing ['bɔrəuiŋ] | Entleihen n; Kreditaufnahme f
  borrowing power | Kreditfähigkeit f
boss [bɔs] | Chef m, Vorgesetzter m
  to boss s.o. around | jdn herumkommandieren
bottleneck ['bɔtlnek] | Engpaß m
  bottleneck in supplies | Versorgungsengpaß m
boundary ['baundəri] | Grenze f, Grenzlinie f
boycott ['bɔikət] | s Boykott m; v boykottieren

bracket [ˈbrækit]   1. (eckige) Klammer *m*;
                         2. Kategorie *f*, Klasse *f*
   salary bracket   Gehaltsgruppe f
branch office [ˈbrɑːntʃ ˌɔfis]   Zweigstelle *f*, Filiale *f*
brand [brænd]   (Schutz-) Marke *f*, Warenzeichen *n*;
                        Markenartikel *m*
   What brand does he smoke?   *Was für eine Sorte raucht er?*
   brand name   *Markenname* m
   branded goods pl   *Markenfabrikate* n pl
breadth [bredθ]   Breite *f*
breakdown [ˈbreikdaun]   Panne *f*, Betriebsstörung *f*;
                        Zusammenbruch *m*, Ausfall *m*;
                        Aufgliederung *f*
   breakdown of costs/cost   *Kostenaufgliederung* f
   breakdown
   breakdown of/in   *Scheitern* n *der Verhandlungen*
   negotiations
brief [briːf]   *a* kurz; *v* einweisen
   in brief   *kurz gesagt*
   Please be brief.   *Bitte fassen Sie sich kurz!*
   briefing   *Einweisung* f, *Unterrichtung* f
briefcase [ˈbriːfkeis]   Aktentasche *f*
brisk [brisk]   lebhaft, flott
   brisk demand   *lebhafte Nachfrage* f
   to sell briskly   *reißenden Absatz finden*
   Business is brisk.   *Das Geschäft geht gut.*
broker [ˈbrəukə]   (Börsen-) Makler *m*
brought forward   Übertrag *m*, Vortrag *m*
[brɔːt ˈfɔːwəd]
budget [ˈbʌdʒit]   Haushaltsplan *m*
   to draw up a budget   *einen Haushaltsplan aufstellen*
   family budget   *Familienbudget* n
   budget-priced   *preisgünstig*
building trade [ˈbildiŋ treid]   Bauindustrie *f*
bulk [bʌlk]   Umfang *m*, Größe *f*; Großteil *m*
   to sell in bulk   *in Bausch und Bogen verkaufen*
   bulk article   *Massenartikel* m
   bulk buying   *Großeinkauf* m
bulky goods *pl* [ˈbʌlki gudz]   sperrige Güter *n pl*
bulletin [ˈbulitin]   Mitteilungsblatt *n*, Bulletin *n*
   news bulletin   *Kurznachrichten* f pl
   bulletin board   *Am Anschlagtafel* f
bumper crop [ˈbʌmpə krɔp]   Rekordernte *f*
bushel [ˈbuʃl] *(8 gallons)*   Scheffel *m (36,35, Am 35.24 Liter)*
buyer [ˈbaiə]   Käufer *m*, Abnehmer *m*
   buyer's market/strike   *Käufermarkt* m/ -*streik* m
by(e)-law [ˈbailɔː]   Satzung *f*; Statuten *n pl*
by-election [ˈbaiiˌlekʃən]   Ersatz-, Nachwahl *f*
by-product [ˈbaiˌprɔdʌkt]   Nebenprodukt *n*

C

cable [ˈkeibl] — s Kabel(depesche f) n;
v kabeln
  by cable — telegraphisch
  cable address — Drahtanschrift f, Telegrammadresse f
  cable order — telegraphische(r) Auftrag m
to calculate [ˈkælkjuleit] — aus-, berechnen, kalkulieren
  They calculated the costs. — Sie kalkulierten die Kosten.
calculation [ˌkælkjuˈleiʃən] — Berechnung f, Kalkulation f; Schätzung f, Voranschlag m
  according to my calculation — nach meiner Berechnung
  I am out in my calculation. — Ich habe mich verrechnet.
  rough calculation — Überschlag m
  calculation of profits — Rentabilitätsberechnung f
call [kɔːl] — s (Telefon-) Anruf m; Zahlungsaufforderung f, Forderung f; Kaufoption f;
v einfordern; kündigen; telefonieren
  at/on call — auf Abruf
  to be called for — postlagernd
  money at call/call money — Tagesgeld n
  long-distance/trunk call — Ferngespräch n
  reversed charge call, Am collect call — R-Gespräch n
  call box — Telefonzelle f
  I called on him at his office. — Ich suchte ihn in seinem Büro auf.
  to call at a port — einen Hafen anlaufen
caller [ˈkɔːlə] — Besucher m; Anrufer m
calling [ˈkɔːliŋ] — Beruf m; Geschäft n
  calling on customers — Kundenbesuch m
  calling card — Am Visitenkarte f
campaign [kæmˈpein] — Feldzug m, Kampagne f
  advertising campaign — Werbefeldzug m
  sales campaign — Verkaufsaktion f
to cancel [ˈkænsəl] — annullieren; abbestellen, stornieren
  until cancelled — bis auf Widerruf
  They cancelled the order. — Sie machten den Auftrag rückgängig.
  The meeting/The appointment was cancelled. — Die Versammlung/Die Verabredung wurde abgesagt.
cancellation [ˌkænsəˈleiʃən] — Annullierung f, Stornierung f, Rückgängigmachung f, Streichung f
  cancellation of an entry — Löschung f eines Eintrags
  cancellation of a postage stamp — Entwertung f einer Briefmarke
to canvass [ˈkænvəs] — (Kunden) besuchen; (Aufträge) hereinholen
  to canvass the town — die Stadt bereisen

capable [ˈkeipəbl]   fähig, tüchtig
  to be capable of   verbesserungsfähig sein
  improvement
capacity [kəˈpæsiti]   Leistungsfähigkeit *f;* Kapazität *f;*
       Fassungsvermögen *n*
  in a managerial capacity   *in leitender Stellung*
  working to capacity   *voll ausgelastet*
  seating capacity of a room   *Fassungsvermögen* n *eines Raumes,*
       Sitzplätze m pl *in einem Raum*
  in his capacity as a chairman   *in seiner Eigenschaft als Vorsitzender*
capital [ˈkæpitl]   Kapital *n,* Vermögen *n,* Geldmittel *n pl*
  invested capital   *Anlagekapital* n
  working capital   *Betriebskapital* n
  capital goods pl   *Produktionsgüter* n pl
  capital market   *Kapitalmarkt* m
carbon copy [ˈkɑːbən ˈkɔpi]   Durchschlag *m*
carbon paper [ˈkɑːbən ˈpeipə]   Kohlepapier *n*
card-index [ˈkɑːdˌindeks]   Kartei *f*
cardboard [ˈkɑːdbɔːd]   Pappe *f*
  cardboard box   *Pappkarton* m
career [kəˈriə]   Laufbahn *f;* Beruf *m*
  to enter upon a career   *eine Laufbahn einschlagen*
  career woman   *berufstätige Frau* f
cargo, *pl* **-oes**   *(Schiff, Flugzeug)* Ladung *f;*
[ˈkɑːgəu, -z]   Fracht(gut *n*) *f*
  mixed cargo   *Stückgut* n
  to discharge a cargo   *eine Ladung löschen*
carriage [ˈkæridʒ]   Transportkosten *pl,* Rollgeld *n;*
       Beförderung *f;* Eisenbahnwagen *m*
  by land carriage   *per Achse*
  carriage-free/-paid   *frachtfrei*
  carriage forward   *Frachtkosten per Nachnahme*
  carriage by rail/by sea   *Eisenbahn-/Seetransport* m
carrier [ˈkæriə]   Spediteur *m,* Rollfuhrunternehmer *m;*
       (Seetransport) Verfrachter *m*

to carry forward   vortragen, übertragen
[ˈkæri ˈfɔːwəd]
  to carry forward to new   *auf neue Rechnung vortragen*
  account
carrying [ˈkæriiŋ]   Transport *m,* Beförderung *f*
  carrying agent   *Spediteur* m
  carrying business   *Speditionsgeschäft* n
  carrying trade   *Transportgewerbe* n
cash [kæʃ]   *s* Bargeld *n;* Kassenbestand *m;*
       v einkassieren, einlösen
  for ready cash   *gegen sofortige Kasse*
  cash in hand   *Bar-, Kassenbestand* m
  cash on delivery (C.O.D.)   *gegen Nachnahme*
  cash account   *Bankguthaben* n, *Kassakonto* n

cash discount — Kassaskonto m, n
to cash a cheque — einen Scheck einlösen
He is out of cash. — Er ist nicht bei Kasse.
cashier [kæˈʃiə] — Kassierer m
to pay the cashier — an der Kasse zahlen
cask [kɑːsk] — Faß n
casual [ˈkæʒjuəl] — zufällig; gelegentlich
casual labourer — Gelegenheitsarbeiter m
catalogue, Am **catalog** [ˈkætəlɔg] — Katalog m
price catalogue — Preisliste f
catalogue price — Listenpreis m
category [ˈkætigəri] — Kategorie f, Klasse f, Gruppe f
to cater (for) [ˈkeitə] — sorgen (für); Lebensmittel liefern
catering industry — Gaststättengewerbe n
to cater to popular taste — dem allgemeinen Geschmack gerecht werden
caution [ˈkɔːʃən] — s Vorsicht f; (polizeiliche) Verwarnung f; Rechtsmittelbelehrung f
v (ver)warnen; belehren
Caution! Men at work! — Vorsicht! Straßenarbeiten!
ceiling [ˈsiːliŋ] — Höchstgrenze f, Maximum n; (Flugzeug) Gipfelhöhe f; (Zimmer-) Decke f
central [ˈsentrəl] — zentral
central bank — Zentralnotenbank f
certificate [səˈtifikit] — Bescheinigung f, Beglaubigung f; (Prüfungs-) Zeugnis n
certificate of origin — Ursprungszeugnis n
to produce a certificate — ein Zeugnis beibringen
to certificate [səˈtifikeit] — bescheinigen; ein Zeugnis ausstellen über
to certify [ˈsəːtifai] — bescheinigen; beglaubigen, beurkunden
This is to certify that... — Hiermit wird bescheinigt, daß...
chain [tʃein] — Kettenunternehmen n, Filialbetriebe m pl
chain store — Kettenladen m
chairman [ˈtʃɛəmən] — Vorsitzender m, Präsident m
chamber(s pl**)** [ˈtʃeimbə(z)] — Richter-, Anwaltszimmer n; Kammer f (Amt)
Chamber of Commerce — Handelskammer f
Chancellor of the Exchequer — Schatzkanzler m (brit. Finanzminister)
channel [ˈtʃænl] — Kanal m
through official channels — auf dem Dienstweg
channels pl *of supply* — Versorgungswege m pl
charge [tʃɑːdʒ] — s 1. finanzielle Belastung f; Preis m, Kosten pl;
2. Beschuldigung f;
3. Verantwortung f;
v 1. belasten, in Rechnung stellen, fordern; 2. beschuldigen

free of charge	kostenlos, unentgeltlich
There is no charge.	Es kostet nichts.
He charged him too much.	Er berechnete ihm zuviel.
Who is in charge of this office?	Wer leitet dieses Büro?
chart [tʃɑːt]	Tabelle f; Diagramm n; graphische Darstellung f
weather chart	Wetterkarte f
organization chart	Organisationsplan m
charter [ˈtʃɑːtə]	s Chartervertrag m; Befrachtung f; v (Schiff, Flugzeug) chartern; mieten; befrachten
charter plane	Charterflugzeug n
chartered accountant	Wirtschaftsprüfer m
check [tʃek]	s Kontrolle, Überprüfung f; Kontrollabschnitt m; Kassenzettel m; Am Scheck m; v drosseln, dämpfen; überprüfen; abhaken
luggage check	Gepäckschein m
coat/hat check	Garderobenmarke f
checkpoint	Grenzkontrollstelle f
checkroom	Am Gepäckaufbewahrung f; Garderobe f
It was necessary to put a check on production.	Es war erforderlich, die Produktion zu drosseln.
to check in/out	sich an-/abmelden
to check baggage	Am Gepäck aufgeben/bei der Aufbewahrung abgeben
cheque, Am **check** [tʃek]	Scheck m
to draw/to endorse a cheque	einen Scheck ausstellen/girieren
to present a cheque for payment	einen Scheck zur Zahlung vorlegen
cheque book	Scheckheft n
cheque to bearer	Inhaberscheck m
crossed cheque	Verrechnungsscheck m
open cheque	Barscheck m
postal cheque	Postscheck m
traveller's cheque	Reisescheck m
circular [ˈsəːkjulə]	s Rundschreiben n; a kreisförmig
circular letter of credit	Reisekreditbrief m
circular ticket/tour	Rundreisefahrschein m/ Rundreise f
to circulate [ˈsəːkjuleit]	in Umlauf bringen
circulation [ˌsəːkjuˈleiʃən]	1. Umlauf m, Verkehr m; 2. Verbreitung f, Absatz m; 3. Auflagenhöhe f (Zeitung)
monetary circulation	Geldumlauf m

The magazine has a wide circulation.	Die Zeitschrift hat eine hohe Auflage/ist weit verbreitet.
circumstance [ˈsəːkəmstəns]	Umstand *m; pl* Umstände *m pl,* Sachverhalt *m;* Verhältnisse *n pl*
in/under these circumstances	unter diesen Umständen
under no circumstances	unter keinen Umständen, auf keinen Fall
civil servant [ˈsivl ˈsəːvənt]	Beamter *m*
civil service [ˈsivl ˈsəːvis]	Staatsdienst *m*
claim [kleim]	*s* Anspruch *m,* Forderung *f,* Anrecht *n;*
	v beanspruchen, fordern; behaupten
to put in a claim	einen Anspruch geltend machen
We lay no claim to that.	Wir erheben keinen Anspruch darauf.
The insurance company paid all the claims against us.	Die Versicherungsgesellschaft beglich alle gegen uns erhobenen Forderungen.
He claimed damages.	Er forderte Schadenersatz.
claim for compensation/damages	Schadenersatzanspruch *m*
classification [ˌklæsifiˈkeiʃən]	Einteilung *f,* Eingruppierung *f,* Aufgliederung *f,* Klassifizierung *f*
to classify [ˈklæsifai]	einstufen, eingruppieren, einordnen
classified advertisements pl	kleine Anzeigen *f pl*
classified directory	Branchenadreßbuch *n*
clear [kliə]	*a* ohne Ladung; ohne Abzug, netto; schuldenfrei, unbelastet;
	v (Schulden) bezahlen, abtragen; netto verdienen; entlasten
to clear a bill	einen Wechsel einlösen
He cleared his luggage at the customs.	Er ließ sein Gepäck zollamtlich abfertigen.
The roads are now clear.	Die Straßen sind jetzt frei.
clear profit/loss	Reingewinn *m*/reiner Verlust *m*
clearance [ˈkliərəns]	Zollabfertigung *f;* Zollschein *m;* *(Schiff)* Auslaufgenehmigung *f; (Flugzeug)* Starterlaubnis *f; (Brücke)* lichte Höhe *f*
clearance sale	Räumungsverkauf *m*
clearing [ˈkliəriŋ]	Verrechnungsverkehr *m*
clearing-house	Verrechnungsstelle *f*
clerical [ˈklerikəl]	Schreib(er)-, Büro-
clerical error	Schreibfehler *m*
clerical work	Büroarbeit *f*
client [ˈklaiənt]	Kunde *m;* Klient *m*
coach [kəutʃ]	Omnibus *m,* Autobus *m;* Personenwagen *m (der Eisenbahn); Am* zweitürige Limousine *f*

code [kəud]   s Kode *m;* Chiffre *f;*
                           v verschlüsseln
   highway code   Straßenverkehrsordnung f
   *post/*Am *zip code*   Postleitzahl f
   code number   Kennziffer f
   S.T.D. (subscriber trunk   Vorwahl f, Ortsnetzkennzahl f
    dialling) code
cold storage [ˈkəuld ˈstɔːridʒ]   Kühlhauslagerung *f*
collaboration [kəˌlæbəˈreiʃən]   Zusammenarbeit *f*
   in collaboration with   zusammen mit
collapse [kəˈlæps]   s Zusammenbruch *m;*
                              v zusammenbrechen; scheitern
to collate [kɔˈleit]   kollationieren
to collect [kəˈlekt]   einkassieren; einziehen, einlösen
   to collect outstanding debts   Außenstände einziehen
   to collect taxes   Steuern erheben
   to collect the luggage   das Gepäck (in der Wohnung)
                                     abholen
   to collect the letters   den Briefkasten leeren
   collect call Am,   R-Gespräch n
    Br *reversed charge call*
collection [kəˈlekʃən]   1. Inkasso *n,* Einziehung *f;*
                                      2. Abholung *f;* Leerung *f (des*
                                      Briefkastens);
                                      3. Sammlung *f*
   The luggage is ready for   Das Gepäck steht zur Abholung
    collection.   bereit.
   collection department   Inkassoabteilung f
   collection of samples   Musterkollektion f
column [ˈkɔləm]   Zahlenkolonne *f;* Kolumne *f,* Spalte *(in*
                                      einer Zeitung); Rubrik *f*
   in the second column on the   in der zweiten Spalte der ersten Seite
    first page
combination [ˌkɔmbiˈneiʃən]   Zusammenschluß *m;* Konzern *m,*
                                      Kartell *n;* Interessengemeinschaft *f*
combine [ˈkɔmbain]   Vereinigung *f;* Konzern *m,*
                                      Kartell *n*
   combine price   *Verbandspreis* m
to combine [kəmˈbain]   (sich) vereinigen,
                                      (sich) zusammenschließen
comment [ˈkɔment]   s Kommentar *m,* Stellungnahme *f;*
                                      Kritik *f;*
                                      v kommentieren
   No comment.   Ich habe nichts dazu zu sagen.
   Did you make any comment   Haben Sie der Presse gegenüber
    to the press?   Stellung dazu genommen?
commercial [kəˈməːʃəl]   s Werbesendung *f;*
                                      a geschäftlich, handeltreibend,
                                      kaufmännisch

commercial aviation	Verkehrsluftfahrt f
commercial correspondence	Handelskorrespondenz f
commercial television	Werbefernsehen n
commercial traveller	Handelsreisender m
commission [kəˈmiʃən]	s Provisions-, Vermittlungsgebühr f; Kommission f, Ausschuß m; Geschäftsvollmacht f; v in Auftrag geben; bevollmächtigen
on a commission basis	auf Provisionsbasis
He is a member of the commission.	Er ist Mitglied der Kommission.
The goods are sold on commission.	Die Waren werden gegen Provision verkauft.
commission agent	Provisionsvertreter m
commitment [kəˈmitmənt]	finanzielle Verpflichtung f, Verbindlichkeit f
without any commitments	unverbindlich
committee [kəˈmiti]	Ausschuß m, Kommission f
to appoint a committee	einen Ausschuß einsetzen, eine Kommission bilden
ad hoc committee	Sonderausschuß m
advisory committee	beratender Ausschuß m
joint committee	gemischte Kommission f
standing committee	ständiger Ausschuß m
steering committee	Lenkungsausschuß m
commodities pl [kəˈmɔditiz]	Waren f pl, Gebrauchsgüter n pl.
common [ˈkɔmən]	gemeinsam, gemeinschaftlich
for the common good	im Interesse der Allgemeinheit
common law	bürgerliches Recht n
the Common Market	der Gemeinsame Markt
common stock	Stammaktien f pl
to communicate (with) [kəˈmjuːnikeit]	tr übermitteln, mitteilen; itr sich in Verbindung setzen (mit)
communication [kəˌmjuːniˈkeiʃən]	Mitteilung f (to an), Nachricht f; Verbindung f, Verkehr m
Communications had been cut.	Die Verbindungen waren unterbrochen worden.
He is in communication with us.	Er steht mit uns in Verbindung.
a means of communication	ein Verkehrsmittel n
company [ˈkʌmpəni]	(Handels-) Gesellschaft f
joint stock company	Br Aktiengesellschaft f
company meeting	Hauptversammlung f
company property	Betriebsvermögen n
to compare [kəmˈpɛə]	vergleichen
That cannot be compared with/to ...	Das ist nicht zu vergleichen mit ...
comparison [kəmˈpærisn]	Vergleich m

to make a comparison
comparison of costs
to compensate (for)
['kɔmpenseit]
compensation
[ˌkɔmpen'seiʃən]
We had to pay compensation.
as/by way of compensation
compensation claim
to compete with [kəm'piːt]
competent ['kɔmpitənt]
competition [ˌkɔmpi'tiʃən]
to enter into competition with
They are in competition with each other.
free/unfair competition
competitive [kəm'petitiv]
on a competitive basis
under fully competitive conditions
competitive price
competitor [kəm'petitə]
completion [kəm'pliːʃən]
near completion
completion date
compliance [kəm'plaiəns]
in compliance with your instructions
to complicate ['kɔmplikeit]
to comply with [kəm'plai]
They complied with his instructions.
to comply with a request/ a wish
to comply with the terms
component (part)
[kəm'pəunənt]
comprehensive
[ˌkɔmpri'hensiv]
compulsory [kəm'pʌlsəri]
computer [kəm'pjuːtə]
to computerize
[kəm'pjuːtəraiz]
to concentrate on
['kɔnsəntreit]
concentration
[ˌkɔnsən'treiʃən]

einen Vergleich anstellen
Kostenvergleich m
ausgleichen, kompensieren; entschädigen (für)

Entschädigung f, Schadenersatz m; Am Vergütung f, Lohn m
Wir mußten Schadenersatz leisten.

als Ersatz/Entschädigung
Schadenersatzanspruch m
konkurrieren mit
sach-, fachkundig; zuständig
Konkurrenz f, Wettbewerb m
in Konkurrenz treten mit

Sie machen sich gegenseitig Konkurrenz.

freier/unlauterer Wettbewerb m
konkurrenzfähig
auf Wettbewerbsgrundlage
unter Bedingungen des freien Wettbewerbs
Konkurrenzpreis m
Konkurrent m, Konkurrenz(firma f) f
Abschluß m, Vollendung f
kurz vor dem Abschluß
Fertigstellungstermin m
Befolgung f; Einwilligung f
Ihren Anordnungen entsprechend

erschweren, komplizieren
einwilligen in
Sie befolgten seine Anordnungen.

einer Bitte entsprechen/einem Wunsch nachkommen
den Bedingungen entsprechen
Bestandteil m

umfassend

obligatorisch, zwingend
Computer m, (Elektronen-) Rechner m
auf Computer umstellen

(sich) konzentrieren auf

Konzentration f, Zusammenfassung f, Zusammenballung f

concession [kənˈseʃən] Entgegenkommen n, Zugeständnis n; Konzession f
  to make no concessions keine Konzessionen machen
to conclude (from) [kənˈkluːd] beenden, abschließen; schließen (aus)
  What do you conclude from his letter? Welchen Schluß ziehen Sie aus seinem Schreiben?
  to conclude an agreement/ a contract ein Abkommen/einen Vertrag schließen
conclusion [kənˈkluːʒən] Ende n; Abschluß m; Schlußfolgerung f
  He has come to the same conclusion. Er ist zu derselben Schlußfolgerung gekommen.
  at the conclusion of his speech am Ende seiner Rede
  to draw a conclusion einen Schluß ziehen
  conclusion of an agreement Vertragsabschluß m
conditional acceptance [kənˈdiʃənl əkˈseptəns] bedingte Annahme f
conduct [ˈkɔndʌkt] Führung f, Leitung f; Verhalten n, Benehmen n
to conduct [kənˈdʌkt] führen, leiten
  to conduct a business ein Geschäft betreiben
  to conduct negotiations Verhandlungen führen
  conducted tour Gesellschaftsreise f
conference [ˈkɔnfərəns] Konferenz f, Verhandlung f, Besprechung f, Tagung f
  at the conference auf der Tagung
  He took part in a conference. Er nahm an einer Konferenz/Besprechung teil.
  to preside at a conference eine Tagung leiten
  conference room/table Konferenzzimmer n/-tisch m
confidential [ˌkɔnfiˈdenʃəl] vertraulich
  private and confidential streng vertraulich
to confirm [kənˈfəːm] bestätigen
  to confirm an order/a report einen Auftrag/Bericht bestätigen
confirmation [ˌkɔnfəˈmeiʃən] Bestätigung f, Bekräftigung f
connection [kəˈnekʃən] Beziehung f, Verbindung f; (Zug) Anschluß m; pl Kundschaft f
  in this connection in diesem Zusammenhang
  in connection with im Zusammenhang mit
  He missed his connection. Er versäumte seinen Anschluß.
  a wrong connection eine falsche Fernsprechverbindung
  He has far-reaching connections. Er hat weitreichende Verbindungen.
  business connections pl Geschäftsbeziehungen f pl
consent [kənˈsent] s Zustimmung f, Bewilligung f; v zustimmen, einwilligen
  by common consent mit allgemeiner Zustimmung
considering [kənˈsidəriŋ] mit Rücksicht auf

consignee [ˌkɔnsaiˈniː] — Empfänger m, Adressat m
consignment [kənˈsainmənt] — Konsignation f, Warenübergabe f, Lieferung f
  on consignment — *in Kommission*
  consignment note — *Frachtbrief* m
consignor [kənˈsainə] — Absender m; Verfrachter m
to construct [kənˈstrʌkt] — bauen, errichten; konstruieren
construction [kənˈstrʌkʃən] — Bau m, Konstruktion f; Bauwerk n
  The road is still under construction. — *Die Straße ist noch im Bau.*
to consult [kənˈsʌlt] — zu Rate ziehen, konsultieren
  to consult a dictionary — *in einem Wörterbuch nachschlagen*
consultant [kənˈsʌltənt] — Gutachter m; Berater m
  marketing consultant — *Vertriebsberater* m
  firm of consultants — *Unternehmensberatung* f (Firma)
to consume [kənˈsjuːm] — verbrauchen, konsumieren
consumer [kənˈsjuːmə] — Verbraucher m, Konsument m
  consumer goods pl — *Konsumgüter* n pl
  consumer industry — *Verbrauchsgüterindustrie* f
  consumer resistance — *Kaufunlust* f
consumption [kənˈsʌmpʃən] — Verbrauch m, Konsum m
  power consumption — *Stromverbrauch* m
contact [ˈkɔntækt] — Kontakt m, Verbindung f
to contact [kənˈtækt] — sich in Verbindung setzen (s.o. mit jdm)
  You can contact me by phone. — *Sie können sich mit mir fernmündlich in Verbindung setzen.*
container [kənˈteinə] — Versandbehälter m, Container m
contract [ˈkɔntrækt] — Vertrag m, Kontrakt m
  by contract — *vertraglich*
  to make/to enter into a contract — *einen Vertrag schließen*
contractor [kənˈtræktə] — Unternehmer m
  building contractor — *Bauunternehmer* m
to contribute [kənˈtribjuː(ː)t] — beitragen, beisteuern; (Geld) zuschießen
contribution [ˌkɔntriˈbjuːʃən] — Einlage(kapital n) f; Beitrag m
  to make a contribution — *einen Beitrag leisten*
  employer's contribution — *Arbeitgeberanteil* m
control [kənˈtrəul] — s Kontrolle f, Lenkung f; Bewirtschaftung f, Überwachung f
  v bewirtschaften, planen, lenken
  control of purchasing power — *Kaufkraftlenkung* f
  price control — *Preiskontrolle* f
  controlled prices pl — *gebundene Preise* m pl
convenience [kənˈviːnjəns] — Belieben n; Bequemlichkeit f, Komfort m
  at your earliest convenience — *sobald wie möglich*
  all modern conveniences — *mit allem Komfort*
convenient [kənˈviːnjənt] — passend, geeignet
  It is not convenient for me to come just now. — *Es paßt mir nicht, gerade jetzt zu kommen.*

conversion [kənˈvəːʃən] Umwandlung f; Konvertierung f; Umstellung f; Umrechnung f
  conversion of a plant to ... Umstellung f einer Fabrik auf ...
  conversion table Umrechnungstabelle f
  conversion loan Umschuldungsanleihe f
to convert [kənˈvəːt] umwandeln; konvertieren; umstellen
  to convert into cash zu Geld machen, flüssigmachen
to cooperate [kəuˈɔpəreit] zusammenarbeiten, mitwirken
cooperation [kəuˌɔpəˈreiʃən] Zusammenarbeit f, Mitwirkung f
cooperative (society) [kəuˈɔpərətiv səˈsaiəti] Genossenschaft f
  (consumer) cooperative Konsumgenossenschaft f
  cooperative bank Genossenschaftsbank f
to co-ordinate [kəuˈɔːdineit] aufeinander abstimmen, koordinieren
to cope with [kəup] fertig werden mit
  He had to cope with the situation. Er mußte die Situation meistern.
copy [ˈkɔpi] Kopie f; Durchschlag m; Pause f; (photographischer) Abzug m; Druckvorlage f
  certified copy beglaubigte Abschrift f
corporation [ˌkɔːpəˈreiʃən] Körperschaft f, eingetragene Gesellschaft f; Am Aktiengesellschaft f
  public corporation Körperschaft des öffentlichen Rechts
  corporation tax Körperschaftssteuer f
correspondence [ˌkɔrisˈpɔndəns] Schriftwechsel m, Korrespondenz f
  I take care of/I handle the correspondence. Ich erledige die Post.
  correspondence clerk Korrespondent m
cost [kɔst] Gestehungskosten pl; pl Unkosten pl, Auslagen f pl, Spesen pl
  cost of living allowance Teuerungszulage f
  cost of living index Lebenshaltungsindex m
  cost free kostenlos
  at cost price zum Selbstkostenpreis m
  cost of production Produktionskosten pl
counter [ˈkauntə] Schalter m; Ladentisch m; Theke f
  to sell over the counter im Laden verkaufen
to countermand [ˌkauntəˈmɑːnd] rückgängig machen, stornieren
coupon [ˈkuːpɔn] Kassenzettel m; Gutschein m; Zinsschein m; Kontrollabschnitt m
  dividend coupon Dividendenschein m
cover [ˈkʌvə] Deckung f, Versicherungsschutz m; Briefumschlag m
  under separate cover mit gleicher Post

coverage [ˈkʌvəridʒ]   (Schadens-) Deckung f,
                                Versicherungsschutz m
   full coverage   *volle Deckung* f
craft [krɑːft]   Gewerbe n, Handwerk n; Fahrzeug n,
                                Schiff n, Flugzeug n
   arts and crafts   *Kunsthandwerk* n
   craftsman   *Handwerker* m
credit [ˈkredit]   Kredit m; Kreditwürdigkeit f;
                                Guthaben n
   credit and debit   *Soll und Haben*
   on credit   *auf Kredit*
   sale on credit   *Verkauf* m *auf Kredit*
   three months credit   *drei Monate Ziel*
   credit with a savings bank   *Sparkassenguthaben* n
   to grant/to open a credit   *einen Kredit bewilligen/eröffnen*
   to the credit of your account   *zugunsten Ihres Kontos*
   credit balance   *Guthaben* n
   credit note   *Gutschriftanzeige* f
creditor [ˈkreditə]   Gläubiger m
crisis, pl **-es** [ˈkraisis, -iːz]   Krise f
   economic/financial crisis   *Wirtschafts-/Finanzkrise* f
currency [ˈkʌrənsi]   Währung f; Geldumlauf m
   currency control/reform   *Währungskontrolle* f/-*reform* f
   foreign currency   *fremde Währung* f; *Devisen* f pl
current [ˈkʌrənt]   laufend; marktgängig; aktuell
   at the current rate of   *zum Tageskurs* (von Devisen)
     exchange
   current account   *laufendes Konto* n,
                                 Kontokorrentkonto n
   current price   *Tagespreis* m
   current events pl   *Tagesereignisse* n pl
custom [ˈkʌstəm]   Kundschaft f, Kundenkreis m;
                                Gewohnheit f
   according to custom   *usancemäßig*
   This shop has little custom.   *Dieser Laden hat einen kleinen*
                                Kundenkreis.
customer [ˈkʌstəmə]   Kunde m, Käufer m, Abnehmer m
   chance/regular customer   *Lauf-/Stammkunde* m
customs [ˈkʌstəmz]   Zoll m; Zollbehörde f
   to pay customs duty   *Zoll bezahlen*
   The passengers went   *Die Passagiere gingen durch den Zoll.*
     through the customs.
   customs clearance   *Zollabfertigung* f
   customs officer   *Zollbeamter* m
cut (cut, cut) [kʌt]   s Kürzung f, Abstrich m;
                                 v kürzen; abbuchen
   to cut prices   *die Preise herabsetzen*
   to cut rates   *die Gebühren senken*
   He has cut his losses.   *Er hat seine Verluste abgeschrieben.*

damage – deal

price cut, cut in prices	Preissenkung f
cut in salary	Gehaltskürzung f

D

damage [ˈdæmidʒ]
s Schaden m, Nachteil m;
v schaden, beeinträchtigen
  He had to pay damages.   Er mußte Schadenersatz leisten.
  to do damage   Schaden anrichten
  action for damages   Schadenersatzklage f
  to sue for damages   auf Schadenersatz klagen
  to claim damages   Schadenersatz fordern
  seriously damaged   schwer beschädigt
danger money [ˈdeindʒə ˌmʌni]   Gefahrenzulage f
data pl (mit v im pl oder sing) [deitə]   Daten n pl, Unterlagen f pl
  personal data   Personalangaben f pl
  data processing   elektronische Datenverarbeitung f
date [deit]   Datum n; Zeitpunkt m; Termin m
  at an early date   möglichst bald
  date as per postmark   Datum des Poststempels
  date of maturity   Fälligkeitstermin m
  date of invoice   Rechnungsdatum n
  delivery date   Lieferungstermin m
day [dei]   Tag m; Termin m
  eight-hour day   Achtstundentag m
  per day   täglich
  pay day   Zahltag m
dead [ded]   ruhig, still, flau
  dead market   lustloser Markt m
  dead weight   Leergewicht n
  dead season   geschäftslose Zeit f
deadline [ˈdedlain]   Stichtag m, letzter Termin m
  He met the deadline.   Er hielt die Frist ein.
  He is always working to a deadline.   Er arbeitet immer unter Termindruck.
deadlock [ˈdedlɔk]   völliger Stillstand m, toter Punkt m; Sackgasse f
deal (with) [diːl]   s Geschäft n, Handel m; Abschluß m; Übereinkommen n;
v ein Geschäft machen, Handel treiben (mit)
  It's a deal!   Abgemacht!
  square deal   ehrliche Abmachung f, reeller Handel m
  He made a lot of money on that deal.   Er hat viel Geld bei diesem Geschäft verdient.

He deals in textiles.	Er handelt mit/Er führt Textilien.
Can you deal with ...?	Können Sie ... absetzen?
They closed the deal.	Sie machten das Geschäft perfekt.
dealer [ˈdiːlə]	Händler *m*, Kaufmann *m*
wholesale dealer	Grossist *m*
used-car dealer	Gebrauchtwagenhändler *m*
dealing [ˈdiːliŋ]	Handel *m*, Geschäft *n*; Geschäftsverkehr *m*; *pl* Umsätze *m pl*
cash deal	Bargeschäft n
dealing in real estate	Grundstückshandel *m*
to have dealings with s.o.	mit jdm zu tun haben/in Geschäftsverbindung stehen
debit [ˈdebit]	*s* Debet-, Schuldposten *m*; Lastschrift *f*; *v* in Rechnung stellen, belasten
to the debit of	zu Lasten *gen*
your debit balance	Saldo zu Ihren Lasten
to debit an account	ein Konto belasten
on the debit side	auf der Debetseite
debtor [ˈdetə]	Schuldner *m*, Debitor *m*
debts *pl* [dets]	Schulden *f pl*; Verbindlichkeiten *f pl*
bad debts	zweifelhafte Forderungen f pl
He is in debt.	Er ist verschuldet.
decimal [ˈdesiməl]	*s* Dezimalzahl *f*; *a* Dezimal-
decline [diˈklain]	*s* Rückgang *m*, Niedergang *m*, Abschwächung *f*; *v* zurückgehen, sich verschlechtern; ablehnen
decline in business	Geschäftsrückgang *m*
decline of/in prices	Preisrückgang *m*
decline in production	Produktionsrückgang *m*
decline in sales	Umsatzrückgang *m*
He declined their offer.	Er lehnte ihr Angebot ab.
declining sales pl	sinkende Umsätze m pl
decrease [ˈdiː-kriːs]	Verminderung *f*, Abnahme *f*, Reduzierung *f*
decrease in population/in prices	Bevölkerungs-/Preisrückgang *m*
decrease in value	Wertminderung f
to be on the decrease	im Abnehmen begriffen sein
to decrease [diːˈkriːs]	vermindern, reduzieren, herabsetzen
Oil consumption has decreased.	Der Ölverbrauch ist zurückgegangen.
to deduct from [diˈdʌkt]	abziehen, absetzen von
Deduct ten per cent.	Ziehen Sie 10% ab!
deduction [diˈdʌkʃən]	Abzug *m*, Absetzung *f* (*from* von), Rabatt *m*, Nachlaß *m*
after deduction of expenses	nach Abzug der Spesen

34 defect – deposit

defect [di'fekt] — Fehler *m*, Defekt *m*, Mangel *m*
defective [di'fektiv] — schadhaft, fehlerhaft, beschädigt
deficit ['defisit] — Fehlbetrag *m*; Defizit *n*, Unterbilanz *f*
  to show a deficit — mit einem Verlust abschließen
definite ['definit] — bestimmt; genau festgelegt; endgültig

  definite booking — feste Bestellung f/Anmeldung f
  definite order — fester Auftrag m
  They came to a definite understanding. — Sie gelangten zu einer endgültigen Vereinbarung.

delivered [di'livəd] — geliefert, zugestellt, übergeben
  delivered free — frei Haus
delivery [di'livəri] — (Ab-, Aus-) Lieferung *f*, Zusendung *f*, Zustellung *f*

  payable on delivery — zahlbar bei Lieferung
  delivery of letters — Briefzustellung f
  delivery note — Lieferschein m

demand (for) [di'mɑ:nd] — Nachfrage *f* (nach); Bedarf *m* (an)
  to be very much in demand — sehr gefragt sein
  supply and demand — Angebot und Nachfrage
  payable on demand — zahlbar auf Verlangen

to demonstrate ['demənstreit] — vorführen, zeigen; darlegen, beweisen
  He'll demonstrate how the machine works. — Er wird vorführen, wie die Maschine arbeitet.

demonstration [,demən'streiʃən] — Vorführung *f*; Demonstration *f*; praktisches Beispiel *n*
  to give a demonstration — vorführen
  demonstration model — Vorführgerät n

department [di'pɑ:tmənt] — Abteilung *f*, Geschäftsbereich *m*; Branche *f*, Geschäftszweig *m*; Amt *n*; Am Ministerium *n*

  accounts/export department — Buchhaltungs-/Exportabteilung f
  sales department — Verkaufsabteilung f
  department store — Warenhaus n

departure (for) [di'pɑ:tʃə] — Abfahrt *f* (nach), Abflug *m* (nach), Abreise *f* (nach)

deposit [di'pɔzit] — s Hinterlegung *f*; (Geld-) Einlage *f*, Einzahlung *f*; Depot *n*; pl Depositengelder *n pl*, -einlagen *f pl*; v einzahlen, hinterlegen *(with s.o.* bei jdm); anzahlen

  to make a deposit at the bank — eine Einzahlung auf der Bank leisten
  to pay/to leave a deposit — eine Anzahlung machen
  He deposited his money in the bank. — Er zahlte sein Geld in der Bank ein.
  deposit account — Sparkonto n; Am Festgeldkonto n
  deposit slip — Einzahlungsbeleg m

depreciation [diˌpriːʃiˈeiʃən]   Abschreibung *f;* Abwertung *f*
depression [diˈpreʃən]   Konjunkturrückgang *m,* Flaute *f; (Börse)* Baisse *f*

  economic depression   Wirtschaftskrise *f*
  market depression   Preisdruck *m*
design [diˈzain]   *s* Formgebung *f;* Konstruktion *f;* Entwurf *m,* Plan *m;* Muster *n,* Dessin *n;* *v* entwerfen, konstruieren

  our latest designs   unsere neuesten Muster/Modelle
  registered design   Gebrauchsmuster *n*
designer [diˈzainə]   Formgestalter *m,* Musterzeichner *m;* Konstrukteur *m*
desk [desk]   Schalter *m;* Schreib-, Ladentisch *m*
  Pay at the cash-desk.   An der Kasse zahlen!
  reception desk   (Hotel) Empfang *m*
destination [ˌdestiˈneiʃən]   Bestimmung(sort *m*) *f;* Ziel *n*
  He reached his destination.   Er erreichte seinen Bestimmungsort.
devaluation [ˌdiːvæljuˈeiʃən]   Abwertung *f*
to devalue [ˈdiːˈvæljuː]   abwerten
device [diˈvais]   Vorrichtung *f,* Gerät *n;* Erfindung *f;* Plan *m,* Vorhaben *n*

  safety device   Sicherheitsvorrichtung *f*
diagram [ˈdaiəgræm]   graphische Darstellung *f,* Schaubild *n;* Tabelle *f*

to dial [ˈdaiəl]   *(Telefon)* wählen
  He dialled the wrong number.   Er hat die falsche Nummer gewählt.

  dialling tone   Amtszeichen *n*
  dialling code   Vorwahl(nummer) *f*
to diminish [diˈminiʃ]   verringern, reduzieren
directory [diˈrektəri]   Adreßbuch *n*
  classified directory   Branchenadreßbuch *n*
  telephone directory   Telefonbuch *n*
disadvantage [ˌdisədˈvaːntidʒ]   Nachteil *m*

  I'm at a disadvantage.   Ich bin im Nachteil.
discount [ˈdiskaunt]   Preisnachlaß *m,* Skonto *m, n,* Rabatt *m;* Diskont *m*

  less discount   abzüglich Skonto
  to raise/to lower the discount   den Diskont(satz) erhöhen/herabsetzen
  cash discount   Kassaskonto *m*
  cash without discount   Barzahlung ohne Abzug
  group discount   Gruppenermäßigung *f*
to dismantle [disˈmæntl]   auseinandernehmen; demontieren
dispatch [disˈpætʃ]   *s* Abfertigung *f,* Versand *m,* Beförderung *f;* Spedition *f;* Telegramm *n;* *v* abschicken, absenden; rasch erledigen

36 display – draw

dispatch department	Versandabteilung f
ready for dispatch	versandfertig
dispatch note	Versandanzeige f
display [dis'plei]	s Auslage f, Dekoration f; Ausstellung f;
	v ausstellen, auslegen; zeigen
window display	Schaufensterauslage f
The goods are on display.	Die Waren sind ausgestellt.
disposal [dis'pəuzəl]	Absatz m, Verkauf m; Verfügung f
for disposal	zum Verkauf
He/It is at your disposal.	Er/Es steht Ihnen zur Verfügung.
to dispose of [dis'pəuz]	verfügen (über), disponieren; verkaufen, abstoßen; erledigen; beseitigen
He disposed of his business.	Er verkaufte sein Geschäft.
We had to dispose of our house.	Wir mußten unser Haus verkaufen.
to dissolve [di'zɔlv]	(Firma, Gesellschaft) auflösen
distribution [ˌdistri'bju:ʃən]	Vertrieb m, Verteilung f
distribution of dividends	Dividendenausschüttung f
distribution of a film	Filmverleih m
distributor [dis'tribjutə]	Groß-, Zwischenhändler m
dividend ['dividend]	Gewinnanteil m, Dividende f
dividend warrant	Gewinnanteilschein m
dock [dɔk]	Dock n; Hafenbecken n; pl Hafenanlagen f pl
dry/floating dock	Trocken-/Schwimmdock n
document ['dɔkjumənt]	Urkunde f; Unterlage f; pl Verlade-, Versand-, Verschiffungspapiere n pl
documentary [ˌdɔkju'mentəri]	urkundlich, dokumentarisch
documentary credit	Dokumentenkredit m
domestic [dəu'mestik]	einheimisch, inländisch
domestic market	Binnenmarkt m
domestic production	Inlandsproduktion f
down [daun]	(Preis) gefallen
down payment	Anzahlung f
downtown	Am Geschäftsviertel n, Innenstadt f
draft [drɑ:ft]	Zahlungsanweisung f; Tratte f, Wechsel m; Entwurf m
draft payable at sight	Sichttratte f
He made a draft on the firm.	Er zog einen Wechsel auf die Firma.
final draft	endgültiger Entwurf m
draw (on) [drɔ:]	s Attraktion f; Verlosung f; v (Geld) abheben (from von); (Wechsel) ziehen, ausstellen (auf); (Gehalt) beziehen
to draw a bill of exchange on s.o.	einen Wechsel auf jdn ziehen/ausstellen; trassieren
to draw a cheque/Am check	einen Scheck ausstellen
to draw money from an account	Geld von einem Konto abheben

drawback - economy

drawback [ˈdrɔːbæk]   Nachteil *m*; Rückvergütung *f*
drive [draiv]   Verkaufskampagne *f*, Werbefeldzug *m*
  sales drive   Absatzsteigerung f, -kampagne f
drop [drɔp]   *s* Sinken *n*, Fallen *n*, Rückgang *m*;
   v fallen, sinken, zurückgehen
  drop in prices/turnover   Preis-/Umsatzrückgang m
  drop in production   Produktionsrückgang m
due [djuː]   fällig, sofort zahlbar; gebührend
  in due course   *fristgerecht*
  The rent is due next month.   *Die Miete ist nächsten Monat fällig.*
  They are due to return today.   *Sie werden heute zurückerwartet.*
  The letter is duly signed.   *Der Brief ist ordnungsgemäß unterschrieben.*
  due date   *Fälligkeitsdatum n*
dues *pl* [djuːz]   Gebühren *f pl*, Abgaben *f pl*
  membership dues   *Mitgliedsbeitrag m*
duplicate [ˈdjuːplikit]   Zweitschrift *f*, Kopie *f*
  in duplicate   *in doppelter Ausfertigung*
  to make out in duplicate   *doppelt ausfertigen*
to duplicate [ˈdjuːplikeit]   eine Abschrift machen von; vervielfältigen

duty [ˈdjuːti]   Abgabe *f*, Gebühr *f*; Zoll *m*
  liable to duty   *zollpflichtig*
  duty-paid   *verzollt, versteuert*
  customs duties pl   *Zollabgaben* f pl
  duty-free shop   *zollfreies Geschäft* (z.B. in einem Flughafen)

E

earnings *pl* [ˈəːniŋz]   Lohn *m*, Gehalt *n*, Verdienst *m*, Einkommen *n*; Einnahmen *f pl*
  annual earnings   *Jahreseinkommen n*
  hourly earnings   *Stundenlohn m*
economic [ˌiːkəˈnɔmik]   wirtschaftlich
  economic conditions pl   *Wirtschaftslage f*
  economic development   *wirtschaftliche Entwicklung* f
  economic recovery   *Wirtschaftsbelebung* f
economical [ˌiːkəˈnɔmikəl]   sparsam, haushälterisch
economics (*pl* mit *sing*) [ˌiːkəˈnɔmiks]   Volkswirtschaft(slehre) *f*
economy [i(ː)ˈkɔnəmi]   Wirtschaft *f*; Wirtschaftlichkeit *f*; Sparsamkeit *f*
  free economy   *freie Wirtschaft* f
  planned economy   *Planwirtschaft* f
  economy class   *Touristenklasse* f
  economy fare   *Preis* m *der Touristenklasse*

education [ˌedju(:)ˈkeiʃən] — Ausbildung *f*; Bildung *f*
  general education — *Allgemeinbildung* f
  professional education — *Berufsausbildung* f
educational [ˌedju(:)ˈkeiʃənl] — erzieherisch
  educational film — *Lehrfilm* m
effect (on) [iˈfekt] — *s* Wirkung *f*, Auswirkung *f* (auf); Ergebnis *n*; *pl* Effekten *f pl*; Vermögenswerte *m pl*; Sachbesitz *m*; *v* bewirken, herbeiführen
  to go/to come into effect, to take effect — in Kraft treten
  This event had an adverse effect on the market. — Dieses Ereignis beeinflußte den Markt ungünstig.
  with effect from — mit Wirkung vom
  to effect payment — Zahlung leisten
  a phone call to the same effect — ein Telefongespräch desselben Inhalts
effective [iˈfektiv] — (rechts)wirksam, rechtskräftig; wirkungsvoll
  effective from/as of January 1st — mit Wirkung vom 1. Januar
  effective immediately — mit sofortiger Wirkung
  to become effective — Gültigkeit erlangen
  effective measures pl — *wirkungsvolle Maßnahmen*
efficiency [iˈfiʃənsi] — Leistungsfähigkeit *f*; Wirtschaftlichkeit *f*; Tauglichkeit *f*
  efficiency expert — *Rationalisierungsfachmann* m
  efficiency bonus — *Leistungszulage* f
efficient [iˈfiʃənt] — leistungsfähig; gut funktionierend; wirtschaftlich, rationell
  He is very efficient in his work. — Er ist in seiner Arbeit sehr tüchtig.
eight-hour day — Achtstundentag *m*
elaborate [iˈlæbərit] — bis ins einzelne ausgearbeitet; sorgfältig durchdacht
  an elaborate scheme — *ein genau überlegter Plan*
to elapse [iˈlæps] — (Zeit) vergehen; (Frist) ablaufen
electrician [ilekˈtriʃən] — Elektrotechniker *m*
electrification [iˌlektrifiˈkeiʃən] — Elektrifizierung *f*
electronic, *adv* **-ally** [ilekˈtrɔnik] — elektronisch
  electronic brain — *Elektronengehirn* n
electronics (*pl* mit *sing*) [ilekˈtrɔniks] — Elektronik *f*
element [ˈelimənt] — Grundbestandteil *m*, wesentlicher Bestandteil *m*; Bauteil *m, n*
  There is always an element of uncertainty involved. — *Es bleibt immer ein Unsicherheitsfaktor.*

eligible [ˈelidʒəbl]
It is difficult to find an eligible candidate.
to eliminate [iˈlimineit]
We had to eliminate all difficulties/the causes.
elimination [iˌlimiˈneiʃən]
to embark (for) [imˈbaːk]
to embark upon s.th.
He embarked upon a business career.
embarkation card [ˌembaːˈkeiʃən]
embassy [ˈembəsi]
to embrace [imˈbreis]
His marketing plans embraced the whole of Western Europe.
to emerge [iˈməːdʒ]
A new plan emerged from the conference.
emergency [iˈməːdʒənsi]

in an emergency/in case of emergency
emergency door/exit
emergency landing
emigrant [ˈemigrənt]
to emigrate to [ˈemigreit]
emigration [ˌemigreiʃən]
employed [imˈplɔid]
to be employed
employee [ˌemplɔiˈiː]
employer [imˈplɔiə]
employment [imˈplɔimənt]

The factory provides employment for many men.
employment agency
employment market
empties *pl* [ˈemptiz]
Empties non returnable.
to enable [iˈneibl]

This enabled him to find a good job.
to enclose [inˈkləuz]
Enclosed please find . . .

bank-, diskontfähig; geeignet, qualifiziert
Es ist schwierig, einen geeigneten Bewerber zu finden.
ausscheiden, ausschließen
Wir mußten alle Schwierigkeiten/die Ursachen beseitigen.
Ausschaltung *f*, Ausscheidung *f*
sich einschiffen (nach)
sich auf etw einlassen
Er wählte den Beruf eines Kaufmanns.

Bordkarte *f*

Botschaft *f*
umfassen, in sich schließen
Seine Verkaufspläne erstreckten sich auf ganz Westeuropa.

in Erscheinung treten, sich herausstellen
Das Ergebnis der Konferenz war ein neuer Plan.
plötzlicher Notstand *m*, Krise *f*, kritische Situation *f*
notfalls, im Notfall

Notausgang m
Notlandung f
Auswanderer *m*
auswandern nach
Auswanderung *f*
angestellt; berufstätig
in Arbeit stehen
Arbeitnehmer *m*; Angestellter *m*
Arbeitgeber *m*, Unternehmer *m*
Beschäftigung *f*; Arbeits-, Dienstverhältnis *n*
Die Fabrik bietet vielen Menschen einen Arbeitsplatz.
Stellen-, Arbeitsvermittlungsbüro n
Stellenmarkt m
Leergut *n*
Leergut wird nicht zurückgenommen.
ermächtigen, befähigen (*s.o.* jdn); ermöglichen
Das verhalf ihm dazu, eine gute Stellung zu finden.
einschließen, umzäunen; umfassen
Beiliegend/In der Anlage erhalten Sie . . .

He enclosed a photograph with his letter.	Er legte seinem Brief ein Foto bei.
enclosure [inˈkləuʒə]	Beilage f, Einlage f; Umzäunung f
encouragement [inˈkʌridʒmənt]	Ermutigung f; Förderung f
by way of encouragement	zur Aufmunterung
to encroach [inˈkrəutʃ]	eingreifen (*upon* in); übermäßig in Anspruch nehmen
That's encroaching upon his rights.	Das greift in seine Rechte ein.
to endanger [inˈdeindʒə]	gefährden
endeavo(u)r [inˈdevə]	s Anstrengung f, Bemühung f; v sich bemühen (*after* um), sich anstrengen
They endeavoured to do their best.	Sie gaben sich alle Mühe.
endless [ˈendlis]	endlos, ohne Ende; ununterbrochen
to endorse [inˈdɔːs]	indossieren, girieren
to endorse a bill of exchange	einen Wechsel indossieren
He endorsed the plan/her opinion.	Er billigte den Plan/pflichtete ihrer Meinung bei.
endorsee [ˌendɔːˈsiː]	Indossatar m, Giratar m
endorsement [inˈdɔːsmənt]	Indossament n, Giro n; Bestätigung f
endorser [inˈdɔːsə]	Indossant m, Girant m
endowment [inˈdaumənt]	Stiftung f
endowment funds	Stiftungsvermögen n
to endure [inˈdjuə]	aushalten, ertragen
to enforce [inˈfɔːs]	Geltung verschaffen; durchsetzen, erzwingen
to enforce a law	ein Gesetz durchführen
to enforce a claim	einen Anspruch gerichtlich geltend machen
enforced sale	Zwangsverkauf m
enforcement [inˈfɔːsmənt]	Durchsetzung f; Vollstreckung f
engaged [inˈgeidʒd]	reserviert, besetzt, belegt; beschäftigt
He is engaged in business.	Er ist geschäftlich tätig.
engaged signal	Besetztzeichen n
The number is engaged.	Die Nummer ist besetzt.
My time is fully engaged.	Ich habe keine freie Minute.
engagement [inˈgeidʒmənt]	Verbindlichkeit f; Verabredung f; Anstellung f, Beschäftigung f
I have another engagement.	Ich habe eine andere Verabredung.
engagement book	Terminkalender m
engineer [ˌendʒiˈniə]	Ingenieur m, Techniker m; Am Lokomotivführer m
consulting engineer	beratender Ingenieur m
engineering [ˌendʒiˈniəriŋ]	Ingenieurwissenschaft f; Technik f; Maschinenbau m
engineering facilities pl	technische Einrichtungen f pl

to enlarge (upon) [inˈlɑːdʒ] — tr vergrößern; erweitern; itr sich auslassen (über)
I don't want to enlarge upon the matter. — Ich möchte mich über die Sache nicht näher auslassen.
He enlarged his business. — Er erweiterte sein Geschäft.
enlargement [inˈlɑːdʒmənt] — Vergrößerung f; Erweiterung f
to enrol(l) [inˈrəul] — registrieren, verzeichnen; (*einen Namen*) einschreiben
to enrol workers — Arbeiter einstellen
to ensure [inˈʃuə] — schützen (*against* gegen); garantieren, gewährleisten
to entail [inˈteil] — nach sich ziehen, zur Folge haben
That entails great expense. — Das verursacht große Ausgaben.
enterprise [ˈentəpraiz] — Unternehmen n, Betrieb m
business enterprise — geschäftliches Unternehmen n
free enterprise — freies Unternehmertum n
a man of enterprise — ein Mann mit Unternehmungsgeist
enterprising [ˈentəpraiziŋ] — unternehmungslustig
to entice (from) [inˈtais] — weglocken (von); abwerben
entitled [inˈtaitld] — berechtigt, ermächtigt
He is entitled to vote. — Er ist stimmberechtigt.
entrepreneur [ˌɔntrəprəˈnəː] — Unternehmer m
to entrust (with) [inˈtrʌst] — anvertrauen; betrauen (mit)
He was entrusted with the sale. — Der Verkauf wurde ihm übertragen.
entry [ˈentri] — Buchung f, Eintragung f; Eingang m (*von Geldern*); Zolldeklaration f
He made an entry in the book. — Er machte eine Buchung.
double-entry book-keeping — doppelte Buchführung f
entry into the Common Market — Beitritt zum Gemeinsamen Markt
credit/debit entry — Gut-/Lastschrift f
upon entry — nach Eingang
no entry — verbotener Eingang
entry form — Anmeldeformular n
entry visa — Einreisevisum n
envelope [ˈenvələup] — Briefumschlag m
to put a letter into an envelope — einen Brief in einen Umschlag stecken
window envelope — Fensterbriefumschlag m
equality [iˈkwɔliti] — Gleichheit f, -berechtigung f
equality of votes — Stimmengleichheit f
equally [ˈiːkwəli] — in gleicher Weise, zu gleichen Teilen
to equip [iˈkwip] — ausrüsten, ausstatten
equipment [iˈkwipmənt] — Ausstattung f, Einrichtung f; Betriebsanlage f; Apparatur f
factory equipment — Betriebseinrichtung f
office equipment — Büroeinrichtung f

equities pl [ˈekwitiz]   Stammaktien f pl
equivalent [iˈkwivələnt]   gleichwertig; entsprechend
    What is $10 equivalent to in   *Was entspricht $ 10,— in deutschem*
    German money?   *Geld?*
era [ˈiərə]   Ära f, Epoche f
    the Christian era   *die christliche Zeitrechnung*
to erase [iˈreiz]   ausradieren; *(Tonband)* löschen
eraser [iˈreizə]   Radiergummi m
to erect [iˈrekt]   errichten, bauen
    to erect a block of flats   *einen Wohnblock bauen*
errand [ˈerənd]   Besorgung f, Botengang m
    to run an errand   *einen Auftrag ausführen, einen Botengang machen*
    errand boy   *Laufbursche m, -junge m*
error [ˈerə]   Irrtum m, Versehen n, Fehler m
    in error   *aus Versehen, irrtümlicherweise*
    Errors excepted.   *Irrtümer vorbehalten.*
essentials pl [iˈsenʃəlz]   das Wesentliche; wesentliche Punkte pl
to establish (o.s.) [isˈtæbliʃ]   begründen, errichten; sich etablieren
    The business was established in 1910.   *Das Geschäft wurde 1910 gegründet.*
    He has established himself as a lawyer.   *Er hat sich als Anwalt niedergelassen.*
establishment [isˈtæbliʃmənt]   Unternehmen n, Firma f, Geschäft n
    banking establishment   *Bankinstitut n*
    industrial establishment   *Industrieunternehmen n*
estate [isˈteit]   Besitz m, Vermögen n; Landsitz m
    real estate   *Immobilien pl, Grundbesitz m*
    estate agent   *Grundstücksmakler m*
esteem [isˈtiːm]   Achtung f
estimate [ˈestimit]   Kostenanschlag m, Voranschlag m
    a rough estimate   *ein grober Überschlag, eine ungefähre Schätzung*
    to make an estimate of the costs   *einen Kostenvoranschlag machen*
to estimate [ˈestimeit]   veranschlagen, bewerten
estimation [ˌestiˈmeiʃən]   Meinung f, Ansicht f; Würdigung f, Beurteilung f
    in my estimation   *meiner Ansicht nach*
European [ˌjuərəˈpiː)ən]   europäisch
    European Community (EC)   *Europäische Gemeinschaft (EG) f*
to evade [iˈveid]   ausweichen, umgehen
    He evaded the question.   *Er umging die Frage/vermied es, die Frage zu beantworten.*
to evaluate [iˈvæljueit]   bewerten, beurteilen, abschätzen
evaluation [iˌvæljuˈeiʃən]   Bewertung f, Wertermittlung f
evidence [ˈevidəns]   Beweismaterial n; Aussage f, Gutachten n
    for lack of evidence   *mangels Beweises*

to give evidence (als Zeuge) *aussagen*
evident [ˈevidənt] offensichtlich, augenscheinlich, klar
It was evident to all of them that... *Es lag für alle klar auf der Hand, daß...*
ex [eks] 1. von, ab;
2. ohne, ausschließlich
ex factory/quay/ warehouse/works *ab Fabrik/Kai/Lager/Werk*
ex interest *ohne Zinsen*
to exaggerate [igˈzædʒəreit] übertreiben
to exceed [ikˈsiːd] überschreiten, übersteigen
He exceeded the speed limit. *Er überschritt die zulässige Höchstgeschwindigkeit.*
except [ikˈsept] *v* ausnehmen, ausschließen; *prp* ausgenommen
exception [ikˈsepʃən] Ausnahme *f*
with the exception of *mit Ausnahme von*
an exception to the rule *eine Ausnahme von der Regel*
The exception proves the rule. *Die Ausnahme bestätigt die Regel.*
exceptional [ikˈsepʃənl] ungewöhnlich, außergewöhnlich
exceptional offer *Vorzugsangebot n*
excess [ikˈses] Übermaß *n*, Überschuß *m*
to excess *im Übermaß*
excess luggage Br/ *baggage* Am *Übergepäck n*
excessive [ikˈsesiv] übermäßig, übertrieben
an excessive amount *ein übertrieben hoher Betrag*
exchange [iksˈtʃeindʒ] *s* Umwechseln *n;* Umtausch *m;* Wechselverkehr *m;* Währung *f;* Wechselkurs *m;*
v um-, austauschen
bill of exchange *Wechsel* m
foreign exchange *Devisen* f pl
exchange rate *Wechsel-, Umrechnungskurs* m
(telephone) exchange *(Telefon-) Vermittlung* f
Exchange [iksˈtʃeindʒ] Börse *f*
to exclude from [iksˈkluːd] ausschließen von
exclusive [iksˈkluːsiv] ausschließlich, alleinig
exclusive agent *Alleinvertreter* m
to have exclusive use of s.th. *etw zur alleinigen Verfügung haben*
to have the exclusive rights *die alleinigen Rechte haben*
to execute [ˈeksikjuːt] aus-, durchführen
to execute an order/a plan *einen Auftrag ausführen/einen Plan durchführen*
to execute a deed *eine Urkunde unterzeichnen*
execution [ˌeksiˈkjuːʃən] Aus-, Durchführung *f;* Ausfertigung *f (einer Urkunde)*

executive [igˈzekjutiv] — s leitender Angestellter m; a ausführend; Am geschäftsführend
   top executive — Spitzenkraft f
executor [igˈzekjutə] — Testamentsvollstrecker m
to exhaust [igˈzɔ:st] — erschöpfen, aufbrauchen
   He exhausted all possibilities. — Er schöpfte alle Möglichkeiten aus.
to exhibit [igˈzibit] — zur Schau stellen, ausstellen; *(Urkunde)* vorlegen
   to exhibit goods — Waren ausstellen
exhibition [ˌeksiˈbiʃən] — Ausstellung f, Schau f; Vorlage f *(von Urkunden)*
   industrial exhibition — Industrieausstellung f
   exhibition hall — Ausstellungshalle f
   exhibition stand — Ausstellungsstand m
exhibitor [igˈzibitə] — Aussteller m, Messeteilnehmer m
exit [ˈeksit] — Ausgang m; Ausreise f; Am (Autobahn-) Ausfahrt f
   exit permit — Ausreiseerlaubnis f
to expand [iksˈpænd] — erweitern, ausdehnen, ausweiten
   He expanded his business. — Er erweiterte sein Geschäft.
expansion [iksˈpænʃən] — Ausdehnung f, Erweiterung f, Ausweitung f; Expansion f
   expansion of credit/of production — Kredit-/Produktionsausweitung f
expenditure [iksˈpenditʃə] — Aufwand m, Ausgaben f pl, Kosten pl
   Limit your expenditure. — Schränke deine Ausgaben ein!
expense [iksˈpens] — Ausgabe f; pl Unkosten pl, Spesen pl
   at great expense — mit großem Geldaufwand
   at the company's expense — auf Kosten der Firma
   after deduction of expenses — nach Abzug der Kosten
expert [ˈekspə:t] — Fachmann m, Experte m
   expert opinion — Sachverständigengutachten n
to expire [iksˈpaiə] — ungültig werden
   When does your passport expire? — Wann läuft Ihr Paß ab?
exploitation [ˌeksplɔiˈteiʃən] — Ausnutzung f, Verwertung f
export [ˈekspɔ:t] — Ausfuhr(handel m) f, Export m
   chief exports pl — Hauptausfuhrgüter n pl
   export industry — Exportindustrie f
   export permit — Ausfuhrgenehmigung f
   export trade — Außenhandel m
to export [eksˈpɔ:t] — ausführen, exportieren
exporter [eksˈpɔ:tə] — Exporteur m
express [iksˈpres] — Eilbeförderung f; Expreßbrief m; D-Zug m
   express delivery — Eilzustellung f
   to send a parcel express — ein Eilpaket aufgeben

to extend [iks'tend]
  to extend credit
  *I should like to have my
   residence permit extended.*

extension [iks'tenʃən]

  to request an extension
  extension of credit
  Extension 226, please.
extensive [iks'tensiv]
  He gave an extensive report.

external [eks'tə:nl]
  external trade
extra ['ekstrə]

  Packing and postage extra.

  *Do you get extra pay for this
   job?*

  to be charged extra
  extra charges pl
  extra work
extract ['ekstrækt]

ausdehnen, erweitern, verlängern
  einen Kredit einräumen
  Ich möchte meine
   Aufenthaltserlaubnis/-genehmigung
   verlängern lassen.
Ausdehnung *f;* Prolongation *f,* (Frist-)
  Verlängerung *f*
  um Zahlungsaufschub bitten
  Kreditverlängerung f
  Bitte Apparat 226!
ausgedehnt, umfassend
  Er erstattete einen eingehenden
   Bericht.
auswärtig, ausländisch
  Außenhandel m
s Sonderleistung *f;* Zuschlag *m;*
pl Nebenausgaben *f pl;*
a zusätzlich
  Verpackung und Porto werden
   gesondert berechnet.
  Bekommen Sie diese Arbeit extra
   bezahlt?/Erhalten Sie eine Zulage für
   diese Arbeit?
  gesondert berechnet werden
  Nebenkosten pl
  Mehrarbeit f
Auszug *m;* Abriß *m*

F

face value [ˌfeis 'vælju:]
to facilitate [fə'siliteit]
  *to facilitate customs
   clearance*
facilities *pl* [fə'silitiz]

  transport facilities
factor ['fæktə]

  foreign/home factor
  key factors pl

  safety factor
fact-finding ['fæktɪfaindiŋ]
  fact-finding commission
factoring ['fæktəriŋ]

Nenn-, Nominalwert *m*
erleichtern, fördern
  die Verzollung erleichtern

Einrichtungen *f pl,* Anlagen *f pl;*
  Vorteile *m pl,* Erleichterungen *f pl*
  Transportmöglichkeiten f pl
Handelsvertreter *m,* Makler *m,*
  Kommissionär *m,* Disponent *m;*
  Faktor *m,* Umstand *m*
  Auslands-/Inlandsvertreter m
  wichtigste Faktoren m pl/
   Umstände m pl
  Sicherheitsfaktor m
Tatsachenfeststellung *f*
  Untersuchungsausschuß m
Factoring n (kombiniertes Finanzierungs-
und Dienstleistungssystem)

failure ['feiljə] Bankrott *m*, Konkurs *m;* Versäumnis *n;* Fehlschlag *m;* Defekt *m*
  failure to pay Nichtzahlung f
fair [fɛə] Messe *f*, Ausstellung *f*
  at the book fair auf der Buchmesse
fall [fɔ:l] Rückgang *m*, Niedergang *m*, Sturz *m*
  a sudden fall in prices ein Preissturz m, Kurseinbruch m
familiar [fə'miljə] vertraut
  He is not familiar with it. Er ist nicht damit vertraut.
family ['fæmili] Familie *f*
  family allowance Familienbeihilfe f, Kinderzulage f
  family name Zu-, Familienname m
fancy goods *pl* ['fænsi‚gudz] Modeartikel *m pl*
fare [fɛə] Fahr-, Flugpreis *m*
  What's the fare? Wie hoch ist der Fahr-/Flugpreis?
  full fare Fahrkarte f zum vollen Preis
  economy fare Preis m der Touristenklasse
fast-selling item gutgehender Artikel *m*
  ['fa:st 'seliŋ 'aitəm]
faulty ['fɔ:lti] mangelhaft, fehlerhaft
feature ['fi:tʃə] wichtiger Bestandteil *m;* Charakteristikum *n*
  distinctive feature Unterscheidungsmerkmal n
fee [fi:] Gebühr *f;* Vergütung *f*
  entrance fee Eintrittsgeld n
to feed [fi:d] *(Material)* zuführen
  to feed into the computer dem Computer eingeben
figure ['figə] Ziffer *f;* Zahl *f;* Betrag *m;* Gestalt *f*
  He is good at figures. Er ist ein guter Rechner.
file [fail] *s* Aktenstück *n*, -bündel *n;* Ablage *f;* *v (Akten)* ablegen; *(Antrag)* einreichen
  on file bei den Akten
  file number Aktenzeichen n
  to file an application einen Antrag einreichen
  filing cabinet Aktenschrank m
  filing clerk Registrator m
final ['fainl] endgültig, schließlich
  final date Schlußtermin m
  final item letzter Punkt m (einer Tagesordnung)
  final result Endergebnis n
finance [fai'næns] Finanzwirtschaft *f;* Geldwesen *n*
  finance department Finanzabteilung f
financial [fai'nænʃəl] finanziell, geldlich
  financial adviser Finanzberater m
  financial condition Finanzlage f
  financial difficulties pl finanzielle Schwierigkeiten f pl
  financial expert Finanzsachverständiger m
  financial standing Kreditfähigkeit f; Kapitalkraft f
  financial status/situation Vermögenslage f

financial year — Geschäftsjahr n
financing [fai'nænsiŋ] — Finanzierung f
findings *pl* ['faindiŋz] — Feststellungen f pl; *jur* richterliche Erkenntnis f
fine [fain] — s Geldstrafe f; v zu einer Geldstrafe verurteilen
finished ['finiʃt] — fertig, abgeschlossen
finished goods pl — Fertigwaren f pl
half-finished products pl — Halbfabrikate n pl
finishing ['finiʃiŋ] — Veredelung f; Zurichtung f; Fertigverarbeitung f
finishing industry — verarbeitende Industrie f
finishing process — Veredelungsverfahren n
first-class ['fə:st'klɑ:s] — erstklassig, ausgezeichnet
first-class references pl — erstklassige Empfehlungen f pl
He travelled first-class. — Er reiste erster Klasse.
first-hand ['fə:st'hænd] — aus erster Hand
first-hand information — Nachricht aus erster Hand
to buy first-hand — aus erster Hand beziehen
first-rate ['fə:st'reit] — erstklassig, ausgezeichnet
first-rate quality — erstklassige Qualität f
fiscal ['fiskəl] — steuerlich, fiskalisch
fiscal year — Rechnungsjahr n
fitness ['fitnis] — Eignung f; Tüchtigkeit f; gute körperliche Verfassung f
fitness test — Eignungsprüfung f
fitter ['fitə] — Mechaniker m, Schlosser m
fitting ['fitiŋ] — Montage f, Installation f; pl Beschläge m pl, Ausstattung f
fixed [fikst] — fest (eingebaut), ortsfest, stationär; unveränderlich
fixed assets pl — feste Anlagen f pl
fixed rate of interest — fester Zinssatz m
fixed salary — Fixum n, festes Gehalt n
fixtures *pl* ['fikstʃəz] — Inventar n, Zubehör n
flexible ['fleksəbl] — elastisch, flexibel
flexible policy — flexible Politik f
flight [flait] — Flug n, -strecke f; Abflug m; Flucht f
connecting flight — Anschluß(flug) m
flight ticket — Flugschein m
floating ['fləutiŋ] — fluktuierend; *(Schuld)* schwebend; *(Geld)* umlaufend
floating capital — Betriebskapital n
flourishing ['flʌriʃiŋ] — blühend
flourishing industry — blühende Industrie f
flourishing trade — schwunghafter Handel m
to fluctuate ['flʌktjueit] — fluktuieren, schwanken
Prices are fluctuating. — Die Preise schwanken.
fluctuation [,flʌktju'eiʃən] — Schwanken n, Fluktuieren n

folder - freight

fluctuations in demand/ in the exchange rate/ in prices — Nachfrage-/ Kurs-/ Preisschwankungen f pl
folder [ˈfəuldə] — Faltprospekt m, -blatt n; Aktendeckel m; Schnellhefter m
follow-up [ˈfɔləuˈʌp] — Nachstoßen n, Nachfassen n
follow-up advertising — Nachfaß-, Erinnerungswerbung f
follow-up letter — nachfassender Werbebrief m
foodstuffs pl [ˈfuːdstʌfs] — Lebensmittel n pl
fool-proof [ˈfuːl-pruːf] — narrensicher, betriebssicher
forced [fɔːst] — erzwungen
forced landing — Notlandung f
forced sale — Zwangsversteigerung f
forecast [ˈfɔːkɑːst] — Vorhersage f; Prognose f; Vorausplanung f
weather forecast — Wettervorhersage f
foreign [ˈfɔrin] — ausländisch
foreign assets pl — Devisenwerte m pl
foreign department — Auslandsabteilung f
foreign currency — Devisen pl, ausländische Währung f
foreign trade — Außenhandel m
foreman [ˈfɔːmən] — Vorarbeiter m; Werkmeister m
to forge [fɔːdʒ] — fälschen, nachmachen
forged money — Falschgeld n
forgery [ˈfɔːdʒəri] — Fälschung f
forgery of documents — Urkundenfälschung f
fortnight [ˈfɔːtnait] — vierzehn Tage
in a fortnight — in 14 Tagen
fortnightly — halbmonatlich, vierzehntägig
forward [ˈfɔːwəd] — a auf Ziel/Zeit/Termin; v ver-, nachsenden
Please forward. — Bitte nachsenden!
forward transaction — Termingeschäft n
forward rate — Kurs m für Termingeschäfte
forwarding [ˈfɔːwədiŋ] — Versand m, Beförderung f
forwarding agent — Spediteur m
forwarding charges pl — Versandspesen pl
forwarding department — Versandabteilung f
forwarding instructions pl — Versandanweisungen f pl
foundation [faunˈdeiʃən] — Gründung f, Errichtung f; Stiftung f
to lay the foundations of — den Grundstock legen für
fragile [ˈfrædʒail] — zerbrechlich
framework [ˈfreimwəːk] — Rahmen m, Gefüge n, System n
within the framework of — im Rahmen von
fraudulent [ˈfrɔːdjulənt] — betrügerisch
fraudulent bankruptcy — betrügerischer Bankrott m
freight [freit] — s Fracht f, -kosten pl; v beladen; verfrachten
freight rate — Frachtsatz m

freight train | Güterzug m
freight transportation | Frachtgutbeförderung f
freeze [fri:z] | Einfrieren n, Stopp m
wage/price freeze | Lohn-/Preisstopp m
fringe benefits pl [frindʒ 'benefits] | freiwillige Sozialleistungen f pl
frozen ['frəuzn] | eingefroren, blockiert
frozen assets pl | eingefrorene Guthaben n pl
frozen food | tiefgekühlte Lebensmittel pl
fuel [fjuəl] | Brennstoff m; Treibstoff m
fuel oil | Heizöl n
to fulfil(l) [ful'fil] | erfüllen, ausführen
to fulfil a contract | einen Vertrag erfüllen
to fulfil a promise | ein Versprechen einlösen
fulfil(l)ment [ful'filmənt] | Erfüllung f
full-time ['ful'taim] | ganztägig; hauptamtlich, -beruflich
full-time job | Ganztagsbeschäftigung f
function ['fʌŋkʃən] | s Tätigkeit f, Funktion f, Aufgabe f; v tätig sein (as als); funktionieren

He has an important function within the firm. | Er spielt eine wichtige Rolle in der Firma.
The machine is not functioning properly. | Die Maschine funktioniert nicht richtig.
administrative function | Verwaltungstätigkeit f
fund [fʌnd] | Kapital n, Vermögen n; Fonds m pl, Geldmittel pl

No funds. | (Scheck) Keine Deckung!
for lack of funds | mangels Barmittel/Deckung
pension fund | Pensionskasse f
sufficient funds pl | ausreichende Deckung f
furnishings pl ['fə:niʃiŋz] | Einrichtungsgegenstände m pl, Mobiliar n

furniture ['fə:nitʃə] | Möbel n pl, Mobiliar n, Einrichtung f
office furniture | Büromöbel n pl
furniture van | Möbelwagen m

G

gains pl [geinz] | Einkommen n, Verdienst n; Einnahmen f pl; Gewinn m
to make gains | Gewinne verzeichnen
gainful ['geinful] | gewinnbringend, einträglich
gainful employment | Erwerbstätigkeit f
He is gainfully employed. | Er ist erwerbstätig.
gap [gæp] | Lücke f
to fill/to stop a gap | eine Lücke ausfüllen, ein Loch stopfen
dollar gap | Dollarlücke f
gas [gæs] | Gas n; Am Benzin n

gas main	*Gasleitung* f
gas station Am	*Tankstelle* f
gate [geit]	Flugsteig m; (Eisenbahn) Sperre f
gauge [geidʒ]	Normalmaß n; Meßgerät n; Spurweite f
general [ˈdʒenərəl]	allgemein; üblich; umfassend
general delivery	Am *postlagernd; postlagernde Sendungen* f pl
general manager	*Generaldirektor* m
general meeting	*General-, Hauptversammlung* f
General Post Office	*Hauptpostamt* n
consul general	*Generalkonsul* m
Consulate General	*Generalkonsulat* n
genuine [ˈdʒenjuin]	echt, unverfälscht
gift token [gift ˈtəukən]	Geschenkgutschein m
Giro [ˈdʒairəu]	Br Postscheckdienst m
giro account	*Girokonto* n
given [ˈgivn]	bestimmt, festgesetzt
at a given time	zu einer festgesetzten Zeit
under the given conditions	unter den gegebenen Umständen
given name	Am *Vorname* m
goal [gəul]	Ziel n
investment goal	*Investitionsziel* n
going [ˈgəuiŋ]	gehend; in Gang, in Betrieb
Going! going! gone!	*Zum ersten, zum zweiten, zum dritten Mal!*
goods pl [gudz]	Güter n pl, Waren f pl
consumer goods pl	*Konsumgüter* n pl
goods pl *in process*	*Halbfabrikate* n pl
goodwill [ˈgudˈwil]	Firmenwert m; Kundschaft f, Klientel f
go-slow [ˈgəuˈsləu]	Bummelstreik m
grade [greid]	Sorte f, Klasse f
high-grade	erstklassig
low-grade	von minderer Qualität
grade label(l)ing	*Güteklassenbezeichnung* f
grant [grɑ:nt]	s Bewilligung f, Gewährung f; Zuschuß m, Subvention f, Beihilfe f; v bewilligen, gewähren
to grant a loan	ein Darlehen geben
to grant permission	die Erlaubnis erteilen
grant-in-aid	Am öffentlicher Zuschuß m
gross [grəus]	brutto, gesamt
gross amount	*Bruttobetrag* m
gross earnings pl	*Bruttoverdienst* m, *-einnahmen* f pl
gross national product	*Bruttosozialprodukt* n
gross weight	*Bruttogewicht* n
group [gru:p]	Gruppe f; Konzern m
age group	*Altersgruppe* f
group discussion	*Gruppendiskussion* f
group insurance	*Gruppenversicherung* f

growth [grəuθ] — Wachstum n; Zunahme f
  rate of growth — *Wachstumsrate* f
  growth in consumption — *Konsumsteigerung* f
guarantee [ˌgærənˈtiː] — s Bürgschaft f, Garantie f;
  v garantieren, verbürgen
  to guarantee a bill — *für einen Wechsel Bürgschaft leisten*
guarantor [ˌgærənˈtɔː] — Bürge m, Garant m
guidance [ˈgaidəns] — Leitung f, Führung f, Anleitung f
  for your guidance — *zu Ihrer Orientierung*
  vocational guidance — *Berufsberatung* f

H

haberdasher [ˈhæbədæʃə] — Kurzwarenhändler m; Am Herrenausstatter m
handbill [ˈhændbil] — Reklamezettel m, Flugblatt n
handicapped [ˈhændikæpt] — behindert, benachteiligt (by durch)
handicraft [ˈhændikrɑːft] — (Kunst-) Handwerk n
to handle [ˈhændl] — handeln mit (Waren), durchführen
  to handle the correspondence — *die Korrespondenz erledigen*
  to handle goods — *Waren führen*
handwriting [ˈhændˌraitiŋ] — Handschrift f
handy [ˈhændi] — geschickt, praktisch; greifbar
  This gadget is very handy. — *Dieses Gerät ist sehr praktisch.*
  Do you have a ballpoint-pen handy? — *Haben Sie einen Kugelschreiber zur Hand?*
hangar [ˈhæŋə] — Flugzeughalle f
hanger [ˈhæŋə] — Kleiderbügel m
harbour dues pl [ˈhɑːbə djuːz] — Hafengebühren f pl
  harbour master/commissioner — *Hafenmeister* m
hard cash [ˈhɑːd ˈkæʃ] — Bargeld n; Hartgeld n
harden [ˈhɑːdən] — (Preise) anziehen
hardware [ˈhɑːd-wɛə] — Haushaltwaren f pl; (Computer) Hardware f
hat stand/Am **tree** [ˈhæt-stænd/triː] — Hutständer m
hatter [ˈhætə] — Hutmacher m
haulage [ˈhɔːlidʒ] — Beförderung f, Transport m
  haulage contractor — *Rollfuhrunternehmer* m
hawker [ˈhɔːkə] — Straßenhändler m
hazard [ˈhæzəd] — Risiko n, Gefahr f
heading [ˈhediŋ] — Briefkopf m; Überschrift f
headline [ˈhedlain] — Schlagzeile f, Überschrift f

head office - imply

head office, headquarters
(sing oder *pl)*
[ˈhedˈɔfis, ˈhedˈkwɔːtəz]
heavy [ˈhevi]
  heavy losses pl
  heavy traffic
helicopter [ˈhelikɔptə]
heliport [ˈhelipɔːt]
hidden defect [ˈhidn]
highest bidder [ˈhaiist]
high-grade [ˈhaiˈgreid]
highway [ˈhaiwei]
  highway code
hire [ˈhaiə]

  to hire a car
  hire purchase
  to buy on hire purchase
to hoard [hɔːd]
holder [ˈhəuldə]
  holder of a bill/of shares
holding company [ˈhəuldiŋ]
home [həum]
  home address
  home demand
  home market
  home produce
hotel reservation [həuˈtel]
hourly wages *pl* [ˈauəli]
household [ˈhaushəuld]
housekeeping [ˈhausˌkiːpiŋ]
housing [ˈhauziŋ]
  housing shortage
hovercraft [ˈhɔvə-krɑːft]

Hauptgeschäftsstelle *f*, Zentrale *f*

beträchtlich, bedeutend, groß
  schwere Verluste m pl
  starker Verkehr m
Hubschrauber *m*
Hubschrauberlandeplatz *m*
verborgener Mangel *m*
Meistbietender *m*
hochwertig; erstklassig
Fern(verkehrs)straße *f*
  Straßenverkehrsordnung f
s Miete *f;* (Arbeits-) Lohn *m;*
v mieten; *(Flugzeug)* chartern;
in Dienst nehmen
  einen Wagen mieten
  Raten-, Abzahlungskauf m
  auf Abzahlung kaufen
horten, anhäufen
Inhaber *m*, Besitzer *m*
  Wechsel-/Aktieninhaber m
Dachgesellschaft *f*
inländisch, einheimisch
  Privatanschrift f
  Inlandsbedarf m
  Binnenmarkt m
  einheimische Erzeugnisse n pl
Zimmerreservierung *f*
Stundenlohn *m*
Haushalt *m*
Haushaltsführung *f*
Wohnung *f*, Unterkunft *f;* Lagerung *f*
  Wohnungsnot f
Luftkissenfahrzeug *n*

I

idle [ˈaidl]
  idle capacity
  idle capital
illegal [iˈliːgəl]
imitation [ˌimiˈteiʃən]
immovable [iˈmuːvəbl]
  immovables pl
implement [ˈimplimənt]
to imply [imˈplai]

  This implies ...

unproduktiv; ungenützt
  ungenützte Kapazität f
  totes Kapital n
ungesetzlich, rechtswidrig
Nachahmung *f;* Fälschung *f*
unbeweglich
  Immobilien pl, *Liegenschaften* f pl
Werkzeug *n*
einbeziehen, in sich schließen;
zu verstehen geben
  Daraus ergibt sich ...

import [ˈimpɔ:t]　　　　　　　Einfuhr f, Import m;
　　　　　　　　　　　　　　　　pl Einfuhrwaren f pl
　import duty　　　　　　　　　Einfuhrzoll m
　import trade　　　　　　　　　Einfuhrhandel m
to import [imˈpɔ:t]　　　　　einführen, importieren
　importing country　　　　　Einfuhrland n
importer [imˈpɔ:tə]　　　　　Importeur m
inactive [inˈæktiv]　　　　　(Börse) flau, lustlos; untätig
incentive [inˈsentiv]　　　　(Leistungs-) Anreiz m, Antrieb m
　incentive bonus　　　　　　Leistungsprämie f
incidentals *pl* [ˌinsiˈdentlz]　Nebenausgaben f pl
included, including　　　　einschließlich
　[inˈkludid, inˈkludiŋ]
　postage included　　　　　　einschließlich Porto
　including value-added tax　einschließlich Mehrwertsteuer
income [ˈinkʌm]　　　　　　Einkommen n, Einkünfte pl
　average income　　　　　　Durchschnittseinkommen n
　earned income　　　　　　　Arbeitseinkommen n
　unearned income　　　　　Kapitaleinkommen n
　yearly income　　　　　　　Jahreseinkommen n
　income group　　　　　　　Einkommensklasse f
　income tax　　　　　　　　Einkommensteuer f
increase [ˈinkri:s]　　　　　Zunahme f, Steigerung f, Wachstum n
　increase in the bank rate　Diskonterhöhung f
　increase in capital/in salary　Kapital-/Gehaltserhöhung f
　price/wage increase　　　　Preis-/Lohnerhöhung f
increasing [inˈkri:siŋ]　　　zunehmend, steigend
　increasing costs pl　　　　zunehmende Kosten pl
　increasingly　　　　　　　　in zunehmendem Maße
to incur [inˈkə:]　　　　　　geraten in
　to incur debts　　　　　　　Schulden machen
　to incur liabilities　　　　Verpflichtungen eingehen
　to incur losses　　　　　　Verluste erleiden
indebted [inˈdetid]　　　　　verschuldet
　He is indebted to me.　　　Er hat Schulden bei mir.
index [ˈindeks]　　　　　　　Index m, Register n, Verzeichnis n;
　　　　　　　　　　　　　　　　Meßziffer f, -zahl f
　index card　　　　　　　　　Karteikarte f
　index number　　　　　　　Kennziffer f; Katalognummer f
　cost-of-living index　　　　Lebenshaltungs(kosten)index m
to indicate [ˈindikeit]　　　anzeigen, bezeichnen
　He indicated the direction.　Er gab die Richtung an.
　as indicated　　　　　　　　wie angegeben
indirect [ˌindiˈrekt]　　　　　indirekt
　indirect tax　　　　　　　　indirekte Steuer f
indispensable for/to　　　　unentbehrlich für
　[ˌindisˈpensəbl]
individual [ˌindiˈvidjuəl]　　s Einzelner m, Individuum n;
　　　　　　　　　　　　　　　　a einzeln, individuell

individual case/member — Einzelfall m/-mitglied n
industrial [in'dʌstriəl] — s Industrieller m; a industriell, gewerblich
　industrial accident — Betriebsunfall m
　industrial potential — Industriepotential n
　industrial wages pl — Industriearbeiterlöhne m pl
industrialize [in'dʌstriəlaiz] — industrialisieren
inefficient [ˌini'fiʃənt] — leistungsschwach; unrationell
inferior [in'fiəriə] — minderwertig; mittelmäßig
　inferior goods pl — *minderwertige Waren* f pl
　in an inferior position — *in untergeordneter Stellung*
inflation [in'fleiʃən] — Inflation f
inflationary [in'fleiʃnəri] — inflationär, inflationistisch
　inflationary trend — *inflationistische Tendenz* f
initial [i'niʃəl] — anfänglich
　initial capital/salary — Anfangskapital n/-gehalt n
initiative [i'niʃiətiv] — Initiative f
　He took the initiative. — *Er ergriff die Initiative.*
inland ['inlənd] — s Binnenland n; a binnenländisch

to insert [in'sə:t] — einfügen
　to insert a coin in the slot — *eine Münze in den Schlitz stecken*
　to insert in brackets — *in Klammern setzen*
insolvent [in'sɔlvənt] — zahlungsunfähig, insolvent
inspection [in'spekʃən] — Prüfung f, Kontrolle f; (Bücher-) Einsicht f
　for inspection — *zur Ansicht*
　inspection test — *Abnahmeprüfung* f
to install [in'stɔ:l] — einbauen, montieren; einen Platz anweisen
　to install a telephone — *ein Telefon einrichten*
installation [ˌinstə'leiʃən] — Einrichtung f, Anlage f
instalment [in'stɔ:lmənt] — Teil-, Ratenzahlung f
　by instalments — *in Raten, ratenweise*
　in monthly instalments — *in monatlichen Raten*
　first instalment — *Anzahlung* f
instance ['instəns] — Beispiel n; Instanz f
　for instance — *zum Beispiel*
　in the first instance — *an erster Stelle; in der ersten Instanz*
institution [ˌinsti'tju:ʃən] — Institution f, Einrichtung f
　banking institution — *Bankinstitut* n
to instruct [in'strʌkt] — informieren, unterrichten
instruction(s pl**)** [in'strʌkʃən(z)] — Anordnung f, Richtlinien f pl
　according to instructions — *weisungsgemäß; vorschriftsmäßig*
insurance [in'ʃuərəns] — Versicherung f
　to take out an insurance — *eine Versicherung abschließen*
　insurance agent — *Versicherungsvertreter* m
　insurance benefit — *Versicherungsleistung* f

insurance claim	Versicherungsanspruch m
insurance company	Versicherungsgesellschaft f
insurance policy	Versicherungspolice f
insurance premium	Versicherungsprämie f
fire/life insurance	Feuer-/Lebensversicherung f
intelligence [in'telidʒəns]	Verständnis n; Mitteilungen f pl, Nachrichten f pl; Auskunft f
intelligence test	Intelligenzprüfung f
interest (in) ['intrist]	Vorteil m, Nutzen m; Beteiligung f, Anteil m (an); Zins(en pl) m; Zinsfuß m; pl Geschäfte n pl; pl Interessenten m pl
to bear/to yield interest	Zinsen tragen
compound interest	Zinseszinsen m pl
credit interest	Habenzinsen m pl
interest on capital/on deposit	Kapital-/Depositenzinsen m pl
interest-bearing	zinsentragend, verzinslich
to interfere [ˌintə'fiə]	beeinträchtigen, behindern; intervenieren, sich einmischen
internal [in'tə:nl]	einheimisch, binnenländisch; innerbetrieblich
internal trade	Binnenhandel m
international [ˌintə(:)'næʃənl]	international
international trade	Welthandel m
international reply coupon	internationaler Postantwortschein m
interpreter [in'tə:pritə]	Dolmetscher m
interview ['intəvju:]	s Befragung f; Unterredung f; v befragen
introduction [ˌintrə'dʌkʃən]	Einführung f, Einleitung f; Vorstellung f (einer Person)
letter of introduction	Empfehlungsschreiben n
introductory [ˌintrə'dʌktəri]	einleitend
introductory remarks pl	einleitende Bemerkungen f pl
inventory ['invəntri]	Inventar n, Bestandsliste f; (Waren-) Bestand m; Schlußinventar n
to draw up an inventory	eine Bestandsliste aufstellen
to invest [in'vest]	investieren
to invest money	Geld anlegen
invested capital	Anlagekapital n
to investigate (into) [in'vestigeit]	tr untersuchen (a crime ein Verbrechen); itr Untersuchungen/Ermittlungen anstellen (über)
investigation [inˌvesti'geiʃən]	Untersuchung f, Nachforschung f
investment [in'vestmənt]	Investition f; Anlage f
long-term/short-term investment	langfristige/kurzfristige Anlage f
investment securities pl	Anlagewerte m pl
investment trust	Investmentgesellschaft f
investor [in'vestə]	Kapital-, Geldanleger m

invisible [in'vizəbl] | unsichtbar
  invisible exports pl | *unsichtbare Exporte* m pl
invoice ['invɔis] | Faktura *f,* Warenrechnung *f*
  as per invoice | *laut Rechnung*
  pro forma invoice | *Proformarechnung* f
to involve (in) [in'vɔlv] | in sich schließen, nach sich ziehen; verwickeln (in)
  He is involved in a lawsuit. | *Er ist in einen Rechtsstreit verwickelt.*
  for all parties involved | *für alle beteiligten Parteien*
irregular [i'regjulə] | uneinheitlich; vorschriftswidrig
  at irregular intervals | *in unregelmäßigen Abständen*
issue ['iʃu:] | *s* Ausstellung *f (eines Wechsels);* Emission *f (von Wertpapieren);* Begebung *f (einer Anleihe);* Streitfrage *f;*
   | *v* in Umlauf setzen; *(Anleihe)* begeben; *(Scheck)* ausstellen
  bank of issue | *Emissionsbank* f
  a point at issue | *ein umstrittener Punkt* m
  to issue a bill of exchange | *einen Wechsel ausstellen*
item ['aitem] | (Rechnungs-) Posten *m;* Artikel *m,* Gegenstand *m;* Punkt *m (der Tagesordnung)*
  a fast-selling/hard-to-sell item | *ein gutgehender/schwer verkäuflicher Artikel* m
  items pl *on the agenda* | *Punkte* m pl *der Tagesordnung*
itinerant exhibition [i'tinərənt] | Wanderausstellung *f*
itinerary [ai'tinərəri] | Reiseroute *f,* -bericht *m*

J

jet [dʒet] | Düsenverkehrsflugzeug *n,* Düsenmaschine *f*
job [dʒɔb] | Beschäftigung *f;* Arbeit *f;* Akkordarbeit *f;* Beruf *m*
  full-time job | *Ganztagsbeschäftigung* f
  job description | *Arbeitsplatzbeschreibung* f
joint [dʒɔint] | gemeinschaftlich, gemeinsam
  joint action | *gemeinsames Vorgehen* n
  joint owner | *Miteigentümer* m
journal ['dʒə:nl] | Journal *n;* Zeitschrift *f,* Zeitung *f*
judicial [dʒu(:)'diʃəl] | gerichtlich
junction ['dʒʌŋkʃən] | (Eisenbahn-) Knotenpunkt *m*
  traffic junction | *Verkehrsknotenpunkt* m
junior ['dʒu:njə] | junior; rangjünger; untergeordnet
  junior clerk | *zweiter Buchhalter* m
  junior partner | *Juniorpartner* m

jurisdiction [ˌdʒuərisˈdikʃən] Rechtsprechung *f*
justification [ˌdʒʌstifiˈkeiʃən] Rechtfertigung *f;* Berechtigung *f*

K

to keep [ki:p] *(Waren)* auf Lager halten; *(Bücher)* führen
  to keep books/an account of   Buch/über Ausgaben Buch führen
  expenses
  to keep a shop   ein Ladengeschäft betreiben
key [ki:] Kennziffer *f,* -wort *n;*
  (Landkarte) Zeichenerklärung *f;*
  Schlüssel *m,* Lösung *f*
  key factor   Hauptfaktor m; *Schlüsselzahl* f
  key industry/position   Schlüsselindustrie f/-position f
kind [kaind] Art *f,* Sorte *f*
  of the same kind   gleichartig
  to pay in kind   in Naturalien zahlen
know-how [ˈnəuhau] Sach-, Fachkenntnisse *f pl*
  industrial know-how   Betriebserfahrung f; *Herstellungs-,*
  Produktionsverfahren n

L

label [ˈleibl] *s* (Anhänge-, Klebe-) Zettel *m,* Etikett *n,*
  Schildchen *n;* Beschriftung *f;*
  v beschriften; etikettieren
  He put labels on his   *Er versah sein Gepäck mit*
  luggage.   *Anhängezetteln.*
labour, *Am* **labor** [ˈleibə] Arbeitskräfte *f pl,* Arbeiter *m pl;*
  Arbeiterschaft *f*
  shortage of labour   *Mangel* m *an Arbeitskräften*
  unskilled/skilled labour   *ungelernte Arbeitskräfte* f pl/
  Facharbeiter m pl
  cost of labour   Lohnkosten pl
  labour conditions pl   Arbeitsbedingungen f pl
  labour exchange   Arbeitsamt n
  labour market   Arbeitsmarkt m
  labour relations pl   Arbeitgeber-Arbeitnehmer-
  Beziehungen f pl
  labour-saving   arbeitsparend
labo(u)rer [ˈleibərə] (ungelernter) Arbeiter *m*
to land [lænd] *tr* ausladen, löschen, an Land bringen;
  itr landen
landing [ˈlændiŋ] Landung *f;* Ausladen *n;* Löschen *n;*
  Ausschiffung *f;* Anlegeplatz *m*
  landing-field   Landeplatz m
  landing-stage   Landungsbrücke f

launch - liability

to launch [lɔ:ntʃ] — (Schiff) vom Stapel lassen
  to launch a business — ein Geschäft gründen
  to launch a product — ein Erzeugnis auf den Markt bringen
  to launch into a discussion — sich in eine Diskussion stürzen
law-suit [ˈlɔ:-sju:t] — Gerichtsverfahren n, Prozeß m
lawyer [ˈlɔ:jə] — Rechtsanwalt m; Jurist m
layout [ˈleiaut] — Planung f; Entwurf m; Anlage f
leader [ˈli:də] — Lock-, Spitzenartikel m; (Zeitung) Leitartikel m
leading [ˈli:diŋ] — führend, tonangebend
  leading firm — führendes Haus n
leaflet [ˈli:f-lit] — Merk-, Flugblatt n, Prospekt m
learner [ˈlə:nə] — Anlernling m; Fahrschüler m
lease [li:s] — Pacht f, Miete f; Verpachtung f; Pacht-, Mietvertrag m
leaseholder [ˈli:shəuldə] — Pächter m
ledger [ˈledʒə] — Hauptbuch n
  to enter in the ledger — in das Hauptbuch eintragen
legal [ˈli:gəl] — gesetzlich, rechtsgültig
  He took legal action. — Er beschritt den Rechtsweg.
  legal adviser — Rechtsberater m
  legal capacity — Geschäftsfähigkeit f
  legal department — Rechtsabteilung f
  legal entity — juristische Person f
lender [ˈlendə] — Darlehens-, Kreditgeber m
letter [ˈletə] — Brief m, Schreiben n; Buchstabe m
  by letter — brieflich
  He answered/acknowledged receipt of her letter. — Er beantwortete/bestätigte ihren Brief.
  to post a letter — einen Brief zur Post bringen/aufgeben
  business letter — Geschäftsbrief m
  capital letter — Großbuchstabe m
  express letter — Eilbrief m
  registered letter — eingeschriebener Brief m
  letter of application — Bewerbungsschreiben n
  letter of credit — Akkreditiv n
  letter of introduction — Empfehlungsschreiben n
  letter-box — Briefkasten m
  letter-head — Briefkopf m
level [ˈlevl] — Niveau n, Stufe f, Ebene f
  on the same level — auf gleicher Höhe
  salary/price level — Gehaltsstufe f / Preisniveau n
liability [ˌlaiəˈbiliti] — Verbindlichkeit f; Haftung f; pl Passiva pl
  assets and liabilities pl — Aktiva und Passiva (Bilanz)
  limited liability — beschränkte Haftung f
  liability insurance — Haftpflichtversicherung f

liable for [ˈlaiəbl] haftbar, verantwortlich für
You are liable to meet with *Sie können leicht in einen Unfall*
an accident. *verwickelt werden.*
liable to taxation *steuerpflichtig*
licence, *Am* **license** [ˈlaisəns] Lizenz *f*, Konzession *f*; Zulassung *f*
The firm applied for a *Die Firma beantragte eine*
licence. *Konzession.*
He was granted a licence. *Es wurde ihm eine Lizenz erteilt.*
driving/driver's licence *Führerschein m*
export/import licence *Ausfuhr-/Einfuhrbewilligung f*
licence plate *Nummernschild n*
to license [ˈlaisəns] lizensieren, (amtlich) genehmigen
licensee [ˌlaisənˈsiː] Lizenznehmer *m*
life, *pl* **lives** [laif, -vz] Leben *n*; Lebensdauer *n*, Haltbarkeit *f*
for life *auf Lebenszeit*
life assurance/insurance *Lebensversicherung f*
limit [ˈlimit] *s* Limit *n*, Preisgrenze *f*; Höchstbetrag *m*;
 v limitieren, begrenzen
lower/upper limit *untere/obere Grenze f*
time limit *zeitliche Begrenzung f*
limitation [ˌlimiˈteiʃən] Begrenzung *f*
line [lain] Branche *f*; Artikel *m*, Sorte *f*; Posten *m*;
 Kollektion *f*; Linie *f*; (Telefon-)
 Verbindung *f*
What line is he in? *In welcher Branche arbeitet er?*
They had to stand in line. *Sie mußten Schlange stehen.*
Hold the line, please. *Bleiben Sie bitte am Apparat!*
line of business *Geschäftszweig m*
liner [ˈlainə] Überseedampfer *m*
link [liŋk] *s* Ketten-, Bindeglied *n*;
 v verbinden, verknüpfen
liquid [ˈlikwid] flüssig, liquid
liquid assets pl *liquide Mittel n pl*
to liquidate [ˈlikwideit] liquidieren; flüssigmachen
liquidity [liˈkwiditi] Liquidität *f*, Flüssigkeit *f*
livestock [ˈlaivstɔk] Viehbestand *m*, lebendes Inventar *n*
living [ˈliviŋ] Lebensunterhalt *m*; Aufenthalt *m*,
 Wohnen *n*
He earns his own living. *Er verdient seinen Unterhalt selbst.*
plain living *einfache Lebensführung f*
cost of living *Lebenshaltungskosten pl*
load [ləud] *s* Last *f*, Ladung *f*; Belastung *f*;
 v beladen, belasten
pay load *Nutzlast f*
loan [ləun] Anleihe *f*, Darlehen *n*
to locate [ləuˈkeit] ausfindig machen
location [ləuˈkeiʃən] Standort *m*, Lage *f*
They had to decide on the *Sie mußten sich über die Lage ihres*
location of their new office. *neuen Büros klarwerden.*

to lodge [lɔdʒ] — (Geld) deponieren; (Gegenstand) in Verwahrung geben; (Güter) lagern
  He lodged an appeal/ a complaint/an objection — Er legte Berufung ein/brachte eine Beschwerde vor/erhob Einspruch.
  to lodge a credit — einen Kredit eröffnen
long [lɔŋ] — lang; langfristig, auf lange Sicht
  long-distance call — Ferngespräch n
  long-distance lorry driver — Fernfahrer m
  long-term bond — langfristige Schuldverschreibung f
  long-term contract — langfristiger Vertrag m
  long-range planning — langfristige Planung f
loose [luːs] — lose; offen, nicht verpackt
  loose change — Kleingeld n
  loose-leaf book — Ringbuch n, Loseblattbuch n
lorry Br [ˈlɔri] — Lastkraftwagen m
lost [lɔst] — verloren; untergegangen; vernichtet
  to get lost — abhanden kommen
  lost property office — Fundbüro n
low [ləu] — nieder, niedrig; (Vorrat) knapp
  He is low on funds. — Er ist nicht gut bei Kasse.
  low-budget — preiswert
  low-grade — minderwertig
  lowest price — äußerster Preis m
to lower [ˈləuə] — senken, herabsetzen
  to lower the rate of interest — den Zinssatz herabsetzen
luggage Br [ˈlʌgidʒ] — Gepäck n
  We registered our luggage. — Wir gaben unser Gepäck auf.
  luggage insurance — Reisegepäckversicherung f
  luggage label — Gepäckadresse f
  luggage ticket — Gepäckschein m
  luggage van — Gepäckwagen m
lump [lʌmp] — Masse f, Menge f; Stück n
  lump of sugar — Stück n Zucker
  lump sugar — Würfelzucker m
  lump sum — Pauschale f, Pauschalbetrag m
lunch, luncheon [lʌntʃ, ˈlʌntʃən] — Gabelfrühstück n, Mittagessen n
  lunch break — Mittagspause f

M

machinery [məˈʃiːnəri] — Maschinenpark m; Maschinerie f
machine-tool [məˈʃiːn tuːl] — Werkzeugmaschine f
magazine [ˌmægəˈziːn] — Speicher m, Warenlager n; Zeitschrift f
mail [meil] — s Post f; Postsendung f; Postsack m; v mit der Post schicken, aufgeben
  by mail — per Post
  by return mail — postwendend
  Please mail the letters. Am — Bitte werfen Sie die Post ein!

The mail is delivered regularly at 10 o'clock.	Die Post wird regelmäßig um 10 Uhr ausgetragen.
incoming/outgoing mail	eingehende/ausgehende Post f
mail-order house	Versandhaus n
mailing list	Adressenkartei f
main [mein]	hauptsächlich, wichtigst
main office	Zentrale f
main road	Hauptverkehrsstraße f
mainly	größtenteils, vorwiegend
to maintain [mein'tein]	1. aufrechterhalten; *(Preis)* halten; 2. instand halten; 3. behaupten, verteidigen
He maintained his claim/opinion.	Er bestand auf seiner Forderung/blieb bei seiner Meinung.
to maintain the roads	die Straßen instand halten
maintenance ['meintənəns]	1. Instandhaltung f, Wartung f; 2. Unterhalt m
maintenance costs pl	Instandhaltungskosten pl
resale price maintenance	Preisbindung f der zweiten Hand
major ['meidʒə]	1. größer; wichtig, bedeutend; 2. volljährig
the major part of his income	der größere Teil seines Einkommens
major road	Hauptverkehrsstraße f
majority [mə'dʒɔriti]	1. Mehrheit f; Mehrzahl f; 2. Volljährigkeit f
in the majority of cases	in der Mehrzahl der Fälle
They are in the majority.	Sie sind in der Mehrzahl.
majority (of votes)	Stimmenmehrheit f
make [meik]	Fabrikat n, Marke f; Bauart f, Typ m; Produktion f
What make is your car?	Was für einen Wagen fahren Sie?
It's a popular make.	Das ist eine gut eingeführte Marke.
standard make	Markenartikel m
maker ['meikə]	Erzeuger m, Hersteller m; *(Wechsel)* Aussteller m
to manage ['mænidʒ]	*(Betrieb)* leiten, lenken, beaufsichtigen; *(Maschine)* handhaben, bedienen
He managed the business for years.	Er hat das Geschäft jahrelang geleitet.
They have to manage on a small sum of money.	Sie müssen mit einem geringen Geldbetrag auskommen.
managing director	Generaldirektor m
management ['mænidʒmənt]	(Betriebs-) Führung f, Leitung f; Direktion f, Geschäftsleitung f
industrial management	Betriebswirtschaft(slehre f) f
top management	oberste Führungskräfte f pl
management consultant	Betriebsberater m
manager ['mænidʒə]	Betriebsleiter m, Geschäftsführer m
assistant manager	stellvertretender Direktor m

managerial – maturity

personnel/staff manager — Personalchef m
sales manager — Verkaufsleiter m
managerial [ˌmænəˈdʒiəriəl] — leitend, geschäftsführend
　He has a managerial position. — Er ist in leitender Stellung.
manpower [ˈmænpauə] — Arbeitskräfte f pl
　shortage of manpower — Mangel m an Arbeitskräften
manufacture [ˌmænjuˈfæktʃə] — s Herstellung f, Fabrikation f; Erzeugnis n; v herstellen, erzeugen
　large-scale manufacture — Massenherstellung f
　manufactured goods pl — Industriewaren f pl
manufacturer [ˌmænjuˈfæktʃərə] — Hersteller m, Fabrikant m
manufacturing [ˌmænjuˈfæktʃəriŋ] — Herstellung f, Fabrikation f
　manufacturing industry — Fertigungsindustrie f
　manufacturing process — Herstellungsverfahren n
margin [ˈmɑːdʒin] — Spielraum m; (Handels-) Spanne f, Marge f, Rand m
　indicated in the margin — nebenstehend vermerkt
　He allowed a margin for incidental expenses. — Er ließ einen Spielraum für Nebenausgaben.
　profit margin — Gewinnspanne f
maritime [ˈmæritaim] — seefahrend
　maritime trade/insurance — Seehandel m/Seeversicherung f
market [ˈmɑːkit] — Markt m; Markthalle f; Absatz m, Verkauf m
　He is in the market for furniture. — Er ist Abnehmer für Möbel/hat Bedarf an Möbeln.
　This item is now on the market. — Dieser Artikel ist zur Zeit auf dem Markt/zu haben/wird zur Zeit angeboten.
　His house will come on the market next month. — Sein Haus wird nächsten Monat verkauft.
　This item has a ready market. — Dieser Artikel findet guten Absatz.
　market price/value — Marktpreis m/-wert m
　market report — Markt-/Börsenbericht m
　market research — Marktforschung f
marketing [ˈmɑːkitiŋ] — Vertrieb m, Absatzförderung f, Marketing n
　marketing consultant — Marketing-Berater m
mass [mæs] — Masse f, Menge f, Hauptteil m
　mass media — Massenmedien n pl
　mass production — Massenproduktion f
maturity [məˈtjuəriti] — Fälligkeit f
　payable at/on maturity — zahlbar bei Verfall

maximum ['mæksɪməm] Höchstbetrag m; Höchstsatz m
maximum speed Höchstgeschwindigkeit f
maximum wage Spitzenlohn m
means pl [miːnz] (Geld-) Mittel n pl, Einkommen n, Vermögen n
measure ['meʒə] 1. Maßeinheit f;
2. Maßnahme f
to take legal measures den Rechtsweg beschreiten
measure of capacity Hohlmaß n
mechanical [mɪ'kænɪkəl] mechanisch
medium, pl **media** Mittel n, Medium n
['miːdjəm, 'miːdjə]
advertising media Werbeträger m pl
medium-priced goods pl Waren f pl der mittleren Preislage
medium-sized mittelgroß
membership ['membəʃɪp] Mitgliedschaft f
membership card/list Mitgliedskarte f/ Mitgliederverzeichnis n
memo(randum) ['meməu Aufzeichnung f, Notiz f
(ˌmemə'rændəm)]
memo pad Notizblock m
merchandise ['məːtʃəndaɪz] Waren f pl
merchant ['məːtʃənt] (Groß-) Kaufmann m
merchant bank/ship Handelsbank f/-schiff n
to merge [məːdʒ] tr, itr fusionieren, verschmelzen
merger ['məːdʒə] Fusion f, Zusammenschluß m, -legung f
messenger ['mesɪndʒə] Bote m
messenger boy Botenjunge m
method ['meθəd] Methode f, System n
mid-week ['mɪd'wiːk] Mitte f der Woche
mileage ['maɪlɪdʒ] Kilometergeld n/-preis m
mileage allowance Kilometerpauschale f
mineral ['mɪnərəl] mineralisch
mineral water Mineralwasser n
minimum, pl **-ma** s Mindestbetrag m, -maß n;
['mɪnɪməm, -mə] a minimal, Mindest-
subsistence minimum Existenzminimum n
minimum price/wage Mindestpreis m/-lohn m
ministry ['mɪnɪstrɪ] Ministerium n
minor ['maɪnə] geringfügig; minderjährig
minor changes pl geringfügige Änderungen f pl
minor repairs pl geringfügige Reparaturen f pl
minor matter Nebensache f
Charles is still a minor. Karl ist noch minderjährig.
minority [maɪ'nɔrɪtɪ] 1. Minderheit f, Minorität f;
2. Minderjährigkeit f
They are in the minority. Sie sind in der Minderheit.
minority group Minderheitengruppe f
minus ['maɪnəs] weniger

minutes *pl* [ˈminits] — Niederschrift *f*, Sitzungsprotokoll *n*
  Mr Smith kept the minutes of the meeting. — Herr Smith führte das Protokoll der Sitzung.
misunderstanding [ˈmisʌndəˈstændiŋ] — 1. Mißverständnis *n*; 2. Mißhelligkeit *f*
mode [məud] — 1. Methode *f*, Verfahren *n*, (Art und) Weise *f*; 2. Mode *f*
model [ˈmɔdl] — Modell *n*, Muster *n*, Vorlage *f*
  model plant — Musterbetrieb m
to modernize [ˈmɔdənaiz] — modernisieren
modification [ˌmɔdifiˈkeiʃən] — Abänderung *f*
  He made some modifications. — Er nahm einige Änderungen vor.
to modify [ˈmɔdifai] — abändern
  to modify the terms of the lease — die Pachtbedingungen abändern
monetary [ˈmʌnitəri] — geldlich, finanziell
  monetary reform — Währungsreform f
money [ˈmʌni] — Geld *n*; Zahlungsmittel *n*
  He is short of money. — Er ist knapp bei Kasse.
  money market — Geldmarkt m
  money order (M.O.) — Postanweisung f
monopoly [məˈnɔpəli] — Monopol *n*, Alleinverkauf *m*
  to hold a monopoly on s.th. — das Alleinverkaufsrecht für etw haben
monthly [ˈmʌnθli] — monatlich
  monthly instalment/ production/report/salary — Monatsrate f/-produktion f/ -bericht m/-gehalt n
mortgage [ˈmɔːgidʒ] — Hypothek *f*
motion [ˈməuʃən] — 1. Antrag *m*; 2. Bewegung *f*
  to propose a motion — einen Antrag stellen
  The motion to adjourn was adopted/carried by a large majority. — Der Antrag auf Vertagung wurde mit großer Mehrheit angenommen.
motor [ˈməutə] — Motor m
  motor-boat — Motorboot n
  motor-car — Automobil n
  motorway — Autobahn f
to move [muːv] — 1. bewegen; 2. einen Antrag stellen auf
  I move that we adjourn. — Ich beantrage Vertagung.
movement [ˈmuːvmənt] — Bewegung *f*; Entwicklung *f*
  downward movement — rückläufige Bewegung f
  upward movement — Aufwärtsbewegung f
multiple [ˈmʌltipl] — vielfach, mehrfach
municipal [mjuː(ː)ˈnisipəl] — städtisch, kommunal
mutual [ˈmjuːtʃuəl] — gegenseitig, wechselseitig
  mutual aid — gegenseitige Hilfe f
  mutual consent — beiderseitiges Einverständnis n

N

nation [ˈneiʃən] — Nation f, Volk n
  nation-wide — das ganze Land umfassend
national [ˈnæʃənl] — s Staatsangehöriger m;
  a national, staatlich
  national economy — Volkswirtschaft f
nationality [ˌnæʃəˈnæliti] — Staatsangehörigkeit f
to nationalize [ˈnæʃnəlaiz] — verstaatlichen
necessity [niˈsesiti] — Notwendigkeit f; Bedürfnis n; Bedarfsartikel m
  necessities pl *of life* — Lebensbedürfnisse n pl
negative [ˈnegətiv] — s Verneinung f;
  a negativ, verneinend
  He answered in the negative. — Er gab eine abschlägige Antwort.
negligence [ˈneglidʒəns] — Nachlässigkeit f, Unachtsamkeit f; Fahrlässigkeit f
negligible [ˈneglidʒəbl] — nebensächlich, unbedeutend; geringfügig
negotiable [niˈgəuʃjəbl] — verkäuflich; übertragbar; bank-, börsenfähig
  not negotiable — nur zur Abrechnung; nicht übertragbar
to negotiate [niˈgəuʃieit] — (Anleihe) unterbringen
  to negotiate a sale — einen Verkauf tätigen
negotiation [niˌgəuʃiˈeiʃən] — Verhandlung f; (Wechsel) Übertragung f, Unterbringung f
  Negotiations were broken off. — Die Verhandlungen wurden abgebrochen.
net [net] — a netto;
  v Gewinn abwerfen
  net income — Nettoeinkommen n
  net proceeds pl — Nettoeinnahmen f pl
  net profit — Reingewinn m
network [ˈnetwəːk] — Netz n
  network of roads/of railways/of canals — Straßen-/Eisenbahn-/Kanalnetz n
to nominate [ˈnɔmineit] — benennen
  They nominated their candidates. — Sie stellten ihre Kandidaten auf.
non-delivery [ˈnɔndiˈlivəri] — Nichterfüllung f
non-stop flight [ˈnɔnˈstɔp ˈflait] — Nonstopflug m
normal [ˈnɔːməl] — normal, üblich
  normally — für gewöhnlich, in der Regel
notary [ˈnəutəri] — Notar m
note [nəut] — s Nota f, Rechnung f; schriftliche Mitteilung f; Nachricht f;
  v notieren, aufzeichnen
  as per note — laut Nota

advice note — Versandanzeige f
bank-note — Banknote f
credit/debit note — Gutschrifts-/Lastschriftsanzeige f
delivery note — Lieferschein m
note-book — Notizbuch n
note-paper — Briefpapier n
notice [ˈnəutis] — 1. Mitteilung f, Nachricht f; Bekanntmachung f; 2. Kündigung f
subject to a month's notice — mit monatlicher Kündigung
at short notice — kurzfristig
I have notice to quit. — Mir ist gekündigt worden.
He gave them notice last week. — Er hat ihnen vergangene Woche gekündigt.
notice-board — Anschlagtafel f, Schwarzes Brett n
to notify [ˈnəutifai] — bekanntmachen; in Kenntnis setzen, benachrichtigen
He should have notified me. — Er hätte mich benachrichtigen sollen.
nuclear [ˈnjuːkliə] — nuklear
nuclear energy — Kern-, Atomenergie f
nuclear power plant — Atomkraftwerk n
number [ˈnʌmbə] — s 1. Zahl f, Ziffer f, Nummer f; 2. Anzahl f; v numerieren; zählen
in large numbers — in großer Anzahl
a large number of people — viele Leute pl
serial/supply number — Fabrik-/Bestellnummer f

O

oath [əuθ] — Eid m
on/under oath — unter Eid
He swore an oath/took an oath. — Er schwor/leistete einen Eid.
objection [əbˈdʒekʃən] — 1. Einwand m, Einspruch m; 2. Reklamation f, Beanstandung f
She didn't raise any objections. — Sie erhob keinen Einwand.
He has no objection. — Er hat nichts einzuwenden.
objective [əbˈdʒektiv] — objektiv, sachlich
obligation [ˌɔbliˈgeiʃən] — 1. Verpflichtung f, Verbindlichkeit f; 2. Schuldverschreibung f, Obligation f
no obligation — unverbindlich
He took on several obligations. — Er ging mehrere Verbindlichkeiten ein.
He cannot meet his obligations. — Er kann seinen Verpflichtungen nicht nachkommen.
obligation to buy — Kaufzwang m

to oblige [əˈblaidʒ]	verpflichten; nötigen, zwingen
Much obliged.	*Danke bestens!*
Could you oblige me with some information?	*Könnten Sie mir eine Auskunft geben?*
to obtain [əbˈtein]	erhalten, bekommen
obvious [ˈɔbviəs]	offensichtlich, einleuchtend, klar
That is obvious.	*Das ist klar/liegt auf der Hand.*
occasional [əˈkeiʒənl]	gelegentlich; zufällig
occupation [ˌɔkjuˈpeiʃən]	Beschäftigung *f;* Beruf *m*
occupational [ˌɔkju(:)ˈpeiʃənl]	beruflich
occupational category	*Berufsgruppe* f
occupational disease	*Berufskrankheit* f
to occur [əˈkəː]	sich ereignen, geschehen
It didn't occur to me.	*Es ist mir nicht eingefallen.*
The name occurred several times.	*Der Name kam mehrfach vor.*
odd [ɔd]	1. restlich, überzählig; 2. ungerade; 3. einzeln; 4. gelegentlich
ten pounds odd	*etwas über zehn Pfund*
odd number	*ungerade Zahl* f
an odd shoe	*ein einzelner Schuh* m
odd jobs pl	*Gelegenheitsarbeiten* f pl
offer [ˈɔfə]	*s* Angebot *n,* Offerte *f;* *v* anbieten, offerieren
He made a written offer.	*Er machte ein schriftliches Angebot.*
He declined the offer.	*Er lehnte das Angebot ab.*
to offer for sale	*zum Verkauf anbieten*
all-inclusive offer	*Pauschalangebot* n
office [ˈɔfis]	1. Büro *n;* 2. Zweigniederlassung *f,* -stelle *f;* 3. Aufgabe *f,* Pflicht *f*
branch/head office	*Zweig-/Hauptgeschäft* n
office building/equipment	*Bürogebäude* n*/-einrichtung* f
office hours pl	*Dienststunden* f pl
to omit [əˈmit]	1. aus-, weglassen; 2. versäumen
one-way traffic [ˈwʌnwei ˈtræfik]	Einbahnverkehr *m*
open [ˈəupən]	*a* offen; *v* öffnen, aufmachen
The firm opened up new markets.	*Die Firma erschloß neue Märkte.*
to open an account/ a business	*ein Konto/ein Geschäft eröffnen*
open-air stand	*Stand* m *unter freiem Himmel*
open competition	*freier Wettbewerb* m

to operate [ˈɔpəreit] in Gang/in Betrieb setzen; bedienen, betätigen; betreiben
  to operate on schedule   *planmäßig arbeiten*
  Do you know how to operate this machine?   *Wissen Sie, wie man diese Maschine in Gang setzt?*
operating [ˈɔpəreitiŋ] betrieblich; in Betrieb befindlich
  operating costs pl/ *expenses* pl   *Betriebskosten* pl
  operating instructions pl   *Betriebsanleitung* f
operation [ˌɔpəˈreiʃən] Betrieb *m*; Geschäft *n*; Unternehmen *n*
  to put into/out of operation   *in Betrieb/außer Betrieb setzen*
  commercial operation   *geschäftliche Unternehmung* f
  continuous operation   *durchgehender Betrieb* m
operator [ˈɔpəreitə] Telefonistin *f*; Unternehmer *m*; (Börse) Spekulant *m*
opinion [əˈpinjən] Meinung *f*; Gutachten *n*
  expert opinion   *Sachverständigengutachten* n
  opinion poll   *Meinungsbefragung* f, -forschung f
optimistic [ˌɔptiˈmistik] zuversichtlich, optimistisch
optimum [ˈɔptiməm] optimal, günstigst
  optimum conditions pl   *günstigste Bedingungen* f pl
option [ˈɔpʃən] Vorkaufs-, Optionsrecht *n*
  He had no option.   *Es blieb ihm keine Wahl.*
order [ˈɔ:də] 1. Auftrag *m*, Bestellung *f*; Order *f*;
2. Ordnung *f*
  by order   *im Auftrag, i. A.*
  made out to order   *an Order lautend*
  He placed an order with the firm.   *Er erteilte der Firma einen Auftrag.*
  They confirmed/filled the order.   *Sie bestätigten den Auftrag/führten den Auftrag aus.*
  order book/form   *Bestellbuch* n/*-schein* m
  money/(bis zu £5) postal order   *Postanweisung* f
organization [ˌɔ:gənaiˈzeiʃən] Organisation *f*; Aufbau *m*, Gliederung *f*
to organize [ˈɔ:gənaiz] organisieren, gestalten
outdoor [ˈautdɔ:] im Freien/draußen (befindlich)
  outdoor advertising   *Außenwerbung* f
outfit [ˈautfit] Ausrüstung *f*
outlet [ˈaut-let] Absatzgebiet *n*, -möglichkeit *f*
outline [ˈaut-lain] Umriß *m*; Entwurf *m*
output [ˈautput] Produktion *f*, Ertrag *m*
  annual/daily output   *Jahres-/Tagesproduktion* f
outstanding [autˈstændiŋ] 1. hervorragend;
2. unerledigt, ausstehend
  outstanding accounts pl   *Außenstände* m pl
overall [ˈəuvərɔ:l] gesamt
  overall result   *Gesamtergebnis* n
overdraft [ˈəuvədrɑ:ft] Kontoüberziehung *f*

to overdraw o.'s account [ˈəuvəˈdrɔ:]   sein Konto überziehen
overdue [ˈəuvəˈdju]   überfällig
  The aircraft is several hours overdue.   *Das Flugzeug hat mehrere Stunden Verspätung.*
overhead [ˈəuvəhed]   allgemein, pauschal
  overheads pl, *overhead costs* pl/*expenses* pl   *Gemein-, Gesamtkosten* pl
overseas [ˈəuvəˈsi:z]   überseeisch
  overseas market   *Überseemarkt* m
overtime [ˈəuvətaim]   Überstunden f pl
  He worked overtime.   *Er machte Überstunden.*
overweight [ˈəuvəweit]   Übergewicht n
owner [ˈəunə]   Eigentümer m
  at owner's risk   *auf Gefahr des Eigentümers*

P

pack [pæk]   s Ballen m, Bündel n; (Zigaretten-) Packung f; Paket n;
   v verpacken, einpacken; beladen; eindosen, konservieren; vollstopfen
  He packed his suitcase.   *Er packte seinen Koffer.*
  packed in like sardines   *wie Heringe zusammengepreßt*
  a pack of cards   *ein Spiel Karten*
  factory-packed   *in Originalpackung*
package [ˈpækidʒ]   Packung f; Verpackung f; Paket n, Kollo n, Gepäck-, Frachtstück n
  package advertising   *Versandwerbung* f
  package tour   *Pauschalreise* f
packet [ˈpækit]   Päckchen n; Paketboot n, Postschiff n
  Send me a packet of tea, please.   *Schicken Sie mir bitte ein Päckchen Tee!*
  registered packet   *Einschreibpaket* n
  wage packet   *Lohntüte* f
packing [ˈpækiŋ]   Verpackung f; Konservierung f
  not including packing   *Verpackung nicht inbegriffen*
  packing paper   *Packpapier* n
pad [pæd]   Polster n; Unterlage f; Schreibblock m
  writing pad   *Schreibunterlage* f
  ink pad   *Farb-, Stempelkissen* n
paid [peid]   bezahlt
  carriage paid   *frachtfrei*
  duty-paid   *verzollt*
pamphlet [ˈpæmflit]   Broschüre f; Prospekt m
paper [ˈpeipə]   1. (Wert-) Papier n; Wechsel m;
   2. Referat n; Schriftstück n
  to show one's papers   *seine Papiere vorzeigen*

paragraph - patent

He wrote a paper on the subject. — *Er schrieb einen Aufsatz über diesen Gegenstand.*
paper-money — *Papiergeld* n
paper-work — *Schreibarbeit* f
paragraph ['pærəgrɑːf] — Abschnitt *m*, Absatz *m*; Notiz *f*
parcel ['pɑːsl] — 1. Posten *m*, Partie *f*; 2. Paket *n*, Päckchen *n*

parcel delivery — *Paketzustellung* f
parcel office — *Gepäckabfertigung* f
parcel post — *Paketpost* f
parent company ['pɛərənt 'kʌmpəni] — Stammhaus *n*; Dachgesellschaft *f*

part [pɑːt] — 1. Teil *m*; Anteil *m*; Einzelteil *m*; 2. Partei *f*

part payment — *Teilzahlung* f
part-time job — *Teilzeitbeschäftigung* f
part-time worker — *Kurzarbeiter* m; *Halbtagskraft* f
partner ['pɑːtnə] — Teilhaber *m*, Gesellschafter *m*, Partner *m*
senior/junior partner — *Senior-/Juniorchef* m
sleeping partner — *stiller Teilhaber* m
partnership ['pɑːtnəʃip] — 1. Mitbeteiligung *f*, Teilhaberschaft *f*; 2. Personalgesellschaft *f*

party ['pɑːti] — Partei *f*
the parties concerned — *die Beteiligten* m pl
a third party — *ein Dritter* m
party line — *Gemeinschaftstelefon* n
pass (to) [pɑːs] — *s* Ausweis *m*; Passierschein *m*; *v tr* vorbeifahren, -gehen an; überschreiten; *itr* übertragen werden, übergehen (auf); anerkannt/angenommen werden; (Zeit) vergehen

The bill was passed. — *Der Gesetzentwurf wurde angenommen.*
The firm passed from father to son. — *Die Firma ging vom Vater auf den Sohn über.*
pass on the left — *links überholen*
free pass — *Freikarte* f
passage ['pæsidʒ] — Durchgang *m*, Passage *f*; Abschnitt *m*
He booked a passage to New York. — *Er löste eine Schiffs-/Flugkarte nach New York.*
passenger ['pæsindʒə] — Fahr-, Fluggast *m*, Passagier *m*
passenger cabin — *Fluggastraum* m
passenger plane — *Verkehrsflugzeug* n
passenger train — *Personenzug* m
passport ['pɑːs-pɔːt] — Reisepaß *m*
passport control — *Paßkontrolle* f
patent (on) ['peitənt] — *s* Patent *n* (auf); *v* patentieren lassen

patron - periodical

patent leather shoes pl	*Lackschuhe* m pl
patent office	*Patentamt* n
patron ['peitrən]	(Stamm-) Kunde m/Gast m; Förderer m
pattern ['pætən]	Vorlage f; Muster n, Warenprobe f; Dessin n; Struktur f
pattern book	*Musterbuch* n
paper pattern	*Schnittmuster* n
pawn [pɔ:n]	s Pfand n; v verpfänden, lombardieren
pay [pei]	s Bezahlung f, Lohn m; v tr bezahlen, begleichen; itr zahlen, Zahlung leisten (for für)
to pay a bill	*eine Rechnung bezahlen*
to pay cash/by cheque	*bar/mit Scheck bezahlen*
to pay damages	*Schadenersatz leisten*
pay packet/roll	*Lohntüte* f/-*liste* f
pay phone	*Münzfernsprecher* m
pay rise	*Gehaltserhöhung* f
payable ['peiəbl]	lohnend, rentabel; zahlbar
payable at sight	*zahlbar bei Sicht*
payer ['peiə]	(Wechsel) Bezogener m, Trassat m
payment ['peimənt]	Zahlung f, Begleichung f; (Wechsel) Einlösung f
on payment	*nach Eingang, gegen Bezahlung*
cash payment	*Barzahlung* f
payment in kind	*Sachleistung* f
terms pl *of payment*	*Zahlungsbedingungen* f pl
peak [pi:k]	Gipfel m, Höhepunkt m
Their shares reached a new peak yesterday.	*Ihre Aktien erreichten gestern einen neuen Höhepunkt.*
peak viewing hours pl	*Zeit* f *der größten Zuschauerdichte*
pension ['penʃən]	Pension f, Ruhegehalt n
to pension off	*in den Ruhestand versetzen*
old-age pension	*Altersversorgung* f
pension fund	*Pensionskasse* f
per [pə:]	per, durch; für
as per	*laut, gemäß*
per annum	*pro Jahr, jährlich*
per capita	*pro Kopf*
per post	*mit der Post*
percentage [pə'sentidʒ]	Prozentsatz m; Prozente n pl
performance [pə'fɔ:məns]	Leistung f; Durchführung f; (Maschine) Arbeitsleistung f
performance of a duty	*Erfüllung* f *einer Pflicht*
period ['piəriəd]	Periode f, Zeitraum m, Frist f
for a period of two months	*für die Dauer von zwei Monaten*
periodical [ˌpiəri'ɔdikəl]	s Zeitschrift f; a regelmäßig erscheinend

monthly/weekly periodical — Monats-/Wochenzeitschrift f
perishable ['periʃəbl] — leicht verderblich
  perishable goods pl — leicht verderbliche Waren f pl/ kurzlebige Verbrauchsgüter n pl
permanent ['pə:mənənt] — ständig, dauernd
permission [pə'miʃən] — Genehmigung f, Erlaubnis f
  by special permission — mit besonderer Erlaubnis
permit ['pə:mit] — Passierschein m; Lizenz f; Aus-/Einfuhrerlaubnis f
  landing permit — Landeerlaubnis f
personal ['pə:snl] — persönlich; privat
  personal call — Gespräch n mit Voranmeldung
  personal data — Angaben f pl zur Person
  personal shares pl — Namensaktien f pl
  personal status — Personenstand m
personnel [ˌpə:sə'nel] — Personal n, Belegschaft f
  personnel department — Personalabteilung f
  personnel files pl — Personalakten f pl
  personnel manager — Personalchef m
petty ['peti] — geringfügig, unbedeutend; kleinlich
  petty cash — Portokasse f
phone [fəun] — s Telefon n; v telefonieren

He contacted me by phone. — Er setzte sich fernmündlich mit mir in Verbindung.
You are wanted on the phone. — Sie werden am Telefon verlangt.
photo-copy ['fəutəuˌkɔpi] — Photokopie f
piece-work ['pi:s-wə:k] — Akkordarbeit f
  They do piece-work. — Sie arbeiten im Akkord.
pier [piə] — Landungsbrücke f, Landesteg m; Mole f
to pigeon-hole ['pidʒinhəul] — zu den Akten legen; verschleppen
pipeline ['paip-lain] — Pipeline f, Rohr-, Ölleitung f
place — s Platz m, Stelle f; Örtlichkeit f; (Unternehmen) Sitz m; Wohnsitz m, Wohnung f; v unterbringen, plazieren
  place of business — Geschäftssitz m
  place of payment/of performance — Zahlungs-/Erfüllungsort m
  to place an order — einen Auftrag erteilen (for für)
  to place shares — Aktien unterbringen
planning ['plæniŋ] — Planung f
plant [plɑ:nt] — (Fabrik-) Anlage f, Fabrik f, Werk n
  plant manager — Betriebsleiter m
  power plant — Kraftwerk n
pledge [pledʒ] — s Pfand n; Bürgschaft f; v verpfänden

He pledged his property. — Er verpfändete sein Hab und Gut.

plus [plʌs] zuzüglich; plus
pocket [ˈpɔkit] s Tasche f; Geldbeutel m;
 v einstecken
He is out of pocket. Er hat Geld verloren.
He pocketed all the profits. Er hat den ganzen Gewinn eingesteckt.
pocketbook Notizbuch n; Brieftasche f, Am
 Geldbeutel m; Taschenbuch n
pocket book (edition) Taschenbuch(ausgabe f) n
pocket money Taschengeld n
policy [ˈpɔlisi] 1. Politik f, Taktik f, einzuschlagendes
 Verfahren n; Klugheit f;
 2. (Versicherungs-) Police f,
 Versicherungsschein m
They adopted a new policy. Sie schlugen einen neuen Kurs ein.
It is my policy to... Es ist mein Grundsatz, daß...
marketing policy Absatzpolitik f
pollster [ˈpəulstə] Am Meinungsforscher m
pool [puːl] s Kartell n, Interessenverband m,
 Ring m; gemeinsamer Fonds m;
 v tr zusammenlegen;
 itr ein Kartell bilden
The partners pooled the Die Partner teilten den Gewinn.
 profits.
Let's pool our savings/our Wir wollen unsere Ersparnisse/unsere
 resources. Geldmittel zusammenlegen/
 zusammenwerfen.
the football pools pl Toto n
motor pool Fahrbereitschaft f
population [ˌpɔpjuˈleiʃən] Bevölkerung f; Bestand m
population movement Bevölkerungsbewegung f
a fall/rise in population eine Abnahme f/eine Zunahme f der
 Bevölkerung
port [pɔːt] See-/Flughafen m
to call at a port einen Hafen anlaufen/einen Flughafen
 anfliegen
port of destination Bestimmungshafen m/ Zielflughafen m
port of registry Heimathafen m
portable [ˈpɔːtəbl] tragbar
portable radio Kofferradio n
portable typewriter Reiseschreibmaschine f
position [pəˈziʃən] Sachlage f, Position f, Situation f;
 Standpunkt m
position as per December Stand vom 31. Dezember
 31st
financial/legal position Finanz-/Rechtslage f
positive [ˈpɔzətiv] konkret; feststehend; zustimmend;
 überzeugt
I'm positive that he will Ich bin sicher/überzeugt/weiß genau,
 come. daß er kommt.

post [pəust]   s 1. Post f, Postamt n, Postsendungen f pl;
2. Posten m, Anstellung f;
v verbuchen, eintragen; mit der Post senden, zur Post geben
   They kept us posted.   *Sie hielten uns auf dem laufenden.*
   postcode   *Postleitzahl* f
   post-free   *portofrei*
   postman   *Briefträger* m
   post office   *Postamt* n
   post-office box, P.O.B.   *Postschließfach* n
postage ['pəustidʒ]   Porto n
   postage paid   *franko, portofrei*
postal ['pəustəl]   postalisch; Post-
   postal order   *Postanweisung* f (bis zu £5)
poster ['pəustə]   Plakat n, Anschlagzettel m
poste restante ['pəust'restɑ:nt]   postlagernd
to postpone [pəust'pəun]   verschieben, hinausschieben; vertagen
postscript, P.S. ['pəusskript]   Postskriptum n, Nachschrift f
potential [pəu'tenʃəl]   s Potential n, Reserven f pl;
a potentiell, möglich, denkbar
   industrial potential   *Industriepotential* n
   potential sales pl   *voraussichtliche Umsätze* m pl
power ['pauə]   (Handlungs-) Vollmacht f; Antriebskraft f
   power of attorney   *Handlungs-, Vertretungs-, Prozeßvollmacht* f
   power consumption   *Stromverbrauch* m
   power station   *Kraft-, Elektrizitätswerk* n
   power supply   *Energieversorgung* f; *Netz(anschluß* m) n
   buying/purchasing power   *Kaufkraft* f
   financial power   *Finanzkraft* f
precaution [pri'kɔ:ʃən]   Vorsichtsmaßregel f
to predict [pri'dikt]   vorhersagen, voraussagen
preferably ['prefərəbli]   vorzugsweise, möglichst
preference ['prefərəns]   Begünstigung f, Priorität f; Meistbegünstigung f; Bevorrechtigung f
   What are your preferences?   *Was ziehen Sie vor?*
   preference share   *Vorzugsaktie* f
preferential [ˌprefə'renʃəl]   bevorrechtigt; bevorzugt
   preferential claim   *bevorrechtigte Forderung* f
preliminary [pri'liminəri]   einleitend; vorläufig
   preliminary discussion   *Vorbesprechung* f
   preliminary remarks pl   *Vorbemerkungen* f pl
premises pl ['premisiz]   Grundstück n, Anwesen n
   on the premises   *an Ort und Stelle; im Lokal*
   business premises   *Geschäftsräume* m pl, *-grundstück* n

premium ['priːmjəm] — Prämie f, Bonus m; Zugabe f; Aufgeld n, Agio n; Belohnung f
  to put a premium on s.th. — einen Preis für etw aussetzen
  to sell at a premium — tr mit Gewinn verkaufen; itr über Pari stehen
  insurance premium — Versicherungsprämie f
prepaid ['priːpeid] — vorausbezahlt; portofrei
to present [priˈzent] — (zur Zahlung) vorlegen, präsentieren; (Klage) einreichen; (eine Person) vorstellen
  He presented the facts as they really were. — Er stellte die Sache so dar, wie sie wirklich war.
  to present a bill for acceptance — einen Wechsel zum Akzept vorlegen
  to present a cheque at the bank — einen Scheck bei der Bank einreichen
presentation [ˌprezenˈteiʃən] — 1. *(Waren)* Aufmachung f; 2. *(Wechsel)* Vorlage f; 3. *(Person)* Vorstellung f
  payable on presentation — zahlbar bei Sicht
president ['prezidənt] — Präsident m, Vorsitzender m; Vorstandsvorsitzer m; Generaldirektor m
pressing ['presiŋ] — dringend, eilig
pressure ['preʃə] — Druck m; Last f; Drang m
  They put/brought pressure to bear on him. — Sie setzten ihn unter Druck.
  economic pressure — wirtschaftlicher Druck m
  pressure of taxation — Steuerlast f, -druck m
  pressure group — Interessengruppe f
to presume [priˈzjuːm] — vermuten, annehmen
  I presume he is at the office. — Vermutlich ist er im Büro.
presumption [priˈzʌmpʃən] — Vermutung f, Annahme f
previous ['priːvjəs] — vorausgehend, früher
  The previous day was a holiday. — Der Tag davor war ein Feiertag.
  previous experience — Vorkenntnisse f pl
  previous month/year — Vormonat m/-jahr n
price [prais] — s *(Kauf-, Markt-)* Preis m; Kosten pl; *(Börse)* Kurs m; v *(Waren)* auszeichnen
  at the current market price — zum Tageskurs
  at a reduced price — herabgesetzt, mit einem Preisnachlaß
  asked/bid price — Brief-/Geldkurs m
  price ceiling — obere Preisgrenze f
  price control — Preiskontrolle f
  price cut — Preissenkung f
  price freeze — Preisstopp m
  price list — Preisliste f

primarily - procedure

price maintenance — Preisbindung f
price stability — Preisstabilität f
primarily ['praimərili] — in erster Linie, vor allem
primary ['praiməri] — hauptsächlich; wichtigst; grundlegend; ursprünglich
That's of primary importance. — Das ist von größter Wichtigkeit.
primary education — Grundschulunterricht m
primary products pl — Grundstoffe m pl
principal ['prinsəpəl] — s 1. Kapital(summe f) n; (Nachlaß-) Masse f;
2. Vorgesetzter m;
3. Geschäftsinhaber m;
a hauptsächlich
principal creditor/debtor — Hauptgläubiger m/-schuldner m
principal and interest — Kapital und Zinsen
principle ['prinsəpl] — Grundsatz m, Prinzip n, Leitsatz m
on principle — grundsätzlich
He stuck to his principles. — Er hielt an seinen Grundsätzen fest.
print [print] — s Druck m; Druckbuchstaben m pl; Druckschrift f; Lichtpause f; (photographischer) Abzug m;
v tr drucken; in Druckschrift schreiben;
itr drucken; Bücher veröffentlichen; gedruckt werden
in print — im Druck; (Buch) vorrätig
out of print — (Buch) vergriffen
to appear in print — im Druck erscheinen
Please print your name. — Schreiben Sie Ihren Namen bitte in Druckschrift!
printed matter — Drucksache f
prior (to) ['praiə] — a früher (als); vordringlich;
adv vor
prior to any discussion — vor Eintritt in die Diskussion
subject to prior sale — Zwischenverkauf vorbehalten
priority [prai'ɔriti] — Dringlichkeit f, Priorität f, Vorrang m
We shall give high priority to your order. — Wir werden Ihren Auftrag besonders vordringlich behandeln.
He was given priority. — Er wurde bevorzugt abgefertigt.
of top priority — von größter Dringlichkeit
priority list — Dringlichkeitsliste f
prize [praiz] — 1. Auszeichnung f, Preis m;
2. (Lotterie-) Gewinn m
to award a prize — einen Preis zuerkennen
He won first prize on the pools. — Er hat den ersten Preis im Toto gewonnen.
consolation prize — Trostpreis m
procedure [prə'si:dʒə] — Verfahren n
usual procedure — übliches Verfahren n

proceeds pl ['prəusi:dz] Erlös m, Ertrag m, Einnahmen f pl
  cash proceeds   Barerlös m
process ['prəuses] s Verfahren n, Arbeitsgang m, Prozeß m; Verlauf m, Vorgang m; v be-/verarbeiten
  in the process of construction   im Bau
  manufacturing process   Herstellungsverfahren n
processing ['prəusesiŋ] Verarbeitung f, Veredelung f
  processing industry   Veredelungsindustrie f
produce ['prɔdju:s] (landwirtschaftliches) Erzeugnis n; Gewinn m, Ertrag m
to produce [prə'dju:s] erzeugen, produzieren; (Gewinn) erzielen; (Urkunde) vorlegen
product ['prɔdʌkt] Fabrikat n, Erzeugnis n, Produkt n
  intermediate product   Zwischenprodukt n
  national product   Nationalprodukt n
production [prə'dʌkʃən] Herstellung f, Produktion f, Fertigung f; Fabrikat n;
  The plant goes into production tomorrow.   Die Fabrik nimmt morgen die Produktion auf.
  We had to curb production.   Wir mußten die Produktion drosseln.
  production costs pl   Gestehungskosten pl
  production manager   Betriebsleiter m
  production planning   Produktionsplanung f
productivity [ˌprɔdʌk'tiviti] Ertragsfähigkeit f, Produktivität f, Leistungsfähigkeit f
  to increase productivity   die Produktivität erhöhen
professional [prə'feʃənl] beruflich; fachlich; freiberuflich
  professional man   Fachmann m
  professional qualifications pl   berufliche Eignung f
  professional training   berufliche Ausbildung f
proficiency [prə'fiʃənsi] Tüchtigkeit f, Fertigkeit f, Leistung f
profit ['prɔfit] Gewinn m, Profit m; pl Ertrag m, Erlös m
  to make a profit   einen Gewinn erzielen
  He sold the house at a profit.   Er verkaufte das Haus mit Gewinn.
  clear profit   Reingewinn m
  profit and loss account   Gewinn- u. Verlustrechnung f, Erfolgsrechnung f
  profit margin   Gewinnspanne f
  profit-sharing   Gewinnbeteiligung f
profitable ['prɔfitəbl] gewinnbringend, rentabel
pro forma [prəu'fɔ:mə] Proforma-
  pro forma invoice   Proformarechnung f
program(me) ['prəugræm] Programm n, Plan m
  (computer) program(me)   (Computer-) Programm n
  manufacturing program(me)   Herstellungsprogramm n

programmer – provide

programmer [ˈprəugræmə] — Programmierer *m*
progressive [prəuˈgresiv] — fortschreitend, fortlaufend; gestaffelt; progressiv, fortschrittlich
  progressive assembly Am — Fließbandmontage *f*
  progressive tax — gestaffelte Steuer *f*
project [ˈprɔdʒekt] — Plan *m*, Projekt *n*; Entwurf *m*
  to carry out a project — einen Plan ausführen
  housing project — geplante Wohnsiedlung *f*
to project [prəˈdʒekt] — planen, entwerfen; projizieren
to promote [prəˈməut] — fördern; werben für
  to promote a company — eine Gesellschaft gründen
  to promote a product — für ein Erzeugnis werben
promotion [prəˈməuʃən] — Gründung *f*; Werbung *f*, Verkaufsförderung *f*
  export/sales promotion — Export-/Verkaufsförderung *f*
  promotion manager — Werbeleiter *m*
prompt [prɔmpt] — sofort, unverzüglich, prompt
  a prompt answer/reply — eine umgehende Antwort
  prompt delivery — unverzügliche/prompte Lieferung *f*
property [ˈprɔpəti] — Eigentum *n*, Besitz *m*; Grundstück *n*
  industrial property — gewerbliches Eigentum n
  personal property — persönliches Eigentum n
  landed property — Immobilien pl, Liegenschaften f pl
proportion [prəˈpɔːʃən] — Verhältnis *n*; (verhältnismäßiger) Anteil *m*; Proportion *f*
  in proportion to — im Verhältnis zu
  to be out of proportion to — in keinem Verhältnis stehen zu
proposal [prəˈpəuzəl] — Angebot *n*, Antrag *m*; Vorschlag *m*
  to make/to reject a proposal — einen Vorschlag machen/ablehnen
to propose [prəˈpəuz] — vorschlagen
  to propose an amendment — eine Ergänzung beantragen
proprietor [prəˈpraiətə] — Eigentümer *m*, Besitzer *m*
  sole proprietor — Alleininhaber *m*
prospect [ˈprɔspekt] — Aussicht *f*; potentieller Kunde *m*, Interessent *m*
  He has no prospect of success. — Er hat keine Erfolgsaussichten.
prospective [prəsˈpektiv] — vorausschauend, zukünftig
  prospective buyer/client — potentieller Käufer *m*/Kunde *m*
prospectus [prəsˈpektəs] — 1. Prospekt *m*, Werbeschrift *f*; 2. *(Wertpapiere)* Subskriptionsanzeige *f*
prosperity [prɔsˈperiti] — Wohlstand *m*, Aufschwung *m*, Prosperität *f*
prosperous [ˈprɔspərəs] — wohlhabend; erfolgreich; günstig
protective [prəˈtektiv] — Schutz-
  protective duty — Schutzzoll m
  protective measures pl — Schutzmaßnahmen f pl
to provide (for) [prəˈvaid] — *tr* beschaffen, liefern; *itr* sorgen (für)

to provide cover	Deckung anschaffen
provided that...	unter der Voraussetzung, daß...
provision [prə'viʒən]	1. Beschaffung f, Bereitstellung f; pl Rückstellungen f pl; 2. Bestimmung f, Vorschrift f; Bedingung f; 3. pl Lebensmittel n pl
with the usual provisions	unter üblichem Vorbehalt
He made provision for his old age.	Er traf Vorsorge für sein Alter.
final provisions pl	Schlußbestimmungen f pl
provisional [prə'viʒənl]	provisorisch, einstweilig
They made a provisional arrangement.	Sie trafen eine vorläufige Vereinbarung.
public ['pʌblik]	öffentlich
in public	in der Öffentlichkeit
public opinion	die öffentliche Meinung
public relations pl	Öffentlichkeitsarbeit f, Kontaktpflege f
public utility	öffentlicher Versorgungsbetrieb m
publicity [pʌb'lisiti]	Werbung f, Reklame f
publicity department/ manager	Werbeabteilung f/-leiter m
to publish ['pʌbliʃ]	veröffentlichen, herausgeben
publisher ['pʌbliʃə]	1. Herausgeber m, Verleger m; 2. pl Verlag m
to punch [pʌntʃ]	lochen
punch card	Lochkarte f
purchase ['pə:tʃəs]	s Kauf m, Anschaffung f, Erwerb m; pl (Bilanz) Wareneingänge m pl; v kaufen, erwerben
purchase price	Kaufpreis m
purchase tax	Kaufsteuer f
purchasing power	Kaufkraft f
purse [pə:s]	Geldbeutel m, Börse f
the public purse	die Staatskasse

Q

qualification (for) [ˌkwɔlifi'keiʃən]	Eignung f, Befähigung f, Qualifikation f (für)
without any qualification	vorbehaltlos
He has the necessary qualifications.	Er entspricht den gestellten Anforderungen.
professional qualifications pl	fachliche Qualifikationen f pl
qualified ['kwɔlifaid]	geeignet, befähigt, qualifiziert
He is not qualified for this position.	Er ist für diese Stelle ungeeignet.

quality [ˈkwɔliti] — Qualität f, Güte(grad m) f, Beschaffenheit f
 to guarantee the quality of a product — die Güte eines Produktes garantieren
 inferior/superior quality — geringere/vorzügliche Qualität f
 quality control/goods pl — Qualitätskontrolle f/-waren f pl
quarter [ˈkwɔːtə] — vierter Teil m; (Stadt-)Viertel n; Vierteljahr n, Quartal n
 business/residential quarter — Geschäfts-/Wohnviertel n
 quarterly — vierteljährlich
quay [kiː] — Kai m, Anlegestelle f
 alongside the quay — längsseits Kai
questionnaire [ˌkwestĭəˈnɛə] — Fragebogen m
 He filled in the questionnaire. — Er füllte den Fragebogen aus.
queue [kjuː] — Reihe f, Schlange f
 to stand/to wait in a queue — Schlange stehen
quota [ˈkwəutə] — Quote f, Kontingent n
quotation [kwəuˈteiʃən] — Preisangabe f; (Kurs-) Notierung f
to quote [kwəut] — (Preis) berechnen, ansetzen; (Börse) notieren; girieren
 Please quote ref. (reference.) — In der Antwort bitte angeben!
 to be quoted officially — amtlich notiert werden

R

radio [ˈreidiəu] — Rundfunk m, Radio n
 radio advertising — Rundfunkwerbung f
railway, Am **railroad** [ˈreilwei, ˈreilrəud] — Eisenbahn f
 railway carriage — Eisenbahnwagen m
 railway crossing — Bahnübergang m
 railway guide — Kursbuch n
 railway junctions — Eisenbahnknotenpunkt m
 railway station — Bahnhof m
random [ˈrændəm] — zufällig, wahllos
 at random — aufs Geratewohl
 random sample — Stichprobe f
range [reindʒ] — Umfang m; Bereich m; Auswahl f; Spielraum m
 The shop keeps a wide range of goods. — Der Laden führt eine große Auswahl von Waren.
 price range — Preislage f, -klasse f
rapid [ˈræpid] — rasch, schnell
 rapid growth/decline — rasches Wachstum n/schneller Rückgang m
rate [reit] — (Steuer-) Satz m; Tarif m; (Börsen-) Kurs m; Preis m, Betrag m; (Kosten-) Anschlag m; Abgabe f, (Gemeinde-) Steuer f

at a cheap rate	zu einem niedrigen Preis
at the most favourable rate	zum günstigsten Kurs
at the present rate	zum gegenwärtigen Tarif
at a reduced rate	zu ermäßigter Gebühr
rate of discount	Diskontsatz m
rate of exchange	Wechsel-, Börsenkurs m
rate of interest	Zinssatz m, -fuß m
bank rate	Bankdiskontsatz m
birth/death rate	Geburten-/Sterbeziffer f

ratio [ˈreiʃiəu]   Verhältnis n
   in the ratio of 2:1   im Verhältnis von 2:1
   cover ratio   Deckungssatz m
rationalization [ˌræʃnəlaiˈzeiʃən]   Rationalisierung f
to rationalize [ˈræʃnəlaiz]   tr rationalisieren
raw [rɔ:]   roh, unverarbeitet
   raw material   Rohmaterial n, -stoff m
re [ri:]   betrifft, betreffs, bezüglich
ready [ˈredi]   1. schnell, rasch;
2. fertig;
3. bereit, willens;
4. verfügbar
   to find a ready market   raschen Absatz finden
   ready-made clothes pl   Fertigkleidung f
   ready money   Bargeld n
real [riəl]   wirklich, echt, wahr
   real estate   unbewegliches Vermögen n, Grundeigentum n
   real silk   echte/reine Seide f
   real wage(s)   Reallohn m
to realize [ˈriəlaiz]   veräußern, zu Geld machen
rebate [ˈri:beit]   Rabatt m; (Preis-) Nachlaß m
receipt [riˈsi:t]   1. Quittung f, Empfangsbestätigung f;
2. Inempfangnahme f;
3. pl Einnahmen f pl, Eingänge m pl
   against receipt   gegen Quittung
   on receipt of the draft   bei Eingang des Wechsels
   He acknowledged receipt of the letter.   Er bestätigte den Empfang/den Eingang des Briefes.
receiver [riˈsi:və]   Empfänger m; Treuhänder m; (Steuer-) Einnehmer m; (Telefon-) Hörer m; (Radio) Empfangsgerät n, Empfänger m
   receiver (of stolen goods)   Hehler m
reception [riˈsepʃən]   Empfang m; Aufnahme f; (Hotel) Rezeption f
   The managing director held a reception for the trade delegation.   Der Geschäftsführer gab einen Empfang für die Handelsdelegation.

reception desk — *Empfangsbüro* n
receptionist [ri'sepʃənist] — Empfangschef *m*, -dame *f*
recession [ri'seʃən] — Konjunkturrückgang *m*, Rezession *f*
to reckon ['rekən] — 1. rechnen, berechnen, kalkulieren;
2. halten für
  to reckon with s.th. — mit etw rechnen
  to reckon upon s.th. — auf etw zählen
  I reckon that... — Ich bin der Meinung, daß...
recommendation [ˌrekəmen'deiʃən] — Empfehlung *f*
  letter of recommendation — *Empfehlungsschreiben* n
record ['rekɔ:d] — 1. Aufzeichnung *f*, Niederschrift *f*;
2. Unterlage *f*, Urkunde *f*; Protokoll *n*;
3. *pl* Akten *f pl*;
4. Register *n*, Verzeichnis *n*;
5. Schallplatte *f*;
6. Rekord *m*
  off the record — nicht für die Öffentlichkeit bestimmt
  He kept a careful record of all expenses. — Er führte über alle Ausgaben genau Buch.
recording [ri'kɔ:diŋ] — Aufzeichnung *f*; Aufnahme *f*, Protokollierung *f*; gespeicherte Information *f*
to reduce [ri'dju:s] — herabsetzen, ermäßigen, reduzieren, verringern
  at a reduced price/rate — zu herabgesetztem Preis, verbilligt
  We must reduce costs/expenses. — Wir müssen unsere Kosten/Ausgaben verringern.
  He reduced his stocks. — Er verringerte sein (Waren-) Lager.
reduction [ri'dʌkʃən] — (Preis-) Nachlaß *m*, Ermäßigung *f*, Herabsetzung *f*
  reduction of expenses — *Kosteneinsparung* f
to refer (to) [ri'fə:] — *tr* verweisen, hinweisen (auf); überweisen (an);
itr sich beziehen, Bezug haben (auf)
  referring to your letter — unter Bezugnahme auf Ihr Schreiben
reference ['refrəns] — Bezugnahme *f*; Hinweis *m*; Referenz *f*
  with reference to — unter Bezugnahme auf
  He has excellent references. — Er hat ausgezeichnete Zeugnisse/Empfehlungen.
  You may quote me as a reference. — Sie können sich auf mich berufen.
  your/our reference — (Brief) *Ihr/unser Zeichen*
  reference book — *Nachschlagewerk* n
  reference number — Akten-, Geschäftszeichen *n*
refund ['ri:-fʌnd] — Rückvergütung *f*, Rückzahlung *f*
to refund [ri:'fʌnd] — zurückerstatten, rückvergüten
  The shopkeeper refunded the full price. — Der Händler erstattete den vollen Preis.

refusal [riˈfjuːzəl]	Ablehnung f, Absage f
a flat refusal	*eine glatte Ablehnung* f
regarding [riˈgɑːdiŋ]	bezüglich, hinsichtlich
regardless of [riˈgɑːdlis]	ohne Rücksicht auf
regardless of expense	*ohne Rücksicht auf die Kosten*
region [ˈriːdʒən]	Region f, Gebiet n, Gegend f; Bereich m
regional [ˈriːdʒənl]	regional, örtlich
register (at, with) [ˈredʒistə]	s Register n, Verzeichnis n;
	v tr registrieren, verbuchen, eintragen;
	(Gepäck) aufgeben;
	itr sich eintragen, sich anmelden (bei)
He registered at the hotel.	*Er hat den Meldezettel im Hotel ausgefüllt.*
registered trade-mark	*eingetragenes Warenzeichen*
cash register	*Registrierkasse* f
commercial register	*Handelsregister* n
a registered letter	*ein eingeschriebener Brief/ Einschreibebrief* m
Registered!	*Einschreiben!*
registration [ˌredʒisˈtreiʃən]	Eintragung f, Anmeldung f, Einschreibung f
registration of luggage	*Gepäckaufgabe* f
registration desk	*Abfertigungsschalter* m
registration fee/form	*Anmeldegebühr* f / *-formular* n
regulation [ˌregjuˈleiʃən]	Regelung f; pl (Dienst-, Betriebs-) Vorschriften f pl; pl Satzung f, Statuten pl
according to/contrary to regulations	*vorschriftsmäßig/-widrig*
traffic regulations pl	*Verkehrsvorschriften* f pl
to reject [riˈdʒekt]	ablehnen, zurückweisen, aussondern
The motion was rejected.	*Der Antrag wurde abgelehnt.*
to reject a cheque/an offer	*einen Scheck/ein Angebot zurückweisen*
rejection [riˈdʒekʃən]	Annahmeverweigerung f; pl Ausschuß, Abfall m
relating to [riˈleitiŋ]	betreffend, bezüglich, in bezug auf
relations pl [riˈleiʃənz]	Beziehungen f pl
to break off all relations	*alle Beziehungen abbrechen*
business relations pl	*Geschäftsbeziehungen* f pl
relative [ˈrelətiv]	verhältnismäßig, relativ; bezüglich
reliability [riˌlaiəˈbiliti]	Zuverlässigkeit f; Sicherheit f; Kreditwürdigkeit f
reliable [riˈlaiəbl]	zuverlässig, verläßlich; kreditwürdig; betriebssicher
It's a reliable firm.	*Es handelt sich um eine solide/ reelle/seriöse Firma.*
to rely on [riˈlai]	sich verlassen, sich stützen (auf)
You can rely on him.	*Sie können sich auf ihn verlassen.*

remainder [ri'meində] — Restbestand m, -betrag m; Rückstand m
reminder [ri'maində] — Erinnerung f, Mahnung f
  letter of reminder — *Mahnbrief* m
to remit [ri'mit] — tr überweisen, übersenden; *(Steuer)* erlassen; itr Deckung anschaffen
  He remitted the £2 through his bank. — *Er hat die 2 Pfund durch seine Bank überwiesen.*
  to remit by cheque — *mit einem Scheck bezahlen*
remittance [ri'mitəns] — Überweisung f, Rimesse f; Anschaffung f
  to make a remittance — *eine Überweisung vornehmen*
  remittance order — *Überweisungsauftrag* m
removal (to) [ri'mu:vəl] — Aus-, Umzug m (nach); Entlassung f
  removal (of business) — *Geschäftsverlegung* f
  removal van — *Möbelwagen* m
to renew [ri'nju:] — erneuern, verlängern; renovieren
  He renewed the bill/the contract. — *Er prolongierte den Wechsel/verlängerte den Vertrag.*
  He should renew his efforts. — *Er sollte erneute Anstrengungen machen.*
renewal [ri'nju(:)əl] — Erneuerung f, Verlängerung f; pl Neuanschaffungen f pl
  renewal bill — *Prolongationswechsel* m
rent [rent] — s Miete f, Pacht f; v vermieten, verpachten; mieten
  We pay £30 rent a month. — *Wir zahlen £30 Miete im Monat.*
  rent-a-car — *Autovermietung* f
rental ['rentl] — Mietbetrag m, Pachtsumme f
reorganization ['ri:ˌɔ:gənai'zeiʃən] — Umgestaltung f, Neuordnung f
to reorganize ['ri:'ɔ:gənaiz] — umgestalten, -bilden, neu ordnen; sanieren
repair [ri'pɛə] — s Ausbesserung f, Instandsetzung f; pl Instandsetzungsarbeiten f pl, Reparaturen f pl; v instand setzen, reparieren
  It's in need of repair. — *Es ist reparaturbedürftig.*
  The house is in good repair. — *Das Haus ist in gutem Zustand.*
  to repair the damage — *den Schaden ausbessern*
to repay ['ri:'pei] — zurückzahlen, (zurück-) erstatten
repayment [ri:'peimənt] — Rückzahlung f, -vergütung f
to replace [ri'pleis] — ersetzen; zurückerstatten
  He replaced the receiver. — *Er legte den Hörer auf.*
replacement [ri'pleismənt] — Ersatz m, Wiederbeschaffung f, Erneuerung f
  replacement cost/price — *Wiederbeschaffungskosten* pl/ *-preis* m
  replacement parts pl — *Ersatzteile* n pl

report (on) [ri'pɔːt] — s Bericht m (über); Nachricht f, Meldung f; v berichten, melden

He gave a detailed report. — Er erstattete einen ausführlichen Bericht.

market report — Markt-, Börsenbericht m

to represent [ˌrepri'zent] — 1. vertreten; 2. darstellen

Mr Fox will represent the firm. — Herr Fox wird die Firma vertreten.

What does this sign represent? — Was bedeutet dieses Zeichen?

to be represented on the board — im Aufsichtsrat vertreten sein

representation [ˌreprizen'teiʃən] — 1. Vertretung f; 2. Darstellung f, Schilderung f

representative [ˌrepri'zentətiv] — (Stell-) Vertreter m

authorized representative — Bevollmächtigter m

reputation [ˌrepju(ː)'teiʃən] — Ansehen n, (guter) Ruf m

request [ri'kwest] — s 1. Bitte f, Ansuchen n, Aufforderung f; 2. Nachfrage f; v bitten um; (Person) ersuchen

by/on request — auf Wunsch/Ansuchen; bei Bedarf

He came at my request. — Er kam auf meine Bitte.

request for payment — Zahlungsaufforderung f

to require [ri'kwaiə] — 1. erfordern, bedürfen, brauchen; 2. fordern, verlangen

What do you require of me? — Was wollen Sie von mir?

They require extra help. — Sie brauchen eine zusätzliche Kraft.

requirements (of) pl [ri'kwaiəmənts] — 1. Bedingungen f pl, Voraussetzungen f pl; 2. Bedarf m (an)

He meets our requirements. — Er entspricht unseren Anforderungen.

This firm is in a position to meet our requirements of raw materials. — Diese Firma ist in der Lage, unseren Rohstoffbedarf zu decken.

resale ['riː'seil] — Wieder-, Weiterverkauf m

resale price — Wiederverkaufspreis m

research [ri'səːtʃ] — Untersuchung f; Forschung f

He does research work. — Er ist in der Forschung tätig.

reservation [ˌrezə'veiʃən] — 1. Vorbestellung f, Reservierung f; 2. Vorbehalt m

without reservation — ohne Vorbehalt

We could not get hotel reservations. — Wir konnten keine Hotelzimmer bekommen.

I have a seat reservation on the 6 o'clock train. — Ich habe eine Platzkarte für den 6-Uhr-Zug.

reserve [ri'zəːv] — s Rücklage f, -stellung f; v vorbestellen; reservieren, vormerken

resign - return

all rights reserved
hidden reserves pl
to resign [ri'zain]

He has resigned as chairman.
resignation [ˌrezig'neiʃən]
He sent in his resignation.
resolution [ˌrezə'luːʃən]
The members adopted the resolution unanimously.
resources pl [ri'sɔːsiz]

He was left to his own resources.
natural resources pl
respectively [ris'pektivli]
responsibility [risˌpɔnsə'biliti]

to delegate responsibility to s.o.
He took the responsibility.

responsible [ris'pɔnsəbl]

He was held responsible for the damage.
to restock ['riː'stɔk]
to restrict (to) [ris'trikt]
They restricted membership.

restriction [ris'trikʃən]
without restrictions
import restriction/restriction on imports
retail (trade) ['riːteil treid]
to sell wholesale and retail
retail dealer/price
retailer [riː'teilə]
to retire [ri'taiə]

He has retired (from work).
return [ri'təːn]

by return of post

alle Rechte vorbehalten
stille Reserven f pl
tr verzichten auf; zurücktreten von; itr sein Amt niederlegen; zurücktreten
Er hat den Vorsitz niedergelegt.

Rücktritt(sschreiben n/-sgesuch n) m
Er erklärte seinen Rücktritt.
Beschluß m; Entschluß m
Die Mitglieder nahmen den Beschluß einstimmig an.
Mittel n pl; Hilfsquellen f pl; Vermögenswerte m pl; Am Aktiva pl
Er war auf sich allein gestellt.

Bodenschätze m pl
respektive, beziehungsweise
Verantwortung f (for/of für); Haftung f; Zahlungsfähigkeit f; pl Verbindlichkeiten f pl
jdm die Verantwortung übertragen

Er übernahm die Verantwortung/Haftung.
verantwortlich (for für); verantwortungsbewußt; zahlungsfähig; geschäftsfähig
Er wurde für den Schaden verantwortlich gemacht.
(Lager) wieder auffüllen
be-, einschränken (auf)
Sie beschränkten die Zahl der Mitglieder.
Ein-, Beschränkung f
uneingeschränkt
Einfuhrbeschränkung f

Einzelhandel m
im Groß- und Einzelhandel verkaufen
Einzelhändler m/Ladenpreis m
Einzel-, Kleinhändler m
in den Ruhestand treten; sich zurückziehen
Er hat sich zur Ruhe gesetzt.
s Rückerstattung f, Rückzahlung f; Entschädigung f, Vergütung f; pl Umsatz m, Einnahmen f pl; v zurückkehren, -kommen
postwendend

in return for	als Gegenleistung für
income tax return	Einkommensteuererklärung f
return postage	Rückporto n
return ticket	Rückfahrkarte f
revaluation [ˈriːvæljuˈeiʃən]	Aufwertung f
revenue office [ˈrevinjuː ˈɔfis]	Finanzamt n
reverse [riˈvəːs]	s Gegenteil n; Rückseite f; a entgegengesetzt; v tr zurückfahren, -stoßen umstehend
on the reverse	umstehend
He reversed the car.	Er fuhr zurück.
reverse side	Rückseite f
review [riˈvjuː]	s 1. Nachprüfung f; 2. Überblick m (*of* über); 3. Rezension f; 4. Rundschau f; v 1. überprüfen, nachprüfen; 2. überblicken; 3. rezensieren
month under review	Berichtsmonat m
rise [raiz]	Steigen n, Zuwachs m; Aufschwung m, Hausse f
rise in prices/in wages	Preisanstieg m/Lohnerhöhung f
risk [risk]	Risiko n; Gefahr f
at one's own risk	auf eigene Gefahr
He took no risks.	Er ging kein Risiko ein.
risk of loss	Verlustrisiko n
rival [ˈraivəl]	Konkurrent m
rival business/firm	Konkurrenzgeschäft n
road [rəud]	(Land-) Straße f
to be on the road	geschäftlich unterwegs sein
Road up!	Straßenarbeiten!
road conditions pl/*traffic*	Straßenzustand m/-verkehr m
road map	Straßenkarte f
road user	Verkehrsteilnehmer m
rough [rʌf]	roh; annähernd, ungefähr
rough calculation	Überschlagsrechnung f
rough estimate	grobe Schätzung f
route [ruːt]	(Fahrt-) Route f, Strecke f; Transportweg m
Which route did they take?	Welchen Weg haben sie eingeschlagen?
routine [ruːˈtiːn]	s Routine f; a routinemäßig
run (on) [rʌn]	s 1. Ansturm (auf), stürmische Nachfrage f; 2. Art f, Sorte f; v itr laufen, gültig sein; tr *(Geschäft)* betreiben

running - saleable

in the long run	auf die Dauer
trial run	Probefahrt f
The licence has two months to run.	Die Lizenz gilt noch zwei Monate.
to run a factory	eine Fabrik betreiben
running ['rʌniŋ]	laufend
running costs pl	Betriebskosten pl
running expenses pl	laufende Ausgaben f pl
rush [rʌʃ]	stürmische Nachfrage f, Andrang m
rush hour	Hauptverkehrszeit f

S

sack [sæk]	s Sack m; Am Beutel m, Tüte f; fam Entlassung f; v in Säcke/Beutel abfüllen; fam entlassen
safe [seif]	s Tresor m, Geldschrank m; a sicher, gefahrlos; zuverlässig
That's a safe estimate.	Das kann man mit einiger/ziemlicher Sicherheit sagen.
to be on the safe side	um ganz sicher zu gehen
safe-deposit box	Bankfach n, Safe m
safety ['seifti]	Sicherheit f, Zuverlässigkeit f
They were brought to safety.	Sie wurden in Sicherheit gebracht.
road safety	Verkehrssicherheit f
safety factor	Sicherheitsfaktor m
safety measures pl	Sicherheitsmaßnahmen f pl
salary ['sæləri]	s Gehalt n; v ein Gehalt bezahlen (s.o. jdm)
He holds a salaried position.	Er ist fest angestellt.
He is a salaried man/an employee.	Er ist Gehaltsempfänger/Angestellter.
increase in salary	Gehaltserhöhung f
top salary	Spitzengehalt n
salary bracket	Gehaltsstufe f
sale [seil]	Verkauf m, Veräußerung f, Vertrieb m; Auktion f; pl Umsatz m; pl Schlußverkauf m
not for sale	unverkäuflich
salesgirl/salesman	Verkäuferin f/ Verkäufer m
sales manager	Verkaufsleiter m
sales promotion	Verkaufsförderung f
salesroom	Verkaufsraum m
sales talk	Verkaufsgespräch n
saleable, Am **salable** ['seiləbl]	verkäuflich; absetzbar

sample [ˈsɑːmpl] — Probe f, Muster m; Stichprobe f
  by sample post — als Warenprobe
  up to sample — probegemäß
  free sample — kostenlose Warenprobe f
  sample book — Musterbuch n
satisfactory [ˌsætisˈfæktəri] — zufriedenstellend, befriedigend
to save [seiv] — sparen; aufbewahren; einbringen; retten
saving [ˈseiviŋ] — Einsparung f; pl Ersparnisse f pl, Spargelder n pl

  He withdrew his savings from the bank. — Er hob seine Spargelder von der Bank ab.
  savings account/bank — Sparguthaben n/-kasse f
  savings deposit — Spareinlage f
scale [skeil] — 1. Skala f; Maßstab m; 2. Waagschale f
  to scale — maßstabgerecht
  on a large scale — in großem Maßstab/Umfang
  drawn to a scale of 1:10 — im Maßstab 1:10 gezeichnet
  wage scale — Lohnskala f
scarce [skɛəs] — knapp, spärlich
  Eggs are scarce at the moment. — Die Eier sind zur Zeit knapp.
schedule [ˈʃedjuːl, Am ˈskedjuːl] — (Arbeits-/Fahr-) Plan m; Liste f, Tabelle f; Produktionsplan m; Einkommensteuerformular n

  on/behind schedule — fahrplanmäßig/verspätet
  The aircraft arrived on schedule. — Das Flugzeug landete pünktlich.
  The train ist scheduled to leave at 8 o'clock. — Der Zug fährt fahrplanmäßig um 8 Uhr ab.
scheme [skiːm] — Entwurf m, Plan m; Schema n, Übersicht f; Tabelle f

  He has a scheme for raising the money. — Er hat einen Plan, um das Geld zusammenzubringen.
scope [skəup] — Ausmaß n, Umfang m; Bereich m; Spielraum m

  within the scope of the law — im Rahmen des Gesetzes
  That job offers you no scope. — Diese Arbeit bietet Ihnen keine Aussichten.
scrap [skræp] — s Schrott m, Abfall m, Ausschuß m; v verschrotten

  a scrap of paper — ein Fetzen Papier
seasonal [ˈsiːzənl] — saisonbedingt
  seasonal demand/unemployment — saisonbedingte Nachfrage f/ Arbeitslosigkeit f
secondary [ˈsekəndəri] — zweitrangig, nebensächlich
  That's a matter of secondary importance. — Das ist nicht so wichtig.
  secondary effect — Nebenwirkung f

secretarial [ˌsekrə'tɛəriəl] — Büro-, Schreib-
   secretarial work —   *Büroarbeit* f
section ['sekʃən] — Abteilung f; Abschnitt m; Paragraph m
   residential section —   *Wohnviertel* n
   section 4 —   *Abschnitt/Paragraph 4*
sector ['sektə] — Sektor m, Abschnitt m, Bereich m
secure (on, by) [si'kjuə] — a sicher;
    v sicherstellen; garantieren (durch); beschaffen
   secured by mortgage —   *hypothekarisch gesichert*
   secure investments pl —   *sichere Kapitalanlagen* f pl
security [si'kjuəriti] — 1. Sicherheit f;
    2. Garantie f, Kaution f, Bürgschaft f;
    3. pl Wertpapiere n pl, Effekten pl
   against security —   *gegen Sicherstellung*
   to provide security —   *Sicherheit leisten; Kaution stellen*
   to lend money on security —   *Geld gegen Sicherheiten ausleihen*
   security market —   *Effektenmarkt* m
to seize [si:z] — beschlagnahmen; ergreifen, packen
select [si'lekt] — a ausgewählt, auserlesen;
    v auswählen
   to select a team —   *eine Gruppe/ein Team auswählen*
   selected goods pl —   *auserlesene Waren* f pl
selection [si'lekʃən] — Auswahl f, -lese f
   They have a large selection of shoes. —   *Sie haben eine große Auswahl an Schuhen.*
self, pl **selves** [self, selvz] — s Ich n, Selbst n;
    a (in Zusammensetzungen) selbst-, Selbst-
   a cheque drawn to self —   *ein eigener Scheck*
   self-contained house —   *Einfamilienhaus* n
   self-employed —   *selbständig*
   self-service (store) —   *Selbstbedienung(sladen* m*)* f
   self-service restaurant —   *Restaurant* n *mit Selbstbedienung*
   self-supporting —   *sich selbst versorgend*
to sell (at) *(sold, sold)* [sel, səuld] — tr verkaufen, absetzen, veräußern;
    (Waren) führen, vertreiben, handeln mit;
    itr sich verkaufen lassen (für); Verkäufe tätigen
   The store is sold out. —   *Der Laden ist ausverkauft.*
   He sold the house at a profit. —   *Er verkaufte das Haus mit Gewinn.*
   The shirts are selling well. —   *Die Hemden lassen sich leicht absetzen/gehen gut.*
   The pipes usually sell for... —   *Die Röhren werden gewöhnlich um/für... verkauft.*
seller ['selə] — Verkäufer m, Händler m
   seller's market —   *Verkäufermarkt* m, *günstiger Absatzmarkt* m

selling ['seliŋ] — s Verkauf m, Verkaufen n; Absatz m; a verkäuflich; Absatz-
  hard selling — aggressive Verkaufsmethoden f pl
  selling methods pl — Absatz-, Vertriebsmethoden f pl
  selling order/price — Verkaufsauftrag m/-preis m
semi-finished ['semi'finiʃt] — halbfertig
  semi-finished product — Halbfabrikat n
semi-skilled ['semi'skild] — angelernt
  semi-skilled worker — angelernter Arbeiter m
sender ['sendə] — Absender m, Übersender m
senior (to) ['si:njə] — s Älterer m, Ältester m; Vorgesetzter m; a älter (als); ranghöher (als)
  senior clerk/partner — Bürovorsteher m/Seniorchef m
separate ['seprit] — getrennt, gesondert
  separate account/print — Sonderkonto n/-druck m
to separate ['sepəreit] — tr trennen, absondern (*from* von); itr sich trennen
series, *pl* **series** ['siəri:z] — Reihe f, Serie f
  in series — serienmäßig
service (to) ['sə:vis] — s Dienst m (an); Bedienung f; Kundendienst m; Versorgung f; Wartung f; Zustellung f; v pflegen, warten, instand setzen
  on His/Her Majesty's service (Abk. O.H.M.S.) — gebührenfreie Dienstsache
  retired from service — außer Dienst (a. D.)
  railway/shipping service — Eisenbahn-/Schiffahrtsverkehr m
  service station — Reparaturwerkstatt m; Tankstelle f
session ['seʃən] — Sitzung f; Tagung f, Konferenz f
  The court is in session. — Das Gericht tagt.
set [set] — s Kollektion f, Garnitur f, Satz m; Sortiment n; Apparat m; a festgesetzt, bestimmt; vorgeschrieben
  at a set time — zu einem bestimmten Termin
  set of cutlery — (Eß-) Besteck m
to settle (with) ['setl] — tr 1. (Rechnung) regeln, begleichen; 2. (Geschäft) erledigen, abwickeln; 3. (Firma) errichten; itr 1. sich niederlassen; 2. einen Vergleich schließen (mit)
  All claims were settled. — Alle Ansprüche wurden befriedigt.
  to settle an account — ein Konto ausgleichen
settlement ['setlmənt] — 1. (Rechnung) Bezahlung f, Begleichung f, Ausgleich m; 2. (Streit) Beilegung f, Schlichtung f, Bereinigung f; 3. Übereinkommen n
  in settlement of all claims — zum Ausgleich aller Forderungen

set up - shipping

in settlement of your account	zur Begleichung Ihrer Rechnung
They came to/reached a settlement.	Sie gelangten zu einem Vergleich.
an out-of-court settlement	ein außergerichtlicher Vergleich
to set up [ˈset ˈʌp]	(Geschäft) gründen, eröffnen; (Rekord) aufstellen
to set up in business	ein Geschäft eröffnen
set-up [ˈsetʌp]	Anordnung f; Aufbau m, Organisation f; Einrichtung f; Am Situation f, Lage f
sham [ʃæm]	s Täuschung f, Nachahmung f; a vorgetäuscht, fingiert; v tr vortäuschen, fingieren; itr sich verstellen
sham bid/sale	Scheingebot n/-verkauf m
share [ʃɛə]	s 1. Beteiligung f, Geschäftsanteil m; 2. Gewinnanteil m, -beteiligung f; 3. Aktie f, Anteilschein m; v teilen; sich beteiligen an
to share equally	gleichmäßig verteilen
They shared the costs.	Sie teilten die Kosten untereinander auf.
He holds shares in the company.	Er ist Aktionär der Gesellschaft.
shareholder [ˈʃɛəˌhəuldə]	Aktionär m
shift (to) [ʃift]	s 1. (Arbeits-) Schicht f; 2. Verschiebung f, Veränderung f, Wechsel m; 3. Ausweg m, Notbehelf m; v tr 1. um-, auswechseln, verlagern; 2. (Betrieb) umstellen (auf); (Steuer) abwälzen; (Güter) umladen; itr 1. sich verlagern, sich verschieben; 2. umziehen
The men on the night shift work from 10 p.m. to 6 a.m.	Die Arbeiter der Nachtschicht arbeiten von 22 Uhr bis 6 Uhr.
ship [ʃip]	s Schiff n; v versenden, aufliefern, verschiffen, verladen; transportieren
The goods were shipped to New York on Friday.	Die Waren sind am Freitag nach New York abgeschickt worden.
shipment [ˈʃipmənt]	Verschiffung f; Versand m; Lieferung f; (Schiffs-) Ladung f
ready for shipment	versandbereit
shipping [ˈʃipiŋ]	Verschiffung f; Verladung f, Verladen n
shipping clerk	Expedient m
shipping department	Versandabteilung f
shipping company	Reederei f
shipping documents pl	Schiffs-, Versandpapiere n pl
shipping instructions pl	Versandvorschriften f pl

shop [ʃɔp] s 1. Laden *m*, Geschäft *n*;
 2. Betrieb *m*, Fabrik *f*, Werk *n*;
 3. Werkstatt *f*
 v einkaufen
He opened/set up a shop. — *Er eröffnete einen Laden/ein Geschäft.*
shop assistant — *Verkäufer(in f) m*
shopkeeper — *Ladenbesitzer m, Geschäftsinhaber m*
shop-window — *Schaufenster n*
shopping [ˈʃɔpiŋ] Einkauf *m*, Einkaufen *n*
She has a lot of shopping to do. — *Sie hat eine Menge Besorgungen zu machen.*
shopping area/street — *Geschäftsgegend f/-straße f*
shopping centre — *Geschäftsviertel n, Einkaufszentrum n*
shortage (of) [ˈʃɔːtidʒ] Verknappung *f*, Mangel *m* (an); Engpaß *m* (in); Gewichtsverlust *m*, Abgang *m*; Fehlbetrag *m*, Defizit *n*
food shortage — *Lebensmittelknappheit f*
housing shortage — *Wohnungsmangel m*
shortage of money — *Geldknappheit f*
shortage of personnel — *Personalmangel m*
shortage of manpower — *Mangel m an Arbeitskräften*
shorthand typist [ˈʃɔːthænd] Stenotypistin *f*
short-term [ˈʃɔːtəːm] kurzfristig
short-term credit — *kurzfristiger Kredit m*
short-term loan — *kurzfristiges Darlehen n*
short-time (work) [ˈʃɔːttaim] Kurzarbeit *f*
showroom [ˈʃəurum] Ausstellungsraum *m*; Musterlager *n*
sight [sait] Sicht *f*; Sichtweite *f*; Sehvermögen *n*
30 days after sight — *30 Tage nach Sicht*
payable at sight — *bei Sicht zahlbar*
bill payable at sight — *Sichtwechsel m*
signature [ˈsignitʃə] Unterschrift *f*, Namenszug *m*
silent [ˈsailənt] still, schweigsam; stillschweigend
silent partner — *stiller Teilhaber m*
site [sait] Bauplatz *m*, Gelände *n*; Lage *f (eines Grundstückes)*
site of an industry — *Sitz m einer Industrie*
site plan — *Lageplan m*
situation [ˌsitjuˈeiʃən] Stellung *f*, Posten *m*; Sachlage *f*
economic situation — *Wirtschaftslage f*
situations vacant — *Stellenangebote n pl*
situations wanted — *Stellengesuche n pl*
size [saiz] *(Kleidung, Schuhe)* Größe *f*, Nummer *f*
the next size — *die nächstgrößere Nummer*
He takes size 7 in gloves/size 10 in shoes. — *Er hat Handschuhgröße 7/Schuhnummer 10.*
skilled (at, in) [skild] gelernt, erfahren, geschickt (in)
skilled labour — *Facharbeiter m pl*
skilled workman — *gelernter Arbeiter m, Facharbeiter m*

sleeping [ˈsliːpiŋ] schlafend
  sleeping accommodation   *Schlafgelegenheit* f
  sleeping car, sleeper   *Schlafwagen* m
  sleeping partner   *stiller Teilhaber* m
slip [slip] 1. Zettel *m;* (Kontroll-) Abschnitt *m;*
  2. Fehler *m,* Panne *f*
  paying-in slip   *Einzahlungsbeleg* m
  slip of the pen   *Schreibfehler* m
slogan [ˈsləugən] Schlagwort *n;* Werbespruch *m,* Slogan *m*
slump [slʌmp] Kurs-, Preissturz *m; (Börse)* Baisse *f;*
Rezession *f;* Krise *f*
  slump in production   *starker Produktionsrückgang* m
smart [smaːt] geschäftstüchtig, gerissen; schick
social [ˈsəuʃəl] sozial, gesellschaftlich
  social background   *soziale Herkunft* f
  social insurance/security   *Sozialversicherung* f
  social legislation   *Sozialgesetzgebung* f
  social security benefit   *Sozialleistung* f
  social services pl   *Sozialeinrichtungen* f pl
  social welfare   *Fürsorge* f, *Wohlfahrt* f
society [səˈsaiəti] Verein *m;* Gesellschaft *f*
  building society   *Baugenossenschaft* f
  co-operative society Br   *Genossenschaft* f
soft [sɔft] weich; *(Kurse)* nachgiebig
  soft currency   *weiche Währung* f
  soft drinks pl   *alkoholfreie Getränke* n pl
sole [səul] allein, einzig; unverheiratet
  sole agency/agent   *Alleinvertretung* f/-vertreter m
  sole bill of exchange   *Solawechsel* m
  solely responsible   *allein verantwortlich*
solicitor [səˈlisitə] Rechtsanwalt *m (bei niederen Gerichten);* Rechtsbeistand *m*
solution [səˈluːʃən] Lösung *f*
  a workable solution   *eine brauchbare Lösung* f
solvency [ˈsɔlvənsi] Zahlungsfähigkeit *f,* Kreditwürdigkeit *f*
solvent [ˈsɔlvənt] zahlungsfähig, kreditwürdig, solvent
source [sɔːs] Quelle *f*
  from a reliable source   *aus zuverlässiger Quelle*
  source of funds/income   *Kapital-/Einkommensquelle* f
  source of supply   *Bezugsquelle* f
space [speis] (Zeit-, Zwischen-) Raum *m;* Platz *m*
  in the space of a year   *innerhalb Jahresfrist*
  advertising space   *Reklamefläche* f
  a blank space   *eine freie Stelle* f
  space industry   *Raumfahrtindustrie* f
spare [spɛə] *a* übrig; Ersatz-, Reserve-;
v sparsam umgehen mit; erübrigen/
entbehren können
  I don't have a minute to spare.   *Ich habe keine Minute übrig/Zeit.*

spare (part)	Ersatzteil n
spare room	Gästezimmer n
spare time	Freizeit f
spare tire	Ersatzreifen m
special [ˈspeʃəl]	s Sonderzug m; Sonderausgabe f; Am Sonderangebot n; a speziell, besondere
special delivery Am	Eilzustellung f
special offer	Sonderangebot n
special train	Sonder-, Extrazug m
speciality [ˌspeʃiˈæliti]	Spezialartikel m, Neuheit f; Am Spezialfach n
to specialize in [ˈspeʃəlaiz]	sich spezialisieren auf
specific [spiˈsifik]	spezifisch; genau, bestimmt; wesentlich
on a specific day	an einem bestimmten Tag
a specific statement	eine klar umrissene Feststellung
specification [ˌspesifiˈkeiʃən]	genaue Angabe f; nähere Bestimmung f; Patentbeschreibung f; pl Baubeschreibung f
to specify [ˈspesifai]	einzeln aufführen/angeben
He specified the exact measurements.	Er gab die genauen Maße an.
specimen [ˈspesimin]	Muster n, Probeexemplar n
specimen copy/letter	Belegexemplar n / Musterbrief m
to speculate (for/on) [ˈspekjuleit]	spekulieren (auf)
He speculated in shares/for a fall.	Er spekulierte in Aktien/auf eine Baisse.
speculation [ˌspekjuˈleiʃən]	Spekulation f
speculation in real estate/in stocks	Grundstücks-/Aktienspekulation f
to speed (sped, sped) [spiːd, sped]	tr beschleunigen; itr (dahin) fahren; zu schnell fahren
He is always speeding.	Er fährt immer zu schnell.
to speed up production	die Produktion erhöhen
speed limit	Höchstgeschwindigkeit f
spending [ˈspendiŋ]	Ausgeben n; Ausgaben f pl
spending money	Taschengeld n
spending power	Kaufkraft f
sphere [sfiə]	Bereich m, Gebiet n
sphere of activity	Tätigkeitsbereich m
sphere of interest	Interessensphäre f
spiral [ˈspaiərəl]	Spirale f
wage-price spiral	Lohn-Preis-Spirale f
sponsor [ˈspɔnsə]	Förderer m, Gönner m; Geldgeber m
spot [spɔt]	s Stelle f, Platz m, Ort m; kurze Werbedurchsage f, Werbe-Spot m; a sofort lieferbar/zahlbar
spot business	Bargeschäft n
spot cash	Barzahlung f

spot goods pl	sofort lieferbare Waren f pl
squeeze [skwi:z]	wirtschaftlicher Engpaß m; (Geld-) Verlegenheit f; Geldknappheit f
credit squeeze	Kreditbeschränkung f
stability [stə'biliti]	Stabilität f, Wertbeständigkeit f
monetary stability	Währungsstabilität f
price stability	Preisstabilität f
staff [stɑ:f]	Mitarbeiterstab m, Angestellte m pl, Belegschaft f
He is on the staff of the firm.	Er ist bei der Firma fest angestellt.
staff manager	Personalchef m
stage [steidʒ]	Stadium n, Phase f, Etappe f
at this stage	zum gegenwärtigen Zeitpunkt
in stages	stufenweise
stagnant ['stægnənt]	lustlos, flau, schleppend
stall [stɔ:l]	(Verkaufs-) Stand m
He has a stall in the market.	Er hat einen Stand auf dem Markt.
stamp [stæmp]	1. Briefmarke f, Postwertzeichen n; 2. Rabatt-, Stempelmarke f; Stempel m; 3. Firmenzeichen n; 4. Aufdruck m
date/official stamp	Datum-/Amtsstempel m
internal revenue stamp	Steuer-, Gebührenmarke f
stamp duty	Stempelgebühr f
stamp collection	Briefmarkensammlung f
stamp collector	Briefmarkensammler m
stamp dealer	Briefmarkenhändler m
stand [stænd]	(Verkaufs-, Messe-) Stand m
newspaper stand	Zeitungsstand m
cabstand	Taxihaltestelle f
standard ['stændəd]	Standard m, Gütegrad m, Norm f; Niveau n, Stand m
above/below standard	über-/unterdurchschnittlich
by present-day standards	nach heutigen Begriffen/Maßstäben
to be up to standard	den Anforderungen entsprechen
standard of living	Lebensstandard m
standard size	übliche Größe f
standard time	Normalzeit f
standing ['stændiŋ]	s Rang m, Stellung f; a feststehend; ständig, dauerhaft
standing committee	ständiger Ausschuß m
standing order	Dauerauftrag m, laufende Order f
standing room	Stehplatz m
standstill ['stændstil]	Stillstand m
Work in the factory has come to a standstill.	Die Arbeit in der Fabrik ist zum Stillstand gekommen.
staple ['steipl]	Haupterzeugnis n, -artikel m, wichtigstes Produkt n, Stapelware f; Rohstoff m; Handelszentrum n

staple commodities pl — *Stapelwaren* f pl
to state [steit] — festlegen, festsetzen; angeben
  as stated above — *wie oben (angegeben)*
  State full particulars. — *Geben Sie genaue Einzelheiten an!*
  at the stated time — *zur festgesetzten Zeit*
statement [ˈsteitmənt] — (Bank-) Ausweis *m*, (Geschäfts-) Bericht *m*; (Konto-) Auszug *m*; (Rechnungs-) Aufstellung *f*; Lohn *m*; Tarif *m*
  according to/as per statement — *laut Bericht/Angabe*
  He made a statement on oath that... — *Er erklärte unter Eid, daß...*
  Do you wish to make a statement? — *Wollen Sie eine Erklärung abgeben?*
  bank/cash statement — *Bank-/Kassenausweis* m
  statement of account — *Kontoauszug* m
  statement of finances — *Gewinn- und Verlustrechnung* f
stationery [ˈsteiʃnəri] — Schreib-, Papierwaren *f pl*, Bürobedarf *m*
statistical [stəˈtistikəl] — statistisch
  to record statistically — *statistisch erfassen*
statistics *pl* [stəˈtistiks] — Statistik(en *pl*) *f*
  commercial/trade statistics — *Handelsstatistik* f
status [ˈsteitəs] — (geschäftliche) Lage *f*; Stellung *f*, Rang *m*
  personal/marital status — *Personen-/Familienstand* m
  financial status — *Vermögenslage* f
stencil [ˈstensl] — (Wachs-) Matrize *f*
step [step] — *s* Schritt *m*, Maßnahme *f*; *v* schreiten, treten
  step by step — *nach und nach, Schritt für Schritt*
  This is a great step forward. — *Das ist ein großer Schritt nach vorn.*
  He is out of step with the times. — *Er geht nicht mit der Zeit.*
  to take steps (to do s.th.) — *Maßnahmen treffen (um etw zu tun)*
  to step up production — *die Produktion ankurbeln*
to stipulate [ˈstipjuleit] — vereinbaren, festsetzen
  as stipulated — *wie vereinbart*
stock [stɔk] — *s* 1. (Waren-) Lager *n*, Bestand *m*, Vorrat *m*; Inventar *n*; 2. Stamm-, Grundkapital *n*; Anleihekapital *n*; *Am* Aktie *f*; 3. *pl* Wertpapiere *n pl*; *pl* Schuldverschreibungen *f pl*; *v (Waren)* vorrätig haben, führen
  We don't stock that brand. — *Wir führen diese Marke nicht.*
  in (out of) stock — *(nicht) vorrätig, (nicht) auf Lager*
  to take stock — *Inventur machen*
  His stock has gone up. — *Seine Aktien sind gestiegen.*

live/dead stock	lebendes/totes Inventar n
rolling stock	rollendes Material n, Wagenpark m
stockbroker	Börsenmakler m
stock exchange	(Wertpapier-) Börse f
stockholder	Aktionär m
stock-in-trade	Warenbestand m; Betriebsmittel n pl
stock list	Kurszettel m
stock market	Effektenmarkt m, Wertpapierbörse f
stock-taking	Bestandsaufnahme f
storage [ˈstɔːridʒ]	Einlagerung f; Lagergeld n; Lagerraum m
in storage	auf Lager
cold storage	Kühlhauslagerung f
storage charges pl/room	Lagergebühren f pl/-raum m
store [stɔː]	s Lager n, Magazin n; Warenhaus n; Geschäft n; pl Vorräte m pl; v einlagern, speichern
ex store	ab Lager
in store	vorrätig, auf Lager
chain store	Kettenladen m
department store	Warenhaus n
to streamline [ˈstriːmlain]	modernisieren, rationalisieren; elegant/schnittig gestalten
strict [strikt]	strikt, streng
strictly confidential	streng vertraulich
in the strictest sense of the word	im engsten Sinne des Wortes
strictly speaking	genaugenommen
strike [straik]	Streik m, Ausstand m
The workers are going on strike/are on strike.	Die Arbeiter treten in den Ausstand/streiken.
structure [ˈstrʌktʃə]	Struktur f, Gefüge n
economic structure	Wirtschaftsstruktur f
price structure	Preisgefüge n
study group [ˈstʌdi ˈgruːp]	Arbeitsausschuß m, -gemeinschaft f
style [stail]	1. Stil m, Mode f; Machart f; 2. Firmenbezeichnung f, Firma f
business style	Geschäftsstil m
the latest style	die neueste Mode
subject [ˈsʌbdʒikt]	s 1. Thema n, Gegenstand m; 2. Grund m, Anlaß m; 3. Staatsangehöriger m; a abhängig (to von)
to change the subject	das Thema wechseln
to broach a subject	ein Thema anschneiden
subject to approval/to your consent	genehmigungspflichtig/vorbehaltlich Ihrer Zustimmung
subject to prior sale	Zwischenverkauf vorbehalten

submit - suit

Prices are␣are subject to change without notice.
Subject:
to submit [səbˈmit]
He submitted a plan/a report.
to submit a proposal
to subscribe (for/to) [səbˈskraib]

to subscribe to a newspaper
subscriber [səbˈskraibə]

subscriber's number
subscription [səbˈskripʃən]

by subscription
to invite subscriptions for a loan
subsidiary [səbˈsidjəri]

subsidiary agreement
to subsidize [ˈsʌbsidaiz]
substantial [səbˈstænʃəl]
a substantial improvement
a substantial progress
substitute (for) [ˈsʌbstitjuːt]

to subtract [səbˈtrækt]
to sue for [sjuː, suː]

to sue for damages
sufficient for [səˈfiʃənt]
"Not sufficient"
suggestion [səˈdʒestʃən]

His suggestion is that...
It's only a suggestion.
suit [sjuːt]

to bring/institute a suit against s.o.
to suit (to) [sjuːt]

Does this suit your taste?
Blue doesn't suit you.

Die Preise sind unverbindlich. — Änderungen vorbehalten.
Betrifft, Betr.:
vorlegen, vortragen; beantragen
Er legte einen Plan/einen Bericht vor.
einen Vorschlag unterbreiten
tr unterschreiben, unterzeichnen;
itr (etw) abonnieren; (etw) vorbestellen; Geld spenden
eine Zeitung abonnieren/beziehen
Unterzeichneter *m*, Unterzeichner *m*;
Abonnent *m*, Bezieher *m*; Spender *m*;
(Fernsprech-) Teilnehmer *m*
Teilnehmernummer f
Unterzeichnung f; Zeichnung f;
Abonnement *n*; Mitgliedsbeitrag *m*
im Abonnement
eine Anleihe (zur Zeichnung) auflegen

s Tochtergesellschaft *f*;
a untergeordnet
Nebenabkommen n
subventionieren
beträchtlich, wesentlich; kapitalkräftig
eine beträchtliche Verbesserung f
ein beachtlicher Fortschritt m
s Stellvertreter *m*; Ersatz *m*;
v tr an die Stelle setzen (von);
itr an die Stelle treten (von)
tr abziehen
tr verklagen auf;
itr klagen auf
auf Schadenersatz klagen
genügend, ausreichend für
(Scheck) „Ungenügende Deckung"
1. Anregung f, Vorschlag *m*; Hinweis *m*;
2. Vermutung *f*;
3. Andeutung *f*;
4. Spur *f*, Hauch *m*
Er schlägt vor, daß...
Es ist nur ein Vorschlag.
Prozeß *m*, Rechtsstreit *m*, Klage *f*, Verfahren *n*
gegen jdn einen Prozeß anstrengen/Klage erheben
tr anpassen (an), abstimmen (auf);
itr passen (*s.o.* jdm)
Entspricht das Ihrem Geschmack?
Blau steht Ihnen nicht.

sum - supply

He is suited to the job of salesman.
The date doesn't suit me.
sum [sʌm]
a sum of $50
lump sum
sum total
to sum up (to) [ˈsʌm ˈʌp]

to sum up
Let me sum up briefly.
sundries *pl* [ˈsʌndriːz]

sundry [ˈsʌndri]
sundry expenses pl
superior (to) [sju(ː)ˈpiərĭə]

Our new typewriter is superior to the old one.
of superior quality
They are superior in numbers.
Is he her superior?
supermarket [ˈsjuːpəˌmɑːkit]

to supervise [ˈsjuːpəvaiz]
supervision (of)
[ˌsjuːpəˈviʒən]
close supervision
supervisor [ˈsjuːpəvaizə]
supplement (to) [ˈsʌplimənt]

supplementary
[ˌsʌpliˈmentəri]
supplementary agreement
supplementary order
supplier [səˈplai-ə]
main supplier
supply (to) [səˈplai]

They supply us with shirts.
The supply of stockings cannot meet the demand.

Er eignet sich als Verkäufer.

Das Datum paßt mir nicht.
Summe *f*, Betrag *m*
ein Betrag von $ 50
Pauschalbetrag m
Gesamtbetrag m
tr zusammenrechnen, -zählen, addieren; zusammenfassen;
itr sich belaufen (auf)
mit einem Wort; alles zusammen
Lassen Sie mich kurz zusammenfassen.
1. Verschiedenes *n*, diverse Unkosten *pl*;
2. Kurz-, Gemischtwaren *f pl*
diverse, verschiedene; allerhand
verschiedene Unkosten pl
s Vorgesetzter *m*;
a 1. höher stehend, vorgesetzt;
2. besser (als); hervorragend;
3. größer (als);
Unsere neue Schreibmaschine ist besser als die alte.
von hervorragender Qualität
Sie sind zahlenmäßig überlegen.

Ist er ihr Vorgesetzter?
Supermarkt *m*, (großes) Selbstbedienungsgeschäft *n*
überwachen, beaufsichtigen
Aufsicht *f*, Kontrolle *f* (über), Inspektion *f*
strenge Überwachung f
Aufseher *m*, Inspektor *m*, Kontrolleur *m*
s Zusatz *m*, Ergänzung *f* (zu); Beilage *m* (einer Zeitung);
v ergänzen; nachliefern
zusätzlich, ergänzend

Zusatzabkommen n
Nachbestellung f
Lieferant *m*
Hauptlieferant m
s Lieferung *f* (an); Versorgung *f*; Angebot *n*; Vorrat *m*; *pl* Bedarf *m*
v liefern, beschaffen; versorgen; nachzahlen
Sie beliefern uns mit Hemden.
Die Strumpflieferungen können den Bedarf nicht decken.

We are running out of supplies.	Unsere Vorräte gehen zu Ende.
market supply	Marktangebot n
office supplies pl	Bürobedarf m
power supply	Energie-, Stromversorgung f
supply and demand	Angebot und Nachfrage
supply price	Lieferpreis m
support [sə'pɔ:t]	s Stütze f; Stützung f, Unterstützung f; v (unter-) stützen; fördern, finanzieren
in support of my motion	zur Begründung meines Antrags
to support a project	ein Projekt finanzieren
financial support	finanzielle Unterstützung f
surcharge ['sə:-tʃɑ:dʒ]	(Steuer-) Zuschlag m; Überpreis m; Nachporto n
surplus ['sə:pləs]	s Überschuß m; Mehrwert m; (unverteilter) Reingewinn m; a überschüssig
budget surplus	Haushaltsüberschuß m
export/import surplus	Ausfuhr-/Einfuhrüberschuß m
surplus population	Bevölkerungsüberschuß m
surplus weight	Übergewicht n
survey (of) ['sə:vei]	Überblick m (über); Erhebung f, Umfrage f; Studie f; Gutachten n; Vermessung f
He made a general survey of the situation/of the market.	Er verschaffte sich einen Gesamtüberblick über die Lage/ eine Marktübersicht.
to survey [sə:'vei]	prüfen, inspizieren; begutachten; vermessen
switch (to) [switʃ]	s Umstellung f, Übergang m; Weiche f; (elektrischer) Schalter m; v tr umstellen (auf), überleiten (auf); itr umschalten; umstellen
to switch over production	die Produktion umstellen
switchboard	Schalttafel f; Klappenschrank m
syndicate ['sindikit]	Syndikat n, Absatzkartell n; Verband m
banking syndicate	Bankenkonsortium n
synthetic [sin'θetik]	s Kunststoff m; a synthetisch
synthetic fibre	Kunstfaser f
system ['sistim]	System n; Verfahren n, Methode f; Anordnung f; Netz n
banking system	Bankwesen n
metric system	metrisches System n
system of railways	Eisenbahnnetz n

T

tab [tæb]	Schildchen *n*, Etikett *n*; Reiter *m (einer Karteikarte)*; *Am* Rechnung *f*; *Am* Kosten *pl*
to keep tabs on Am	kontrollieren, beobachten
table [ˈteibl]	*s* Verzeichnis *n*, Liste *f*, Tabelle *f*; *v* ein Verzeichnis anlegen von; *Am* auf die lange Bank schieben; verschieben
to table a motion	*einen Antrag einbringen*
table of contents	*Inhaltsverzeichnis* n
table of exchange rates/of charges	*Kurs-/Gebührentabelle* f
tacit [ˈtæsit]	stillschweigend
tacit approval	*stillschweigende Billigung* f
tag [tæg]	*s* Anhänger *m*, Etikett *n*, Schildchen *n*; *v* etikettieren, auszeichnen; markieren
price tag	*Preisschild* n
taker [ˈteikə]	Käufer *m*, Abnehmer *m*
takings *pl* [ˈteikiŋz]	Einnahmen *f pl*
tally [ˈtæli]	*s* 1. (Ab-, Gegen-) Rechnung *f*; 2. Marke *f*, Etikett *n*, Anhänger *m*; Kontrollzeichen *n*; *v tr* abhaken; etikettieren; *itr* übereinstimmen
tally sheet	*Kontrolliste* f
tape [teip]	(Papier-) Streifen *m*; Meßband *n*; Lochstreifen *m*; (Ton-) Band *n*
tape-recorder	*Tonbandgerät* n
target [ˈtɑːgit]	Ziel *n*
tariff [ˈtærif]	Tarif *m*, Gebührenverzeichnis *n*; *(Hotel)* Preisliste *f*; Zolltarif *m*, -gebühr *f*
as per tariff	*laut Tarif*
tariff barriers pl	*Zollschranken* f pl
tariff protection	*Zollschutz* m
tariff regulations pl	*Zollbestimmungen* f pl
tax (on) [tæks]	*s* (Staats-) Steuer *f* (auf); Besteuerung *f*; Abgabe *f*, Gebühr *f*; *v* besteuern mit
corporation tax	*Körperschaftssteuer* f
income tax	*Einkommensteuer* f
supertax	*Zuschlagsteuer* f
value-added tax (VAT)	*Mehrwertsteuer* f
He had to pay £ 500 in taxes.	*Er mußte 500 £ (an) Steuern bezahlen.*
taxpayer	*Steuerzahler* m
taxation [tækˈseiʃən]	Besteuerung *f*; Steueraufkommen *n*
subject to taxation	*steuerpflichtig*

team [tiːm] (Arbeits-) Gruppe f, Arbeitsgemeinschaft f, Team n
  teamwork   *Gruppen-, Zusammenarbeit* f
technical [ˈteknikəl] technisch
  technical difficulties pl   *technische Schwierigkeiten* f pl
technician [tekˈniʃən] Techniker m
technique [tekˈniːk] Verfahren n, Technik f
technology [tekˈnɔlədʒi] Technik f, Technologie f
telecommunications pl Fernmeldewesen n
[ˈteli-kəˌmjuː(ː)niˈkeiʃənz]
telegram [ˈteligræm] Telegramm n
  by telegram   *telegraphisch*
telephone [ˈtelifəun] s Fernsprecher m, Telefon n;
v anrufen, antelefonieren

  on the telephone   *am Apparat*
  over the telephone   *per Telefon*
  He does all his business by telephone.   *Er erledigt alle seine Geschäfte telefonisch.*
  telephone booth/box   *Fernsprechzelle* f
  telephone call   *fernmündlicher Anruf* m
  telephone conversation   *Telefongespräch* n
  telephone directory   *Telefonbuch* n
  telephone subscriber   *Fernsprechteilnehmer* m
telephonist [tiˈləfənist] Telefonist(in f) m
teleprinter, Fernschreiber m
  Am **teletypewriter**
[ˈteliˌprintə, ˈteliˈtaipˌraitə]
  by teleprinter   *fernschriftlich*
television [ˈteliˌviʒən] Fernsehen n
  television advertising   *Werbefernsehen* n
  television audience   *Fernsehpublikum* n
  television broadcast   *Fernsehsendung* f
  television station   *Fernsehstation* f
telex [ˈteleks] Telex n; Fernschreibnetz n
teller [ˈtelə] Kassierer m, Kassen-, Schalterbeamter m

temporary [ˈtempərəri] vorläufig, einstweilig; vorübergehend
  temporary credit   *Zwischenkredit* m
tenant [ˈtenənt] Pächter m, Mieter m
  landlord and tenant   *Vermieter und Mieter*
to tend (to, towards) [tend] tendieren, neigen (zu)
tendency [ˈtendənsi] Tendenz f, Neigung f (*to* für)
  downward/upward tendency   *Baisse-/Haussetendenz* f
tender [ˈtendə] s 1. Angebot n, Offerte f; Kostenanschlag m;
2. Zahlungsmittel n;
v tr (als Zahlung) anbieten;
itr sich an einer Ausschreibung beteiligen

by tender	auf dem Submissionsweg, durch Ausschreibung
The company invited tenders for the project.	Die Gesellschaft hat das Projekt ausgeschrieben.
to tender one's resignation	seinen Rücktritt erklären
legal tender	gesetzliches Zahlungsmittel n
tentatively ['tentətivli]	versuchsweise
term [tə:m]	1. (Fach-) Ausdruck m, Bezeichnung f; 2. Laufzeit f, Dauer f; 3. Quartalstermin m; 4. pl Wortlaut m; pl Preis m, Honorar n; pl Bestimmungen f pl
under the terms of the article	auf Grund der Bestimmungen des Artikels
term of office	Amtsdauer f
on term	auf Ziel
on easy terms	zu günstigen Bedingungen
He only thinks in terms of money.	Er denkt nur an Geld/hat nur Geld im Sinn.
What are your terms?	Was verlangen Sie?
to fix a term	eine Frist setzen
terms of delivery/of payment	Lieferungs-/Zahlungsbedingungen f pl
term of payment	Zahlungsfrist f
long-/short-term	lang-/kurzfristig
subscription terms pl	Beitritts-, Abonnementsbedingungen f pl
terminal ['tə:minl]	Endstation f
air terminal	Air Terminal n (Abfertigungsgebäude im Stadtzentrum)
bus terminal	Autobusbahnhof m
test [test]	s Testverfahren n; Prüfung f; Stichprobe f; v prüfen, untersuchen
by means of a test	mittels Stichproben
to take a test	eine Prüfung ablegen
aptitude test	Eignungsprüfung f
driving test	Fahrprüfung f
test conditions pl	Versuchsbedingungen f pl
textiles pl ['tekstailz]	Textilien pl
theft [θeft]	Diebstahl m
to be guilty of theft	des Diebstahls schuldig sein
theft insurance	Diebstahlversicherung f
theft risk	Diebstahlgefahr f
thrifty ['θrifti]	sparsam, wirtschaftlich
through [θru:]	Durchgangs-
through freight	Durchgangsfracht f
through train	direkter Zug m
No through road.	Sackgasse!

ticket [ˈtikit] 1. Fahr-, Flugkarte *f;* Gepäckschein *m;*
2. Etikett *n,* Schildchen *n,* Zettel *m;*
3. gebührenpflichtige Verwarnung *f,* Strafzettel *m*
  to buy a ticket   eine Fahrkarte lösen
  price ticket   Preiszettel m
  boarding/landing ticket   Flugsteig-/Landungskarte f
  ticket office   Fahrkartenschalter m
tight [tait]   knapp
  tight money market   angespannte Lage auf dem Geldmarkt
  Money is tight.   Das Geld ist knapp.
time [taim]   Zeitdauer *f,* -abschnitt *m;* Frist *f;* Arbeitszeit *f;* Lehrzeit *f*
  at a given time   zu einem festgesetzten Zeitpunkt
  in due time   termingemäß
  overtime   Überstunden f pl
  Your time is up.   Ihre Zeit ist abgelaufen.
  time of arrival   Ankunftszeit f
  time bargain   Termingeschäft n
  time limit   Frist f, Zeitraum m
  timetable   Fahrplan m
timing [ˈtaimiŋ]   zeitliche Abstimmung *f,* richtige Zeit-/Terminwahl *f*
title to [ˈtaitl]   Rechtsanspruch *m*/-titel *m* auf
  title deed   Eigentumsurkunde f
toll [təul]   (Transport-, Hafen-) Gebühr *f;* Straßenbenutzungsgebühr *f;* Wege-, Brückenzoll *m;* Gebühr *f* für ein Ferngespräch; Standgeld *n*
  The accident took a heavy toll of life.   Der Unfall hat viele Menschenleben gefordert.
  toll bridge   Zollbrücke f
ton [tʌn]   Tonne *f,* Tonnage *f*
  by the ton   tonnenweise
tools *pl* [tu:lz]   Handwerkszeug *n,* Werkzeug *n*
top [tɔp]   *s* oberste Stelle *f;* Gipfel *m;* Höchststand *m;*
a oberst, höchst, best; erstklassig;
v überragen, übersteigen
  top executive   leitender Angestellter m
  top-grade quality   erste Wahl f
  top management   Führungsspitze f
  top salary   Spitzengehalt n
topic [ˈtɔpik]   (Gesprächs-) Thema *n,* Gegenstand *m*
total [ˈtəutl]   *s* Gesamtbetrag *m,* -summe *f,* -menge *f;*
a gesamt, total, gänzlich;
v sich belaufen auf; zusammenzählen
  to total up expenses   die Ausgaben zusammenzählen
  sum total   Gesamtbetrag m

total receipts pl/value	Gesamteinnahmen f pl/-wert m
total weight	Gesamtgewicht n
tour [tuə]	Tour f, (Rund-) Reise f
conducted/package tour	Gesellschafts-/Pauschalreise f
tour of inspection	Besichtigungsreise f
tourism ['tuərizm]	Fremdenverkehr m
tourist ['tuərist]	Reisender m, Tourist m
tourist agency/office	Reisebüro n/Verkehrsamt n
tourist class	Touristenklasse f
tourist industry	Fremdenindustrie f
track [træk]	Gleis n, Schienenstrang m; Fahrrinne f; Route f
The train ran off the track.	Der Zug entgleiste.
trade [treid]	s 1. Handel m; 2. Geschäft n; Gewerbebetrieb m; 3. Gewerbe n, Handwerk n; 4. Branche f, Geschäftszweig m; 5. (the trade) die Geschäftswelt; die Kundschaft; v tr eintauschen; itr handeln, Handel treiben (in s.th. mit etw; with s.o. mit jdm)
He is a carpenter by trade.	Er ist Tischler/Schreiner von Beruf.
This article is only supplied to the trade.	Dieser Artikel wird nur an Wiederverkäufer abgegeben.
He does a good trade.	Er macht gute Geschäfte.
He traded in his used car.	Er gab seinen Gebrauchtwagen in Zahlung.
foreign/home trade	Außen-/Binnenhandel m
trade and industry	Handel und Wirtschaft
trade-mark	Warenzeichen n, Schutzmarke f
trade name	Firmenname m; Handelsbezeichnung f
trade union	Gewerkschaft f
trader ['treidə]	Händler m, Kaufmann m
trading ['treidiŋ]	s Handel m (in s.th. mit etw; with s.o. mit jdm); a handeltreibend
trading company	Handelsgesellschaft f
trading stamp	Rabattmarke f
traffic (in) ['træfik]	Handel m (mit); Güteraustausch m; Verkehr m; beförderte Personenzahl f; Kundenverkehr m
air traffic	Flugverkehr m
freight traffic	Güterverkehr m
heavy traffic	starker Verkehr m
traffic control/jam	Verkehrskontrolle f/-stockung f
traffic light	Verkehrsampel f
traffic regulations pl	Verkehrsregeln f pl
trained [treind]	ausgebildet, gelernt

trainee - transportation 107

trained personnel — *Fachkräfte* f pl
trainee [trei'ni:] — Praktikant *m*
training ['treiniŋ] — Ausbildung *f*, Schulung *f*
training period — *Praktikum* n, *Vorbereitungszeit* f
transaction [træn'zækʃən] — Geschäftsabschluß *m*, Geschäft *n*; pl Umsatz *m*; pl Abschlüsse *m pl*
cash transaction — *Kassaverkauf* m; pl *Barumsätze* m pl
transfer ['trænsfə(:)] — Überweisung *f*, Transferierung *f*; Übertragung *f*, Abtretung *f*
transfer deed — *Übertragungsurkunde* f
to transfer [træns'fə:] — überweisen, transferieren; übertragen; umbuchen; verlegen
He transferred the money to his brother's account. — *Er überwies das Geld auf das Konto seines Bruders.*
to transfer by endorsement — *durch Indossament übertragen*
to transform [træns'fɔ:m] — umgestalten, umwandeln
transit ['trænsit] — Transit *m*, Durchfuhr *f*; Durchgangsverkehr *m*, -straße *f*
dammaged/lost in transit — *auf dem Transport beschädigt/ verlorengegangen*
transit of goods — *Warentransit* m
transit camp — *Durchgangslager* n
transit duty — *Transit-, Durchfuhrzoll* m
transit traffic/visa — *Durchgangsverkehr* m/-*visum* n
translator [træns'leitə] — Übersetzer *m*
transmission [trænz'miʃən] — Versand *m*, Übersendung *f*; Übermittlung *f*; (Rundfunk-, Fernseh-) Sendung *f*
transmission of news — *Nachrichtenübermittlung* f
transmission of a radio/ television programme — *Ausstrahlung* f *eines Rundfunk-/ Fernsehprogramms*
to transmit [trænz'mit] — übersenden; befördern; transferieren; *(Programm)* übertragen, ausstrahlen
to transmit a message — *eine Botschaft übermitteln*
The BBC transmits radio and TV programmes. — *Die BBC strahlt Rundfunk- und Fernsehprogramme aus.*
transport ['trænspɔ:t] — Beförderung *f*, Transport *m*, Versand *m*; Transportschiff *n*, -flugzeug *n*;
door-to-door transport — *Beförderung* f *von Haus zu Haus*
rail/road transport — *Eisenbahn-/Straßentransport* m
cost of transport — *Versand-, Transportkosten* pl
to transport [træns'pɔt] — befördern, transportieren, versenden, verschiffen
Our goods are transported by plane. — *Unsere Waren werden mit dem Flugzeug befördert.*
transportation [ˌtrænspɔ:'teiʃən] — Beförderung *f*, Versand *m*; Am Beförderungsmittel *n*, -kosten *pl*
Do you have transportation? Am — *Haben Sie eine Fahrgelegenheit?*

freight transportation	Frachtgutbeförderung f
transportation rate	Frachttarif m, -satz m
travel (for) ['trævl]	s Reise f; Reiseverkehr m; v tr (Gebiet) bereisen; itr Reisender sein, als Reisender arbeiten (für)
He is travelling on business.	Er ist geschäftlich unterwegs.
travel agent's/agency/bureau	Reisebüro n
traveller, Am **traveler** ['trævlə]	(Handlungs-) Reisender m
commercial traveller	Handlungsreisender m
traveller's cheque, Am traveler's check	Reisescheck m
travelling ['trævliŋ]	reisend; fahrbar
travelling salesman	Handlungsreisender m, Reisevertreter m
travelling bag/case	Reisetasche f/-koffer m
travelling clock	Reisewecker m
travelling expenses pl	Reisekosten pl
treasurer ['treʒərə]	Kassenwart m, Schatzmeister m; Leiter m der Finanzabteilung
treaty ['tri:ti]	(Staats-) Vertrag m
commercial treaty	Handelsvertrag m, Wirtschaftsabkommen n
trend [trend]	Tendenz f, Trend m, Entwicklung f
downward/upward trend	rückläufige/steigende Tendenz f
trend of prices	Preisentwicklung f
trial ['traiəl]	1. Versuch m, Probe f; 2. Gerichtsverfahren n, Prozeß m
on trial	auf Probe; versuchsweise
Give him a month's trial.	Geben Sie ihm einen Monat Probezeit!
trial order	Probeauftrag m
triplicate ['triplikit]	Drittausfertigung f
in triplicate	in dreifacher Ausfertigung
truck [trʌk]	1. Am Last(kraft)wagen m; 2. offener Güterwagen m; 3. Tauschhandel m
truck driver, trucker	Am Fernlastfahrer m
truly ['tru:li]	aufrichtig, herzlich
I am truly sorry.	Es tut mir aufrichtig leid.
Yours (very) truly/Very truly yours... Am	Hochachtungsvoll.../Mit freundlichen Grüßen
trunk [trʌŋk]	1. Koffer m; 2. (Telefon) Fernverbindung f, -leitung f; 3. (Eisenbahn) Hauptlinie f, -strecke f
trunk call	Ferngespräch n
trunk road	Fernverkehrsstraße f

trust (in) [trʌst]
1. Vertrauen *n* (auf);
2. Trust *m*, Konzern *m*, Kartell *n*;
3. Kredit *m*;
4. Stiftung *f*; Treuhandvermögen *n*

in/on trust   *zu treuen Händen, zur Verwahrung*
to turn over [tə:n]   *(Waren)* umsetzen; einen Umsatz haben von

He turns over $10,000 a week.   *Er hat einen wöchentlichen Umsatz von $ 10 000.*

turnover [ˈtə:nɪəuvə]
1. Umsatz *m*, Umschlag *m*;
2. Umstellung *f*, Umgruppierung *f*

last year's turnover   *der Vorjahresumsatz*
turnover tax   *Umsatzsteuer* f

type [taip]   *s* 1. Modell *n*, Typ *m*; Bauart *f*;
2. Buchstabe *m*;
v tr mit der Maschine schreiben;
itr tippen, Maschine schreiben

in bold type   *in Fettdruck*
typewriter   *Schreibmaschine* f
typist [ˈtaipist]   Stenotypistin *f*

U

unable [ˈʌnˈeibl]   außerstande, unfähig
He is unable to work/to pay.   *Er ist arbeits-/zahlungsunfähig.*
unanimous [ju(:)ˈnæniməs]   einstimmig
His proposal was accepted with unanimous approval.   *Sein Vorschlag wurde einstimmig angenommen.*
under [ˈʌndə]   unter
under no circumstances   *unter keinen Umständen*
under the provisions of the law   *nach den gesetzlichen Bestimmungen*
under separate cover   *mit gleicher Post*
The road is under construction.   *Die Straße ist im Bau.*
Is everything under control?   *Ist alles in Ordnung?*
to underrate [ˌʌndəˈreit]   unterschätzen; zu niedrig bewerten
understaffed [ˌʌndəˈstɑ:ft]   unterbesetzt, zu schwach besetzt
We are understaffed.   *Wir haben Personalmangel.*
understanding [ˌʌndəˈstændiŋ]   Übereinkunft *f*, Vereinbarung *f*
on the understanding that ...   *unter der Voraussetzung, daß ...*
They came to an understanding with the firm.   *Sie kamen mit der Firma zu einer Einigung/Verständigung.*
to undertake (-took, -taken) [ˌʌndəˈteik]   unternehmen; *(e-e Verpflichtung)* übernehmen
to undertake to do s.th.   *sich verpflichten etw zu tun*

undertaking [ˌʌndəˈteikiŋ] — Unternehmen n; Betrieb m
   industrial undertaking — Gewerbe-, Industriebetrieb m
unemployed [ˈʌnimˈplɔid] — 1. arbeitslos, unbeschäftigt; 2. ungenützt
   unemployed capital — brachliegendes Kapital n
   the unemployed — die Arbeitslosen
unemployment [ˈʌnimˈplɔimənt] — Arbeits-, Erwerbslosigkeit f
   unemployment benefit/compensation/relief — Arbeitslosenunterstützung f
union [ˈjuːnjən] — Vereinigung f, Verband m
   Universal Postal Union — Weltpostverein m
   trade union — Gewerkschaft f
   union rights pl — Rechte n pl der Gewerkschaft
unit [ˈjuːnit] — Einheit f, Stück n; Bauelement n
   unit of account — Rechnungseinheit f
   unit furniture — Anbaumöbel n pl
   unit price — Einheits-, Stückpreis m
unlawful [ˈʌnˈlɔːful] — ungesetzlich, rechtswidrig
unlimited [ʌnˈlimitid] — unbeschränkt; nicht limitiert
   for an unlimited period — unbefristet
to unload [ˈʌnˈləud] — aus-, entladen
   to unload a ship — eine Ladung löschen
unofficial [ˈʌnəˈfiʃəl] — inoffiziell
   unofficial news (mit sing) — eine unbestätigte Nachricht f
unpaid [ˈʌnˈpeid] — unbezahlt, rückständig
   unpaid capital — noch nicht eingezahltes Kapital n
   unpaid interest — rückständige Zinsen m pl
unprofitable [ʌnˈprɔfitəbl] — unrentabel, unvorteilhaft
unreliable [ˈʌnriˈlai-əbl] — unzuverlässig; unreell
unskilled [ˈʌnˈskild] — ungelernt
   unskilled worker — ungelernter Arbeiter m
up-to-date [ˈʌptədeit] — 1. modern, zeitnah;
pred **up to date** [ˈ--ˈ-] — 2. auf dem laufenden
   Are your books up to date? — Sind Ihre Bücher auf dem neuesten Stand?
upkeep [ˈʌpkiːp] — Instandhaltung f; Unterhalt m
upward(s *adv*) [ˈʌpwəd(-z)] — *a* steigend; *adv* aufwärts
   Prices are tending upwards. — Die Preise tendieren nach oben.
   upward movement/trend — Aufwärtsbewegung f/-tendenz f
urban [ˈəːbən] — städtisch
   urban area — Stadtgebiet n
usage [ˈjuːzidʒ] — Brauch m, Usus m, Gepflogenheit f
   commercial usage — Handelsbrauch m
use [juːs] — Benutzung f, Verwendung f; Nutzen m; Nutznießung f
   in common use — allgemein gebräuchlich
   ready for use — gebrauchsfertig

Is this of any use to you?	*Können Sie das brauchen?*
to come into use	*in Gebrauch kommen*
to go out of use	*außer Gebrauch kommen*
instructions pl *for use*	*Gebrauchsanweisung f*
useful [ˈjuːsful]	brauchbar, nützlich, zweckdienlich
user [ˈjuːzə]	Verbraucher m, Konsument m, Bedarfsträger m
ultimate user	*Endverbraucher m*
usury [ˈjuːʒuri]	Wucher m; Wucherzinsen m pl
utility [juː(ː)ˈtiliti]	Nutzen m
marginal utility	*Grenznutzen m*
utility goods pl	*Gebrauchsgüter n pl*
to utilize [ˈjuːtilaiz]	ausnutzen, verwerten
utmost [ˈʌtməust]	äußerst
to the utmost	*aufs äußerste*
He did his utmost.	*Er tat sein möglichstes.*

V

vacancy [ˈveikənsi]	freie Stelle *f*; pl Stellenangebote *n* pl
to fill a vacancy	*eine freie Stelle besetzen*
vacant [ˈveikənt]	unbesetzt, offen, frei; unbewohnt
He applied for the vacant position.	*Er bewarb sich um die freie Stelle.*
vacant possession	*sofort beziehbar*
vacation [vəˈkeiʃən]	(Gerichts-) Ferien pl; Am Urlaub m
He is on vacation. Am	*Er ist im Urlaub.*
valid [ˈvælid]	gültig, rechtskräftig
valid until recalled	*gültig bis auf Widerruf*
to become valid	*rechtskräftig werden*
valid argument	*stichhaltiges Argument n*
valid claim	*berechtigter Anspruch m*
value [ˈvæljuː]	Wert m; Preis m, Betrag m; Währung f
for value received...	*Betrag erhalten...*
book/commercial value	*Buch-/Handelswert m*
value-added tax	*Mehrwertsteuer f*
van [væn]	Lastwagen m; geschlossener Güterwagen m
delivery van	*Lieferwagen m*
variable [ˈvɛəriəbl]	unterschiedlich; veränderlich, wechselnd
variable cost	*veränderliche/bewegliche Kosten pl*
variety [vəˈraiəti]	Vielfalt f; Auswahl f
a wide variety of hats	*eine große Auswahl an Hüten*
to vary [ˈvɛəri]	tr unterschiedlich gestalten, variieren; itr sich (ver)ändern; schwanken
varying prices pl	*schwankende Preise m pl*
vehicle [ˈviːikl]	Fahrzeug n
motor vehicle	*Kraftfahrzeug n*

venture - wastage

venture [ˈventʃə] — geschäftliches Unternehmen n; Risiko n; Spekulation f
   He has a share in the venture. — Er ist an dem Geschäft beteiligt.
vested interest/right [ˈvestid ˈintrist/rait] — wohlerworbenes Recht n
vice-chairman/-president [ˈvaisˈtʃɛəmən/ˈprezidənt] — stellvertretender Vorsitzender m/ Vizepräsident m
view (of, on) [vjuː] — 1. Untersuchung, Prüfung f; 2. Meinung f, Ansicht f (über)
   in my view — meines Erachtens
   Our views differ. — Unsere Ansichten gehen auseinander.
   viewpoint — Gesichts-, Standpunkt m
visa [ˈviːzə] — Visum n, Sichtvermerk m
visible [ˈvizəbl] — sichtbar
   visible imports pl — sichtbare Einfuhr f
visiting [ˈvizitiŋ] — besichtigend
   visiting card — Visitenkarte f
visitor [ˈvizitə] — Besucher m, Gast m, Tourist m
   visitor's book — Fremden-, Gästebuch n
vocational [vəuˈkeiʃənl] — beruflich
   vocational guidance — Berufsberatung f
   vocational training — Berufsausbildung f
void [vɔid] — 1. ungültig, nichtig; 2. leer
   null and void — null und nichtig
volume [ˈvɔljum] — Volumen n, Umfang m
   volume of business/trade — Geschäfts-/Handelsvolumen n
voting [ˈvəutiŋ] — Abstimmung f
   voting paper — Stimmzettel m
   voting stock — stimmberechtigtes Aktienkapital n

W

wage(s pl**)** [weidʒ(iz)] — Lohn m; Lohnanteil m
   minimum wage — Mindestlohn m
   wage claim/earner — Lohnforderung f/-empfänger m
   wage increase — Lohnerhöhung f
warehouse [ˈwɛəhaus] — 1. Lagerhaus n, Magazin n, Speicher m; 2. Kaufhaus n, Großhandelsgeschäft n
   ex warehouse — ab Lager
   customs warehouse — Zollniederlage f
warning [ˈwɔːniŋ] — 1. Warnung f; 2. Ankündigung f
   to give s.o. fair warning — jdn rechtzeitig verständigen
   without warning — unerwartet, ohne vorherige Ankündigung
wastage [ˈweistidʒ] — Verschwendung f, Vergeudung f
   wastage of food — Vergeudung f von Lebensmitteln

waterproof [ˈwɔːtəpruːf] — s Regenmantel m; a wasserdicht
way-bill [ˈweibil] — Frachtbrief m; Passagierliste f
wear and tear [ˈwɛərənˈtɛə] — 1. Abnützung f, Verschleiß m; 2. Abschreibung f
weather [ˈweðə] — Wetter n, Witterung f
  weather conditions pl — Wetterlage f
  weather forecast — Wetterbericht m
weekly [ˈwiːkli] — wöchentlich
  weekly paper/report — Wochenzeitschrift f/-bericht m
  weekly wage — Wochenlohn m
welfare work [ˈwelfɛə] — Wohlfahrtspflege f, Fürsorge f
wharf, pl **wharves** [wɔːf, wɔːvz] — Kai m; Lagerhaus n
white-collar worker [ˈwaitˈkɔlə] — Büroangestellter m; Schreibtischarbeiter m
wholesale [ˈhəul-seil] — s Großhandel m; a im großen, en gros; pauschal
  wholesale business/trade — Großhandel m
  wholesale dealer, wholesaler — Großhändler m, Grossist m
  wholesale price — Großhandelspreis m
winding-up [ˈwaindiŋˈʌp] — Liquidation f, Auflösung f (eines Geschäftes)
window [ˈwindəu] — Fenster n; Schalter m
  Inquire at window number three, please. — Erkundigen Sie sich bitte an Schalter 3!
  window display — Schaufensterauslage f
  window dresser — Schaufensterdekorateur m
  window dressing — Schaufensterdekoration f
  window envelope — Fensterbriefumschlag m
  window-shopping — Schaufensterbummel m
wire [ˈwaiə] — Draht m; Telegramm n
  by wire — telegraphisch
wireless [ˈwaiəlis] — s Radioapparat m; a drahtlos
  on the wireless — im Radio
  wireless message — Funkspruch m
to withdraw [wiðˈdrɔː] — tr (Geld) abheben, entnehmen; (Kredit) kündigen; (Klage) zurücknehmen; itr sich zurückziehen, zurücktreten
  He withdrew his motion. — Er hat seinen Antrag zurückgezogen.
  He wishes to withdraw his offer. — Er möchte sein Angebot zurücknehmen.
  to withdraw money from the bank — Geld von der Bank abheben
withdrawal [wiðˈdrɔːəl] — Abhebung f, Entnahme f; Rücktritt m
witness [ˈwitnis] — Zeuge m
wording [ˈwəːdiŋ] — Wortlaut m, Fassung f; Formulierung f

work - year

work [wə:k]
s Arbeit *f*, Beschäftigung *f*;
pl (mit sing) Fabrikanlage *f*, Werk *n*, Betrieb *m*; *pl* Baustelle *f*, Bauten *m pl*;
v arbeiten; funktionieren

at work	bei der Arbeit
He is out of work.	Er ist arbeitslos.
The computer is not working.	Der Computer ist außer Betrieb.
clerical work	Büroarbeit f
piece work	Akkordarbeit f
total work in hand	Gesamtaufträge m pl
work day	Arbeits-, Werktag m
work done	geleistete Arbeit f
workforce	Arbeitskräfte f pl
worker/workman	Arbeiter m
workshop	Werkstatt f; Arbeitsgemeinschaft f
work to rule	Bummelstreik m; Dienst m nach Vorschrift

working ['wə:kiŋ] Arbeiten *n*; *(Maschine)* Funktionieren *n*

working capital	Betriebskapital n
working clothes pl	Arbeitskleidung f
working conditions pl	Arbeitsbedingungen f pl
working cost/expenses pl	Betriebskosten pl
working hour	Arbeitsstunde f; pl Arbeitszeit f

world [wə:ld] Welt *f*

the business world	die Geschäftswelt f
World Bank	Weltbank f
world depression/economic crisis	Weltwirtschaftskrise f
world economy/production	Weltwirtschaft f/-produktion f
world market	Weltmarkt m
world-wide	weltweit

worth [wə:θ] Wert *m*, Preis *m*
  worthless   wertlos
to write off ['rait'ɔ:f] vollständig abschreiben
writing ['raitiŋ] Schreiben *n*; *pl* Schriftstücke *n pl*; Schrift *f*

to put in writing	schriftlich niederlegen
writing pad/paper	Schreibunterlage f/-papier n

wrongful ['rɔŋful] widerrechtlich, ungesetzlich
wrongly ['rɔŋli] irrtümlicherweise

Y

yarn [jɑ:n] Garn *n*
  dyed in the yarn   im Garn gefärbt
year [jə:] Jahr *n*
  from year to year   Jahr für Jahr

for years — jahrelang, seit Jahren
yearly — a/adv *jährlich*
financial/fiscal year — *Geschäfts-, Rechnungsjahr* n
yield [jiːld] — s *Ertrag* m; *Ernte* f;
v *hervorbringen, (Früchte) tragen*
average yield — *Durchschnittsertrag* m
tax yield — *Steueraufkommen* n
The shares yielded a dividend of 10%. — *Die Aktien brachten eine Dividende von 10 %.*
profit-yielding — *gewinnbringend*

Z

zero, *pl* **zeros** [ˈziərəu, -z] — Null *f*
zip code *Am* [ˈzip kəud] — Postleitzahl *f*
zone [zəun] — Zone *f*; Abschnitt *m*; Postzustellbezirk *m*; Tarifzone *f*

I. Retail and Wholesale Trade — Einzel- und Großhandel

1. Retail Trade — Einzelhandel

retail trading	Einzel-/Detailhandel *m (als Tätigkeit)*
retail business	Einzelhandels-/Detailgeschäft *n*, Einzelhandelsunternehmen *n*
retail shop/store	Einzel-/Kleinhandelsgeschäft *n*
retail establishment, small-scale enterprise	Einzelhandels-/Kleinhandelsunternehmen *n*
retail outlet, point of sale	kleines Einzelhandelsgeschäft *n*, Verkaufsstelle *f*
specialized trade	Fachhandel *m*
single line store, speciality shop	Fachgeschäft *n*
unit shop	Familien-/Einmannbetrieb *m*
over-the-counter store, corner shop	Laden *m* an der Ecke
sole trader	Einzelunternehmer *m*, Einzelhändler *m*
retail trader, retailer	Einzel-/Kleinhändler *m*
the buying public	die Konsumenten *m pl*
ultimate consumer	Letzt-/Endverbraucher *m*
final consumption	Endverbrauch *m*
retail customer	Einzelhandelskunde *m*
shopper	Käufer *m*
errand-boy	Laufbursche *m*
independents *pl*	selbständige Einzelhändler *m pl*
purchasing association	Einkaufsgenossenschaft *f*

Retail sale — *Ladenverkauf*

retail sales *pl*/turnover	Einzelhandelsumsatz *m*
sales volume	Umsatzvolumen *n*
increase in sales	Umsatzsteigerung *f*
annual sales *pl*	Jahresumsatz *m*
retail (selling) price	Laden-/Einzelhandelspreis *m*
retail ceiling price	Verbraucherhöchstpreis *m*
markup	Handelsspanne *f*, Kalkulationsaufschlag *m*, Rohgewinnaufschlag *m*
retail discount	Einzelhandelsrabatt *m*
merchandise offerings *pl*	Warenangebot *n*
commodity group	Warengruppe *f*
seal of approval	Gütesiegel *n*
private brand	Hausmarke *f*

testing of products, product testing	Warentest *m*
shopping basket	Einkaufskorb *m*
goods shelf	Ladenregal *n*
show-case, glass case	Vitrine *f*
till, *Am* cash box	Ladenkasse *f*
book of stamps	Rabattmarkenheft *n*
shoplifting	Ladendiebstahl *m*
shop/business hours *pl*	Geschäftsstunden *f pl*, Öffnungszeiten *f pl*
closing-time	Ladenschluß *m*
assortment	Sortiment *n*, Kollektion *f*
line of goods	Warensortiment *n*, Artikelserie *f*
fast/slow seller	Renner *m*/Ladenhüter *m*
food retailing	Verkauf *m* von Lebensmitteln
perishables *pl*	leicht verderbliche Waren *f pl*
convenience goods *pl*	Verbrauchs-/Bedarfsdeckungsgüter *n pl*, Waren *f pl* des täglichen Bedarfs
luxury goods *pl*, high-price merchandise	Luxusgüter *n pl*
deep freezer	Tiefkühltruhe *f*, Tiefkühlschrank *m*
refrigerator, *Am* ice box	Kühlschrank *m*
window lighting	Schaufensterbeleuchtung *f*
window display/dressing	Schaufensterdekoration *f*
display material	Verkaufsförderungsmaterial *n*
retail drawing	Stückauszeichnung *f*
attention-getter, attention-gaining device, gimmick	Blickfang *m*, Knüller *m*
dummy, mock	Attrappe *f*
bracket	Schaufensterständer *m*

Different kinds of shops *Verschiedene Läden*

grocer's shop, grocery	Lebensmittelgeschäft *n*, Gemischtwarenhandlung *f*
delicatessen (shop)	Feinkosthandlung *f*/-geschäft *n*
butcher's shop	Fleischer-/Metzgerladen *m*
bakery, baker's shop	Bäckerei *f*, Bäckerladen *m*
creamery, milk shop, dairy	Milchgeschäft *n*, -laden *m*
greengrocer's shop, greengrocery	Obst- und Gemüsehandlung *f*
seafood market/fishmonger	Fischhandlung *f*/-händler *m*
liquor store *Am*	Spirituosenhandlung *f*
tobacconist's shop, *Am* tobacco store	Tabakwarenhandlung *f*
drugstore *Am*	Drugstore *m*, Apotheke *f*, Drogerie *f*

118 Retail and Wholesale Trade

hairdresser, *(Männer)* barber	Friseur *m*
hairdresser's shop, barbershop	Friseursalon *m*
florist/florist's shop, flower shop	Blumenhändler *m*/-handlung *f*
stationer's shop, stationery store	Schreibwarenhandlung *f*
jewellery store	Juweliergeschäft *n*
men's wear, *Am* clothing store	(Herren-) Bekleidungsgeschäft *n*
women's outfitter, ladies' wear	Damenbekleidungsgeschäft *n*
ironmongery, hardware store	Eisenwarenhandlung *f*
household supply store	Haus- und Küchengeräte *n pl*
electrical supply store	Elektrowarengeschäft *n*
sporting goods store	Sportartikelgeschäft *n*
service station	Tankstelle *f*
to retail, to sell by/*Am* at retail	im Einzelhandel/en detail verkaufen
to buy retail	en detail/im kleinen kaufen
to sell direct to retailers/to the public	direkt an Einzelhändler/an Konsumenten verkaufen
to order goods from the wholesaler	Waren beim Großhändler bestellen
to stock only goods with a quick turnover	nur sich rasch umsetzende Waren auf Lager nehmen
to operate on a small scale	in beschränktem Umfang tätig sein
to earn/to leave a profit	einen Gewinn erzielen/abwerfen
to sell at a loss	mit Verlust verkaufen
to pay at the cash desk	an der Kasse zahlen
to test goods	Waren testen
to cater for/to	*(Lebensmittel)* liefern/*(Bedürfnisse)* befriedigen
to solicit/to fill orders	sich um Aufträge bemühen/Aufträge ausführen
to patronize a store	in einem Laden regelmäßig einkaufen/Stammkunde in einem Laden sein
to forfeit customers' goodwill	Kundschaft verlieren
to get more display space	zusätzlichen Ausstellungsraum gewinnen
to rearrange the display of goods	die Warenausstellung umstellen
to pre-plan	vorausplanen
to cluster together	in Gruppen zusammenstellen
to reorder staple goods	die gängigsten Waren nachbestellen
to place orders for new items	neue Artikel bestellen
to disperse orders among several suppliers	Aufträge auf verschiedene Lieferanten aufteilen
to bring rapid turnover of merchandise	zu einem raschen Warenumschlag führen
to stimulate customers' interest	das Interesse der Käufer wecken

Einzel- und Großhandel

to induce the customer to order the merchandise	den Kunden veranlassen, die Waren zu bestellen
to have marked seasonal swings	deutliche saisonale Schwankungen aufweisen
to keep in touch with the market	mit dem Markt in enger Verbindung bleiben
to maximize the sales efforts	die Verkaufsanstrengungen maximieren
by retail	en detail/stückweise/ im einzelnen
shop-soiled/-worn	angeschmutzt, beschädigt
perishable	(leicht) verderblich
fashionable	modisch, elegant
out of stock	nicht vorrätig

Sätze und Redewendungen:

The retailer sells to the consumer.	Der Einzelhändler verkauft an den Verbraucher.
The consumer must make a choice from the different brands of goods.	Der Kunde muß unter den verschiedenen Marken wählen.
Brand names, trade-marks, and labels are also a kind of advertising.	Markennamen, Warenzeichen und Etiketten sind auch eine Art Werbung.
Labels often contain useful information.	Etiketten/Aufklebezettel vermitteln oft nützliche Informationen.
the lines that the house carries	das Sortiment, das die Firma führt
A higher price can be charged for the article.	Für den Artikel kann ein höherer Preis angesetzt werden.
Underpurchasing means lost sales, overpurchasing results in end-of-season leftovers.	Kauft man zu geringe Mengen ein, so bedeutet das entgangene Umsätze, kauft man zuviel, so bleiben am Ende der Saison Waren liegen.
Small retailers buy whenever their wholesalers' salesmen call on them.	Kleinhändler decken sich immer dann ein, wenn die Verkäufer ihrer Großhändler bei ihnen vorsprechen.
No credit is given.	Kredit wird nicht eingeräumt.
This new pattern sells well.	Dieses neue Muster verkauft sich gut.
The retailer concentrated all orders with a single supplier.	Der Einzelhändler erteilte alle Aufträge einem einzigen Lieferanten.
Small stores obtain no quantity discounts.	Kleine Läden erhalten keinen Mengenrabatt.

2. Large-scale Trading — Einzelhandel im großen

multiple shop, chain store	Kettenladen *m*
multiples *pl*	Supermarktkette *f*
superette	Supermarkt *m* mit einem Umsatz unter einer halben Million
hypermarket	großer Supermarkt *m*
automatic vending machine	Warenautomat *m*
co-operative store	Konsumgeschäft *n*
department store	Warenhaus *n*
extrashop	Spezialshop *m*
sales force	Verkaufspersonal *n*
floor space	Nutzfläche *f*
sales area	Verkaufsfläche *f*
check-out (point)	Kassierstelle *f* am Ausgang
escalator	Rolltreppe *f*
air-conditioning	Klimatisierung *f*
frozen food	tiefgekühlte Lebensmittel *pl*
freezer centre	Kühlbereich *m*, Tiefkühlanlage *f*
see-through pack	Klarsichtpackung *f*
parking space	Parkfläche *f*
pram park	Abstellplatz *m* für Kinderwagen
peak buying time	Einkaufsspitze *f*
factual information	Sachinformation *f*
hire-purchaser	Käufer *m* auf Raten
hire-purchase/credit-sale agreement	Ratenkauf-/Kreditkauf-/Teilzahlungsvertrag *m*
conditional agreement	(Raten-)Kaufvertrag *m* mit Eigentumsvorbehalt
hire-purchase finance company	Geldinstitut *n* zur Finanzierung von Ratenkäufen
cash price	Barpreis *m*
H.P. price	Preis *m* bei Ratenzahlung
doorstep sales *pl*	Verkäufe *m pl* an der Haustür
memorandum	Vertragsurkunde *f*
right of cancellation	Recht *n* der Annullierung/Stornierung
to pay at the cash desk	an der Kasse zahlen
to bail goods to s.o.	jdm Waren vertragsmäßig übergeben
to sign a hire-purchase agreement	einen Ratenzahlungsvertrag unterschreiben
to budget for the purchase	den Kauf einplanen
to have the money ready	das Geld bar auf der Hand haben
to postpone a purchase	einen Kauf verschieben
to pay goods by instalments	Waren auf Teilzahlung/Raten kaufen
to protect the consumer	den Verbraucher schützen

Einzel- und Großhandel

to terminate the agreement	den Vertrag kündigen
to have a lien on the goods	ein Zurückbehaltungsrecht an den Waren haben
by equal instalments	in gleichen Raten
price/cost conscious	preis-/kostenbewußt
on the end of the hire	nach Entrichtung der letzten Rate

Sätze und Redewendungen:

He is skilled in his trade.	Er ist fachlich ausgebildet.
Women at work have a preference for self-service stores.	Berufstätige Frauen haben eine Vorliebe für Selbstbedienungsläden.
Hire-purchase increases turnover/keeps demand high.	Der Ratenkauf erhöht den Umsatz/sorgt für rege Nachfrage.
The seller has to tell the buyer in writing the cash price of the goods.	Der Verkäufer ist verpflichtet, dem Käufer schriftlich den Barpreis der Waren anzugeben.
The property in the goods does not pass to the buyer until the final instalment is paid.	Das Eigentum an den Waren geht auf den Käufer erst nach Entrichtung der letzten Rate über.
A credit-sale agreement is an agreement to sell goods by five or more instalments, the property passing to the new owner at once.	Ein Kreditkaufvertrag ist ein Übereinkommen, Waren gegen fünf oder mehr Ratenzahlungen zu verkaufen, wobei die Waren sofort in das Eigentum des neuen Besitzers übergehen.
For the customer, the shopping centre has great appeal.	Für den Kunden ist das Einkaufszentrum ein Anziehungspunkt.
Shopping centres have on-site parking as a common feature of their layout.	Einkaufszentren verfügen unmittelbar auf ihrem Gelände über einen Parkplatz, der zur Anlage gehört.
all the products on display	alle ausgestellten Waren
Supermarkets are self-service stores with a minimum selling area of 2,000 square feet.	Supermärkte sind Selbstbedienungsläden mit einer Mindestverkaufsfläche von 2000 Quadratfuß.
Department stores have 25 or more persons engaged in selling clothing and at least four other major commodity groups.	Warenhäuser beschäftigen 25 oder mehr Personen im Verkauf von Kleidung und mindestens vier weiteren wichtigeren Warengruppen.
It has been alarming to see gaping spaces left on shelf in some stores.	Es war erschreckend, in manchen Läden gähnend leere Stellen in den Regalen zu sehen.

3. Wholesale Trade

Großhandel

wholesale price index	Großhandelspreisindex *m*
wholesale cooperative (society)	Großeinkaufsgenossenschaft *f*
wholesale representative	Großhandelsvertreter *m*
cooperative buying/marketing/selling association	Einkaufs-/Absatz-/Verkaufsgenossenschaft *f*
farmers' marketing cooperative	landwirtschaftliche Absatzgenossenschaft *f*
middleman	Zwischenhändler *m*, Vermittler *m*, Makler *m*
intermediary	Mittelsmann *m*, Mittelsperson *f*
mail-order wholesaler/firm	Versandgroßhändler *m*/Versandhaus *n*
general/specialist wholesaler	Sortimenter *m*/Fachgroßhändler *m*
local wholesaler	Großhändler *m* am Platz
cash-and-carry supermarket/warehouse	Abholgroßmarkt *m* (AGM)
distribution costs *pl*/expenses *pl*	Vertriebskosten *f pl*
distribution network	Vertriebsnetz *n*
services to the retailer/to the public	Dienstleistungen *f pl* für Einzelhändler/für Konsumenten
chain wholesaling	Großhandelskette *f*
to (sell) wholesale	*tr* en gros verkaufen; *itr* Großhandel treiben
to buy goods wholesale	Waren im Großhandel einkaufen
to carry on a wholesale business	ein Großhandelsgeschäft betreiben
to display a wide variety of goods	ein reiches Angebot an Waren ausstellen
to operate a fleet of vehicles	über einen Fahrzeugpark verfügen
to grade/to pre-pack goods	Waren nach Güteklassen einstufen/im voraus fertig verpacken
to specialize in distribution	sich auf den Vertrieb spezialisieren
to act as liaison between retailers and producers	die Verbindung zwischen Einzelhändlern und Produzenten herstellen
to take supplies into stock	Vorräte auf Lager nehmen
to take bulk supplies	Waren in großen Mengen abnehmen (*from* von)
to release supplies from stock	Lagerbestände abgeben
to settle promptly with cash	prompt bar begleichen
to market the goods by advertising	die Waren durch Werbung absetzen
to offer price advantages	Preisvorteile anbieten
to operate on lower markups	mit niedrigeren Handelsspannen arbeiten

Sätze und Redewendungen:

He breaks bulk to the requirement of the retailer.	Er packt die Waren entsprechend den Bedürfnissen des Einzelhändlers um.
He carries stock which is readily available.	Er führt Waren, die jederzeit lieferbar sind.
He delivers goods to the retailer when required.	Er beliefert den Einzelhändler nach Bedarf.
He releases goods when they are in short supply.	Er gibt Waren ab, wenn sie knapp sind.
He bridges the time gap between production and consumption.	Er überbrückt die Spanne zwischen Produktion und Verbrauch.
He evens out the flow of goods in times of glut or shortage.	Er gleicht Überangebot und Knappheit an Waren aus.
Sometimes he sells at cut prices.	Manchmal verkauft er zu stark herabgesetzten Preisen.
He enables the consumer to obtain a steady flow of goods at steady prices.	Er ermöglicht dem Konsumenten, Güter regelmäßig zu stabilen Preisen zu beziehen.
Mail-order wholesalers eliminate the retailer and sell direct to the consumer in his own home.	Versandgroßhändler schalten den Einzelhändler aus und verkaufen direkt an den Konsumenten in dessen Wohnung.
Mail-order houses operate through agents working on commission.	Versandhäuser tätigen ihre Geschäfte mit Hilfe von Vertretern, die auf Provisionsbasis arbeiten.
The Cooperative Wholesale Society is the largest unit in wholesale trade, catering for the needs of the retail societies which are members.	Die Einkaufsgenossenschaft der Konsumgenossenschaften ist der größte Verband im Großhandel, der die Bedürfnisse der angeschlossenen Einzelhandelsgenossenschaften befriedigt.

II. Import and Export Trade — Einfuhr- und Ausfuhrhandel

1. Import Trade — Einfuhrhandel

principal imports *pl*	Haupteinfuhrwaren *f pl*
total imports *pl*	Gesamteinfuhr *f*
invisible imports *pl*	unsichtbare Einfuhr *f*
direct importation	direkte Einfuhr *f*

124 Import and Export Trade

import agent/credit	Importvertreter *m*/-kredit *m*
import list/quota	Einfuhrliste *f*/-kontingent *n*
import regulations *pl*/ restrictions *pl*	Einfuhrbestimmungen *f pl*/ -beschränkungen *f pl*
importation in bond	Einfuhr *f* unter Zollverschluß
imported article/commodities *pl*	Importartikel *m*/Einfuhrwaren *f pl*
importing country/firm	Einfuhrland *n*/Importfirma *f*
importer/import merchant	Importeur *m*/Importhändler *m*
import commission agent	Einfuhrkommissionär *m*
import broker	Importmakler *m*
free trade	Freihandel *m*
volume of imports	Einfuhrvolumen *n*
bonded warehouse	Zollspeicher *m*
account sales (A/S)	Verkaufsabrechnung *f (eines Kommissionärs)*
to ensure regular supplies of raw materials	die regelmäßige Belieferung mit Rohstoffen sicherstellen
to dispose of the goods at a profit	die Waren mit Gewinn absetzen
to buy at competitive prices	zu konkurrenzfähigen Preisen einkaufen
to seek (sought; sought) a market	Absatzmöglichkeiten suchen
to promote free trade	den Freihandel fördern
to dump goods on the British market	Waren zu Dumping-Preisen auf dem englischen Markt absetzen
to trade freely around the world	mit der ganzen Welt ungehindert Handel treiben
to check imports	der Einfuhr Hindernisse in den Weg legen
to reduce/to abolish trade barriers	Handelsschranken abbauen/beseitigen
to remove monetary obstacles to trade expansion	Währungsschwierigkeiten beseitigen, die einer Ausweitung des Handels hinderlich sind

Sätze und Redewendungen:

The import merchant buys goods or products from growers or manufacturers.	Der Importeur kauft Waren oder Erzeugnisse von Produzenten oder Fabrikanten.
He stages exhibitions.	Er veranstaltet Ausstellungen.
The import commission agent deals with goods for foreign exporters on a consignment basis.	Der Einfuhrkommissionär handelt mit Waren für ausländische Exporteure auf Kommissionsbasis.
He imports goods at the overseas dealer's risk.	Er importiert Waren auf Gefahr des Händlers in Übersee.

Einfuhr- und Ausfuhrhandel 125

The agent sells the goods at the best price he can obtain.	Der Kommissionär verkauft die Waren zum besten erzielbaren Preis.
He assumes the risk of bad debts.	Er übernimmt das Risiko für zweifelhafte/uneinbringliche Forderungen.
The agent remits the net proceeds to his overseas client.	Der Kommissionär überweist den Nettobetrag seinem Kunden in Übersee.

2. Export Trade

Ausfuhrhandel

export, exportation	Export *m*, Ausfuhr *f*
exports *pl*	Export *m*, Ausfuhr(en) *f (pl)*
export agent/broker	Exportvertreter *m*/-makler *m*
export bounty	Ausfuhrprämie *f*
export business	Exportgeschäft *n*
export contract	Exportvertrag *m*
export control	Ausfuhrkontrolle *f*, -lenkung *f*
exporting country	Ausfuhrland *n*
export credit	Exportkredit *m*
export department	Exportabteilung *f*
export duty	Ausfuhrzoll *m*, Ausfuhrabgabe *f*
export earnings *pl*	Ausfuhrerlöse *m pl*
export figures *pl*	Exportziffern *f pl*
export financing	Exportfinanzierung *f*
export firm/house	Exportfirma *f*
export goods *pl*	Exportgüter *n pl*
export incentives *pl*	Anreize *m pl* für den Export
export increase, increase in exports	Ausfuhrsteigerung *f*
decrease in exports	Ausfuhrrückgang *m*
export manager	Leiter *m* der Exportabteilung
export market	Auslandsmarkt *m*/-absatz *m*
exporter/export merchant	Exporteur *m*/Exportkaufmann *m*, Exporthändler *m*
export order	Exportauftrag *m*
export promotion	Exportförderung *f*
export quota	Ausfuhrkontingent *n*
export regulations *pl*	Ausfuhrbestimmungen *f pl*
export shipments *pl*	Exportlieferungen *f pl*
export volume	Exportvolumen *n*
export licence	Ausfuhrgenehmigung *f*
total exports *pl*	Gesamtausfuhr *f*
home-produced goods *pl*	im Inland hergestellte Güter *n pl*
overseas bank	Überseebank *f*
overseas countries *pl*	überseeische Länder *n pl*
overseas competitors *pl*	überseeische Konkurrenten *m pl*

126 Import and Export Trade

overseas customers *pl*	überseeische Kunden *m pl*
overseas markets *pl*	Überseemärkte *m pl*
risk of non-payment/of theft	Risiko *n* der Zahlungsverweigerung/Diebstahlsrisiko *n*
buying mission	Einkaufsdelegation *f*
sales/marketing area	Absatzgebiet *n*
freight forwarding agent	Güterspediteur *m*
export commission merchant/agent/house	Ausfuhrkommissionär *m*
British week	Britische Woche *f*
free trade area	Freihandelszone *f*
customs union	Zollunion *f*
informative literature	Informationsmaterial *n*
technical handouts *pl*	technische Broschüren *f pl*
to encourage exports	die Ausfuhr fördern
to sell overseas	Waren in Übersee absetzen
to narrow/to reduce the trade gap	die Außenhandelslücke verringern
to enter an export market	einen Exportmarkt erschließen
to release foreign exchange	Devisen freigeben
to eat into/to cut profit margins	die Gewinnspanne schmälern
to base buyers in a foreign country	ein Einkaufsbüro im Ausland errichten
to be competitively priced	konkurrenzfähige Preise aufweisen
to supply the overseas buyer	den Abnehmer in Übersee beliefern
to secure orders from abroad	Aufträge aus dem Ausland beschaffen
to employ a sales agent	einen Handelsvertreter/Reisenden anstellen/einsetzen
to appoint a representative	einen Vertreter anstellen
to promote overseas trade	den Außenhandel fördern
to develop sales to the maximum	den Absatz maximal steigern
to develop an overseas market	einen Auslandsmarkt erschließen
to grant a long-term credit	einen langfristigen Kredit einräumen
to finance the export sales	die Auslandsverkäufe finanzieren
to arrange an insurance policy with Lloyd's	bei Lloyds eine Versicherung abschließen
to pay bounties to exporters	den Exporteuren Prämien zahlen
exportable	für die Ausfuhr geeignet
large-scale	umfangreich, großangelegt

Sätze und Redewendungen:

They compete in the home market with other nations.	Sie stehen auf dem Inlandsmarkt mit anderen Nationen in Wettbewerb.

An exporter supplies goods at a fixed price.	Ein Exporteur liefert Waren zu einem festen Preis.
Risks are assumed by insurers.	Risiken werden von Versicherungsträgern übernommen.
Overseas competition is fierce.	Die Konkurrenz im Ausland ist äußerst hart.
Guarantees are given by the Export Credits Guarantee Department (ECGD).	Kreditbürgschaften werden von der staatlichen Ausfuhrkreditversicherung (ECGD) übernommen.
Invisible exports are e.g. insurance, shipping, consultant services, supervision of maintenance on capital projects.	Zu den unsichtbaren Ausfuhren gehören z.B. Versicherung, Schiffstransport, Beratung, Überwachung der Instandhaltung bei Investitionsvorhaben.
Large firms set up an overseas base.	Große Firmen errichten eine Niederlassung in Übersee.
The main documents used in the export trade are: the bill of lading, the customs specification, the port rates schedule, the shipping note, the certificate of origin, the insurance certificate, and the air waybill.	Die wichtigsten im Exporthandel erforderlichen Unterlagen sind: Seefrachtbrief/Konnossement, Zollpapiere, Aufstellung der Hafengebühren, Warenbegleitschein, Ursprungszeugnis, Versicherungsbescheinigung und Luftfrachtbrief.
The property of the cargo vests with the holder of the bill of lading, to which the policy and invoice are attached.	Das Eigentum an der Ladung ist an den Besitz des Konnossements und der beigefügten Police und Rechnung geknüpft.

III. Markets, Fairs and Exhibitions

Märkte, Messen und Ausstellungen

1. Markets

Märkte

open-air market	Markt *m* im Freien
covered market	Markthalle *f*
market day	Markttag *m*, Wochenmarkt *m*
market place/town	Marktplatz *m*/-flecken *m*
market regulations *pl*	Marktordnung *f*
stand/booth	Marktstand *m*/-bude *f*
black/grey market	Schwarzmarkt *m*/grauer Markt *m*
black marketeer	Schwarzhändler *m*
market-dominating enterprise	marktbeherrschendes Unternehmen *n*
market gap	Marktlücke *f*

Markets, Fairs and Exhibitions

saturation of the market	Sättigung *f* des Marktes
fair market price	marktgerechter Preis *m*
market capacity	Aufnahmefähigkeit *f* des Marktes
market condition/analysis/value	Marktlage *f*/-analyse *f*/-wert *m*
buyer's/seller's market	Käufer-/Verkäufermarkt *m*
producer market	Erzeugermarkt *m*
domestic market	Binnen-, Inlandsmarkt *m*
sale in the open market	freihändiger Verkauf *m*
price fluctuations *pl*	Preisschwankungen *f pl*
standard quality	Standardqualität *f*
fall in value	(plötzlicher) Wertverlust *m*
marketing costs *pl*	Absatzkosten *pl*
marketing organization	Absatz-/Vertriebsorganisation *f*
to be in the market for	an etw Bedarf haben, für etw Abnehmer sein
to market	einkaufen, verkaufen, absetzen
to come into/on the market	auf den Markt kommen
to command/to conquer the market	den Markt beherrschen/erobern
to do o.'s marketing	seine Einkäufe erledigen
to congest/to glut the market	den Markt überschwemmen
to open up new markets	neue Märkte erschließen
to throw on the market	auf den Markt werfen
to preserve world prices	an den Weltmarktpreisen festhalten
to find a market	Absatz finden
to meet with a ready market	guten Absatz finden
in the market	auf dem Markt
marketable	marktgängig, absetzbar
at market price	zum Marktpreis

Sätze und Redewendungen:

Buyers and sellers are brought into contact with one another.	Käufer und Verkäufer kommen miteinander in Kontakt.
She went to (the) market to buy food for the family.	Sie ging auf den Markt, um Nahrungsmittel für die Familie zu kaufen.
The next market is on the 1st of June.	Der nächste Markt wird am 1. Juni abgehalten.

2. Fairs and Exhibitions — Messen und Ausstellungen

fair	Messe *f*
exhibition, *Am* exposition	Ausstellung *f*
visitor to a fair, fairgoer	Messebesucher *m*
fair authorities *pl*/management	Messeleitung *f*
fairground, fairsite	Messe-, Ausstellungsgelände *n*

Märkte, Messen und Ausstellungen

exhibition building	Messe-, Ausstellungsgebäude *n*
exhibition catalogue/directory	Ausstellungskatalog *m*
planning/organization/holding of a fair	Planung *f*/Organisation *f*/Veranstaltung *f* einer Messe
duration of a fair	Ausstellungsdauer *f*
exhibition regulations *pl*	Messeordnung *f*
fair pass	Messeausweis *m*
exhibit	Ausstellungsstück *n*
specialized fair	Fachmesse *f*
trade/commercial fair	Handelsmesse *f*
sample fair	Mustermesse *f*
industrial/electrical goods/furs fair	Industrie-/Elektro-/Rauchwarenmesse *f*
textile goods/leather goods/toy fair	Textil-/Lederwaren-/Spielwarenmesse *f*
British Industries Fair	Britische Industriemesse *f*
world fair	Weltausstellung *f*
agricultural fair	Landwirtschaftsausstellung *f*
postage stamps fair	Briefmarkenmesse *f*
to attend/to visit a fair	eine Messe besuchen
to hold a fair	eine Messe abhalten
to participate in a fair	sich an einer Messe beteiligen
to send goods to a fair for display	eine Messe beschicken
to display/to exhibit goods at a fair	Waren auf einer Messe ausstellen
to apply for exhibition space	sich um Ausstellungsfläche bewerben
to open/to organize a fair	eine Messe eröffnen/veranstalten
to stimulate existing outlets	bestehende Absatzgebiete neu beleben
at the fair	auf der Messe
on display	ausgestellt

Sätze und Redewendungen:

The fair is held.	Die Messe wird abgehalten.
The fair takes place.	Die Messe findet statt.
Trade fairs help to promote the flow of trade both nationally and internationally.	Handelsmessen fördern den Handelsverkehr im nationalen und internationalen Bereich.
A trade fair caters mainly for professional buyers and sellers.	Eine Handelsmesse wendet sich hauptsächlich an Facheinkäufer und -verkäufer.
The primary object of exhibitions is to enhance prestige and goodwill.	Das Hauptziel von Messen besteht in der Steigerung des Ansehens und der Ausweitung des Kundenkreises einer Firma.

The fair presents the prospective buyer with a range of products.	Die Messe orientiert den potentiellen Käufer über ein Sortiment/ eine Auswahl von Erzeugnissen.
Contacts between buyer and manufacturer encourage new designs.	Kontakte zwischen Käufer und Hersteller führen zu neuen Designs/Mustern.
The fair provides a useful way of bringing goods to the notice of a wide circle of potential customers.	Die Messe ist eine gute Gelegenheit, Waren einem weiten Kreis von Interessenten bekanntzumachen.

IV. Commercial Practice — Kaufmännische Praxis

1. Business Correspondence — Handelskorrespondenz

inquiry	Anfrage *f*
further inquiry	Rückfrage *f*
list of products/of customers/of suppliers	Warenverzeichnis *n*/Kunden-/Lieferantenliste *f*
description of goods	Warenbezeichnung *f*
specification, *Am* itemization	detaillierte Aufstellung *f*
details *pl*, particulars *pl*	nähere Angaben *f pl*
buying/selling conditions *pl*	Einkaufs-/Verkaufsbedingungen *f pl*
preliminary announcement	Vorankündigung *f*, Voranzeige *f*
request for a price-list	Anforderung *f* einer Preisliste
commercial guide	Branchenverzeichnis *n*
leaflet, handout	Werbeblatt *n*, Handzettel *m*
booklet	Werbebroschüre *f*
instruction booklet	Bedienungsanleitung *f*
instruction for use	Gebrauchsanweisung *f*
brochure [ˈbrəuʃjuə]	Broschüre *f*
range of samples	Musterkollektion *f*
selection of samples	Auswahlmustersendung *f*
sample of no value	Muster *n* ohne Wert
certificate of inspection/of guarantee	Prüfbescheinigung *f*/Garantieschein *m*
accompanying/covering letter	Begleitbrief *m*
copy block	Notizblock *m*
letter sheet	Briefbogen *m*
letter of acknowledgement	Bestätigungsschreiben *n*
reference/purchase letter	Bezugs-/Bestellschreiben *n*
firm offer	verbindliches/festes Angebot *n*
offer without engagement	unverbindliches Angebot *n*
special offer	Sonderangebot *n*
written/oral offer	schriftliches/mündliches Angebot *n*
previous/suitable offer	früheres/geeignetes Angebot *n*

detailed/exceptional offer	detailliertes/außergewöhnliches Angebot *n*
estimate	Kostenvoranschlag *m*
counter-offer	Gegenangebot *n*
export order	Exportauftrag *m*
ordering firm	Bestellfirma *f*
receipt of order	Auftrags-, Bestellungseingang *m*
reply coupon	Antwortschein *m*
repeat order	Nachbestellung *f*
follow-up order	Anschlußauftrag *m*
orders on hand	Auftragsbestand *m*
refusal/cancellation/withdrawal of an order	Ablehnung *f*/Stornierung *f*/ Widerruf *m* einer Bestellung
confirmation of order	Auftragsbestätigung *f (eigener, erteilter Auftrag)*
acknowledgement of order	Auftragsbestätigung *f (fremder, erhaltener Auftrag)*
to initiate business relations	Geschäftsverbindungen anknüpfen
to address an inquiry to	eine Anfrage richten an
to send out inquiries	Anfragen verschicken
to make special arrangements	besondere Vereinbarungen treffen
to contact manufacturers	sich mit Herstellern in Verbindung setzen
to replenish stocks	das Lager (wieder) auffüllen/ ergänzen
to invite/solicit offers	Angebote einholen
to offer for sale	zum Verkauf anbieten
to make a firm offer	ein verbindliches Angebot machen
to send/submit an offer	ein Angebot schicken/unterbreiten
to accept/reject an offer	ein Angebot annehmen/ablehnen
to sample	(be)mustern; probieren
to check/examine samples	Muster prüfen
to draw samples	Muster ziehen/entnehmen
to send samples on request	Muster auf Verlangen zusenden
to accept an order	einen Auftrag annehmen
to order by telephone/telegram, cable/teleprint message	telefonisch/telegrafisch/über Fernschreiber bestellen
to book an order	einen Auftrag vormerken
to enter an order	einen Auftrag eintragen/buchen
to complete an order	einen Auftrag fertigstellen
to execute an order carefully/properly/according to instructions	einen Auftrag sorgfältig/ordnungsgemäß/weisungsgemäß erledigen/ausführen
to execute an order in time	einen Auftrag rechtzeitig erledigen/ausführen
to cope with the rush of orders	mit dem starken Bestelleingang fertig werden
to send out an advice of dispatch	eine Versandanzeige absenden

132 Commercial Practice

to quote best possible/competitive prices	bestmögliche/konkurrenzfähige Preise angeben
payable to	zahlbar an
subject to prior sale	Zwischenverkauf vorbehalten
subject to goods being unsold	solange der Vorrat reicht
subject to alteration of prices without notice	Preisänderungen ohne vorherige Ankündigung vorbehalten
for immediate ordering only	nur bei sofortiger Bestellung
in accordance with the attached list	in Übereinstimmung mit der beiliegenden Liste

Sätze und Redewendungen:

Your name was given to us by ...	Ihr Name wurde uns von ... mitgeteilt.
Your firm was recommended to us by ...	Ihre Firma wurde uns von ... empfohlen.
We should be glad to receive details of your prices.	Wir möchten gern Näheres über Ihre Preise erfahren.
Please let us have a quotation for the supply of two engines.	Bitte nennen Sie uns den Preis für die Lieferung von zwei Maschinen.
Would you be kind enough to let us have samples.	Würden Sie uns bitte Muster zugehen lassen.
Full information regarding export prices, terms of payment, earliest delivery date and discounts for regular purchases would be appreciated.	Wir wären Ihnen dankbar für ausführliche Angaben über Exportpreise, Zahlungskonditionen, frühestes Lieferdatum und Skonti bei regelmäßigen Abschlüssen.
We have great pleasure in enclosing our catalogue.	Wir erlauben uns, Ihnen in der Anlage unseren Katalog zu übersenden.
A catalogue and a price-list are enclosed.	Beiliegend finden Sie Katalog und Preisliste.
We need the goods most urgently.	Wir brauchen die Waren sehr dringend.
He was in arrears with the execution of orders.	Er war mit der Auftragserledigung im Rückstand.
We shall be glad to give you a trial order.	Wir möchten Ihnen einen Probeauftrag übermitteln.
You may rely on our best efforts.	Sie können sich darauf verlassen, daß wir unser möglichstes tun werden.
May we draw your attention to the enclosed catalogue.	Dürfen wir Sie auf den beiliegenden Katalog hinweisen.

Kaufmännische Praxis 133

2. Sales Contract — Kaufvertrag

sales/supply contract	Kauf-/Liefervertrag *m*
terms of contract	Vertragsbedingungen *f pl*
period/duration of contract	Vertragsdauer *f*
fulfilment of contract	Vertragserfüllung *f*
non-fulfilment/breach of contract	Nichterfüllung *f* des Vertrages/ Vertragsbruch *m*
expiration of contract	Vertragsablauf *m*
renewal of contract	Vertragserneuerung *f*
the contracting parties *pl*	die vertragschließenden Parteien *f pl*
draft agreement	Vertragsentwurf *m*
cash/credit sale	Bar-/Kreditverkauf *m*
sale on approval	Kauf *m* auf Probe
sale by sample	Kauf *m* nach Muster
sale or return	Kauf *m* mit Rückgaberecht
transfer/reservation of title	Eigentumsübertragung *f*/-vorbehalt *m*
transfer of risk	Risikoübergang *m*
to contract	ein Geschäft abschließen; vertraglich vereinbaren
to conclude a contract	einen Vertrag schließen
to enter into an agreement	zu einem Abkommen gelangen
to stipulate/negotiate the conditions of a contract	die Vertragsbedingungen festlegen/aushandeln
to renew/extend a contract	einen Vertrag erneuern/verlängern
to cancel/revoke/break a contract	einen Vertrag stornieren/widerrufen/brechen
to draft/to draw up a document	eine Urkunde aufsetzen
to support by documents	urkundlich belegen
to fear rapid changes in demand	rasche Änderungen der Nachfrage befürchten
to judge the demand for furniture	den Bedarf an Möbeln schätzen
contractual	vertraglich
by mutual agreement	in beiderseitigem Einverständnis
according/contrary to regulations	vorschriftsmäßig/-widrig

Sätze und Redewendungen:

We thank you for your order No ... received today.	Wir danken Ihnen für Ihren Auftrag Nr. ..., der heute bei uns eingegangen ist.
The consignment is being dispatched by rail today and should reach you on 11th of May.	Die Lieferung geht heute mit der Bahn ab und sollte am 11. Mai bei Ihnen eintreffen.

134 Commercial Practice

We have for acknowledgement your order No ...	Wir bestätigen Ihren Auftrag Nr....
We reserve title to the goods delivered pending payment in full.	Wir behalten uns das Eigentum an den gelieferten Waren bis zur vollständigen Bezahlung vor.
We reserve the right to cancel the order if delivery is not made by 1st March.	Wir behalten uns das Recht vor, die Bestellung zurückzunehmen, wenn die Lieferung nicht bis zum 1. März erfolgt.
Your careful attention to our instructions will be appreciated.	Für genaue Beachtung unserer Anweisungen wären wir Ihnen dankbar.

3. Invoicing and Payment — Fakturierung und Bezahlung

commercial invoice	Handels-, Warenrechnung *f*
customs/consular invoice	Zoll-/Konsulatsfaktura *f*
duplicate invoice	Duplikat *n* der Rechnung
invoice form/number	Rechnungsformular *n*/-nummer *f*
date of invoice	Rechnungsdatum *n*
invoice item/amount	Rechnungsposten *m*/-betrag *m*
invoice total	Gesamtbetrag *m* der Rechnung
net invoice value	Nettofakturenwert *m*
E. & O. E. (= errors and omissions excepted)	Irrtümer *m pl* und Auslassungen *f pl* vorbehalten
invoice/billing department	Rechnungsabteilung *f*
billing machine	Fakturiermaschine *f*
payment of invoices/accounts	Begleichung *f* von Rechnungen/Verbindlichkeiten
means of payment (*sing* and *pl*)	Zahlungsmittel (sing *n* und *pl*)
method/mode of payment	Zahlungsweise *f*
payment in advance	Vorauszahlung *f*
payment on account	Akonto-, Abschlagszahlung *f*
spot cash	sofortige Barzahlung *f*
net cash	netto Kassa
ready money down (R.M.D.)	nur gegen bar
cash with order (C.W.O.)	Zahlung *f* bei Auftragserteilung
30 days net	30 Tage netto
3% discount for payment within 10 days	3% Skonto *m, n* bei Zahlung innerhalb von 10 Tagen
2/10 – R.O.G. (= receipt of goods)	2% Skonto innerhalb von 10 Tagen *(vom Tag des Eingangs der Ware an gerechnet)*
trade/quantity discount	Wiederverkäufer-/Mengenrabatt *m*
remittance by money order	Zahlung *f* durch Postanweisung
payment by cheque/bill of exchange	Zahlung durch Scheck/Wechsel
documentary draft/bill of exchange	Dokumententratte *f*

Kaufmännische Praxis 135

commercial letter of credit (L/C)	Warenakkreditiv *n*
documents against acceptance (D/A)	Dokumente *n pl* gegen Akzept
documents against payment (D/P)	Dokumente *n pl* gegen Zahlung
documentary acceptance credit	Rembourskredit *m*
documentary credit	Dokumentenakkreditiv *n*
unconfirmed letter of credit	unbestätigtes Akkreditiv *n*
payment by instalments	Ratenzahlung *f*
down/first payment	Anzahlung *f*
collection of outstanding amounts	Einzug *m* von Außenständen
dunning/collection letter, demand note	Mahnbrief *m*, -schreiben *n*
collection sequence	Reihe *f* von Mahnbriefen
factory price/price ex works	Fabrikpreis *m*, Preis *m* ab Werk
net/gross/average price	Netto-/Brutto-/Durchschnittspreis *m*
total/list/catalogue price	Gesamt-/Listen-/Katalogpreis *m*
recommended price	unverbindlicher Richtpreis *m*
fixed/firm price	Festpreis *m*
sales/selling price	Verkaufspreis *m*
maximum/seasonal/clearance price	Höchst-/Saison-/Ausverkaufspreis *m*
trend of prices	Preisentwicklung *f*
upward trend of prices	Preisauftrieb *m*
increase/rise in prices	Preiserhöhung *f*/-anstieg *m*/-steigerung *f*
excessive prices *pl*	überhöhte Preise *m pl*
price fluctuations *pl*	Preisschwankungen *f pl*
closest price	äußerster Preis *m*
reasonable/favourable price	angemessener/günstiger Preis *m*
cost price	Selbstkostenpreis *m*
to invoice, to bill	in Rechnung stellen, berechnen
to make out an invoice/a receipt	eine Rechnung/Quittung ausstellen
to enter on the invoice	auf die Rechnung setzen
to pay promptly/within the stipulated time	prompt/innerhalb der vereinbarten Zeit bezahlen
to remit/to transfer an amount	einen Betrag überweisen
to suspend payments	Zahlungen einstellen
to be in arrears with one's payments	mit seinen Zahlungen im Rückstand sein
to meet o.'s payment obligations	seinen Zahlungsverpflichtungen nachkommen
to resume payments	Zahlungen wiederaufnehmen
to grant/to allow a cash discount	Skonto einräumen
to deduct/to take advantage of a cash discount	Skonto abziehen
to ask for an extension	um Zahlungsaufschub bitten
to consider prices too high	Preise als zu hoch ansehen
to cut the prices fine	knapp kalkulieren

Commercial Practice

to meet a customer	einem Kunden (im Preis) entgegenkommen
to allow a credit	einen Kredit einräumen/gewähren
to open a credit	einen Kredit eröffnen
in payment of your account/invoice	zum Ausgleich Ihres Kontos/zur Begleichung Ihrer Rechnung
... d/s (=days after sight)	... Tage nach Sicht
... m/s (=months after sight)	... Monate nach Sicht
for account of	für Rechnung von
in favour of	zugunsten von
irrevocable [iˈrevəkəbl]	unwiderruflich
confirmed	bestätigt
above/below market price	über/unter dem Marktpreis
at the expense of your firm	zu Lasten Ihrer Firma
at my/our/your expense	auf meine/unsere/Ihre Kosten
all expenses included	einschließlich aller Spesen

Sätze und Redewendungen:

The firm surrendered the shipping papers.	Die Firma übergab die Versandpapiere.
He entrusted the presentation and collection of the bill to a bank.	Er beauftragte eine Bank mit Vorlage und Einzug des Wechsels.
The engineer paid off the instalments punctually.	Der Ingenieur hielt die Ratenzahlungen pünktlich ein.
The importer had difficulties in collecting outstanding accounts.	Der Importeur hatte Schwierigkeiten beim Einzug von Außenständen.
The car dealer reminded him of an overdue account.	Der Autohändler erinnerte ihn an eine überfällige Forderung.
Buy now — pay later!	Jetzt kaufen - später zahlen!
No down payment!	Keine Anzahlung!
In payment of your invoice we enclose a crossed cheque for £200.	Zum Ausgleich Ihrer Rechnung senden wir Ihnen in der Anlage einen Verrechnungsscheck über 200 Pfund.
Please note that we have instructed the bank to open an irrevocable credit for £300 in your favour.	Bitte merken Sie vor, daß wir die Bank beauftragt haben, ein unwiderrufliches Akkreditiv über 300 Pfund zu Ihren Gunsten zu eröffnen.
Please draw on us as agreed for the full amount of your invoice, and attach the following documents to your draft: Bill of Lading, Commercial Invoice, Insurance Policy.	Bitte ziehen Sie wie vereinbart für den vollen Rechnungsbetrag einen Wechsel und legen Sie folgende Dokumente bei: Konnossement, Handelsfaktura, Versicherungspolice.

4. Packing and Delivery — Verpackung und Lieferung

packing instructions *pl*	Verpackungsvorschriften *f pl*
packing note/list	Packschein *m*/-liste *f*
packing material	Verpackungsmaterial *n*
original packing	Originalverpackung *f*
customary packing	handelsübliche Verpackung *f*
special/export packing	Spezial-/Exportverpackung *f*
seaworthy/waterproof packing	seemäßige/wasserdichte Verpackung *f*
proper/careful packing	sachgemäße/sorgfältige Verpackung *f*
improper/careless packing	unsachgemäße/nachlässige Verpackung *f*
bad/defective/faulty packing	schlechte/mangelhafte/falsche Verpackung *f*
gross/net weight, tare [tɛə]	Brutto-/Nettogewicht *n*, Tara *f*
wrapping	Umhüllung *f*
wrapping paper	Packpapier *n*
cardboard, pasteboard	Karton *m*, Pappe *f*
corrugated/crinkled cardboard	Wellpappe *f*
tissue/wax/oil paper	Seiden-/Wachs-/Ölpapier *n*
oil cloth	Wachstuch *n*
canvas	Segeltuch *n*
box	Schachtel *f*
wooden case/box	Holzkiste *f*
plywood box	Sperrholzkiste *f*
tin can	Blechdose *f*, Konservendose *f*
tin-case	Blechkiste *f*
crate	Lattenkiste *f*, Holzverschlag *m*
paper/plastic bag	Papier-/Plastiksack *m*
carrier bag	Tragtasche *f*
basket	Korb *m*
small/medium-size/big glass-bottle	kleine/mittelgroße/große Glasflasche *f*
unbreakable/shatterproof bottle	unzerbrechliche/bruchsichere Flasche *f*
barrel, cask	Faß *n*
tube	Tube *f*
filler, filling material	Füllmaterial *n*
paper shavings *pl*	Papierabfälle *m pl*
glass padding, glass-wool, fibre-glass	Glaswolle *f*
wood shavings *pl*	Holzwolle *f*
keg/carboy	Fäßchen *n*/Korbflasche *f*
foam, foam-rubber	Schaumstoff *m*, -gummi *m*
thread	dünner Faden *m*
twine, string	Schnur *f*, Bindfaden *m*

Commercial Practice

adhesive tape	Klebestreifen *m*
steel strapping	Stahlbandumreifung *f*
wire tying/strapping	Drahtverschnürung *f*
marking of cases	Markierung *f*/Beschriftung *f* von Kisten
exact marking instructions *pl*/requirements	genaue Markierungsanweisungen *f pl*/-vorschriften *f pl*
shipping marks *pl*	Markierungszeichen *n pl*, Versandmarkierung *f*

Caution marks — *Vorsichtsmarkierungen* (für Transportverpackung)

Top; This side up	Oben
Bottom	Unten
Open here	Hier öffnen
Lift here	Hier anheben
Handle with care	Vorsicht!
Glass! Handle with care	Vorsicht Glas!
Inflammable	Feuergefährlich
Liquids — do not tilt — keep in cool place	Flüssigkeit – nicht kippen – kühl lagern
Keep dry	Trocken lagern
Do not store in damp place	Vor Nässe schützen
to deliver from stock/ex works/ex factory	ab Lager/Werk/Fabrik liefern
to furnish	(be)liefern, versenden, ausrüsten, ausstatten
to send (off), to ship	(ab)senden, versenden, verschiffen
to dispatch without delay	unverzüglich absenden
to distribute goods	Waren verteilen
to open a letter of credit in favour of the supplier	ein Akkreditiv zugunsten des Lieferanten eröffnen
to supply only goods of best quality	nur Waren bester Qualität liefern
to deliver on receipt of order	nach Bestelleingang ausliefern/zustellen
to deliver at a later date	zu einem späteren Zeitpunkt liefern
to deliver goods direct or through a forwarding agent	Waren direkt oder über einen Spediteur ausliefern
to speed up/accelerate delivery	die Lieferung beschleunigen
to effect delivery by a specified date	die Lieferung bis zu einem bestimmten Zeitpunkt durchführen
to honour/keep delivery dates	Liefertermine einhalten
to provide goods for immediate delivery	Waren zur sofortigen Lieferung bereitstellen

Kaufmännische Praxis 139

deliverer	Überbringer *m*
time/period of delivery	Lieferfrist *f*
delivery date	Liefertermin *m*, -tag *m*
date of shipment	Versanddatum *n*
delivery on call	Lieferung *f* auf Abruf
delivery instructions *pl*	Liefer-/Versandanweisungen *f pl*
part(ial) delivery	Teillieferung *f*
delay in delivery	Lieferverzug *m*
dispatch/shipping department	Versandabteilung *f*

Incoterms (International Commercial Terms)	*Incoterms*
free/franco house, free domicile	frei Haus/frei Domizil
free customer's warehouse	frei Lager des Kunden
f.o.r. (= free on rail)	frei Waggon Versandbahnhof
f.o.t. (= free on truck)	frei LKW
f.a.q. (= free alongside quay)	frei Längsseite Kai Versandhafen
f.a.s. (= free alongside ship)	frei Längsseite Schiff Versandhafen
f.o.b. (= free on board)	frei an Bord Versandhafen
c. & f. (= cost and freight)	Kosten und Fracht *(bedingt frachtfrei: Versicherung und Ausladekosten sind nicht enthalten)*
c.i.f. (= cost, insurance, freight)	Kosten, Versicherung, Fracht *(frei Empfangs-, Bestimmungshafen)*
c.i.f.c. (= cost, insurance, freight and commission)	Kosten, Versicherung, Fracht und Provision *(frei Empfangshafen, einschließlich Provision)*
c.i.f.c. & i. (= cost, insurance, freight, commission and interest)	frei Empfangshafen, einschließlich Provision und Zinsen

to make/carry out part deliveries	Teillieferungen vornehmen
to meet the cost of storage	die Lagerhaltungskosten begleichen
to pack separately	getrennt verpacken
to wrap up, to cover	einwickeln, einhüllen
to unpack, to unwrap	auspacken
to charge packing material at cost price	Verpackungsmaterial zum Selbstkostenpreis berechnen
to box	in Kartons/Schachteln verpacken
to case	in Kisten verpacken
to stack cases	Kisten aufstapeln
to crate	in Lattenkisten verpacken
to sack, to bag	in Säcke abfüllen
to press in bales	in Ballen pressen
to bottle	in Flaschen abfüllen
to barrel	in Fässer füllen
to mark cases	Kisten beschriften

140 Commercial Practice

to mark with a brush	mit dem Pinsel beschriften
to mark cases with the name of the place of destination	Kisten mit dem Namen des Bestimmungsortes versehen
available	lieferbar, erhältlich
unavailable	nicht erhältlich
carriage paid (C.P.)	frachtfrei
carriage forward	Frachtkosten per Nachnahme
duty paid	verzollt
o/s (= out of stock)	nicht auf Lager, Vorrat erschöpft
deliverable	zustellbar
undeliverable	unzustellbar
ready for delivery	lieferbereit
(un)restricted in supply	(un)beschränkt lieferbar

Sätze und Redewendungen:

We are pleased to advise that the goods you ordered were dispatched by ship this morning.	Wir freuen uns, Ihnen mitteilen zu können, daß die bestellten Waren heute morgen per Schiff versandt wurden.
We hope the consignment will arrive safely.	Wir hoffen, daß die Sendung wohlbehalten bei Ihnen ankommt.
Your consignment has been packed, and we are enclosing herewith a detailed list of the contents to facilitate customs clearance at your end.	Ihre Lieferung wurde verpackt, und um Ihnen die Verzollung zu erleichtern, legen wir eine genaue Liste des Inhalts bei.

5. Complaints and Adjustments, Apologies / Beschwerden und deren Erledigung, Entschuldigungen

complaint, claim	Beschwerde *f*, Beanstandung *f*, Reklamation *f*, Mängelrüge *f*
deficiency claim	Mängelrüge *f*
letter of complaint, claim letter	Beschwerdebrief *m*
supplement/adjustment of a complaint	Erledigung *f*/Bereinigung *f* einer Beanstandung
serious complaint about a mistake	ernsthafte Beschwerde *f* über einen Fehler
defect, fault	Mangel *m*, Schaden *m*, Defekt *m*, Fehler *m*
defect in material/workmanship	Material-/Fabrikationsfehler *m*
latent/hidden defects *pl*	versteckte Mängel *m pl*
fraudulent concealment	arglistiges Verschweigen *n*
non-agreement with previous offer	Nichtübereinstimmung *f* mit dem vorausgegangenen Angebot

Kaufmännische Praxis 141

non-conformity with sample	Nichtübereinstimmung f mit dem Muster
inferior/poor quality	minderwertige Qualität f
error in the invoice	Rechnungsfehler m
rough handling/treatment	grobe/unsachgemäße Behandlung f
wrong delivery	Falsch-, Fehllieferung f
non-contractual delivery	nicht vertragsgemäße Lieferung f
to complain of/about	sich beklagen/beschweren über
to lodge a complaint	Beschwerde/Klage erheben
to sue for damages	auf Schadensersatz klagen
to keep the goods at reduced prices	die Waren zu ermäßigten Preisen behalten
to make an allowance	einen Preisnachlaß gewähren
to ask for a replacement	eine Ersatzlieferung verlangen
to place the goods at the seller's disposal	die Waren dem Verkäufer zur Verfügung stellen
to keep the goods on sale or return	die Waren kommissionsweise behalten
to return the goods at our risk and expense	die Waren auf unsere Gefahr und Rechnung zurückschicken
to take the goods back	die Waren zurücknehmen
to exchange the goods	die Waren umtauschen
to adjust a complaint	eine Beschwerde regeln
to apologize to the buyer for the trouble caused	sich beim Käufer wegen der entstandenen Unannehmlichkeiten entschuldigen
(un)justified	(un)berechtigt
well-founded	begründet
unfounded	unbegründet
(il)legitimate	(un)gerechtfertigt

Sätze und Redewendungen:

On examining the consignment we found that ...	Beim Überprüfen der Lieferung stellten wir fest, daß ...
Some articles are missing from the consignment.	Bei der Sendung fehlen einige Artikel.
The packing was extremely defective.	Die Verpackung war äußerst mangelhaft.
The goods arrived in bad condition.	Die Waren kamen in schlechtem Zustand an.
The goods have suffered in transit.	Die Waren haben während des Transports Schaden genommen.
We will take the matter up with the shippers.	Wir werden die Angelegenheit mit der Schiffahrtsgesellschaft besprechen.

We should be very much obliged if you would rectify this error/send us replacements.

Unless this shipment arrives here by the 10th of July we will have to cancel, as we cannot wait any longer for delivery.

The error occurred in our dispatch department and was due to our reorganization programme.

Please accept our apologies for this error/the inconvenience caused/ this delay in delivery.

Wir wären Ihnen sehr verbunden, wenn Sie Ihren Irrtum berichtigen/Ersatzlieferungen senden würden.

Sollte diese Sendung nicht bis spätestens 10. Juli hier eintreffen, sehen wir uns genötigt, den Auftrag zu stornieren, da wir nicht länger auf die Lieferung warten können.

Der Irrtum entstand in unserer Versandabteilung und ist auf unser Reorganisationsprogramm zurückzuführen.

Bitte entschuldigen Sie diesen Irrtum/die entstandenen Unannehmlichkeiten/diesen Lieferverzug.

V. Banking

Bankwesen

1. General Terms

Allgemeine Begriffe

bank loan
bank customer/manager
bank connections pl/operations pl

bank balance/charges pl
money at call/at short notice

collateral security/credit

branch banking
commercial bank
joint-stock bank
private/public deposits pl
demand/time deposit
short-term/medium-term/long-term deposit
deposit book (DPB), savings book, passbook
depositor

credit/lending policy
credit expansion/limit/restriction/ squeeze

Bankkredit m, -darlehen n
Bankkunde m/-direktor m
Bankverbindungen f pl/-geschäfte n pl

Bankguthaben n/-spesen pl
täglich fälliges/kurzfristig kündbares Geld n

zusätzliche Sicherheit f/Lombardkredit m

Filialbanksystem n
Geschäftsbank f
Aktienbank f (GB)
private/öffentliche Guthaben n pl
Sicht-/Termineinlage f
kurz-/mittel-/langfristige Einlage f

Sparbuch n, Depositenbuch n

Hinterleger m, Einzahler m; Konto-/Depositeninhaber m

Kreditpolitik f
Kreditausweitung f/-rahmen m/-einschränkung f/-knappheit f

Bankwesen 143

savings/foreign exchange/loan/ securities department	Spar-/Devisen-/Kredit-/Effektenabteilung *f*
investment business/consultant/ fund/stocks *pl*	Anlagegeschäft *n*/-berater *m*/Investmentfonds *m*/-papiere *n pl*
investment management	Effektenverwaltung *f*, Verwaltung *f* von Kapitalanlagen
investment portfolio	Wertpapierbestand *m*, Effektenportefeuille *n*
account holder/number/turnover	Kontoinhaber *m*/-nummer *f*/-umsatz *m*
loan/credit/deposit/savings/time deposit account	Darlehens-/Kredit-/Depositen-/Spar-/Festgeldkonto *n*
blocked/frozen/overdrawn account	gesperrtes/eingefrorenes/überzogenes Konto *n*
clearing account	Verrechnungskonto *n*
securities payment counter	Wertpapierschalter *m*
deposit/exchange/teller's counter	Einzahlungs-/Geldumtausch-/Kassenschalter *m*
loose-leaf statement	Kontoauszug *m* in loser Blattform
credit card	Kreditkarte *f*
safe custody	sicherer Gewahrsam *m*
bank safe	Banktresor *m*
safe-deposit box	Schließfach *n*
strong-room, vault	Tresorraum *m*
cash dispenser	Bargeldausgeber *m*
to lend money at interest	Geld gegen Zinsen ausleihen
to close/to reopen the banks	die Banken schließen/wiedereröffnen
to run an overdraft	ein Konto überziehen
to advance funds to the customer	dem Kunden Mittel vorschießen/vorstrecken
to be in need of funds	Kapital benötigen
to lend sums of money	Geldbeträge ausleihen
to accept deposits	Geldeinlagen entgegennehmen
to make regularly recurring payments	regelmäßig wiederkehrende Zahlungen vornehmen
to expand credit	Kredit ausweiten
to contract/to draw in a loan	einen Kredit aufnehmen/kündigen
to maintain branch offices	Zweigstellen unterhalten
to create purchasing power	Kaufkraft schaffen
below current bank rate	unter dem gegenwärtigen Diskontsatz
illiquid	illiquide, nicht flüssig
creditworthy	kreditfähig, -würdig
insolvent	zahlungsunfähig
local	örtlich
leading	führend
at maturity	bei Fälligkeit

Banking

Sätze und Redewendungen:

What credit would you give them in this case?	Welchen Kredit würden Sie ihnen in diesem Falle einräumen?
My money is in the bank.	Mein Geld liegt auf der Bank.
I'd like to open a bank account.	Ich möchte ein Bankkonto eröffnen.
You should deposit this money in a bank.	Sie sollten dieses Geld bei einer Bank einzahlen.
The depositor can pay money into his account at any branch in the country.	Der Kontoinhaber kann bei jeder Filiale im Lande Geld auf sein Konto einzahlen.
We keep our money in a bank for safety.	Wir legen unser Geld aus Sicherheitsgründen auf die Bank.
Whom do you bank with?	Mit welcher Bank stehen Sie in Verbindung?
I had to wait at the teller's counter at the bank.	Ich mußte am Kassenschalter in der Bank warten.
His bank statement showed a considerable overdraft.	Aus dem Kontoauszug war zu ersehen, daß er sein Konto erheblich überzogen hatte.
The banks are obliged to charge higher interest.	Die Banken müssen höhere Zinsen berechnen.
The customer withdraws money.	Der Kunde hebt Geld ab.
Banks cash cheques for their depositors.	Banken lösen Schecks für ihre Kunden ein.

2. Merchant Bank — Merchantbank

acceptance house	Rembours-, Akzeptbank *f*
investment adviser	Anlage-, Effektenberater *m*
insurance/issue/foreign exchange market	Versicherungs-/Emissions-/Devisenmarkt *m*
issuing bank/house	Emissionsbank *f*
issuer	Emittent *m*, Aussteller *m*
issue price	Ausgabekurs *m*
issue of a loan	Begebung *f* einer Anleihe
issue of securities	Effektenemission *f*
gold and silver bullions *pl*	Gold- und Silberbarren *m pl*
to secure payment for the goods	Zahlung für die Waren sicherstellen
to perform banking functions	die Aufgaben einer Bank übernehmen
to offer shares and debentures	Aktien und Obligationen anbieten
to hedge against currency fluctuations	sich gegen Kursschwankungen absichern

Sätze und Redewendungen:

The price of gold is fixed daily at a meeting whose chairman is the representative of one of the merchant-banking firms.

Merchant bankers are frequently called in to assist in mergers and take-overs.

The acceptance houses have close links with the shipping world, the insurance markets, the foreign exchange market and the money market.

Acceptance houses are those merchant banks "whose acceptance of a bill is one condition of the bill's eligibility for rediscount at the Bank of England, and who are members of the Accepting Houses Committee".

A confirming house is an intermediary between an overseas buyer and his British supplier.

Der Goldpreis wird täglich in einer Sitzung festgelegt, bei der ein Vertreter einer der Merchantbanken den Vorsitz hat.

Merchantbanken werden häufig bei Fusionen und Geschäftsübernahmen hinzugezogen.

Remboursbanken stehen in enger Verbindung mit der Schiffahrt, den Versicherungen, dem Devisen- und Währungsmarkt.

Remboursbanken sind Akzeptbanken, „deren Akzept auf einem Wechsel für die Rediskontierbarkeit bei der Bank von England unbedingt erforderlich ist und die Mitglieder im Remboursbankkomitee sind".

Ein Confirming House ist Vermittler zwischen dem Käufer in Übersee und seinem englischen Lieferanten.

3. The Bank of England

Die Bank von England

clearing house	Abrechnungsstelle f
Federal Reserve Bank	Zentralbank f der USA
gilt-edged market	Markt m für mündelsichere Wertpapiere
issue of notes	Banknotenausgabe f
issue department	Emissions-, Ausgabeabteilung f
fiduciary issue	ungedeckte Notenausgabe f
gold reserves pl	Goldreserven $f\,pl$
gold standard	Goldstandard m, -währung f
notes pl in circulation	Banknotenumlauf m
weekly bank return	wöchentlicher Bankausweis m
exchange control	Devisenbewirtschaftung f
drain on the reserves	Inanspruchnahme f von Reserven
net indebtedness	Nettoverschuldung f
hot money	Fluchtgeld n, heißes Geld n
to bank with s.o.	mit jdm in Bankverbindung stehen
to keep on the gold standard	den Goldstandard beibehalten
to advise on the finance of companies	Gesellschaften bei der Finanzierung beraten

to assist in forecasts of the economic situation	bei Prognosen über die Wirtschaftslage mitarbeiten
to withdraw worn notes	beschädigte Banknoten aus dem Verkehr ziehen
to register the transfer of gilt-edged securities	die Übertragung von mündelsicheren Wertpapieren registrieren
to have a large portfolio of stocks	einen großen Bestand an Wertpapieren haben
to tender for Treasury bills	die Ausgabe von Schatzwechseln übernehmen
to create a fund	einen Fonds schaffen
to have repercussions on the liquidity	Auswirkungen auf die Liquidität haben
fiduciary [fiˈdjuːʃəri]	treuhänderisch, fiduziarisch

Sätze und Redewendungen:

The Bank of England was founded in 1694.	Die Bank von England wurde 1694 gegründet.
In 1946, Parliament brought the Bank of England into public ownership.	1946 überführte das Parlament die Bank von England in öffentliches Eigentum.
The Governor, Deputy Governor and 16 Directors, who form the Court of Directors, are appointed by the sovereign on the recommendation of the Prime Minister.	Der Gouverneur, der Vizegouverneur und 16 Direktoren, die das Direktorium bilden, werden vom König auf Vorschlag des Premierministers ernannt.
The Bank of England is known as "The Old Lady of Threadneedle Street".	Die Bank von England ist unter der Bezeichnung „The Old Lady of Threadneedle Street" bekannt.
Ministerial accounts are kept at the Bank.	Konten der Ministerien werden bei der Bank von England geführt.
The major expenses of the government departments are disbursed through these accounts.	Die wichtigsten Ausgaben der Ministerien werden über diese Konten abgewickelt.
The government borrows the sums required by issuing Treasury bills or selling stocks.	Die Regierung beschafft sich die benötigten Summen durch Ausgabe von Schatzwechseln oder durch Verkauf von Wertpapieren.
A fiduciary issue is one that has no gold to back it but is backed only by other coins and securities.	Fiduziarisch ausgegebene Banknoten sind nicht durch Gold, sondern nur durch andere Münzen und Wertpapiere gedeckt.
The bank rate is a rate at which the Bank will rediscount first-class bills of exchange.	Der Diskontsatz ist ein fester Zinssatz, zu dem die Bank von England erstklassige Wechsel rediskontiert.

Bankwesen 147

The value of the pound dropped against the dollar.	Das Pfund fiel gegenüber dem Dollar.

4. Discount Market — Diskontmarkt

discount house	Diskont-, Wechselbank f
clearing bank	Clearing-, Girobank f
discount broker	Wechselmakler m
bill-broking	Wechselhandel m, Diskontgeschäft n
portfolio	Portefeuille n, Wechselbestand m
security portfolio	Wertpapierportefeuille n
discount of a bill	Wechseldiskont m
discount charges pl/credit	Diskontspesen pl/-kredit m
discount terms pl	Diskontbedingungen f pl
increase in the discount rate	Diskonterhöhung f
lowering of the discount rate	Diskontsenkung f
discount/bank bill	Diskont-/Bankwechsel m
Treasury bill	Schatzwechsel m, Schatzanweisung f
trade bill	Kunden-, Waren-, Handelswechsel m
foreign currency bill	Fremdwährungswechsel m
short-term gilt-edged securities pl	kurzfristige mündelsichere Wertpapiere n pl
corporation stock	Stadtanleihe f, Kommunalwerte m pl
paper securities pl	Papierwerte m pl, Effekten pl
provision of short-term money on the market	Versorgung f des Marktes mit kurzfristigem Geld
short-term stock investment	kurzfristiger Aktienbesitz m
surplus money	Geldüberhang m
to discount bills	Wechsel diskontieren
to issue short-term bills and bonds	kurzfristige Wechsel und Schuldverschreibungen ausgeben
to accept full liability on a bill	volle Haftung für einen Wechsel übernehmen
to be accepted/endorsed by a respectable bank	von einer angesehenen Bank akzeptiert/indossiert werden
to have a large portfolio of bills	einen großen Wechselbestand haben
to build a balanced portfolio of investment	einen ausgeglichenen Bestand an Wertpapieren zusammenstellen
to pay out interest	Zinsen auszahlen
to borrow money at a worthwhile rate of interest	Geld zu einem günstigen Zinssatz borgen
to lend at a higher rate of interest	zu einem höheren Zinssatz ausleihen
to force interest rates up	Zinssätze hinauftreiben

148 Banking

to repay within a month	innerhalb eines Monats zurückzahlen
to raise money	Geld aufbringen
to ease the shortage of cash	den Mangel an Bargeld beseitigen
to require funds	Kapital benötigen
to secure funds	sich Kapital verschaffen
to be forced into the Bank	gezwungen sein, bei der Bank von England Geld aufzunehmen
to be in debt	verschuldet sein
discountable	diskontfähig, diskontierbar

Sätze und Redewendungen:

The discount market consists of eleven firms who are members of the London Discount Market Association.	Der Diskontmarkt besteht aus 11 Firmen, die Mitglieder der L.D.M.A. sind.
The savings of the ordinary public are concentrated in the hand of banks, insurance companies, and building societies.	Die Ersparnisse der Durchschnittsbevölkerung befinden sich zu einem erheblichen Teil bei Banken, Versicherungen und Baugenossenschaften.
The discount house puts the customer in funds.	Die Diskontbank versorgt den Kunden mit Geldmitteln.
Almost all deals are by word of mouth only.	Beinahe alle Geschäfte werden nur mündlich abgemacht.
Money is not allowed to lie idle.	Geld darf nicht brach liegen.

5. Accounts — Konten

bank deposits *pl*	Bankeinlagen *f pl*, Bankguthaben *n* (*sing* und *pl*)
deposit banking	Depositengeschäft *n*
current account/bank giro	Kontokorrent-/Girokonto *n*
cash deposit	Bareinlage *f*
demand deposit *Am*	Sichteinlage *f*
deposit account (D. A.)	Depositen-, Einlagekonto *n*
savings deposit	Spareinlage *f*
current account advance, credit in current account	Kontokorrentkredit *m*
interest rates for current account credits	Kontokorrentkreditzinsen *m pl*
deposits on current account	Kontokorrenteinlagen *f pl*
current account balance	Kontokorrentguthaben *n*
balance of account	Kontostand *m*
current account customer	Kontokorrentkunde *m*

Bankwesen 149

depositor	Konto-, Depositeninhaber *m*
deposits and drawings *pl*	Einzahlungen *f pl* und Abhebungen *f pl*
deposits at notice	Einlagen *f pl* mit Kündigungsfrist *f*
deposit money, *Am* current account money	Giral-/Buchgeld *n*
paying-in book/slip	Einzahlungsbuch *n*/-beleg *m*
credit/debit slip	Gutschrift-/Lastschriftzettel *m*
stub	Kontrollabschnitt *m*
coded number	Code-Nummer *f*
post office savings bank	Postsparkasse *f*
post office savings account	Postsparkonto *n*
postal savings deposit	Postsparkassenguthaben *n*
postal giro central office	Postscheckzentrale *f*
postal giro office/service	Postscheckamt *n*/-verkehr *m*
postal giro account, *Am* postal check account	Postscheckkonto *n*
post office/postal money order	Postanweisung *f*
payment order	Zahlkarte *f*
direct debiting	automatischer Rechnungseinzug *m*
to have a current account with s.o.	mit jdm in laufender Rechnung stehen
to deposit money/to make a deposit	Geld einzahlen/eine Einzahlung leisten
to accept a deposit	eine Geldeinlage entgegennehmen
to enter a deposit in s.o.'s account	eine Einlage auf jds Konto verbuchen
to issue a cheque book	ein Scheckbuch ausstellen
to open a bank account	ein Bankkonto eröffnen
to pay into the current account	auf das Kontokorrentkonto einzahlen
to pay out sums of money from s.o.'s account	Geldbeträge von jds Konto auszahlen
to present to the cashier	an der Kasse vorlegen
to check a slip	einen Beleg überprüfen
to record on the customer's account	auf das Kundenkonto eintragen
to withdraw money	Geld abheben
to give notice	kündigen
to verify an account	ein Konto prüfen
to create bank money	Giralgeld schöpfen
to bear the bank stamp/the cashier's initials	den Bankstempel/das Namenszeichen des Kassenbeamten aufweisen
to make out a paying-in slip in duplicate	einen Einzahlungsbeleg in doppelter Ausfertigung ausstellen
free of charge	spesenfrei, kostenlos, unentgeltlich

on current account	im Kontokorrent; für laufende Rechnung
at long/at short notice	lang-/kurzfristig
in the back of the cheque book	hinten im Scheckbuch

Sätze und Redewendungen:

He was regarded as reliable.	Er wurde als verläßlich/kreditwürdig angesehen.
The bank extended current-account services to the new customer.	Die Bank eröffnete dem neuen Kunden ein Kontokorrentkonto.
He was asked for a reference.	Er wurde um eine Empfehlung gebeten.
He was recommended by his employer.	Er wurde von seinem Arbeitgeber empfohlen.
The balance of the account changes from day to day.	Der Kontostand ändert sich von Tag zu Tag.
Slips are provided to customers in handy booklets.	Belege erhalten die Kunden in praktischen Heftchen.
Slips are available on the counter.	Belege liegen auf dem Zahltisch.
The cashier stamps and initials both the stub and the credit slip.	Der Kassierer stempelt und unterzeichnet Kontrollabschnitt und Einzahlungsbeleg.
The cashier tears off the credit slip.	Der Kassierer trennt den Einzahlungsbeleg ab.
Dividends are paid direct to the holder's current account.	Dividenden werden direkt auf das laufende Konto des Inhabers einbezahlt.
a receipt for the safe delivery of a sum of money	eine Quittung für die zuverlässige Ablieferung eines Geldbetrages
a receipt for the amount paid in	eine Quittung über den eingezahlten Betrag
The cashier accepted the sum paid in.	Der Kassierer nahm die eingezahlte Summe entgegen.
The customer withdrew money from the account.	Der Kunde hob Geld vom Konto ab.
The banker makes an advance.	Die Bank gewährt einen Kredit.

6. Cheque — Scheck

drawer, issuer	Aussteller *m*, Trassant *m*
payee	Zahlungsempfänger *m*
payer	Bezogener *m*
presenter	Vorzeiger *m*
transferor	Indossant *m*
transferee [ˌtrænsfəˈriː]	Indossatar *m*

confirmed cheque *(bears the mark 'good')*	bestätigter Scheck *m (mit Gutvermerk)*
endorsement in blank	Blankoindossament *n*
specimen signatures *pl*	Unterschriftsproben *f pl*
cheque number	Schecknummer *f*
bank cheque, cashier's cheque	Bankscheck *m*
payment by cheque	Scheckzahlung *f*
crossed cheque	Verrechnungs-/Überweisungsscheck *m*
cheque card	Scheckkarte *f (z.B. Access, Barclaycard)*
order cheque	Orderscheck *m*
cheque — not to order	Rektascheck *m*
forgery of a cheque	Scheckfälschung *f*
to sign/to complete/to pass on a cheque	einen Scheck unterschreiben/ausfüllen/weitergeben
to pay by cheque	mit einem Scheck bezahlen
to fill in the amount both in words and in figures	den Betrag in Worten und Zahlen eintragen
to cross a cheque	einen Scheck kreuzen
to endorse a cheque	einen Scheck girieren/indossieren
to cover/to honour a cheque	für einen Scheck Deckung anschaffen/einen Scheck einlösen
to obtain cash	Bargeld erhalten
to collect the money	das Geld einziehen/kassieren
to fall due	fällig werden
to pay in funds	Beträge einzahlen
to waive charges	keine Gebühren erheben, auf Gebühren verzichten
to embezzle money	Geld unterschlagen
payable on demand/at a later date	auf Verlangen/zu einem späteren Zeitpunkt zahlbar
not negotiable [nɪˈgəʊʃjəbl]	nicht übertragbar, nur zur Verrechnung
dishonoured cheque	nicht eingelöster Scheck
post-dated cheque	vordatierter Scheck
a busy account	ein Konto mit vielen Umsätzen
to order	an Order
on presentation	bei Vorlage, bei Sicht
on the back of the cheque	auf der Rückseite des Schecks

Sätze und Redewendungen:

Specimen signatures must be lodged with the bank.	Unterschriftsproben müssen bei der Bank hinterlegt sein.

Two signatures are required.	Es sind zwei Unterschriften erforderlich.
A cheque can be safeguarded by crossing it.	Ein Scheck kann durch Kreuzen gesichert werden.
He signed his name on the back of the cheque.	Er setzte seinen Namen auf die Rückseite des Schecks.
The bank cleared the cheque.	Die Bank löste den Scheck ein.
The presenter of the cheque is known to the cashier.	Der Vorzeiger des Schecks ist dem Kassierer bekannt.
"Pay T. A. Doe ... or Order"	„Zahlen Sie T. A. Doe ... oder an Order"
"a/c Payee only"	„nur zur Verrechnung"
R. D. means "Refer to Drawer".	R. D. bedeutet „Zurück an Aussteller".
The cheque falls due at the end of the month.	Der Scheck wird am Ende des Monats fällig.
The cheque was cleared into his bank account.	Der Scheck wurde seinem Konto gutgeschrieben.
He paid the cheque into his account.	Er zahlte den Scheck auf sein Konto ein.
The firm has a sizable balance on its current account.	Die Firma hat ein beträchtliches Guthaben auf ihrem Kontokorrentkonto.
The bank keeps accounts free of charge.	Die Bank führt Konten spesenfrei.
The cashier ensures that forgeries do not remain undetected.	Der Kassierer sorgt dafür, daß Fälschungen nicht unentdeckt bleiben.
He committed the crime of forgery.	Er beging eine Fälschung.
Customers are advised that the bank reserves the right at its discretion to postpone payment of cheques drawn against uncleared effects which may have been credited to the account.	Die Kunden werden davon in Kenntnis gesetzt, daß sich die Bank das Recht vorbehält, nach ihrem Ermessen die Einlösung von Schecks zurückzustellen, die auf noch nicht verrechnete Gutschriften gezogen wurden.
Cheque cards/Bankers' cards guarantee customers' cheques up to a maximum of £30.	Scheckkarten sind eine Garantie für die Zahlung eines Kundenschecks bis zur Höhe von £ 30.
The cheque is drawn for £50.	Der Scheck lautet auf 50 Pfund.

7. Bill of Exchange (B/E)

Wechsel

bills in portfolio [pɔː'fəuljəu]	Wechselbestand *m*
bills payable/receivable	Wechselschulden *f pl* /-forderungen *f pl*
drawer/issuer of a B/E	Wechselaussteller *m* /-geber *m*, Trassant *m*
drawee [drɔː'iː], acceptor	Wechselbezogener *m*, Trassat *m*
payee [pei'iː]	Zahlungsempfänger *m*, Remittent *m*
unconditional order	unbedingte Anweisung *f*

Bankwesen

negotiable instrument	begebbares Papier n
Bills of Exchange Act	Wechselrecht n
discount banker	diskontierende Bank f, Diskontbank f
face/back of a bill	Vorder-/Rückseite f eines Wechsels
place and date of issue	Ausstellungsort m und -datum n
time of payment/maturity	Zahlungsfrist f/Fälligkeit f
name and address of the drawee/drawer	Name m und Anschrift f des Bezogenen/Ausstellers
stamp duty	Wechselmarke f
endorsement	Indossament n, Indossierung f
negotiation [nɪˌgəʊʃiˈeiʃən]	Begebung f, Weitergabe f
endorsee [ˌendɔːˈsiː]	Indossatar m
endorser	Indossant m
prolongation, renewal	Prolongation f
protest/noting of a B/E	Wechselprotest m
protest for non-acceptance/non-payment	Protest m mangels Annahme/Zahlung
three days of grace pl	drei Respekttage m pl, drei Tage Nachfrist f
recourse	Regreß m, Rückgriff m
discounting of a B/E	Wechseldiskontierung f
proceeds pl of discounting	Diskonterlös m
acceptance credit	Akzeptkredit m

Types of Bills of Exchange (Am *Drafts*)   *Wechselarten*

inland/domestic bill	Inlandswechsel m
foreign/external bill (Am bill)	Auslandswechsel m
bill at sight, sight bill/draft	Sichtwechsel m
bill after date	Datowechsel m
bill after sight, time draft	Nachsichtwechsel m
bill of credit	Kreditbrief m
clean bill/draft	Tratte f ohne Dokumente
documentary bill/draft	Dokumententratte f
commercial/trade bill, Am trade acceptance	Handels-/Warenwechsel m
fine trade bill	erstklassiger Handelswechsel m
finance bill	Finanzwechsel m
usance bill, bill at usance	Usowechsel m
short/long bill	Wechsel m mit einer Laufzeit bis/über 10 Tage
accommodation bill	Gefälligkeitstratte f
promissory note (P/N)	Eigen-, Solawechsel m, Schuldschein m
I.O.U. ("I Owe You")	Schuldschein m
to accept a bill	einen Wechsel annehmen

154 Banking

to be due on ...	fällig sein am ...
to endorse/negotiate a B/E	einen Wechsel indossieren/weitergeben
to discount a bill with a bank	einen Wechsel bei einer Bank diskontieren
to honour/to dishonour a bill on date	einen Wechsel bei Fälligkeit einlösen/nicht einlösen
to give notice of non-acceptance	Nichtannahme vormerken
to spread out payment over a long period	Zahlung auf einen langen Zeitraum verteilen
to specialize in acceptance	sich auf das Akzept spezialisieren
to have a bill protested	einen Wechsel zu Protest gehen lassen
to have recourse to s.o.	auf jdn Rückgriff nehmen
on demand	auf Verlangen
on presentation	bei Sicht
on due date	bei Fälligkeit
revocable/irrevocable	widerruflich/unwiderruflich
negotiable/non-negotiable	begebbar/nicht begebbar
eligible for discount	diskontfähig

Sätze und Redewendungen:

The firm presented the bill of exchange to the acceptance house named by the customer.	Die Firma legte den Wechsel der vom Kunden angegebenen Akzeptbank vor.
The credit will be confirmed by a British bank.	Der Kredit wird von einer englischen Bank bestätigt werden.
Confirming houses offer acceptance of bills as a further service to exporters.	C. H. übernehmen für Exporteure als zusätzliche Dienstleistung das Akzept von Wechseln.
Merchant bankers are prepared to accept bills within a reasonable limit.	Remboursbanken akzeptieren Wechsel bis zu einer annehmbaren Höchstgrenze.
The exporter draws funds up to the agreed limit by means of bills of exchange.	Der Exporteur beschafft sich durch Wechsel Geldmittel bis zu einem festgesetzten Höchstbetrag.
The drawer, before negotiating or before handing a B/E to the payee, sends it to the drawee for acceptance.	Bevor der Aussteller den Wechsel indossiert oder an den Begünstigten weitergibt, sendet er ihn dem Bezogenen zum Akzept.
The drawee accepts by writing his name across the face of the bill.	Der Bezogene akzeptiert dadurch, daß er seinen Namen quer über die Vorderseite des Wechsels schreibt.
The holder presents the bill for payment when it is due.	Der Wechselinhaber legt den Wechsel bei Fälligkeit zur Zahlung vor.

The drawer has to wait until the bill matures.
If the drawee does not pay the sum specified, the owner of the bill may resort to endorsers.

The bill falls due for payment three months and three days after date.
The foreign bill of exchange is drawn in a set of three, known respectively as the First, Second and Third of Exchange.

Der Aussteller muß warten, bis der Wechsel fällig wird.
Falls der Bezogene die angegebene Summe nicht bezahlt, kann der Wechselinhaber auf die Indossanten zurückgreifen.
Der Wechsel wird drei Monate und drei Tage nach Ausstellungsdatum zur Zahlung fällig.
Der Auslandswechsel wird in drei Exemplaren ausgestellt, die der Reihe nach als Prima, Sekunda und Tertia bekannt sind.

VI. Stock Exchange

1. General Terms

stock exchange, Am stock market
commodity exchange
share market
bond market

auction sale
exchange regulations pl
exchange rate
stock prices pl and yields pl
trend of the market
daily list, Am stock list
market price/value
nominal/par value
official quotation
bid price
take-over bid
placing (of a loan)

covering purchase
bargain
bargain book
stamp duty, transfer tax Am
boom/bull market
slump/bear market
moderate/sharp rise
sharp fall

Börse

Allgemeine Begriffe

Wertpapierbörse f
Warenbörse f
Aktienmarkt m
Markt m für festverzinsliche Wertpapiere, Pfandbriefmarkt m, Rentenmarkt m

Versteigerung f
Börsenordnung f
Börsenkurs m
Börsenkurse m pl und Erträge m pl
Börsentendenz f
Börsenbericht m, -zettel m
Kurswert m, Börsenkurs m
Nominal-/Nennwert m
Notierung f, amtlicher Kurs m
gebotener Kurs m, Geldkurs m
Übernahmeangebot n
Unterbringung f, Plazierung f (einer Anleihe f)

Deckungskauf m
(Börsen-) Abschluß m
Schlußnotenregister n
Börsenumsatzsteuer f
Hausse f
Baisse f
leichter/starker Kursanstieg m
starker Rückgang m

156 Stock Exchange

share certificate, *Am* stock certificate	Anteilschein *m*, Aktienzertifikat *n*, Kapitalanteilschein *m*
account/settlement/making-up day, ticket-day	Börsenabrechnungstag *m*, Liquidationstag *m*
making-up price	Abrechnungs-, Liquidationskurs *m*
speculative operation/transaction	Spekulationsgeschäft *n*
cash/spot transaction	Kassageschäft *n*
future/forward transaction, option dealing	Termingeschäft *n*
contango	Reportgeschäft *n*
backwardation	Deportgeschäft *n*
call/put option	Vor-/Rückprämiengeschäft *n*
Baltic (*Mercantile and Shipping*) Exchange	Getreidemarkt *m* (*in London*)
the London Tea Auctions (*in Plantation House*)	Londoner Teemarkt *m*

2. Persons Involved

Beteiligte

stock exchange agent	Börsenvertreter *m*
stock exchange speculator/operator	Berufsspekulant *m*
jobber, dealer	Effektenhändler *m*
jobber's turn	Gewinn *m* des Effektenhändlers
bull	Haussier *m*, Haussespekulant *m*
bear	Baissier *m*, Baissespekulant *m*
stag	Konzertzeichner *m*
underwriter	Garant *m* einer Effektenemission
short seller	Leerverkäufer *m*, Baissier *m*
forward seller	Terminverkäufer *m*
admission to quotation/permission to deal	Börsenzulassung *f*
institutional investors *pl*	Kapitalsammelstellen *f pl*

3. Types of Securities

Effektenarten

a) Fixed interest securities

Festverzinsliche Wertpapiere

debentures *pl*	Schuldverschreibungen *f pl*, Obligationen *f pl*
fixed debentures *pl*	festverzinsliche Schuldverschreibungen *f pl*
simple/naked debentures *pl*	ungesicherte Schuldverschreibungen *f pl*
redeemable/irredeemable bond	tilgbare/untilgbare Obligation *f*
mortgage debenture/bond	hypothekarisch gesicherte Obligation *f*
premium/convertible bond	Prämien-/Wandelanleihe *f*

Börse   157

Treasury bond	Schatzwechsel *m*
consols *pl*	Staatsanleihen *f pl*
bearer/registered bonds *pl*	Inhaber-/Namensobligationen *f pl*
industrial bonds *pl*	Industrieobligationen *f pl*
baby bonds *pl Am*	Kleinobligationen *f pl (bis zu $100)*

b) Shares   *Aktien*

issue of shares	Aktienemission *f*
subscription right/option on new shares	Bezugsrecht *n* auf neue Aktien
bonus issue	Ausgabe *f* von Gratisaktien
yield to redemption	Effektivverzinsung *f*
majority of shares	Aktienmehrheit *f*
blue chips *pl*	Spitzenpapiere *n pl*/-werte *m pl*
steels/chemicals/textiles *pl*	Stahl-/Chemie-/Textilwerte *m pl*
equity shares *pl*, equities *pl*	Dividendenpapiere *n pl*
ordinary shares *pl*	Stammaktien *f pl*
preference shares *pl*, preferred stock	Vorzugsaktien *f pl*
founder shares *pl*	Gründeraktien *f pl*
bearer/registered share	Inhaber-/Namensaktie *f*
investment shares *pl*	Investmentanteile *m pl*
to turn fixed capital into cash	Anlagekapital in Bargeld verwandeln
to buy/to sell securities/shares	Wertpapiere/Aktien kaufen/verkaufen
to buy/to sell at best	bestens kaufen/verkaufen
to sell short	bei fallendem Kurs verkaufen, fixen
to sell at a fixed price	zu einem festgesetzten Kurs verkaufen
to be admitted to the Stock Exchange	börsenfähig/zur Börse zugelassen sein
to trade on the Stock Exchange	an der Börse handeln
to put in a tender	ein Angebot einreichen
to sell at a premium	über dem Nennwert/über pari verkaufen
to be at par	al pari stehen
to earn 6 per cent for the holder	dem Inhaber 6% einbringen
to sell shares at the best possible price	Aktien zum bestmöglichen Kurs verkaufen
to make a note in the bargain book	eine Eintragung in das Schlußnotenregister vornehmen
to be easier	schwächer liegen
to be in great demand	stark gefragt sein
to hold up well	sich gut halten
to plough back profits	Erträge wieder anlegen
to expect a fall in share prices	einen Rückgang der Aktienkurse erwarten

Stock Exchange

to carry over	prolongieren
to apply for quotation	Notierung beantragen
to scrutinize companies rigorously	Gesellschaften streng prüfen
to service a loan	Zinsen und Amortisationsdienst für eine Anleihe bestreiten
to float/to launch an issue	eine Anleihe auflegen
to subscribe to/to oversubscribe an issue	eine Anleihe zeichnen/überzeichnen
to place an issue	eine Anleihe unterbringen
to hedge	sich absichern
to even up	glattstellen
to take in shares	Aktien hereinnehmen
fixed interest bearing	festverzinslich
redeemable	kündbar, tilgbar
irredeemable	unkündbar, untilgbar, nicht zurückzahlbar
bearish	auf Baisse gerichtet
bullish	steigend, haussierend
lively, buoyant, brisk	lebhaft
dull, sluggish	lustlos
low/high period	niedrig/hoch notierend
firm	fest
patchy	uneinheitlich
defaulting	zahlungsunfähig, im Verzug, säumig
at a discount, under pari	unter pari, unter dem Nennwert
marketable	börsenfähig
cum-div, with dividend	mit Dividendenausschüttung
ex-div, without dividend	ohne Dividendenausschüttung

Sätze und Redewendungen:

The company kept its list of shareholders up-to-date.	Die Gesellschaft hielt das Aktionärsverzeichnis auf dem laufenden.
The buyer acquired large blocks of shares.	Der Käufer erwarb große Aktienpakete.
Investments change hands quickly.	Wertpapiere wechseln schnell den Besitzer.
Loans are floated at regular intervals.	Anleihen werden in regelmäßigen Abständen aufgelegt.
Bonds pay a fixed rate of interest throughout their lives.	Obligationen werfen während ihrer Laufzeit feste Zinsen ab.
A mortgage debenture carries a mortgage on the assets of a company.	Eine hypothekarisch gesicherte Schuldverschreibung ist mit einer Hypothek auf die Vermögenswerte einer Gesellschaft verbunden.

Börse 159

Only experts may deal on commodity markets.	Nur Fachleute sind an Warenbörsen zugelassen.
Products such as tea and wool must be sampled by the buyers.	Die Käufer müssen bei Tee und Wolle Proben entnehmen.
They deal in the British commodity markets.	Sie tätigen an englischen Warenbörsen Geschäfte.
They auction their lots.	Sie versteigern ihre Waren(posten).
The highest bid wins./Sales are made to the highest bidder.	Der Meistbietende erhält den Zuschlag.
They decide the limits of prices to which they will go.	Sie legen die Preisgrenzen fest, bis zu denen sie gehen wollen.
Sugar prices fluctuate widely.	Zuckerpreise schwanken stark.
Vegetables are sold at rock-bottom prices.	Gemüse wird zu Schleuderpreisen abgesetzt.
They face serious losses.	Sie riskieren erhebliche Verluste.
Futures are sold at firm prices.	Termingeschäfte werden zu festen Preisen abgeschlossen.
Buyers and sellers are brought into contact with one another.	Käufer und Verkäufer kommen miteinander in Kontakt.
The broker strikes a bargain with the jobber.	Der Börsenmakler wickelt mit dem Effektenhändler ein Geschäft ab.
Jobbers specialize in particular fields.	Effektenhändler spezialisieren sich auf besondere Bereiche.
The market is bullish.	Der Markt zeigt steigende Tendenz.
He urgently needs to sell shares.	Er ist gezwungen, Aktien zu verkaufen.
The firm they have invested in is not in too sound a position.	Die Firma, in die sie investiert haben, steht nicht besonders günstig.
The price rises steeply.	Der Kurs geht sprunghaft in die Höhe.
Confidence declines.	Das Vertrauen schwindet.
Prices begin to slip.	Die Kurse fangen an, abzubröckeln.
All bargains must be settled on the Account Day.	Alle Abschlüsse müssen am Liquidationstag abgewickelt sein.
The speculators sell in booms and buy in slumps.	Die Spekulanten verkaufen bei steigenden und kaufen bei fallenden Kursen.
The companies whose shares are dealt with on the Stock Exchange ...	Die Gesellschaften, deren Aktien an der Börse gehandelt werden ...
The Stock Exchange year is divided into twenty-four Accounts.	Das Börsenjahr wird in 24 Liquidationstermine eingeteilt.

VII. Insurance — Versicherungswesen

1. General Terms — Allgemeine Begriffe

insurance contract/business	Versicherungsvertrag m/-geschäft n
contract of indemnity	Garantievertrag m
personal insurance	Personenversicherung f
property insurance	Sach-/Schadensversicherung f
insurance commission	Versicherungsprovision f
compulsory insurance	Zwangsversicherung f
indemnity	Entschädigung f, Schadenersatz m
subrogation	Gläubigerwechsel m, Forderungsübergang m, -abtretung f
premium rate/income	Prämiensatz m/-eingang m
settlement of a claim	Schadensregulierung f
in the event of damage or loss	im Schadensfall m
damage to property	Sachschaden m
indemnity sum	Entschädigungsbetrag m
depreciation in value	Wertminderung f
assessment of damage	Schadensfeststellung f (Wert)
calculation of probabilities	Wahrscheinlichkeitsrechnung f
expectation of loss	Schadenserwartung f
incidence of loss	Schadenshäufigkeit f
actuarial theory	Versicherungsmathematik f
actuary	Versicherungsmathematiker m
statistician [ˌstætisˈtiʃən]	Statistiker m
statistical records pl	statistische Unterlagen f pl
mortality	Sterblichkeit f
sickness	Krankheit f
retirement	Ruhestand m

2. Persons Involved — Beteiligte

the insured	der Versicherte m
insurer/underwriter	Versicherer m, Versicherungsträger m
individual underwriter	Einzelversicherer m
Lloyd's (Corporation), Lloyd's underwriters	Lloyds (Vereinigung privater Einzelversicherer)
beneficiary [ˌbeniˈfiʃəri]	Begünstigter m
aggrieved party	Geschädigter m
claimant	Forderungsberechtigter m
policy holder	Inhaber m einer Versicherungspolice/Versicherungsnehmer m
applicant for insurance, proposer of a contract	Antragsteller m

Versicherungswesen 161

insurance broker	Versicherungsmakler *m*
general average adjuster	Dispacheur *m*
surveyor [səˈveiə]	Havariekommissar *m*
home-service agent	Vertreter *m* der Kleinlebensversicherung

3. Documents / Dokumente

proposal form	Versicherungsantrag *m*
standard/floating/open policy	Normal-/Pauschal-/Generalpolice *f*
cover note	Deckungsbestätigung *f*
insurance certificate	Versicherungszertifikat *n*
survey report	Schadenszertifikat *n*
reinsurance policy	Rückversicherungspolice *f*
comprehensive policy	Vollkaskoversicherung *f*

4. Types of Insurance / Versicherungsarten

a) Marine insurance / Seeversicherung

hull/cargo/freight insurance	Kasko-/Kargo-/Frachtversicherung *f*
general average (G. A.)	große Havarie *f*
particular average (P. A.)	besondere Havarie *f*
petty average	kleine Havarie *f*
W. P. A. (= With Particular Average)	„mit besonderer Havarie"
F. P. A. (= Free of Particular Average)	„frei von Beschädigung (außer im Strandungsfall)"
T. L. O. (= Total Loss Only)	„nur gegen Totalverlust"
A. A. R. (= Against All Risks)	All-Risks-Klausel *(bes. Risiken, jedoch nur gegen Zuschläge)*
"warehouse to warehouse"	„von Haus zu Haus"

b) Fire insurance, insurance against fire / Feuerversicherung, Brandschadenversicherung

fire loss	Brandschaden *m*
fire office	Brandkasse *f*
fire insurance on domestic and business premises	Feuerversicherung *f* auf Haus- und Geschäftsräume
fire protection	Feuerschutz *m*
fire brigade	Feuerwehr *f*

c) Life assurance/insurance / Lebensversicherung

expectation of life	Lebenserwartung *f*
life office, life insurance company	Lebensversicherungsanstalt *f*

Insurance

whole life insurance	Todesfallversicherung *f*
endowment insurance	Erlebensfallversicherung *f*
group life insurance	Gruppenversicherung *f*, (betriebliche) Pensionsversicherung *f*
annuity	Rente *f*
mutual benefit society	Versicherungsverein *m* auf Gegenseitigkeit
mutual life offices	Lebensversicherungsverein *m* auf Gegenseitigkeit
industrial life offices/home service offices	Kleinlebensversicherung *f*

d) Motor vehicle insurance — *Kraftfahrzeugversicherung*

accident insurance	Unfallversicherung *f*
third-party insurance, *Am* liability insurance	Haftpflichtversicherung *f*
third-party, fire and theft	Haftpflicht- und Teilkaskoversicherung *f*
fully comprehensive cover	Vollkasko- und Insassenversicherung *f*
$100 deductible	100 Dollar Selbstbehalt *m*

e) Other types of insurance — *Andere Versicherungsarten*

burglary insurance	Einbruchdiebstahlversicherung *f*
household and personal effects insurance	Hausratversicherung *f*
hail/windstorm/rain insurance	Hagel-/Sturm-/Regenversicherung *f*
National Insurance (*GB*)	Sozialversicherung *f*
old-age pension	Altersrente *f*
disability benefits *pl*	Invalidenrente *f*
hospital expense	Krankenhauskosten *pl*
sickness benefits *pl*	Krankengeld *n*
unemployment benefits *pl*	Arbeitslosenunterstützung *f*
aviation insurance	Luftfahrtversicherung *f*
products' liability insurance	Produktversicherung *f*
credit insurance	Kreditversicherung *f*
fidelity guarantee insurance	Kautionsversicherung *f*
employers' liability insurance	Haftpflichtversicherung *f* des Arbeitgebers
to insure	*tr* versichern lassen/*itr* Versicherung gewähren
to fill in a proposal form	einen Versicherungsantrag ausfüllen
to effect/to take out insurance	eine Versicherung abschließen
to be insured with a company	bei einer Gesellschaft versichert sein

Versicherungswesen

to be insured against fire	gegen Feuer versichert sein
to suffer a loss	einen Verlust erleiden
to minimize losses	Verluste klein halten
to offer cover	Deckung bieten
to underwrite a risk	ein Risiko versichern
to indemnify s.o. for a loss	jdn für einen Verlust entschädigen
to pay out/to provide compensation	Schadensersatz auszahlen/gewähren
to substantiate the claim	den Schadensnachweis erbringen
to have fully comprehensive cover	Vollkasko, einschließlich Insassen, versichert sein
to incur liability	die Haftpflicht übernehmen
to charge s.o. a fair premium	jdm eine angemessene Prämie berechnen
to refund the premium	die Prämie zurückerstatten
to raise s.o.'s premium	jds Prämie erhöhen
to share economic risks	wirtschaftliche Risiken teilen
to warrant the truth of the statements	die Richtigkeit der Erklärungen bescheinigen
to take account of depreciation	die Wertminderung berücksichtigen
to commence at death	zum Zeitpunkt des Todes beginnen
to cover death or retirement of the insured	Tod oder Ruhestand des Versicherten decken
to put in a claim against s. o.	gegen jdn eine Schadensersatzforderung einbringen
insurable	versicherbar
non-insurable	nicht versicherbar
sufficiently/insufficiently covered by insurance	ausreichend/ungenügend durch Versicherung gedeckt
voidable	anfechtbar
susceptible to insurance	versicherungsfähig
up to a certain limit	bis zu einer gewissen Grenze
at a pre-arranged rate	zu einem vorher vereinbarten Satz
recoverable	einziehbar
payable at death	zahlbar im Todesfall
liable to pay damages	schadenersatzpflichtig

Sätze und Redewendungen:

Every insurance policy defines the risk that is being insured against.	Jede Versicherungspolice legt das Risiko fest, das versichert wird.
He is fully insured against fire.	Er ist gegen alle Schäden durch Feuer versichert.
The claims were paid promptly and in full.	Die Ansprüche wurden prompt und in voller Höhe bezahlt.

An applicant fills in a proposal form.
False answers to the questions render the policy voidable.
He was suspected of fraudulent intent.
No claim arises.
Your claim will fail.

He died before the policy matured.

The sum will be paid out to widows and orphans, when death occurs.
He is entitled to be indemnified for the loss.
Policies covering not only fire but storm and tempest, burst pipes, explosions and burglary were introduced.

Building societies insist that mortgages must be backed by life assurances.
Reinsurance through London as a hedge against possible heavy claims is a normal practice.

Lloyd's underwriters engage as principals in the sale of insurance cover.
Insurance companies have stood considerable losses.

Ein Antragsteller füllt einen Versicherungsantrag aus.
Falsche Angaben machen die Police anfechtbar.
Er wurde betrügerischer Absichten verdächtigt.
Es entsteht kein Anspruch.
Ihr Anspruch wird abgelehnt werden.

Er starb, bevor die Versicherung fällig wurde.

Im Todesfalle wird die Summe an Witwen und Waisen ausbezahlt.
Er hat ein Recht auf Entschädigung für den Verlust.
Man führte Versicherungen ein, die nicht nur Feuer-, sondern auch Sturm- und Unwetterschäden, Wasserrohrbruch, Explosionen und Einbruch decken.

Bausparkassen verlangen, daß Hypotheken durch Lebensversicherungen gedeckt werden.
Rückversicherung bei einer Londoner Versicherungsgesellschaft gegen eventuelle hohe Versicherungsansprüche ist allgemein üblich.

Einzelversicherer von Lloyd's schließen als Unternehmer Versicherungen ab.
Versicherungsgesellschaften haben beträchtliche Verluste hinnehmen müssen.

VIII. Customs

Zollwesen

1. Tariffs and Duties

Zölle und Abgaben

customs (authorities)/administration
customs area/territory
customhouse, customs office
customs duty/charges *pl*
customs convention/regulations *pl*

G.A.T.T. *(General Agreement on Tariffs and Trade)*

Zollbehörde *f*/-verwaltung *f*
Zollgebiet *n*
Zollamt *n*
Zollgebühren *f pl*
Zollabkommen *n*/-bestimmungen *f pl*

GATT *(Allgemeines Zoll- und Handelsabkommen n)*

most-favoured-nation clause	Meistbegünstigungsklausel f
customs/tariff union	Zollunion f
tariff policy/protection	Zollpolitik f/-schutz m
tariff preferences pl/concessions pl	Zollpräferenzen f pl/-zugeständnisse n pl
tariff negotiations pl	Zollverhandlungen f pl
abolition of tariff walls	Beseitigung f der Zollschranken
tariff legislation/information	Zollgesetzgebung f/-auskunft f
tariff nomenclature/agreement	Zolltarifschema n/-abkommen n
customs tariff	Zolltarif m
tariff classification	Tarifierung f
increase of customs	Zollerhöhung f
customs documents pl	Zollpapiere n pl
customs declaration	Zollinhaltserklärung f/(Paket-)Inhaltserklärung f
customs examination	Zollrevision f
bill of entry/customs entry	Zolleinfuhrschein m
transire [trænsˈaiəri]	Zolldurchlaßschein m
customs bond note	Zollbegleitschein m
customs bill of clearance	Zollabfertigungsschein m
permit	Zollfreischein m
customs warrant/debenture	Zollauslieferungsschein m/Rückschein m
customs formalities pl/receipt	Zollformalitäten f pl/-quittung f
customs invoice/facilities pl	Zollfaktura f/-erleichterungen f pl
entrepôt trade	Transithandel m

2. Types of Tariffs

Zollarten

specific tariff	spezifischer Zoll m
revenue duty	Finanzzoll m
preferential duty/tariff	Vorzugs-/Präferenzzoll m
sliding-scale tariff	Gleitzoll m
protective duty	Schutzzoll m
export/import tariff	Ausfuhr-/Einfuhrzoll m
external/internal tariff	Außen-/Binnenzoll m
ad valorem tariff	Wertzoll m
customs receipts pl/revenue	Zolleinnahmen f pl
tariff quota	Zollkontingent n
rate of customs, rate of duty, customs rate	Zollsatz m
customs reduction, tariff cut	Zollsenkung f
tariff heading	Tarifposition f
customs shed/store	Zollschuppen m/-speicher m
goods in bond, bonded goods pl	Waren f pl unter Zollverschluß
bonding	Zolleinlagerung f
customs seal	Zollverschluß m/-plombe f
customs offence/penalty	Zollvergehen n/-strafe f

166 Customs

evasion of customs	Zollhinterziehung f
confiscation/forfeiture of undeclared goods	Beschlagnahme f/zollamtliche Einziehung f nicht deklarierter Waren
customs drawback	Zollrückvergütung f
Free Port	Freihafen m
transshipment	Umschlag m, Umladung f
to collect/to levy customs duty	Zoll einziehen/erheben
to be subject to duty	zollpflichtig sein
to impose duty on s. th.	etw mit Zoll belegen
to pay duty on s. th.	etw verzollen/Zoll zahlen für etw
to enter goods at the customs office	Güter zur Verzollung beim Zollamt anmelden
to furnish/to submit customs documents	Zolldokumente vorlegen
to attend to the customs formalities	die Zollformalitäten erledigen
to pass through the customs	durch den Zoll gehen
to clear goods through the customs	Waren zollamtlich abfertigen
to decrease/to lower customs	Zölle senken
to increase/to raise customs	Zölle erhöhen
to smuggle	schmuggeln
to warehouse	unter Zollverschluß bringen
to be in bond	im Zollverschluß liegen
to be engaged in entrepôt trade	im Transithandel tätig sein
to transship	umschlagen, umladen
customs cleared	zollamtlich abgefertigt
duty-paid	verzollt
dutiable, customable, liable to duty	zollpflichtig
non-dutiable	nicht zollpflichtig
deceptive, misleading	irreführend

Sätze und Redewendungen:

the collection of duties, taxes and fees due on imported merchandise	der Einzug von Zöllen, Steuern und Abgaben auf Importwaren
The Bureau of Customs (Am) is charged with the inspection of all export declarations and permits.	Das Bureau of Customs hat die Aufgabe, alle Ausfuhrerklärungen und -bewilligungen zu prüfen.
Customs barriers are abolished within a customs union.	Innerhalb einer Zollunion gibt es keine Zollschranken.
A common tariff policy is maintained by the members of a customs union.	Die Mitglieder einer Zollunion verfolgen eine gemeinsame Zollpolitik.

Specific duties are imposed on a commodity per unit of the quantity imported.	Spezifischen Zöllen wird die Stückzahl der importierten Menge einer Ware zugrunde gelegt.
Ad valorem duties are imposed on the value of the merchandise.	Wertzölle werden vom Wert der Ware erhoben.
A country can give most-favoured-nation treatment to a particular country.	Ein Land kann einem speziellen Land Meistbegünstigung einräumen.
Goods arriving in the United Kingdom must be entered for customs clearance on a form known as an "Entry".	Waren, die in das Vereinigte Königreich eingeführt werden, müssen zur Verzollung in ein als „Entry" bezeichnetes Formular eingetragen werden.
"Entry" forms are prepared in quadruplicate.	„Zollerklärungen" werden vierfach ausgefertigt.
The customs return one copy of the "Entry" to the importer on payment of duty.	Die Zollbehörde gibt dem Importeur nach Bezahlung des Zolls eine Ausfertigung der Zollerklärung zurück.
Duty is payable in advance.	Zoll muß im voraus bezahlt werden.
Customs duties represent an increase in the price of goods to home consumers.	Zölle haben für den Konsumenten im Inland eine Erhöhung des Warenpreises zur Folge.
The amount of duty paid can be claimed as a drawback from the customs authorities.	Der bezahlte Zoll kann als Rückvergütung von der Zollbehörde zurückverlangt werden.
Bonded warehouses permit the landing of cargo on which duty has not been paid.	Zollspeicher bieten die Möglichkeit, unverzollte Waren zu löschen.
The owner of bonded warehouses gives a bond to the Government promising not to release goods from the warehouse until the duty has been paid.	Der Eigentümer von Zollspeichern verpflichtet sich der Regierung gegenüber, keine Waren vor Bezahlung des Zolls freizugeben.
The bond names a penalty to be paid should any infringement occur.	Die Verpflichtungserklärung bestimmt eine Geldstrafe, die bei Übertretung bezahlt werden muß.
The duty is payable only on removal of the goods from the bonded warehouse for sale on the home market.	Der Zoll muß nur dann bezahlt werden, wenn die Waren dem Zollspeicher zum Verkauf auf dem Inlandsmarkt entnommen werden.
The value-added tax is assessed on the c.i.f. duty-paid value of the goods.	Die Mehrwertsteuer wird vom cif-Wert der verzollten Ware berechnet.
A rate of 6 per cent is applicable to certain foods.	Auf bestimmte Nahrungsmittel wird eine Abgabe von 6% erhoben.

For the determination of the dutiable value customs officials may require additional documents.
No special form is prescribed for the certificate of origin.

Zur Festsetzung des zollpflichtigen Werts können Zollbeamte zusätzliche Unterlagen verlangen.
Für das Ursprungszeugnis ist kein spezielles Formular vorgeschrieben.

IX. Transport

1. General Terms

means of transport/of conveyance
mode of transportation
public (means of) conveyance
risk of conveyance
carriage/conveyance of goods
road haulage
long-distance road haulage, long-distance hauling *Am*
transit
transit cargo/goods *pl*
transit traffic
overland/intercity transportation
surface transport(ation)
inland carriage
transcontinental traffic
transport route
transport industry/trade
common carrier, haulier

haulage firm
transporter
contract of carriage
transport costs/rates *pl*
carrier's charges *pl*
liability of the carrier
transport loss/insurance
quantity of available traffic
total transports *pl*
transportation speed
voyage distance
back loads *pl*
place of dispatch/of destination
date of dispatch/of delivery

Transportwesen

Allgemeine Begriffe

Transport-/Beförderungsmittel *n* *(sing* und *pl)*
Transportart *f*
öffentliches Verkehrsmittel *n*
Transportgefahr *f*
Gütertransport *m*
Güterkraftverkehr *m*
Güterfernverkehr *m*, Fernlastverkehr *m*
Transit *m*, Durchfuhr *f*
Transitladung *f*/-waren *f pl*
Transitverkehr *m*
Überlandverkehr *m*
Landtransport *m*
Binnenverkehr *m*
transkontinentaler Verkehr *m*
Transportweg *m*
Transportgewerbe *n*
Transportunternehmer *m*, (öffentlicher) Frachtführer *m*/Spediteur *m*
Transportunternehmen *n*
Transportfahrzeug *n*
Transportvertrag *m*
Transportkosten *pl*/-tarif *m*
Speditionsgebühren *f pl*
Transporthaftung *f*
Transportschaden *m*/-versicherung *f*
Verkehrsaufkommen *n*
Transportvolumen *n*
Transportgeschwindigkeit *f*
Fahrkilometer *m pl*
Rückfracht *f*
Versand-/Bestimmungsort *m*
Versanddatum *n*/Liefertermin *m*

freight list	Versandliste *f*
advice of dispatch	Versandanzeige *f*
delivery service	Zustelldienst *m*
large-scale/low-cost transportation	Transport *m* im großen/zu niedrigen Preisen
transport policy/planning	Verkehrspolitik *f*/-planung *f*
to convey	befördern, transportieren *(Güter und Personen)*
to haul	transportieren, befördern *(Güter)*
to transport by land/by sea/by air	auf dem Land-/See-/Luftweg befördern
to contract for the carriage of goods	einen Vertrag über die Beförderung von Waren abschließen
to provide the necessary transport	die erforderlichen Transportmittel beschaffen
to group freight, to consolidate shipments	Sammelladungen zusammenstellen
to shift	verschieben, verlagern
to be damaged in transport	auf dem Transport Schaden leiden
transportable	transportierbar
movable	beweglich
containerized	in Container verpackt
from door to door	von Haus zu Haus
in transit	auf dem Transport, unterwegs
at destination	am Bestimmungsort
at regular times	zu bestimmten Zeiten, fahrplanmäßig
at a very high speed	mit sehr großer Geschwindigkeit
by public transport	mit öffentlichen Verkehrsmitteln

Sätze und Redewendungen:

The function of transport is to move goods and passengers from one place to the other.	Das Transportwesen hat die Aufgabe, Güter und Menschen von einem Ort zum anderen zu befördern.
Transport satisfies wants by making goods available.	Die Transportwirtschaft befriedigt Bedürfnisse, indem sie Waren verfügbar macht.
Transport increases the size of a market.	Durch den Transport wird ein größerer Markt geschaffen.
Transport makes possible an increase in the scale of production.	Der Transport ermöglicht eine Ausweitung des Produktionsumfangs.
Speed reduces the company's storage expenses.	Geschwindigkeit verringert die Lagerkosten der Gesellschaft.

Transport

transfer of goods from vehicle to vehicle	Umladen von Gütern von einem Fahrzeug zum andern
A contractor makes special contracts of carriage with his individual customers.	Ein Unternehmer schließt mit jedem seiner Kunden spezielle Frachtverträge ab.
Substantial public funds are used to help public transport.	Erhebliche öffentliche Mittel werden zugunsten der öffentlichen Verkehrsmittel aufgewendet.
Fares are responsible for the bulk of the revenue.	Das Fahrgeld stellt den größten Teil der Einnahmen dar.
An increase in fares results in a reduction in passengers.	Eine Erhöhung des Fahrgelds führt zu einer Verringerung der Zahl der Fahrgäste.
Public transport has a permanent part to play.	Öffentliche Verkehrsmittel werden stets eine Rolle spielen müssen.
An integrated system of transport is operated by a central authority.	Eine zentrale Stelle verwaltet ein Verkehrs-Verbundsystem.
There are vast sums of capital invested in transport systems.	Im Transportwesen sind erhebliche Kapitalien investiert.
The National Freight Corporation is responsible for all public-sector freight traffic.	Der „N.F.C." *(in England)* ist für den gesamten Güterverkehr auf dem öffentlichen Sektor verantwortlich.
Local Passenger Transport Authorities (P.T.A.'s) integrate and develop bus and rail services.	Örtliche P.T.A. *(in England)* schaffen ein Verbundsystem zwischen Bus- und Schienenverkehr und bauen es weiter aus.
TAKE CARE	VORSICHT! (*auf Kisten*)
The London International Freight Terminal (LIFT) was established by British Rail.	Die Londoner Internationale Frachtsammelstelle wurde von den britischen Eisenbahnen eingerichtet.

2. Motor Transport — Kraftfahrzeugverkehr

road transport, transport of goods by road	Straßentransport *m*, Güterverkehr *m* mit LKW, Transport *m* per Achse
road transport industry	Straßenverkehrsgewerbe *n*
commercial motor vehicle	gewerblich genutztes Fahrzeug *n*
motor vehicle user	Kraftfahrzeugbenutzer *m*
local/intercity carriage	Orts-/Überlandverkehr *m*
short/long hauls *pl*	Nah-/Fernverkehr *m*
feeder line	Zubringerdienst *m*
property/passenger carriage	Güter-/Personenverkehr *m*
piggyback hauling *Am*	Huckepackverkehr *m*
pickup/delivery service	Abhol-/Zubringerdienst *m*
bulk haulage	Massengüterverkehr *m*

Transportwesen 171

volume of goods carried	beförderte Gütermenge *f*
truck freight *Am*	LKW-Fracht *f*
bus/truck terminal	Autobusbahnhof *m*/Autohof *m*
roll-on, roll-off ferry	Ro-Ro-Fähre *f*
concentration/distribution point	Sammel-/Verteilerpunkt *m*
transshipment, changeover	Umschlagen *n*/Umladen *n*
transshipment charge/point	Umladegebühr *f*/Umschlagplatz *m*
forwarding route	Beförderungsweg *m (Güterverkehr)*
routing	Festlegung *f* des Transportwegs
route chart	Strecken-, Leitkarte *f*
for-hire transportation	gewerbliches Transportunternehmen *n*
freight forwarder, *Am* shipper	Gütersprediteur *m*
motor carrier	LKW-Transportunternehmer *m*
urban bus service	städtischer Autobusbetrieb *m*
motor pool	Fahrbereitschaft *f*
car park	Parkplatz *m*, Autopark *m*
truck fleet	Fuhrpark *m*
vanman, trucker *Am*	Fernlastfahrer *m*
bus operator/driver	Busfahrer *m*
motor fitter, mechanic	Autoschlosser *m*
motorist/motorcyclist	Auto-/Motorradfahrer *m*
assistant driver	Beifahrer *m*
driver-accompanied vehicle	begleitetes Fahrzeug *n (bei der Überfahrt von England)*
petrol, *Am* gas/Diesel engine	Benzin-/Dieselmotor *m*
fuel	Kraftstoff *m*, Treibstoff *m*
filling/petrol/*Am* gas station	Tankstelle *f*
petrol consumption	Benzinverbrauch *m*
motor industry, *Am* automotive industry	Autoindustrie *f*
motor show	Automobilausstellung *f*
car dealer	Autohändler *m*
used car	Gebrauchtwagen *m*
car hiring service	Autovermietung *f*
rented car	Mietwagen *m*
car rental	Wagenmiete *f*
taxi, *Am* cab	Taxe *f*
(motor-)scooter/motor-cycle	Motorroller *m*/Motorrad *n*
roadworthiness	Verkehrstauglichkeit *f*
motor accident	Autounfall *m*
motoring offence	Verkehrsdelikt *n*
vehicle tax/taxation	KFZ-Steuer *f*/-Besteuerung *f*
bottleneck	verengte Fahrbahn *f*
area congestion	(Verkehrs-) Stau *m*
underground/multi-stor(e)y car park	Tiefgarage *f*/Parkhochhaus *n*

Transport

Specialized vehicles — *Spezialfahrzeuge*

long-distance lorry/*Am* truck	Fernlaster *m*
truck tractor	Sattelzugmaschine *f*
semi-trailer, tractor truck, trailer-tractor unit	Sattelschlepper *m*
truck trailer	LKW-Anhänger *m*
trailer	Wohnwagen *m*; Anhänger *m*
tanker, tanktrailer, *Am* tank truck	Tankwagen *m*
tractor	Zugmaschine *f*
road train, motor freight train	Lastzug *m*
general-purpose truck	Mehrzweckwagen *m*
refrigerator truck	Kühlwagen *m*
flat-bed truck/trailer	Tieflader *m*
station-wag(g)on	Kombiwagen *m*
ambulance, motor ambulance	Kranken-, Unfallwagen *m*
dust cart, *Am* garbage truck	Müllabfuhrwagen *m*
furniture van, *Am* moving van	Möbelwagen *m*
to route (via)	befördern, dirigieren (über)
to motorize	motorisieren
to run o.'s own fleet	über einen eigenen Wagenpark verfügen
to pick up loads/passengers	Ladungen/Fahrgäste mitnehmen
to pass into/around large cities	in große Städte hineinfahren/große Städte umfahren
to move large consignments	große Frachten befördern
to fill a container	einen Großbehälter/Container füllen
to stack goods on top of one another	Güter aufeinanderstapeln
to take the wheel	(Auto) fahren
to rent a car	einen Wagen mieten
to back a car	einen Wagen zurückstoßen
motor-driven	mit Motorantrieb
motorless	ohne Motor, motorlos
by road	per LKW
in/on the road	auf der Landstraße
en route	unterwegs
two-door/four-door	zwei-/viertürig
single-/two-axle	ein-/zweiachsig
two-/four-wheeled	zwei-/vierrädrig
at the wheel	am Steuer
air-conditioned	mit Klimaanlage versehen

Sätze und Redewendungen:

I'll pick you up at your house.	Ich hole Sie zu Hause ab.

Motor vehicles can serve almost all points in the country.	Kraftfahrzeuge können beinahe jeden Ort im Lande beliefern.
Delivery is made direct at the consignee's premises.	Auslieferung erfolgt unmittelbar auf dem Gelände des Empfängers.
The maintenance of a fleet of vans is expensive.	Die laufende Unterhaltung eines LKW-Parks ist kostspielig.
The trailer is hauled by highway to the place of unloading.	Der Anhänger wird auf der Landstraße zum Entladeort gebracht.
cost of operating a vehicle	Betriebskosten für ein Fahrzeug
the highest hourly volume of traffic	das höchste Verkehrsaufkommen pro Stunde
Truck transport reduces the number of handlings of packages.	Die Beförderung mit LKW erspart mehrfaches Umladen der Versandstücke.
Computerized route charts give the most economic route to be followed.	Mit dem Computer zusammengestellte Streckenkarten geben die günstigste Strecke an.
Truck transport provides a highly flexible, speedy, and economical service.	Die Beförderung mit LKW ist höchst anpassungsfähig, rasch und wirtschaftlich.
Road transport is particularly suitable for small loads over short distances.	Der Güterverkehr mit LKW ist besonders für kleine Ladungen über kurze Entfernungen geeignet.
Closed-circuit TV cameras allow dispatchers to observe the loading and unloading of vehicles.	Mittels einer betriebsinternen Fernsehanlage kann der Expedient das Be- und Entladen der Wagen verfolgen.
A wide range of standardized containers is available.	Eine große Auswahl genormter Container steht zur Verfügung.
The basic advantages of containers are low freight charges and door-to-door security.	Die grundlegenden Vorteile von Containern liegen in den niedrigen Frachtgebühren und der sicheren Beförderung von Haus zu Haus.
Containers must be strong enough to take the weight.	Container müssen so stabil sein, daß sie das Gewicht aushalten.
Goods are off-loaded or re-handled.	Güter werden entladen oder umgeladen.

3. Rail Transport

Eisenbahnverkehr

railway network/line Eisenbahnnetz *n*/-strecke *f*
train journey/staff Bahnfahrt *f*/Zugpersonal *n*
railway guard Zugschaffner *m*

174 Transport

railway/rail traffic	Schienenverkehr m
rail transport(ation)	Eisenbahngütertransport m
main line, Am trunk route/branch line	Haupt-/Nebenstrecke f
overhead/elevated railway	Hochbahn f
suburban line	Vorortbahn f
traffic density	Verkehrsdichte f
dense traffic routes pl	stark befahrene Strecken f pl
railway junction/connection	Eisenbahnknotenpunkt m/-anschluß m
Inter-City train	Intercity-Zug m, Städtezug m
freightliner train Am	Container-Zug m
boat train	Zug m mit Schiffsanschluß
corridor/express/fast/Am vestibule train	D-, Schnellzug m
passenger/slow/stopping/Am way train	Personen-, Bummelzug m
morning/early train	Morgen-/Frühzug m
high-speed streamliner Am	Stromlinienzug m mit großer Geschwindigkeit f
Motorail	*Autoreisezug-Service* m *der British Rail*
goods/Am freight train	Güterzug m
train speed	Zuggeschwindigkeit f
wag(g)on load, Am carload lot	Waggonladung f
carriage of goods by rail	Gütertransport m per Bahn
railway rates pl	Eisenbahntarif m
consignment note, Am waybill	Frachtbrief m
railway guide	Kursbuch n
timetable	Fahrplan m
dependability of rail service	Zuverlässigkeit f des Eisenbahnbetriebs

Rolling stock — *Rollendes Material*

railway carriage, Am railroad car	Eisenbahnwagen m
goods wag(g)on, Am freight car	Güterwagen m
coach, Am passenger car	Personenwagen m
sleeping car, Am sleeper	Schlafwagen m
roomette Am	Schlafwagenkabine f
dining car, Am diner	Speisewagen m
chair/club/Am lounge car	Salonwagen m
observation/Am dome car	Aussichtswagen m
mail van, Am mail car	Postwagen m
refrigerator car	Kühlwagen m
covered wag(g)on, Am box car	gedeckter Güterwagen m
open wag(g)on, truck, Am gondola car	offener Güterwagen m
van	geschlossener Güterwagen m

Transportwesen 175

luggage van, *Am* baggage car	Gepäckwagen *m*
platform car, *Am* flatcar	Plattform-, Flachwagen *m*
automobile/rack car	Autowaggon *m*
hopper car/side-stanchion car	Fallboden-/Rungenwagen *m*
cattle truck, *Am* stock car	Viehwagen *m*
tank car/container car	Kessel-/Behälterwagen *m*
caboose *Am*	Dienstwagen *m (für Personal bei Güterzügen)*
steam/Diesel/electric/switching locomotive	Dampf-/Diesel-/elektrische/Rangierlokomotive *f*
dieselization	Umstellung *f* auf Dieselbetrieb
axle load	Achsdruck *m*
motive power	Antriebskraft *f*
pull	Zugkraft *f*
engine driver, engineman, motorman, *Am* engineer	Lok(omotiv)führer *m*
air brake	Luftdruckbremse *f*
braking capacity	Bremsleistung *f*

Fixed installations   *Ortsfeste Anlagen*

roadbed	Bahnkörper *m*
rails *pl*	Gleise *n pl*
standard/narrow ga(u)ge	Normal-/Schmalspur *f*
cross-tie, sleeper	Eisenbahnschwelle *f*
curve in track, curvature [ˈkə:vətʃə]	Gleiskrümmung *f*, Kurve *f*
rail-highway bridge	kombinierte Eisenbahn- und Straßenbrücke *f*
switch	Weiche *f*
block	Blockstrecke *f*
block signal	Blocksignal *n*
marshalling/shunting/*Am* railroad yard	Rangier-/Verschiebebahnhof *m*
siding, *Am* sidetrack	Neben-/Abstellgleis *n*
elevated hump	Ablaufberg *m*
goods station, goods yard, *Am* freight yard	Güterbahnhof *m*
loading platform/ramp	Verladerampe *f*
switchtower monitor, signal box	Stellwerk *n*
terminus, *pl* -ni, terminal station	End-/Kopfbahnhof *m*
level crossing, *Am* grade crossing	schienengleicher Übergang *m*
to forward by rail	mit der Eisenbahn befördern
to take on passengers	Reisende zusteigen lassen
to be in motion	in Bewegung sein
to accelerate/to decelerate	beschleunigen/verlangsamen
to bring trains to a safe stop	Züge sicher zum Halten bringen

Transport

to brake a train	einen Zug abbremsen
to apply the brakes	die Bremse ziehen
to resume speed	wieder an Geschwindigkeit gewinnen
to run through a stop signal	ein Haltesignal überfahren
to call for speed restrictions	Geschwindigkeitsbeschränkungen erfordern
to run at frequent intervals	in kurzen Zeitabständen fahren
to carry huge loads	große Lasten befördern
to go into service, to be placed in service	in Betrieb genommen/in Dienst gestellt werden
to detour ['di:tuə]	umleiten
to clear a block	eine Strecke nicht belegen
to disconnect cars from a train	Waggons von einem Zug abkuppeln
to assemble cars into a train	Waggons zu einem Zug zusammenstellen
to break a train down into individual cars	einen Zug auflösen
to classify cars	Waggons umgruppieren
to be on the train	im Zug sitzen
to take a train to Liverpool	mit dem Zug nach Liverpool fahren
to run at regular times	fahrplanmäßig fahren
to collect/to pitch up a consignment	eine Sendung abholen
to deliver a consignment	eine Sendung abliefern
to expedite the handling of goods	die Beförderung von Gütern beschleunigen
to transfer containers from rail to road haulage	Behälter vom Waggon auf Straßenfahrzeuge umschlagen
to cut local trains	Personenzüge abschaffen
to operate at a deficit	mit Verlust arbeiten
to refrigerate	tiefkühlen *(Nahrungsmittel)*
by wag(g)on	per Waggon
on heavy grades	bei starken Steigungen
stainless	nicht rostend
lightweight	leicht
streamlined	stromlinienförmig
atop	zuoberst, obenauf
glass-enclosed	mit Glas umgeben
articulated	gelenkig; Gelenk-
Diesel powered	mit Dieselantrieb
high-speed	schnellaufend; Hochleistungs-
motive	bewegend, treibend
wheelless	ohne Räder
standardized	genormt
by goods train, *Am* by slow freight	als Frachtgut
by passenger train, *Am* by fast freight	als Eilgut

Transportwesen 177

embedded in ballast	in Schotterbettung
off the track	entgleist
at (a) low speed	mit geringer Geschwindigkeit
overhead	oben, oberirdisch
allowable	zulässig
at starting	bei Anfahrt
single-/double-track	ein-/zweigleisig
slack	schlaff, lose
incoming	einfahrend

Sätze und Redewendungen:

Goods are loaded and unloaded at terminals.	An Umschlagplätzen werden Güter ein- und ausgeladen.
If goods are to go a long way, rail transport is probably best.	Wenn Güter über eine weite Strecke befördert werden sollen, so ist der Transport mit der Bahn wohl am günstigsten.
The change-over from road to rail is effected by completely mechanical means at special rail terminals.	Der Umschlag von Straße zu Schiene wird voll mechanisiert an besonderen Umschlagplätzen der Bahn vorgenommen.
Trains transport passengers, baggage, mail, express goods, and general freight.	Züge befördern Reisende, Gepäck, Postsendungen, Eilgut und das übliche Frachtgut.
Stephenson's Rocket attained a speed of 29 miles per hour.	Stephensons Rocket erreichte eine Geschwindigkeit von 29 Meilen in der Stunde.
The cars are used in local and commuter service.	Die Waggons werden im Nah-/Bezirks- und Vorortverkehr eingesetzt.
The standard ga(u)ge is 4 ft. 8.5 in.	Die Normalspur beträgt 4 Fuß 8,5 Zoll.
Box cars are built for 40- and 50-ton capacity.	Gedeckte Güterwagen werden für eine Ladefähigkeit von 40 und 50 Tonnen gebaut.
6,000 to 7,000 horsepower (hp.) is available in modern locomotives.	Moderne Lokomotiven haben eine Leistung von 6000 bis 7000 PS.
the railroad's share of freight traffic	der Anteil der Eisenbahn am Frachtaufkommen
the average railroad freight charge per ton-mile	die durchschnittlichen Eisenbahnfrachtgebühren pro Tonnen-Meile
This train conveys both passengers and goods.	Dieser Zug befördert Personen und Güter.
Passenger traffic is measured in passenger-miles.	Der Personenverkehr wird nach Personenmeilen (-kilometern) berechnet.

178 Transport

High speed trains for inter-city services carry up to 444 passengers in air-conditioned comfort.	Sehr schnelle Inter-City Züge befördern bis zu 444 Reisende in bequemen Wagen mit Klimaanlage.
Other trains make more intermediate calls.	Andere Züge halten unterwegs öfters.
There is no supplementary fare.	Ein Zuschlag wird nicht erhoben.

4. Air Transport — Luftverkehr

a) Aviation — *Luftfahrt*

air transport/service	Flugverkehr *m*/Luftverkehrsdienst *m*
airline	Fluglinie *f*; Luftverkehrsgesellschaft *f*
air space	Luftraum *m*
air traffic control	Flugsicherung *f*
air travel	Flugreise *f*
intercontinental network	interkontinentales Streckennetz *n*
air carriage	Beförderung *f* auf dem Luftweg
international carriage by air	Beförderung *f* im internationalen Luftverkehr
air bridge	Luftbrücke *f*
charter airline	Charterfluggesellschaft *f*
air charter	Charterflugverkehr *m*
passenger/transport plane	Passagier-/Transportflugzeug *n*
airliner	Verkehrsflugzeug *n*
air coach	Passagierflugzeug *n* der Touristenklasse
jumbo jet	Riesendüsenflugzeug *n*, Jumbo-Jet *m*
jet (airplane)	Düsenflugzeug *n*
jet propulsion unit	Düsentriebwerk *n*
propeller-driven/supersonic airplane	Propeller-/Überschallflugzeug *n*
airfreighter, cargo-plane, all-cargo aircraft	Frachtflugzeug *n*
aerobus [ˈɛərəʊbʌs]	Airbus *m*
air taxi	Lufttaxi *n*
feeder-service aircraft	Zubringerflugzeug *n*
vertical take-off aircraft	Senkrechtstarter *m*
seaplane	Wasserflugzeug *n*
air raft/screw	Rettungsfloß *n*, Schlauchboot *n*/ Luftschraube *f*
air speed indicator	Fahrtmesser *m*
helicopter/heliport	Hubschrauber *m*/-landeplatz *m*

Transportwesen 179

cockpit	Kanzel *f*
passenger cabin	Passagier-, Fluggastkabine *f*
fuselage	Flugzeugrumpf *m*
airfoil	Tragfläche *f*
wing	Flügel *m*
retractable landing gear/undercarriage	einziehbares Fahrwerk *n*
take-off	Start *m*
instrument flying/landing	Blindflug *m*/Instrumentenlandung *f*
landing/cruising speed	Lande-/Reisegeschwindigkeit *f*
supersonic speed	Überschallgeschwindigkeit *f*
altitude	Flughöhe *f*
ceiling	Gipfelhöhe *f*, Wolkenuntergrenze *f*
flying range/speed	Flugbereich *m*/-geschwindigkeit *f*
distance flown	zurückgelegte Flugstrecke *f*
duration of flight	Flugdauer *f*
flight schedule/timetable	Flugplan *m*
non-stop flight	Flug *m* ohne Zwischenlandung
stop-over	Zwischenaufenthalt *m*
scheduled/regular flight	planmäßiger Flug *m*
flying safety	Flugsicherheit *f*
security/preventive measures *pl*	Sicherheitsvorkehrungen *f pl*/vorbeugende Maßnahmen *f pl*
traffic restrictions *pl*	Verkehrseinschränkungen *f pl*
plane crash	Flugzeugabsturz *m*
crash landing	Bruchlandung *f*
hijacking	Flugzeugentführung *f*

b) Airport — *Flughafen*

commercial airport	Zivilflughafen *m*
airfield, *Am* airdrome	Flugplatz *m*
airpark, *Am* airstrip	Kleinflughafen *m*, Behelfsflugplatz *m*
airport charge	Flughafengebühr *f*
airport of dispatch/of destination/of entry	Abfertigungs-/Bestimmungs-/Zollflughafen *m*
air terminal	Endstation *f* des Zubringerdienstes vom und zum Flugplatz, Flughafenabfertigungsdienst *m*, Air Terminal *m*
city terminal	City Terminal *m*
control tower	Kontrollturm *m*
air traffic controller	Fluglotse *m*
airfield lighting	Flugplatzbefeuerung *f*
airway/air lane/air route	Flugstrecke *f*, Luft-, Flugschneise *f*
air corridor	Luftkorridor *m*, Einflugschneise *f*
polar airline	Polarroute *f*

180 Transport

airworthiness	Lufttüchtigkeit *f*
runway	Start- und Landebahn *f*, Piste *f*
taxiway	Rollbahn *f*
walkway	Laufgang *m* (zum Flugzeug)
hangar, air shed	Flugzeughalle *f*
flying/ground personnel	fliegendes Personal/Bodenpersonal *n*
flight dispatcher	Abfertigungsbeamter *m*
airman	Flieger *m*
aircrew, flight crew	Flugzeugbesatzung *f*
flying experience/hours *pl*	Flugerfahrung *f*/-stunden *f pl*
cabin personnel	Personal *n* im Fluggastraum
air-hostess	(Luft-) Stewardeß *f*
flight captain	Flugkapitän *m*
flight engineer, air-mechanic	Bordmechaniker *m*
co-pilot	Kopilot *m*
navigator	Navigator *m*

c) Clearance — *Abfertigung*

airport restaurant	Flughafenrestaurant *n*
duty-free shop	Zollfreiladen *m*
airport customs office	Flughafenzollamt *n*
baggage check	Fluggepäckabschnitt *m*
checked baggage	aufgegebenes Gepäck *n*
free-baggage allowance	Freigepäck *n*
excess baggage	Übergepäck *n*
baggage in excess	die Freigepäckgrenze übersteigendes Gepäck *n*
hand-luggage	Handgepäck *n*
latest check-in time	Meldeschluß *m*
late passenger arrival	verspätete Ankunft *f* eines Fluggastes
passport/visa/customs/health/currency regulations *pl*	Pass-/Visa-/Zoll-/Gesundheits-/Währungsvorschriften *f pl*
booking/air ticket office	Buchungsstelle *f*
ticket sales office	Flugscheinverkaufsstelle *f*
travel agent/agency	Reisebüro *n*, -agentur *f*
coupon, air flight ticket	Flugkarte *f*, -schein *m*
changes to tickets *pl*	Umschreibungen *f pl*
validity to tickets	Flugscheingültigkeit *f*
tourist/economy class	Touristen-/Economy-Klasse *f*
reduced return fare	ermäßigter Retourtarif *m*
round-trip excursion fare	Rundreisetarif *m*
family-fare plan	Familientarif *m*
waiting list	Warteliste *f*
seating capacity	verfügbare Sitzplätze *m pl*
teleregister	elektronische Platzbelegung *f*
bus service to the airport	Busverbindung *f* zum Flughafen

Transportwesen 181

seasonal demand	saisonbedingter Bedarf *m*
peak days *pl*	Verkehrsspitze *f*
boarding card	Bordkarte *f*
aircraft passenger insurance	Fluggastversicherung *f*
permanent total disablement	bleibende Ganzinvalidität *f*
conditions *pl* of carriage	Beförderungsbedingungen *f pl*

d) *Meteorological/Weather conditions* — *Wetterbedingungen*

meteorological services *pl*, weather service	Wetterdienst *m*
meteorological observation	Wetterbeobachtung *f*
weather report/forecast	Wetterbericht *m*/-vorhersage *f*
weather chart/map	Wetterkarte *f*
weather bureau *Am*	Wetteramt *n*
air bump	Bö *f*
air-hole/-pocket	Luftloch *n*
cold/warm front	Kalt-/Warmfront *f*

e) *Air cargo* — *Luftfracht*

cargo office	Luftfrachtbüro *n*
pay load	Nutzlast *f*
pay-load capacity	Ladefähigkeit *f*
air cargo/freight	Luftfracht *f*
air-freight service, freighter services *pl*, cargo services *pl*	Frachtflugverkehr *m*, Frachtendienste *m pl*
through pallet service	durchgehend palletierter Service *m*
scheduled overnight cargo flight	planmäßiger Nacht-Frachtflug *m*
air-freight space	Luftfrachtraum *m*
cargo pit	Frachtraum *m* im Flugzeug
plane load	Flugzeugladung *f*
air-freight charges *pl*/tariff	Luftfrachtkosten *pl*/-tarif *m*
air express/tariff	Luftexpressfracht *f*/-tarif *m*
air-cargo shipment	Luftfrachtsendung *f*
air waybill, air consignment note	Luftfrachtbrief *m*
air carrier, air-freight forwarder	Luftfrachtführer *m*
airmail rate/service/letter/stamp	Luftposttarif *m*/-dienst *m*/-brief *m*/-marke *f*
air letter *Am*	Luftpostleichtbrief *m*
air parcel	Luftpostpaket *n*
revenue from the carriage of mail	Einnahmen *f pl* aus der Luftpostbeförderung
to airlift, to transport by air	auf dem Luftweg transportieren
to go by air, to take a flight	fliegen

182 Transport

to fly, to pilot	*(ein Flugzeug)* steuern/fliegen
to taxi/to take off	rollen/starten
to airdrop	*(mit dem Fallschirm)* abwerfen
to air-seal	luftdicht verschließen
to air-cool	durch Luft kühlen
to arrive by air	im Flugzeug ankommen
to land safely	sicher landen
to flight-test	einfliegen
to issue a ticket	einen Flugschein ausstellen
to reserve seats at an approved travel agency	Plätze bei einer anerkannten Reiseagentur belegen
to confirm/to cancel a seat	einen Platz bestätigen/streichen
to proceed to the waiting room in good time	sich frühzeitig in den Warteraum begeben
to board a plane	sich an Bord eines Flugzeugs begeben
to debar from transportation	von der Beförderung ausschließen
to attach to air tickets	den Flugscheinen beigeben
to meet with an accident	einen Unfall erleiden, verunglücken
to travel half-fare	zum halben Preis fliegen
to avoid mix-ups	Verwechslungen vermeiden
to mark o.'s baggage with o.'s name and address	sein Gepäck mit Name und Anschrift versehen
to take security precautions	Sicherheitsvorkehrungen treffen
to examine passengers' baggage	das Passagiergepäck untersuchen
to search s.o.	eine Leibesvisitation durchführen
to put on a waiting-list	auf eine Warteliste setzen
to pre-plan flights	Flüge im voraus planen
to embark/to debark	an Bord/von Bord gehen
to accommodate 400 passengers	für 400 Fluggäste Platz bieten
to ensure schedule reliability	für flugplanmäßige Abwicklung sorgen
airborne	im Flugzeug befördert
airproof, airtight	luftdicht
air-ground ...	Bord-Boden- ...
air-minded	flugbegeistert
airsick	luftkrank
air-void	luftleer
airworthy	lufttüchtig
airy	luftig, windig
upon arrival	nach Ankunft
on short routes	auf kurzen Strecken
above the weather	über der Wetterzone

Sätze und Redewendungen:

Fasten your seat-belts, please!	Bitte anschnallen!
Please present at each intermediate stop.	Bitte bei jeder Zwischenlandung vorweisen.
You assume responsibility for completeness and correctness of the information.	Sie übernehmen die Verantwortung für die Vollständigkeit und Richtigkeit der Information.
You are entitled to a free-baggage allowance of 20 kg.	Sie haben ein Anrecht auf Beförderung von 20 kg Freigepäck.
Carrier's address shall be the airport of departure.	Als Anschrift des Luftfrachtführers gilt der Abflughafen.
Checked baggage will be delivered to bearer of the baggage check.	Aufgegebenes Gepäck wird dem Inhaber des Gepäckscheins ausgehändigt.
In case of damage to baggage complaint must be made in writing to carrier.	Gepäckschäden sind dem Luftfrachtführer schriftlich anzuzeigen.
This ticket is good for carriage for one year from date of issue.	Dieser Flugschein ist ein Jahr ab Ausstellungstag gültig.
The fare for carriage is subject to change prior to commencement of carriage.	Der Flugpreis unterliegt etwaigen sich vor Beförderungsbeginn ergebenden Änderungen.
Times shown in timetable or elsewhere are not guaranteed.	Es wird keine Garantie für die in Flugplänen oder sonstwo angegebenen Verkehrszeiten übernommen.
Passenger shall present exit, entry and other required documents.	Der Fluggast muß die erforderlichen Ausreise-, Einreise- und sonstigen Dokumente vorweisen.
latest check-in time at airport	Meldeschluß am Flughafen
Articles which may be carried free in addition to the free-baggage allowance:	Zusätzlich zum Freigepäck können folgende Gegenstände mitgenommen werden:
equivalent amount paid	entrichteter Gegenwert
baggage liability limitations	Haftungsbeschränkungen für Gepäck
Carriers assume no liability for fragile or perishable articles.	Die Luftfrachtführer übernehmen keine Haftung für zerbrechliche oder leicht verderbliche Gegenstände.
We are obliged for the earliest possible cancellation.	Wir sind für eine möglichst frühzeitige Annullierung dankbar.
Requests to board a flight are made 10 to 20 minutes before scheduled departure time.	Der Abruf zum Einsteigen erfolgt 10 bis 20 Minuten vor der flugplanmäßigen Abflugzeit.
Passengers arriving too late for clearance forfeit their claim to transportation.	Fluggäste, die zu spät bei der Abfertigung eintreffen, verlieren das Recht auf Beförderung.
Seats are available.	Plätze können gebucht werden.

5. Water Transport

a) Navigation

Transport zu Wasser

Schiffahrt, Seefahrt, Navigation, Ortung

shipping	Verschiffung *f*, *Am* Versand *m*, Verfrachtung *f*, Spedition *f*; Schiffsbestand *m*; Schiffsverkehr *m*
seaborne trade/traffic	Seehandel *m*/Seeschiffahrt *f*
merchant/mercantile marine	Handelsmarine *f*
merchant fleet/service	Handelsflotte *f*/-schiffahrt *f*
water-borne traffic	Schiffahrtsverkehr *m*
merchantman, merchant/trading ship	Handelsschiff *n*
shipping route, ocean lane	Schiffahrtsstraße *f*, -weg *m*
tonnage	Schiffstonnage *f*
scarcity of tonnage	Schiffsraummangel *m*
idle/laid-up shipping	aufgelegte Tonnage *f*
Lloyd's register	Lloyd's Schiffsregister *n*
shipping business	Seehandel *m*; Reederei *f*
shipping company, steamship company	Schiffahrtsgesellschaft *f*, Reederei *f*
shipping line	Schiffahrtslinie *f*
shipping shares *pl*	Schiffahrtsaktien *f pl*
overseas shipment	Überseetransport *m*
shipping news/intelligence	Schiffahrtsnachrichten *f pl*
shipment of goods	Warenversand *m*, Güterbeförderung *f*
shipping trade	Reedereibetrieb *m*, *Am* Speditionsgeschäft *n*; Seehandel *m*
shipping agent	Schiffsmakler *m*, *Am* Spediteur *m*, Transportmakler *m*
shipping clerk	Expedient *m*, *Am* Spediteur *m*
shipping charges *pl*/expenses *pl*	Verschiffungs-/Verlade-/*Am* Versandkosten *pl*
shipping board	Schiffahrtsbehörde *f*
shipowner	Reeder *m*, Schiffseigner *m*
ship broker, shipping master	Schiffsmakler *m*
ship brokerage	Frachten-/Schiffsmaklergeschäft *n*
ship chandler	Lieferant *m* von Schiffsbedarf
crew	(Schiffs-) Besatzung *f*
ship's company	(Schiffs-) Mannschaft *f*
(sea) captain, skipper, master (mariner)	Schiffs-/Handelskapitän *m*
seaman, mariner, sailor	Matrose *m*
ship's articles *pl*	Heuervertrag *m*
shore leave	Landurlaub *m*
navigator	Steuermann *m*

Transportwesen 185

pilot	Lotse *m*
pilotage	Lotsengebühr *f*
stevedore	Schauermann *m*, Stauer *m*
dockworker, docker, *Am* long-shore-man	Hafenarbeiter *m*
quarantine ['kwɔrənti:n]	Quarantäne *f*
clean bill of health	einwandfreies Gesundheitszeugnis *n*

b) Vessels — *Wasser-/Seefahrzeuge, Schiffe*

steamer, steamship (S.S., s.s.), steamboat	Dampfschiff *n*
sea-going/ocean-going vessel	Hochseedampfer *m*
coaster, coasting vessel	Küstendampfer *m*
motor ship (M.S.), motor vessel (M.V.)	Motorschiff *n*
turbine steamer	Turbinendampfer *m*
nuclear-powered ship	durch Atomkraft getriebenes Schiff *n*
craft	(kleines) Fahrzeug *n*/Schiff *n*
boat	(kleines oder großes) Schiff *n*, Dampfer *m*, Boot *n*, Kahn *m*
tug(-boat)	Schleppdampfer *m*, Schlepper *m*
barge	Leichter *m*, Schleppkahn *m*
passenger liner/ship	Passagier-/Fahrgastschiff *n*
freighter, cargo vessel, cargo steamer, cargo carrier	Frachtdampfer *m*, Dampfer *m*
transport ship/vessel	Transport-/Frachtschiff *n*, Truppentransporter *m*
bulk carrier	Frachter *m* für Massengüter
passenger-cargo ship/vessel	Passagier- und Frachtschiff *n*
tramp (steamer)	Trampschiff *n*
mammoth oil-tanker	Riesenöltanker *m*
refrigerator ship	Kühlschiff *n*
collier, coal freighter	Kohlendampfer *m*
icebreaker	Eisbrecher *m*
train/car ferry	Zug-/Autofähre *f*
container ship	Containerschiff *n*
lash	Lash-Schiff *n*
seabee	Frachtschiff *n* für die Beförderung beladener Barken nach dem Huckepacksystem
hovercraft ['hɔvə-krɑ:ft]	Luftkissenboot *n*
seaworthiness	Seetüchtigkeit *f*
cargo capacity	Ladefähigkeit *f*
full ship	beladenes Schiff *n*
draught, *Am* draft	Tiefgang *m*
displacement	Wasserverdrängung *f*

186 Transport

registered/net/gross tonnage	Registertonnen *f pl* (Handelsschiffe)/Netto-/Bruttoregistertonnage *f*
deadweight tonnage	Gesamtzuladungsgewicht *n*
nautical mile *(= 6,080 ft.)*	Seemeile *f* (= 1.852 m)
knot *(= 1 nautical mile/hour)*	Knoten *m* (= 1 Seemeile/Stunde)
hull	Schiffsrumpf *m*
hold	Laderaum *m*
loading/cargo hatch	Ladeluke *f*
ship's loading gear/loading tackle	Ladegeschirr *n*
derrick	Ladebaum *m*
windlass, winch	Ladewinde *f*
capstan ['kæpstən]	Ankerwinde *f*
rail	Reling *f*
porthole	Bullauge *n*
bulkhead	Schott *n*
bottom	Schiffsboden *m*
bow [bau]	Bug *m*
stern	Heck *n*
port	Backbord *n*
starbord	Steuerbord *n*
keel/bilge	Kiel *m*/-raum *m*
forecastle ['fəuksl]	Vorderdeck *n*, Logis *n*
rudder	Steuerruder *n*
gang-plank, gang-board	Laufplanke *f*, Landungssteg *m*
gangway	Fallreep *n*
shipbuilder	Schiffbauer *m*
shipyard, shipwright's wharf	Werft *f*
shipbuilding industry/order	Schiffbauindustrie *f*/-auftrag *m*
ship damage	Havarie *f*, Schiffsschaden *m*

c) Seafreight

Seefracht

freight/cargo/shipping space	Frachtraum *m*
demand for freight space	Nachfrage *f* nach Schiffsraum
shipper	Befrachter *m*, Ablader *m*, *Am* Versender *m*
carrier	Verfrachter *m*
ship's insurance	Schiffsversicherung *f*
ship's protest	Havarieerklärung *f*
contract of affreightment	(See-) Frachtvertrag *m*
charter party	Chartervertrag *m*, Charterpartie *f*
clean bill of lading	reines Konnossement *n*
unclean/foul/dirty bill of lading	unreines Konnossement *n*
received-for-shipment bill of lading	Übernahmekonnossement *n*
on-board bill of lading	Bordkonnossement *n*
shipping bill/shipper's memorandum	1./2. Kopie *f* des Konnossements
ship's freight/load	Schiffsfracht *f*/-ladung *f*

pooled/partial shipment	Sammel-/Teilladung *f*
dry cargo	Trockenfracht *f*
bulk/deck cargo	Massengut-/Deckladung *f*
bulk commodities *pl*	Massengüter *n pl*
shipper's manifest/order/papers *pl*/ representative	Ausfuhrdeklaration *f*/Eigentumsvorbehalt *m* des Spediteurs/Verladepapiere *n pl*/Speditionsagent *m*
shipping advice/bill/date/order/port	Versandanzeige *f*/Warenbegleitschein *m*/Versandtag *m*/Versandauftrag *m*/Versandhafen *m*
delivery alongside the vessel	Längsseitlieferung *f*
contract/tariff rates *pl*	Kontrakt-/Tariffrachten *f pl*
shipping prices *pl*	Verladepreise *m pl*
freight bill/note	Frachtrechnung *f*
reduction of freight	Frachtermäßigung *f*
loading charges *pl*	Verladegebühr *f*
lighterage	Leichtergebühr *f*
discharge	Löschen *n*
ship's day	Entladetag *m*
laydays *pl*	Liegetage *m pl*
demurrage [diˈmʌridʒ]	Überliegegeld *n*

d) Harbo(u)r, port — *Hafen*

port of departure/of shipment	Abgangs-/Verschiffungshafen *m*
port of exportation/of importation	Ausfuhr-/Einfuhrhafen *m*
port of call/of entry/of destination	Anlauf-/Einlauf-/Bestimmungshafen *m*
port of trans(s)hipment	Umschlaghafen *m*
port of delivery/of discharge	Löschhafen *m*
port of registry/of distress	Heimat-/Nothafen *m*
open-water port	Hafen *m* am offenen Meer
river harbour	Hafen *m* an einer Flußmündung
free port	Freihafen *m*
port dues *pl*/charges *pl*	Hafengebühren *f pl*
anchorage (dues *pl*)	Liegegebühren *f pl*
port authority	Hafenbehörde *f*
clearance inwards/outwards	Ein-/Ausklarierung *f*
cargo tonnage handled	umgeschlagene Gütermenge *f*
port entrance	Hafeneinfahrt *f*
anchorage	Ankerplatz *m*
berth	1. Liege-/Ankerplatz *m*; 2. (Schlaf-) Koje *f*, Kajütenbett *n*; 3. Schiffsplatz *m*
basin, inner port	Hafenbecken *n*, Innenhafen *m*
harbour/port regulations *pl*	Hafenordnung *f*
harbour master/police	Hafenmeister *m*/-polizei *f*
docks *pl*	Hafenanlagen *f pl*

Transport

quay, dock, wharf	Kai *m*
pier, jetty	Pier *m*, Landebrücke *f*
breakwater, mole, jetty, pier	Hafendamm *m*, Mole *f*, Wellen-/Flutbrecher *m*
dock gate	Schleusentor *n*
harbour tug	Hafenschlepper *m*
warehouse	Lagerhaus *n*
bonded warehouse	(Zoll-) Speicher *m*, Lager *n*
railway switch tracks *pl*	Bahnanschluß(-gleise *n pl*) *m*
dockyard, shipyard	Werft *f*
dry/floating dock	Trocken-/Schwimmdock *n*
shipway	Helling *f*, Stapel *m*
floating/jib/pillar/travelling crane	Schwimm-/Ausleger-/Turm-/Laufkran *m*
band/belt conveyer	Transport-/Förderband *n*
ship canal	Seekanal *m (für Ozeanschiffe)*
canal lock	Kanalschleuse *f*
lockage, lock-charges *pl*	Schleusengeld *n*
lighthouse	Leuchtturm *m*
beacon	Bake *f*
buoy	Boje *f*

e) Inland water transport, inland navigation
Binnenschiffahrt(sverkehr)

interior/inland waters *pl*	Binnengewässer *n pl*
inland waterways *pl*	Binnenwasserstraßen *f pl*
coastal waterways *pl*	Küstenschiffahrtswege *m pl*
navigable rivers *pl*	schiffbare Flüsse *m pl*
inland water carrier	Binnenschiffahrtsunternehmen *n*
inland marine insurance	Binnentransportversicherung *f*
inland harbour/port	Binnenhafen *m*
towing vessel	Schleppschiff *n*, Schlepper *m*
channel freight	Kanalfracht *f*
canal traffic	Kanalverkehr *m*
width and depth of a canal	Breite *f* und Tiefe *f* eines Kanals
navigation channel	Fahrrinne *f*/-wasser *n*
lock chamber	Schleusenkammer *f*
dam	Damm *m*, Deich *m*
embankment	Eindeichung *f*, Uferstraße *f*, Kai *m*
aqueduct ['ækwidʌkt]	Aquädukt *m*
mooring pier	Anlegestelle *f*
to launch a ship	ein Schiff vom Stapel lassen
to anchor/to moor a ship	ein Schiff vor Anker legen
to cast/to come to/to drop anchor	vor Anker gehen
to lie/to ride at anchor	vor Anker liegen
to weigh anchor	den Anker lichten
to put in dock	ins Dock bringen

Transportwesen 189

to berth a ship	ein Schiff am Kai festmachen
to tow a ship	ein Schiff ins Schlepptau nehmen
to bring up a ship	ein Schiff aufbringen
to come alongside a ship	an ein Schiff anlegen
to dress/to fit out a ship	ein Schiff beflaggen/ausrüsten
to put a ship in commission	ein Schiff in Dienst stellen
to be shipwrecked	Schiffbruch erleiden
to fly a flag	unter einer Flagge fahren
to touch bottom	auf Grund auflaufen
to load/to discharge/to trans(s)hip/ to stow	verladen/löschen/umladen/verstauen
to ply rivers, canals and lakes	auf Flüssen, Kanälen und Seen verkehren
to book freight space	Frachtraum buchen
to charter a vessel	ein Schiff chartern
to call forward a shipment	eine Sendung abrufen
to ship goods	Güter auf dem Wasserweg befördern
to take shippings	an Bord nehmen/laden
to call at a port, to enter a port	einen Hafen anlaufen
to clear port, to leave port, to put to sea	auslaufen
to go to sea	in See stechen
to follow the sea	zur See fahren
to be in the shipping line	Reederei betreiben
to take ship	an Bord gehen
to leave the ship/to go on shore	von Bord/an Land gehen
to dredge a channel	eine Fahrrinne ausbaggern
to be protected by jetties	durch Molen geschützt sein
ex ship	ab Schiff
on board ship/on board	auf dem Schiff/an Bord
bound for	bestimmt nach
leaving	abgehend
ocean-going	hochseetüchtig
ready for shipment/shipping	versandbereit
incoming/outgoing	ein-/ausgehend
when shipped	nach Verladung
on shore/in shore	an(s) Land/in Küstennähe
shoreward/leeward	küstenwärts/leewärts
on the port quarter/bow/beam	Backbord achtern/voraus/dwars *(quer)*
on the quay	am Kai
on an even keel	auf ebenem Kiel, gleichmäßig
shipwrecked	schiffbrüchig, gescheitert
mercantile	kaufmännisch, handeltreibend
navigable	schiffbar
beyond the seas	nach/in Übersee
in the open sea	auf hoher See
on the sea	zur See, an der See

Transport

Sätze und Redewendungen:

When does the next boat sail for New York?	Wann fährt das nächste Schiff nach New York?
Boats carry very large loads.	Schiffe befördern sehr große Ladungen.
A number of barges are sometimes lashed together.	Eine Reihe Schleppkähne werden manchmal zusammen geschleppt.
Sea-shipping charges are relatively low.	Frachtraten für den Transport auf dem Wasserweg liegen verhältnismäßig niedrig.
a ship sailing under the British flag	ein unter britischer Flagge fahrendes Schiff
Rio de Janeiro has one of the most beautiful harbours in the world.	Rio de Janeiro hat einen der schönsten (natürlichen) Häfen in der Welt.
Passenger ships are not being eliminated by competition from airplanes.	Fahrgastschiffe werden durch die Konkurrenz der Flugzeuge nicht gänzlich verdrängt.
About 60 per cent of the world's merchant ships are freighters.	Ungefähr 60% der Handelsflotte der Welt bestehen aus Frachtschiffen.
ship in difficulty/in distress	Schiff in Seenot
received for shipment	zur Verschiffung übernommen
The ship displaces 75,000 tons.	Das Schiff hat eine Wasserverdrängung von 70.000 t.
to unload deep draft vessels onto shallow draft carriers	Ladungen von Schiffen mit großem Tiefgang auf Frachter mit geringem Tiefgang umladen
The most important shipping companies are Cunard, Ellerman's, Furness Withy, and Peninsular and Oriental.	Die wichtigsten Schiffahrtsgesellschaften *(in England)* sind: Cunard, Ellerman, Furness Withy und Peninsular und Oriental.
Ships take on passengers and cargo.	Schiffe nehmen Passagiere und Fracht an Bord.
Three ships were calling at the port.	Drei Schiffe liefen den Hafen an.
Shipping is highly competitive.	Die Schiffahrt steht unter starkem Konkurrenzdruck.
cargo to and from the major ports of the world	Fracht nach und von den wichtigsten Häfen der Welt
A canal shortens the voyage distance.	Ein Kanal verkürzt die Fahrstrecke.
The gates are kept closed when the tide goes out.	Die Schleusentore sind geschlossen, wenn Ebbe einsetzt.
Only ships built in the United States can be registered as American vessels.	Nur in den Vereinigten Staaten gebaute Schiffe können als amerikanische Schiffe registriert werden.

The high cost of operating ships placed vessels at a competitive disadvantage.	Die hohen Betriebskosten bei Schiffen hatten Wettbewerbsnachteile zur Folge.
A ship needs to re-fuel and replenish its stores of water and food.	Ein Schiff muß Treibstoff auftanken und Wasser- und Nahrungsmittelvorräte ergänzen.

6. Other Means of Transport

Andere Transportmittel

pipeline	Pipeline *f*, Rohr-/Ölleitung *f*
pipeline transportation	Beförderung *f* mittels Pipeline
pumping station	Pumpstation *f*
storage tanks *pl*	Vorratsbehälter *m pl*/-tanks *m pl*
fluid	Flüssigkeit *f*
crude oil	Rohöl *n*
natural gas	Erdgas *n*
passenger lift, *Am* elevator	Personenaufzug *m*/-fahrstuhl *m*
goods lift, *Am* freight elevator	Lastenaufzug *m*
elevator car/cage	(Aufzug-) Kabine *f*
elevator shaft	Aufzugschacht *m*
escalator, moving staircase	Rolltreppe *f*
parachute ['pærəʃu:t]	Fallschirm *m*
funicular/cable railway	Drahtseilbahn *f*
tram, *Am* streetcar	Straßenbahn *f*
trolley bus	Oberleitungsbus *m*, Obus *m*
motorman	Wagenführer *m*
monorail	Einschienenbahn *f*
underground railway, tube *(in London)*, *Am* subway	Untergrundbahn *f*
conveyer belt/band	Transport-/Förder-/Fließband *n*

X. Business Enterprise

Unternehmen

1. General Terms

Allgemeine Begriffe

free enterprise economy	freie Marktwirtschaft *f*
business undertaking/enterprise	Unternehmen *n*
privately-owned enterprise	Privatunternehmen *n*
state-owned enterprise	staatliches Unternehmen *n*
municipal enterprise	städtisches Unternehmen *n*
nationalized company	verstaatlichte Gesellschaft *f*
sole trader	Einzelkaufmann *m*
sole-trader enterprise	Einzelunternehmen *n*, Einmannunternehmen *n*
sole proprietorship	Alleinbesitz *m*, Einzelunternehmen *n*

192 Business Enterprise

large-scale enterprise	Großunternehmen *n*
enterprise affiliation	Unternehmensverflechtung *f*
enterprise liability	Unternehmenshaftung *f*
assessment of credit-worthiness	Einschätzung *f* der Kreditfähigkeit
accountability	Haftpflicht *f*, Rechnungslegungspflicht *f*
insolvency proceedings *pl*	Vergleichsverfahren *n*
business share	Geschäftsanteil *m*
capital gains *pl*	Kapitalgewinne *m pl*
entrepreneur's profit	Unternehmergewinn *m*
corporate form	Gesellschaftsform *f*

2. Partnerships — Personengesellschaften

commercial/trading/mercantile partnership	Handelsgesellschaft *f*
ordinary/*Am* general partnership	offene Handelsgesellschaft *f*, OHG
limited partnership	Kommanditgesellschaft *f*, KG
joint venture	Gemeinschaftsunternehmen *n*, *Am* Gelegenheitsgesellschaft *f*
active/dormant, silent partner	aktiver/stiller Gesellschafter *m*
nominal partner	Scheingesellschafter *m*
general/limited partner	Komplementär *m*, Vollhafter *m*/Kommanditist *m*, Teilhafter *m*
senior/junior partner	firmenälterer/firmenjüngerer Gesellschafter *m*
managing partner	geschäftsführender Teilhaber *m*/Gesellschafter *m*
partnership agreement/deed	Gesellschaftsvertrag *m*
partnership share/interest	Gesellschaftsanteil *m*
contributions *pl* of the partners, funds *pl* invested by the partners	Gesellschaftseinlagen *f pl*
equity/proprietory capital	Eigenkapital *n*
borrowed capital	Fremdkapital *n*
liability of the partners	Haftung *f* der Gesellschafter
joint liability	gesamtschuldnerische Haftung *f*
meeting of the partners	Gesellschafterversammlung *f*
partnership assets *pl*/property	Gesellschaftsvermögen *n*
limited partner's share	Kommanditanteil *m*
partnership capital/debts *pl*	Kapital *n*/Schulden *f pl* der Gesellschaft
profit sharing	Gewinnbeteiligung *f*
share of profits	Gewinnanteil *m*
dissolution of the partnership	Auflösung *f* der Gesellschaft

Unternehmen 193

3. Companies and Corporations

Kapitalgesellschaften

non-profit-making company	gemeinnützige Gesellschaft *f*
registered/*Am* incorporated company	eingetragene Gesellschaft *f*, rechtsfähige Handelsgesellschaft *f*, *Am* Aktiengesellschaft *f*
joint-stock company	Aktiengesellschaft *f*, AG *(ab 7 Aktionären)*, *Am* Handelsgesellschaft *f* ohne eigene Rechtspersönlichkeit
public (limited) company, *Am* stock company	Aktiengesellschaft *f*, AG
private (limited) company	Gesellschaft *f* mit beschränkter Haftung, GmbH *(2 - 50 Aktionäre)*
close company, *Am* close corporation	Gesellschaft *f* mit beschränkter Haftung, GmbH *(bis zu 35 Aktionäre)*
company law	Gesellschaftsrecht *n*
articles *pl* of association/ *Am* of incorporation	Gesellschaftsstatuten *pl*, Satzung *f* *(einer AG)*
memorandum of association	Gründungsurkunde *f*
by(e)laws *pl*	Statuten *n pl*
rules *pl* of procedure	Geschäftsordnung *f*
shareholder, *Am* stockholder	Aktionär *m*/Gesellschafter *m* *(einer GmbH)*
register of the shareholders	Aktionärsverzeichnis *n*
share in a company	Gesellschaftsanteil *m*
monetary/cash subscription	Bar-/Geldeinlage *f*
Registrar of Companies	Registerbeamter *m*
registration	Eintragung *f*
trading/business capital, *Am* capital stock	Gesellschaftskapital *n*
minimum capital	Mindestkapital *n*
share capital	Aktienkapital *n (einer AG)*, Stammkapital *n (einer GmbH)*
increase in the share capital	Erhöhung *f* des Aktien-/Stammkapitals
corporate assets *pl*, property of a company	Gesellschaftseigentum *n*
head/registered/principal office	Gesellschaftssitz *m*
firm/company/*Am* corporate name	Gesellschaftsname *m*
Register of Business Names	Gesellschaftsregister *n*
corporate purpose	Gesellschaftsziel *n*/-zweck *m*
the first meeting	Gründungsversammlung *f*
financial/fiscal year	Geschäftsjahr *n*

194 Business Enterprise

company records *pl*	Gesellschaftsunterlagen *f pl*
business report	Geschäftsbericht *m*
annual account	Jahresabschluß *m*
annual statement/balance-sheet	Jahresbilanz *f*
profit and loss account	Gewinn- und Verlustrechnung *f*
corporate earnings *pl*/profits *pl*	Gesellschaftsgewinne *m pl*
annual general meeting	Hauptversammlung *f (AG)*/Gesellschafterversammlung *f (GmbH)*
distribution/division of profits	Gewinnausschüttung *f*/-verteilung *f*
corporate debts *pl*/liabilities *pl*	Gesellschaftsschulden *f pl*/-verbindlichkeiten *f pl*
statutory reserves *pl*	gesetzliche Rücklagen *f pl*
provision, reserve	Rückstellung *f*
corporate tax	Gesellschaftssteuer *f*

Types of shares   *Aktienarten*

equity shares *pl*, equities *pl*	Dividendenpapiere *n pl*
ordinary share	Stammaktie *f*
founder's share	Gründeraktie *f*
deferred share/*Am* stock	Nachzugsaktie *f*
bonus share	Gratisaktie *f*
preference share, *Am* preferred stock	Vorzugsaktie *f*
cumulative preference share	kumulative/nachzugsberechtigte Vorzugsaktie *f*
participating preference share	Vorzugsaktie *f* mit zusätzlicher Gewinnbeteiligung
participating share, *Am* profit sharing stock	gewinnberechtigte Aktie *f*
personal/registered share	Namensaktie *f*
bearer share	Inhaberaktie *f*
voting share	Stimmrechtsaktie *f*
fresh/new share	neue Aktie *f*
mining share	Bergwerksaktie *f*, Kux *f*
investment shares *pl*	Investmentanteile *m pl*
share certificate	Aktienurkunde *f*
shareholding	Aktienbesitz *m*/Beteiligung *f*
share prices *pl*	Aktien-/Börsenkurse *m pl*
increase/decrease in share prices	Kursanstieg *m*/-abschwächung *f*
fall/drop in share prices	Kursrückgang *m*
subscription to shares	Aktienzeichnung *f*
share purchase	Aktienkauf *m*
parcel/block of shares	Aktienpaket *n*
right to receive a dividend	Dividendenanspruch *m*
stock warrant *Am*	Aktienbezugsschein *m*
subscription right, *Am* shareholder's preemptive right	Bezugsrecht *n*

dividend warrant	Dividendenschein *m*
interest coupon	Zinsschein *m*
share/stock redemption	Rückkauf *m* von Aktien
shares at current quotation, value of stock	Kurswert *m*
rate of issue	Ausgabe-, Emissionskurs *m*
oversubscription	Überzeichnung *f*
payment in full	Vollzahlung *f*
right to vote	Stimmrecht *n*
single/plural vote	einfaches/mehrfaches Stimmrecht *n*
right to object/protest	Einspruchsrecht *n*
publication of the prospectus	Veröffentlichung *f* des Prospekts

4. Business Combinations — Unternehmenszusammenschlüsse

pool, combination, combine	Unternehmenszusammenschluß *m*
holding company	Dachgesellschaft *f*
amalgamation, fusion, merger, integration	Fusion *f*, Verschmelzung *f*
trust	Trust *m*
concern	Konzern *m*
cartel	Kartell *n*, internationaler Trust *m*
syndicate	Konsortium *n*
banking syndicate	Bankenkonsortium *n*
vertical/horizontal integration	vertikaler/horizontaler Zusammenschluß *m*
optimum size	optimale Größe *f*
monopoly enterprise	marktbeherrschendes Unternehmen *n*
price agreement/combination	Preisabsprache *f*/-kartell *n*
demarcation of markets	Abgrenzung *f* der Verkaufsgebiete
purchasing combine	Abnehmerkartell *n*
decartelization	Konzernentflechtung *f*
corporate combination	Konzernzusammenschluß *m*
interlocking combine	Konzernverflechtung *f*
parent company	Muttergesellschaft *f*
subsidiary (company)	Tochter-/Konzerngesellschaft *f*

5. Management — Betriebs-, Geschäftsführung

managerial staff	Betriebs-, Geschäftsleitung *f*
managing director	leitender/geschäftsführender Direktor *m*
acting director	stellvertretender Direktor *m*
business manager	Geschäftsführer *m*
management consulting	Unternehmensberatung *f*

196 Business Enterprise

management policy	Unternehmenspolitik f
operations research	Unternehmensforschung f
management planning	Unternehmensplanung f
management engineering Am	Betriebstechnik f
managerial functions pl	Unternehmerfunktionen f pl
managerial position	leitende Stellung f
chairman of the board of directors	Vorsitzender m des Verwaltungsrates

6. Financing — Finanzierung, Kapitalbeschaffung

preliminary/interim financing	Vor-/Zwischenfinanzierung f
self-financing	Eigenfinanzierung f
bond issue	Emission f von Schuldverschreibungen
bondholder	Wertpapier-/Obligationeninhaber m
bonded debt	Obligations-/Anleiheschuld f
convertible bonds pl	Wandelschuldverschreibungen f pl, -obligationen f pl
debenture	Schuldverschreibung f (einer Handelsgesellschaft)
debenture bonds pl Am	festverzinsliche Schuldverschreibungen f pl
debenture to bearer	Inhaberschuldverschreibung f
debenture holder	Inhaber m einer Schuldverschreibung/Pfandbriefinhaber m
debenture stock Am	Anleiheschuld f
debenture conditions pl	Ausgabebedingungen f pl
security holdings pl/ownership	Wertpapierbestände m pl/-besitz m
security market	Wertpapiermarkt m
security underwriter	Emissionshaus n
mortgage debt	Hypotheken-/Grundschuld f
mortgage claim/creditor	Hypothekenforderung f/-gläubiger m
mortgage interest	Hypothekenzinsen m pl
mortgages pl receivable/payable	Hypothekenforderungen f pl/-schulden f pl (Bilanz)
current assets pl/liabilities pl	Umlaufvermögen n/kurzfristige Verbindlichkeiten f pl
fixed assets pl/liabilities pl	Anlagevermögen n/langfristige Verbindlichkeiten f pl
surplus	Reingewinn m einschließlich Rücklagen
earned surplus	Rücklagen f pl aus Jahresüberschüssen und Gewinn
paid-in surplus	Kapitalzuführung f über den Nennbetrag hinaus

Unternehmen 197

borrowed funds *pl*	Fremdmittel *n pl*
borrowing cost/requirement	Kreditkosten *pl*/-bedarf *m*
undistributed/undivided profits *pl*	nicht ausgeschütteter Gewinn *m*
book value/loss/profit	Buchwert *m*/-verlust *m*/-gewinn *m*
capitalized value	Ertragswert *m*
capitalization	Kapitalisierung *f (einer Gesellschaft)*
to found/to establish/to form a company	eine Gesellschaft gründen
to set up/to start a business	ein Geschäft gründen
to join a firm as partner	bei einer Firma als Partner eintreten
to retire/to withdraw from a partnership	als Gesellschafter ausscheiden
to manage/to operate/to conduct a company	eine Gesellschaft leiten
to earn a profit on a business	aus einem Geschäft Gewinn erzielen
to own an enterprise	Eigentümer eines Unternehmens sein
to apply/to subscribe for shares	Aktien zeichnen
to invite the public to subscribe for shares	Aktien öffentlich zur Zeichnung auflegen
to hold shares	Aktien besitzen
to issue/to allot shares	Aktien ausgeben/zuteilen
to deal in shares	Aktien handeln
to place an issue	eine Emission unterbringen
to pay up a share	eine Aktie voll einbezahlen
to part-pay a share	eine Aktie teilweise einbezahlen
to draw up detailed Articles of Association	ins einzelne gehende Satzungen aufsetzen
to lodge documents with the Registrar	Unterlagen beim Registergericht einreichen
to incorporate	als juristische Person eintragen
to summon/to hold a general meeting	eine Hauptversammlung einberufen/abhalten
to form/to constitute a quorum	beschlußfähig sein
to relieve the board of managers	den Vorstand entlasten
to declare/to distribute a dividend	eine Dividende festsetzen/ausschütten
to be accountable to s.o.	jdm gegenüber verantwortlich sein
to merge, to amalgamate, to absorb	fusionieren, sich zusammenschließen
to co-operate	zusammenarbeiten
to fix minimum prices	Mindestpreise festlegen
to restrain/to stifle competition	den Wettbewerb beschränken
to cut the manufacturing cost	die Herstellungskosten senken
to reap huge profits	riesige Gewinne einheimsen/einstecken

Business Enterprise

to inflate the selling price	den Verkaufspreis künstlich erhöhen
to recoup [ri'ku:p] a loss	einen Verlust ausgleichen
to be in a state of insolvency/to become insolvent	zahlungsunfähig sein/werden
to declare o.'s insolvency	sich für zahlungsunfähig erklären
to declare o.s. insolvent	seine Zahlungen einstellen
to be adjudged insolvent	für bankrott erklärt werden
to go bankrupt	in Konkurs geraten/bankrott machen
to go into voluntary or compulsory liquidation	in freiwillige oder in Zwangsliquidation treten
to wind up/to liquidate a company	die Liquidation einer Handelsgesellschaft durchführen
to dissolve a company	eine Gesellschaft auflösen
to institute proceedings for dissolution	das Verfahren zur Auflösung/*Am* Entflechtung einleiten
to restore the confidence of investors	das Vertrauen des Anlagepublikums zurückgewinnen
to have a right to information	ein Anrecht auf Information haben
managing	geschäftsführend
in a managerial capacity	in leitender Stellung
limited	mit beschränkter Haftung
personally/fully liable	persönlich/unbeschränkt haftend
unlimited	unbeschränkt
nominal	nominell
contractual	vertraglich
incorporated/Inc.	handelsgerichtlich/als juristische Person eingetragen
retiring, outgoing	ausscheidend
entitled to a dividend	dividendenberechtigt
at a premium, above par	über dem Nennwert, über pari
at a discount, below par	unter dem Nennwert, unter pari
vulnerable to recession	rezessionsempfindlich
on a commercial basis	auf kommerzieller Grundlage
at reasonable prices	zu vernünftigen Preisen
for the benefit of	zugunsten von
at meetings	bei Sitzungen
undesirable	nicht wünschenswert, unerwünscht
unbusinesslike	unkaufmännisch, nicht geschäftsmäßig
voluntary	freiwillig
compulsory	obligatorisch
domestic	inländisch, binnenwirtschaftlich
insolvent	zahlungsunfähig

Sätze und Redewendungen:

A sole trader enters business on his own account.	Ein Inhaber einer Einzelfirma nimmt seine geschäftliche Tätigkeit auf eigene Rechnung auf.
A licence must be obtained for certain classes of business.	Für bestimmte Geschäftszweige ist eine Konzession erforderlich.
The name of the business must be registered.	Die Firmenbezeichnung muß eingetragen sein.
The partnership is particularly suitable for professional people.	Die Personengesellschaft/Sozietät ist besonders für Angehörige der freien Berufe geeignet.
The partner is personally liable to the full extent of his private wealth for the debts of the business.	Der Gesellschafter haftet persönlich mit seinem ganzen Privatvermögen für die Schulden der Firma.
Partners may not use firm funds for their own benefit.	Gesellschafter dürfen firmeneigene Mittel nicht für eigene Zwecke benutzen.
A real partner shares in the profits of the firm and is liable for losses.	Ein aktiver Teilhaber ist am Gewinn der Firma beteiligt und haftet für Verluste.
A limited partner is responsible only for the amount that he has contributed to the organization.	Ein beschränkt haftender Gesellschafter haftet nur für den Betrag, den er in die Firma eingebracht hat.
Liability is limited to the contribution.	Die Haftung ist auf die Einlage beschränkt.
The Registrar will issue a Certificate of Incorporation which bestows upon the company a separate legal personality.	Der Registerbeamte stellt dann eine Registrierbescheinigung aus, die der Gesellschaft eigene Rechtspersönlichkeit verleiht.
Invitations to the public to subscribe for shares are made in a prospectus.	Die Aufforderung an die Öffentlichkeit zur Zeichnung von Aktien geschieht mit einem Prospekt.
The prospectus must be registered with the Registrar before the public are invited to subscribe.	Der Prospekt muß vom Registerbeamten in das Register eingetragen sein, ehe die Öffentlichkeit zur Zeichnung aufgefordert wird.
The public send in for shares and allotments are made.	Das Publikum fordert Aktien an, worauf Zuteilungen erfolgen.
Dividends are declared.	Dividenden werden festgesetzt.
All limited companies have to file a copy of their balance sheet with their annual report.	Alle Kapitalgesellschaften, bei denen die Haftung der Gesellschafter beschränkt ist, müssen ihrem Jahresbericht ein Exemplar der Bilanz beilegen.

Share prices move up/increased further/were maintained/weakened.

Die Aktienkurse werden fester/zogen weiter an/hielten sich/gaben nach.

The shares showed an uneven tendency/are down.

Die Aktien tendierten uneinheitlich/stehen niedrig.

All directors are elected by majority vote.

Alle Direktoren werden mit Stimmenmehrheit gewählt.

Creditors must be prompt in presenting claims.

Gläubiger müssen Forderungen umgehend einreichen.

XI. Advertising — Werbung

advertising	Werbewesen n, Werbung f, Reklame f
sales promotion	Absatz-, Verkaufsförderung f
advertising media pl	Werbeträger m pl
media research	Werbeträgerforschung f
advertising agency	Werbeagentur f
advertising department	Werbeabteilung f
advertising material	Werbematerial n
advertising campaign/drive	Werbekampagne f/-feldzug m
advertising consultant	Werbeberater m
advertising manager	Werbeleiter m/-direktor m
advertising expenditures pl	Werbekosten pl
market structure	Marktstruktur f
sales analysis	Verkaufsanalyse f
test campaign	Versuchskampagne f
announcement/initial campaign	Einführungskampagne f
circulation	Verbreitung f eines Werbeträgers
circulation area	Verbreitungsgebiet n
copy	Text m
copy department	Textabteilung f
copy writer	Texter m
announcement	Ankündigung f
advertising message	Werbebotschaft f, -aussage f, Nachricht f
advertising research	Werbeforschung f
audience	Leserschaft f, Publikum n
audience analysis	Leseranalyse f
coverage	erfaßter Personenkreis m
dispersion	Streuung f *(eines Werbemittels)*
product image	Produktimage n
product test	Produkttest m
visualiser, draughtsman	Gestalter m
time schedule, date plan	Terminplan m
impact	Stoßkraft f, Wirksamkeit f

density	Dichte *f*
publicity value, advertising appeal	Werbekraft *f*

a) Audience research — Hörer-, Leser-, Zuschauerforschung

questionnaire [ˌkwestʃəˈnɛə]	Fragebogen *f*
leading question	Suggestivfrage *f*
alternative question	Alternativfrage *f*
informant/interviewee/respondent	Befragter *m*
interviewer	Befrager *m*, Interviewer *m*
sample	Stichprobe *f*
area sample	Flächenstichprobe *f*
sampling, sampling-technique	Auswahl-, Stichprobenverfahren *n*
sampling fraction	Stichprobenanteil *m*
consumer survey	Konsumentenbefragung *f*
retail survey	Einzelhändlerbefragung *f*
income group	Einkommensgruppe *f*
head of household	Haushaltsvorstand *m*
prospect, prospective customer	möglicher Kunde *m*, Interessent *m*
buying motive/motivation	Kaufmotiv *n*
shopping/buying behaviour	Kaufverhalten *n*
buying habits *pl*	Kaufgewohnheiten *f pl*
client/consumer behaviour	Kunden-/Verbraucherverhalten *n*
buyer's resistance	Kaufhemmung *f*
sales resistance	Kaufunlust *f*
brand image	Markenbild *n*/-profil *n*
brand preference	Bevorzugung *f* einer Marke, Vorliebe *f* für eine Marke
brand loyalty	Markentreue *f*

b) Direct advertising — Direktwerbung

direct mail advertising	Direktwerbung *f* durch die Post; Postversandwerbung *f*
mailing/address list	Adressenliste *f*
institutional advertising	Firmenwerbung *f*
mass advertising	geballte Werbung *f*
outdoor advertising	Außenwerbung *f*
opportunity advertising	Gelegenheitswerbung *f*
supplementary advertising	zusätzliche Werbung *f*, Ergänzungswerbung *f*
transport(ation) advertising	Verkehrsmittelwerbung *f*, Werbung *f* in Verkehrsmitteln
point-of-sale advertising	Werbung *f* am Verkaufsort
mail order advertising	Versandhauswerbung *f*
cooperative advertising	Gemeinschaftswerbung *f*
retail advertising	Einzelhandelswerbung *f*
tie-up advertising	kombinierte Werbeaktion *f*

202 Advertising

classified ad(vertisement)	kleine Anzeige f
wall sign	Wandzeichen n
poster, bill	Plakat n, Affiche f
permanent poster	Dauerplakat n
station poster	Bahnhofsplakat n
show-card	Aufstellplakat n
car card	Straßenbahn-/Omnibusplakat n
poster pillar	Litfaß-/Anschlagsäule f
billboard, panel, poster hoarding	Werbetafel f, Anschlagtafel f, -zaun m
broadside	großer Faltprospekt m
booklet	Werbebroschüre f, Prospekt m
folder	Faltprospekt m
package insert	Packungsbeilage f
sales letter	Werbebrief m
mail-out	Reklamedrucksache f
follow-up letter	nachfassender Werbebrief m
advertising reply card	Werbeantwortkarte f
circular	Reklamerundschreiben n
streamer	Streifenanzeige f
leaflet, pamphlet	Flugblatt n
handbill	Reklamezettel m
advertising pamphlet	Werbebroschüre f
mail-order catalog(ue)	Versandkatalog m
contest	Preisausschreiben n, Wettbewerb m
free gift	Zugabe f, Werbegeschenk n
novelty	Werbegeschenkartikel m
free sample	Werbemuster n
introductory price	Werbe-/Einführungspreis m
knock-down price	Reklamepreis m
bargain sale	Reklameverkauf m; Verkauf m zu herabgesetzten Preisen

c) Advertiser — *Inserent*

press advertising	Anzeigenwerbung f
insertion order	Anzeigen-/Insertionsauftrag m
professional magazine, specialist periodical	Fachzeitschrift f, -blatt n
class magazine	Zeitschrift f für eine bestimmte Gruppe
weekly (paper)	Wochenzeitung f
periodical, magazine	Zeitschrift f
house organ	Hauszeitschrift f
window lettering	Schaufensterbeschriftung f
newsprint	Zeitungspapier n
average circulation	durchschnittliche Auflage f
closing date, copy date, copy deadline	Anzeigenschluß m
release date	Veröffentlichungstermin m

publication date	Erscheinungsdatum *n*
front page, title page	Titelseite *f*
display advertisement	Großanzeige *f*
full-page advertisement	ganzseitige Anzeige *f*
double page spread	doppelseitige Anzeige *f*
want ads *pl*	Suchanzeigen *f pl*
repeat (ad)	Wiederholungsanzeige *f*
newspaper space	Zeitungsanzeigenteil *m*
advertising space	Werbefläche *f*
insert, inset, tip-in	Beilage *f*
insertion	Einschaltung *f*
advertising slogan	Werbeslogan *m*
copy point	Werbeargument *n* im Text
running text	fortlaufender Text *m*
newspaper layout, type area	Satzspiegel *m*
type face	Schriftart *f*
column	Spalte *f*
caption	Bildunterschrift *f*, Zwischentitel *m*
head(ing), headline	Überschrift *f*
make-up	Umbruch *m*
blow up, enlargement	Vergrößerung *f*
line drawing	Strichzeichnung *f*
specimen copy	Probeexemplar *n*, -nummer *f*
complimentary copy	Werbenummer *f*
voucher copy	Belegexemplar *n*
press cuttings *pl*/clippings *pl*	Anzeigenausschnitte *m pl*
box/code/key number	Chiffrenummer *f*, Kennziffer *f*
sliding scale	Rabattstaffel *f*
series discount	Wiederholungsrabatt *m*

d) Television advertising — *Fernsehwerbung*

commercial/pay television	Werbefernsehen *n*
radio announcement	Werbedurchsage *f*
radio advertising	Rundfunkwerbung *f*
spot broadcasting *Am*	örtlich beschränkte Rundfunkreklame *f*
live broadcast	Direktübertragung *f*
listener research	Hörerforschung *f*
sponsor	Sponsor *m*, Geldgeber *m*
spot (announcement)	Kurzwerbung *f*, Spot *m*
commercial	Werbedurchsage *f*
screen advertising	Filmwerbung *f*
news-reel	Wochenschau *f (Kino)*
cartoon film	Zeichentrickfilm *m*
slide advertising	Diapositiv-Werbung *f*
neon sign	Neon-Leuchtwerbung *f*
spectacular	*(bewegliche)* Leuchtwerbung *f*; großformatige Anzeige *f*

demonstration	Vorführung f
to insert, to publish	annoncieren, inserieren
to make propaganda	die Werbetrommel rühren
to place advertisements	Anzeigen unterbringen/aufgeben
to advertise widely	eine großzügige Werbung betreiben
to create demand	Bedarf schaffen/hervorrufen
to boom/to boost s.th.	für etw Reklame machen
to run an advertising campaign	einen Reklamefeldzug durchführen
to bring a campaign to a successful issue	einen Werbefeldzug erfolgreich abschließen
to emphasize a trade-mark	eine Handelsmarke herausstreichen/-stellen
to batter down sales resistance	gegen die Kaufunlust mit allen Mitteln ankämpfen
to contain vigorous sales appeals	einen kräftigen Verkaufsappell ent-/beinhalten
to release to the press	für die Presse freigeben
to urge hesitating prospects to take action	unschlüssige potentielle Käufer zu einem Entschluß veranlassen
to interest children in a product	Kinder für ein Produkt interessieren
to persuade dealers	Händler überzeugen
to feature qualities	Qualitäten heraus-/in den Vordergrund stellen
to present selling points	Verkaufsargumente herausstellen
to give information about merchandise	Auskunft über Waren erteilen
to attract prospective buyers to the store	potentielle Käufer veranlassen, den Laden zu betreten
to induce people to buy a product	ein Produkt bei der Bevölkerung einführen
to introduce a new product	ein neues Produkt einführen
to increase sales during off-season	den Absatz in der stillen Zeit steigern
to speed up the sale of slow sellers	den Verkauf von Waren mit geringer Umschlagshäufigkeit beschleunigen
to extend the use of commodities	den Anwendungsbereich von Waren ausweiten
to meet price competition	der Preiskonkurrenz entgegentreten
effective	werbewirksam
attractive	zugkräftig
convincing	überzeugend
persistent	nachhaltig; anhaltend
consistent	übereinstimmend, einheitlich, konsequent
pertinent	sachdienlich, zweckdienlich

plausible	einleuchtend, vertrauenerweckend
timely	aktuell; rechtzeitig
specific	spezifisch, speziell, bestimmt
selective	gezielt
accessory	zusätzlich
editorial	redaktionell
bi-monthly	zweimonatlich
bi-weekly	zweiwöchentlich, vierzehntäglich
discriminatory	diskriminierend
deceptive, misleading	irreführend
for advertising purposes	für/zu Werbezwecken

Sätze und Redewendungen:

The chief objective of advertising is to arouse and stimulate new wants.	Die Hauptaufgabe der Werbung besteht darin, neue Bedürfnisse anzuregen und zu wecken.
The main purpose of an advertisement is to catch the eye of the potential buyer.	Das wesentliche Ziel einer Anzeige besteht darin, die Aufmerksamkeit potentieller Käufer zu fesseln.
Market research classifies potential purchasers in terms of age, sex, locality, income level, and social status.	Die Marktforschung teilt potentielle Käufer nach den Gesichtspunkten Alter, Geschlecht, Wohnort, Einkommen und soziale Stellung ein.
The primary function of radio advertising is to familiarize the audience with the name of the product and the manufacturer.	Der Haupzweck der Rundfunkwerbung besteht darin, die Hörer mit dem Namen des Produkts und des Herstellers bekanntzumachen.
Direct advertising is a selling force that will produce immediate action.	Direktwerbung ist eine Verkaufsmethode, die eine unmittelbare Reaktion hervorrufen möchte.
The most important part of a circular or a follow-up letter is the first line.	Der entscheidende Teil eines Rundschreibens oder eines Nachfaßbriefes ist die erste Zeile.
The newspaper is a medium for obtaining quick sales.	Die Zeitung ist ein Werbemittel, um den Umsatz zu beschleunigen.
The inspection of merchandise is invited without obligation to purchase.	Eintritt ohne Kaufzwang.
Heavily advertised commodities are soaps and detergents, cigarettes and tobacco, soft drinks, sweets and chocolates.	Zu den Produkten, für die am stärksten geworben wird, zählen Seifen und Waschmittel, Zigaretten und Tabak, alkoholfreie Getränke, Süßigkeiten und Schokolade.

206 Communications

Advertising keeps the advertiser's name and his product before the consumer.	Die Werbung erinnert den Konsumenten ständig an Name und Produkt des Werbetreibenden.
He inserted an advertisement in a newspaper.	Er gab eine Anzeige in einer Zeitung auf.
Mr Smith is in the advertising line.	Mr Smith ist im Werbefach tätig.
The firm spends a lot of money on television advertising.	Die Firma gibt viel Geld für Fernsehwerbung aus.
He ran an advertisement only once.	Er hat ein Einzelinserat aufgegeben.

XII. Communications — Nachrichtenverkehr

1. Postal Service — Postdienst

a) General terms — Allgemeine Begriffe

communication service	Nachrichtensystem *n*/-dienst *m*
communication engineering	Fernmeldetechnik *f*
communication centre	Fernmeldestelle *f*
communication satellite	Nachrichtensatellit *m*
Universal Postal Union, UPU	Weltpostverein *m*, WPV
UPU Congress	Weltpostkongress *m*
postal transport	Postbeförderung *f*
international postal service	internationaler Postdienst *m*
internal postal service	Inlandspostdienst *m*
internal/domestic service	Inlandsverkehr *m*
local delivery area/zone	Ortszustellbereich *m*
local postal service	Ortspostdienst *m*
rural postal service	Landpostdienst *m*
urban postal service	Stadtpostdienst *m*
directory of post offices	Verzeichnis *n* der Postämter
postal establishment	Postdienststelle *f*
office of posting/mailing	Aufgabepostamt *n*
office of origin	Aufgabestelle *f*
sorting/distributing office	Versandamt *n*/Umleitamt *n*
office of reforwarding/redispatch	Umschlagamt *n*
self-service kiosk	stummes Postamt *n*
travelling/railway post office	Bahnpost *f*
General Post Office, G.P.O.	Hauptpost(amt *n*) *f*
postal van/truck; mail storage car/storage van	Postwagen *m*
van/car/truck with postal compartment	Packwagen *m* mit Postabteil
mail car/van	Bahnpostwagen *m*

Nachrichtenverkehr

international service	Auslandsverkehr m
(postal) item	Postsendung f
make-up of items	Beschaffenheit f der Sendung
posting/mailing time	Aufgabezeit f
box collection	Kastenleerung f
pigeonhole	Verteil-/Sortierfach n
sorting machine	Sortiermaschine f
size of items	Maße f pl der Sendungen
bulk posting	Masseneinlieferung f, -aufgabe f
bulk entry/advice/billing of items	summarische Eintragung f/Kartierung f der Sendungen
delay of an item	Verzögerung f einer Sendung
postal/mail delivery	Postzustellung f
delivery times/schedule of deliveries	Zustellzeiten f
withdrawal from a P.O.B.	Postfachabholung f
post office counter	Postschalter m
counter transaction/operation	Schalterdienst(verrichtung f) m
withdrawal at the counter	Abholung f am Schalter
issue of postage stamps	Ausgabe f von Postwertzeichen
latest posting time, mail closing time	Postschluß m
postman's walk, carrier's route	Zustellgang m
private letter-box	Hausbriefkasten m
postal employee	Postbediensteter m, -beamter m
service instruction/regulation	Dienstvorschrift f
service indication	Dienstvermerk m
detailed regulations pl	Vollzugsordnung f
inviolability of the mail	Unverletzlichkeit f des Briefgeheimnisses
postal secrecy	Postgeheimnis n
dispatching, sending	Versand m
forwarding/transmission of items	Übermittlung f von Sendungen
dispatch/forwarding/routing of mail	Leitung f der Postsendung
route of dispatching/of forwarding a mail	Leitweg m eines Kartenschlusses
surface mail	Postsendungen f pl (außer Luftpost)
circulation of bags	Umlauf m der Säcke
collective bag/sack	Sammelsack m
rerouting of mails	Umleitung f von Kartenschlüssen
sampling, (Statistik) spot check	Stichprobe f
coding, codification	Kodierung f
code mark/sign	vereinbartes Kennzeichen n
article found	Fundgegenstand m
scale of postal charges/rates	Gebührenstufen f pl
rate fixing/tariff structure	Gebührensystem n
sliding scale of charges	degressiver Tarif m

208 Communications

single rate of postage	einfache Gebühr *f*
basic charge	Grundgebühr *f*
delivery free of charges	gebühren- und abgabenfreie Aushändigung *f*
customs clearance fee	Verzollungsgebühr *f*

b) Letter/Parcel post — *Brief-/Paketpost*

user of the post	Postbenutzer *m*
addressee [ˌædreˈsiː]	Empfänger *m*
abbreviated address	Kurzanschrift *f*
correspondence	Briefsendungen *f pl*
collective envelope	Sammelumschlag *m*
window envelope	Fensterbriefumschlag *m*
method of address	Wortlaut *m* der Adresse
incorrect/incomplete address	fehlerhafte/unvollständige Anschrift *f*
correction of address	Berichtigung *f* der Anschrift
business address	Geschäftsadresse *f*
home/private address	Privatanschrift *f*
mailing address, post office address	Postanschrift *f*
change of address	Adressenänderung *f*
addressing machine, addressograph [əˈdresəugrɑːf]	Adressiermaschine *f*
letter card	Kartenbrief *m*, Briefkarte *f*
reply-paid postcard	Postkarte *f* mit Antwortkarte
reply postcard	Antwortpostkarte *f*
item in wrapper	Sendung *f* unter Streifband
stamped wrapper	Streifband *n* mit eingedrucktem Postwertzeichen
printed papers *pl*/printed matter	Drucksache *f*
sample of merchandise	Warenmuster *n*, -probe *f*
phonopost [ˈfəunəpəust]	Sprechbrief *m*, Phonopostsendung *f*
official correspondence	Dienstschreiben *n*
poste restante/*Am* general delivery item	postlagernde Sendung *f*
free postage	Gebühren-/Portofreiheit *f*
(pre)payment of postage	Frankierung *f*, Freimachung *f*
prepayment in cash/money	Barfrankierung *f*/-freimachung *f*
sale of postage stamps/reply coupons	Verkauf *m* von Postwertzeichen/Antwortscheinen
roll of postage stamps	Briefmarken-/Wertzeichenrolle *f*
charity postage stamp	Wohltätigkeitsmarke *f*
face value of a postage stamp	Nennwert *m* eines Postwertzeichens
commemorative postage stamp	Gedenkmarke *f*

perforation	Zähnung *f*
watermark	Wasserzeichen *n*
postage stamp overprint	Überdruck *m* eines Postwertzeichens
flaw in printing	Fehldruck *m*
period of validity	Gültigkeitsdauer *f*
gummed seal	Siegelmarke *f*
stamping/postmarking of items	Stempeln *n* der Sendungen
date-stamp/date-stamp impression	Datumstempel *m*/-abdruck *m*
cancellation/date-stamping of a postage stamp	Entwertung *f* eines Postwertzeichens
stamp-cancelling machine	Stempelmaschine *f*
postal franking impression/postage-paid imprint	Frankier-/Freimachungsaufdruck *m*
franking machine/postage meter	Frankier-/Freistempelmaschine *f*
embossing stamp	Trockenstempel *m*
publicity/propaganda/advertising slogan	Werbeflagge *f*/-stempel *m*
underpayment, insufficient postage, short payment	ungenügende Frankatur *f*/Freimachung *f*
unpaid correspondence	unfrankierte/nicht freigemachte Briefsendung *f*
absence of postage	fehlende Freimachung *f*
unstuck/invalidated postage stamp	abgefallene/für ungültig erklärte Briefmarke *f*
ordinary item	gewöhnliche Sendung *f*
unenclosed item	lose/bloßgehende Sendung *f*
undeliverable item, returned letter	unzustellbare/unanbringliche Sendung *f*
period of retention of items awaiting delivery	Lagerfrist *f* der lagernden Sendungen
warehousing charge	Lagergebühr *f*
mail storage compartment	Stauraum *m* für Kartenschlüsse
address/business card	Geschäftskarte *f*
commercial papers *pl*	Geschäftspapiere *n pl*
postal subscription	Postbezug *m*/-abonnement *n*
printed enclosure/insert	Zeitungsbeilage *f*
subscription period	Abonnementsdauer *f*
direct subscription	Verlagsstück *n*
subscription rate	Bezugspreis *m*
impression in relief for the blind	Blindenschriftsendung *f*
airmail item	Luftpostsendung *f*
air surcharge	Luftpostzuschlag *m*
airmail correspondence	Luftpostbriefsendung *f*
express item	Eilsendung *f*
registered item	Einschreibsendung *f*
insured item	Wertsendung *f*
declaration of value	Wertangabe *f*

insurance fee	Wert-/Versicherungsgebühr f
insured letter	Wertbrief m
determination of responsibility	Feststellung f der Verantwortung/Haftung
waiving of claim/waiver by the sender	Verzicht m des Absenders
right of appeal/recourse	Rückgriffsrecht n
compensation/indemnity for damage	Schadenersatz m
postal parcel, *Am* package	Postpaket n
ordinary parcel	gewöhnliches Paket n
grouped packet	Mischsendung f
dispatch note	Paketkarte f, Begleitadresse f
parcel bill	Frachtkarte f für Pakete
insured parcel	Wertpaket n
cumbersome/bulky parcel	sperriges Paket n
cash/collect on delivery; COD item/parcel	Nachnahmesendung f/-paket n
abandoned parcel	preisgegebenes Paket n
customs examination of mail	Zollabfertigung f der Postsendung

c) Forms for the use of the public

Formblätter/Formulare für Postbenutzer

enquiry form	Laufzettel-/Nachfrageformular n/-formblatt n
unsuccessful enquiries *pl*	erfolglose Nachforschungen f pl
reference slip	Hinweiszettel m
receipt/acknowledgement	Empfangsschein m/-bestätigung f
attestation	Bescheinigung f
accompanying documents *pl*	Begleitpapiere n pl
advice/notice of loading/of shipment	Verschiffungsbescheinigung f
advice of delivery, return receipt, A.R. (= *avis de réception*)	Rückschein m
verification note, bulletin of verification	Rückmeldung f
transit bulletin	Durchgangszettel m
stamped paper	Stempelpapier n
authorized annotation	zugelassene Ergänzung f
sticker, label	Klebezettel m, Vignette f
tie-on label, fly-tag	Anhängeadresse f
punched card	Lochkarte f
postal identity card	Postausweiskarte f
indelible/copying-ink pencil	Tintenstift m
to put into bags/sacks	einsacken
to forward, to send on	nachsenden

Nachrichtenverkehr

to missend a dispatch	eine Sendung fehlleiten
to raise a charge on s.th.	etw mit einer Gebühr belegen
to give a discharge/receipt	quittieren
to relieve s.o. from responsibility	jdn entlasten
unclaimed, abandoned	nicht abgeholt, preisgegeben
moved/gone away	verzogen/abgereist
deceased	gestorben
unknown	unbekannt
insufficient	ungenügend
unsorted, in bulk, loose	ungeordnet
fortuitous	unvorhergesehen
defaulting	säumig
refused	verweigert
confiscated	beschlagnahmt
by express, by special delivery	durch Eilboten
by/via airmail	mit Luftpost
care of, c/o	zu Händen von
in case of change of address	falls verzogen
according to requirements of the service	nach den Diensterfordernissen
ready for printing, passed for press	druckreif
for the records, as a reminder	(als) Vermerk
properly/fully prepaid	ordnungsgemäß freigemacht
postage free	porto-/gebührenfrei
exempt from charges	von Gebühren befreit
surcharged/unsurcharged	zuschlagpflichtig/-frei
unpaid	unfrankiert
at the exchange rate of	zum Umrechnungskurs von

Sätze und Redewendungen:

Deliver to addressee only/in person.	Eigenhändig zustellen.
Postage paid, PP.	Gebühr bezahlt.
The sender's address should appear both inside the parcel and on the cover.	Die Anschrift des Absenders ist im Innern des Pakets und auf der Außenseite anzubringen.
Sometimes the wrapping becomes damaged.	Gelegentlich wird die Verpackung beschädigt.
Parcels should be fastened either with strong string or stout adhesive tape.	Pakete sollten entweder mit starkem Bindfaden verschnürt oder mit kräftigem Klebestreifen verklebt werden.
The postage on a parcel must be prepaid.	Ein Paket muß freigemacht sein.
A parcel must not be posted in a letter-box.	Ein Paket darf nicht in einen Briefkasten geworfen werden.

Communications

A parcel should be marked "Parcel Post".	Ein Paket muß mit der Aufschrift „Paketpost" versehen sein.
He handed his parcel to the clerk at the post office counter.	Er übergab sein Paket dem Beamten am Schalter des Postamtes.
The sender must affix the postage stamps himself.	Der Absender muß die Briefmarken selbst aufkleben.
The sender should see that weight, size and postage are in order.	Der Absender hat darauf zu achten, daß Gewicht, Maße und Porto den Vorschriften entsprechen.

2. Postal Cheque/*Am* Check Office — Postscheckamt

a) Current postal account — *Postscheckkonto*

rightful holder of an account	rechtmäßiger Kontoinhaber *m*
postal cheque/*Am* check	Postscheck *m*
authenticity of the signature	Echtheit *f* der Unterschrift
drawer of a bill	Unterzeichner *m* eines Eigenwechsels
cheque payable to order	Orderscheck *m*
instruments *pl* deposited at postal cheque offices	bei Postscheckämtern domizilierte/zahlbar gestellte Papiere *n pl*
deposit of instruments	Zahlbarstellung *f* von Wertpapieren
interest on overdue payments	Verzugszinsen *m pl*
prescribed period	Verjährungsfrist *f*
due date	Verfalltag *m*
advice/notice of entry	Gutschriftanzeige *f*
advice/notice of transfer	Gutschriftzettel *m*
extract/statement of account	Kontoauszug *m*
credit balance	Kontoguthaben *n*/Habensaldo *m*
total	Endbetrag *m*
application for transfer	Antrag *m* auf Guthabenübertragung *f*
closing of an account	Aufhebung *f*/Löschung *f* eines Kontos
central clearing bank	Girozentrale *f*
clearing transactions *pl*	Giroverkehr *m*
transfer department	Giroabteilung *f*
deposits *pl* on a transfer account	Giroeinlagen *f pl*
counter banking transaction	Schalterdienst *m* des Zahlungsdienstes

b) Savings contract / Sparvertrag

savings deposit note, notice of savings deposit	Spareinzahlungsschein *m*
postal savings bank book	Postsparbuch *n*
current savings account	Sparkonto *n*
rightful holder of a savings book	rechtmäßiger Inhaber *m* eines Sparbuchs
settlement of accounts by offsetting	Rechnungsausgleich *m* durch Aufrechnung
acceptance of an account	Anerkennung *f* einer Rechnung
additional costs *pl*	Nebenkosten *pl*
recovery of charges *pl*	Einziehung *f* der Auslagen
conversion table	Umrechnungstabelle *f*
conversion of currency	Währungsumrechnung *f*
small coins/change	Kleingeld *n*
arrears *pl*	Rückstände *m pl*
objection to a payment	Sperren *n* einer Zahlung
authority to pay	Zahlungsermächtigung *f*
advice/notice of payment	Auszahlungsschein *m*/-bestätigung *f*
debit balance	Schuldsaldo *m*
transferring bank	Ursprungssparkasse *f*

c) Postal/Money order / Postanweisung

issue of a postal/money order *Am*	Ausstellung *f* einer Zahlungsanweisung
COD money order	Nachnahmepostanweisung *f*
collection money order	(Einzugs-) Auftragspostanweisung *f*
card money order	Kartenanweisung *f*
beneficiary	Zahlungsempfänger *m*
collection of amounts/of sums due	Einziehung *f* von fälligen Beträgen/der Postauftragspapiere
cancellation or reduction of the COD charge	Streichung *f* oder Herabsetzung *f* des Nachnahmebetrags
to provide a service	einen Dienst ausführen
to settle with/to indemnify the sender	den Absender entschädigen
to credit an account	einem Konto gutschreiben
to debit an account	ein Konto belasten
to keep an account	ein Konto führen
to present for collection	durch Postauftrag einziehen
to have legal authority	Rechtskraft haben

Communications

Sätze und Redewendungen:

The remittance services of the post-office provide a convenient means of transmitting sums of money by post.	Der Zahlungsverkehr über die Post bietet eine bequeme Möglichkeit, Geld postalisch zu überweisen.
Postal orders are available in certain fixed values.	„Postal orders" (Zahlungsanweisungen für Beträge bis zu 21 sh.) sind für bestimmte festgesetzte Beträge erhältlich.
Money orders can be drawn for any sum up to the authorized maximum.	„Money orders" (Zahlungsanweisungen für Beträge bis zu 50 £) können bis zu einem amtlich festgesetzten Höchstbetrag ausgestellt werden.
Money orders may also be transmitted by telegraph.	„Money orders" können auch telegraphisch überwiesen werden.
A counterfoil is provided on every postal order.	Jeder „postal order" hat einen Kontrollabschnitt.
The issuing officer will, if requested, impress the counterfoil with the date-stamp of the office of issue at the time of purchase.	Auf Verlangen drückt der ausgebende Beamte den Datumstempel der Ausgabestelle mit dem Datum des Ankaufstages auf den Kontrollabschnitt.
Postal orders will be paid at any post-office in the place named.	„Postal orders" werden bei jedem Postamt an dem angegebenen Ort eingelöst.
Postal orders are not negotiable; only the rightful owner may cash a postal order.	„Postal orders" sind nicht übertragbar; nur der rechtmäßige Eigentümer kann einen „postal order" einlösen.
Crossed postal orders may be paid only through a bank.	Gekreuzte „postal orders" können nur durch eine Bank eingelöst werden.
Postal orders are valid for a period of six months from the last day of the month of issue.	„Postal orders" behalten ihre Gültigkeit für einen Zeitraum von sechs Monaten vom letzten Tag des Ausgabemonats an gerechnet.

3. Mass Communication Media

a) Telephone traffic

telephone service	Telefondienst m
telephone directory	Telefon-, Fernsprechbuch n
London Yellow Pages Classified	Londoner Branchenverzeichnis
telephone call	(fernmündlicher) Anruf m
call number/signal	Rufnummer f/-zeichen n
dial(ling) tone	Amtszeichen n
engaged/busy signal	Besetztzeichen n
telephone subscriber	Fernsprechteilnehmer m
subscriber's telephone/telephone connection	Fernsprechanschluß m/-verbindung f
telephone extension	Fernsprechnebenstelle f, -nebenanschluß m
telephone switchboard	Klappenschrank m, Schaltschrank m
dial telephone	Selbstwähltelefon n
local call number, STD code	Vorwahl f
telephone line/circuit	Telefonleitung f
caller	Anrufer m
called subscriber	angerufener Teilnehmer m
conference call	Konferenzgespräch n
duplex telephony	Gegensprechverkehr m
shared service, party line	Sammelanschluß m
recall	Rückruf m
personal call	XP-Gespräch n mit Voranmeldung
reversed charge call	R-Gespräch n
emergency call	Notruf m
telephone booth/number/receiver	Fernsprechzelle f/-nummer f/-hörer m
coin-box telephone, Am pay station	Münzfernsprecher m
public telephone, call box	Fernsprechstelle f
telephone answering service	Fernsprechauftragsdienst m
telephone exchange	Telefonzentrale f
automatic/manual exchange	automatische Vermittlung f/Handvermittlung f
telephone charges pl/rates pl	Fernsprechgebühren $f\,pl$
telephone bill	Telefonrechnung f
trunk call, toll call, Am long-distance call	Ferngespräch n
trunk exchange, Am long-distance operator	Fernamt n
subscriber trunk dial(l)ing (STD), Am long-distance dial(l)ing	Selbstwählfernverkehr m

Massenkommunikationsmittel

Telefonverkehr

Communications

call unit	Gesprächseinheit *f*
walkie-talkie	tragbares Funksprechgerät *n*
earphone, headphone	Kopfhörer *m*
earpiece	Hörmuschel *f*
telephone recorder, ipsophone, automatic answering set	Telefon-/Anrufbeantworter *m*
wire tapping	Anzapfen *n* von Telefonleitungen
radio telephony	drahtlose Telefonie *f*
to ring s.o. up on the telephone	jdn anrufen
to telephone a message	eine Mitteilung fernmündlich durchgeben
to be on the telephone	am Apparat sein, telefonisch erreichbar sein
to inform s.o. by telephone	jdn fernmündlich benachrichtigen
to book a call	ein Gespräch anmelden
to put a call through	ein Ferngespräch herstellen
to answer the telephone	ans Telefon gehen
telephonic, by telephone	telefonisch, fernmündlich
on the telephone	durch Fernsprecher, am Telefon
over the telephone	per Telefon

Special telephone services — *Fernsprechansagedienst*

the speaking clock, time service, TIM	Normalzeit *f*
weather forecast service	Wettervorhersage *f*
weather information and forecast	Wetterdienst *m*
a recorded daily cooking service, recipe service	Küchenrezepte *n pl*, Kochrezept *n* des Tages
motoring	Straßenzustandsbericht *m*
Financial Times index and business	Börsenkurse *m pl*, Devisen- und Valutenkurse *m pl*
dial-a-disc	Schallplatte *f* des Tages
news summary — updated four times daily	Zusammenfassung *f* der Nachrichten – viermal täglich auf neuestem Stand
test matches	Länderspiele *n pl* (Cricket)
teletourist service — what's on in Town and around	aktueller Dienst für Touristen – was ist los in Stadt und Land?
alarm call	Weckdienst *m*
freephone *(you pay in advance for incoming calls)*	vorausbezahlte Anrufe *m pl*
advice of duration and charge/ADC	Gebührenansage *f*

Nachrichtenverkehr

telephone information service
999 emergency dialling services
(fire, police, ambulance, coastguard, lifeboat and rescue services)
telephone call service

Fernsprechnachrichtendienst *m*
Notruf 999 *(Feuerwehr, Polizei, Krankenwagen, Küstenwache, Lebensrettung)*

Fernsprechauftragsdienst *m*

Sätze und Redewendungen:

My friend answered the telephone.
Did anyone telephone me?
Telephone me tomorrow.
You are wanted on the telephone.

He replaced the receiver.
A public radiotelephone service enables the users of vehicles to make calls to, or receive them from any telephone in the United Kingdom network.
Call directory enquiries.
For the Operator dial 100.

For emergency calls dial 999.

Calls to emergency services are free.
He dialled the telephone number.

Subscribers obtain connections by turning a dial on their telephone.

Mary is on the phone *(fam)*.
He decided to telephone her.
I am going to telephone Mr Garrison.
We can telephone to your mother for a car.
Always write your telephone number exactly as it appears on your phone.
Self-dialled calls save time and money.
Any hold-ups on the way?
Synchronize your watches.

Mein Freund hob den Hörer ab.
Hat mich jemand angerufen?
Rufen Sie mich morgen an.
Sie werden am Telefon verlangt.
Er legte den Hörer wieder auf.
Über Funkfernsprecher können Fahrzeugbenutzer jeden dem englischen Telefonnetz angeschlossenen Apparat anrufen oder von dort angerufen werden.
Rufen Sie die Auskunft an.
Das Amt erreichen Sie unter der Nummer 100.
Den Notruf erreichen Sie unter der Nummer 999.
Notrufe sind gebührenfrei.

Er wählte die Fernsprechnummer.
Fernsprechteilnehmer stellen Verbindungen dadurch her, daß sie die Wählscheibe ihres Telefons drehen.
Mary ist am Telefon.
Er entschloß sich, sie anzurufen.
Ich will Mr. Garrison anrufen.

Wir können deine Mutter wegen eines Wagens anrufen.
Geben Sie Ihre Fernsprechnummer stets genau so an, wie sie auf Ihrem Apparat steht.
Der Selbstwählverkehr spart Zeit und Geld.
Gibt es einen Stau?
Vergleichen Sie die genaue Uhrzeit!

Communications

How to use the telephone:	*Benutzung des Fernsprechers:*
Be sure of the number before calling; use the directory.	Vor Abheben des Handapparates Rufnummer feststellen; Telefonbuch verwenden.
Speak into the mouthpiece.	In die Muschel sprechen.
Don't shout — the telephone was made for normal speech.	Nicht schreien – das Telefon ist für normale Sprechweise eingerichtet.
Identify yourself by name or business firm — not just "Hello".	Melden Sie sich mit Ihrem Namen oder Ihrer Firma – nicht mit „Hallo".
Hang up gently; slamming down the receiver is discourteous.	Legen Sie den Hörer vorsichtig auf; es ist unhöflich, ihn hinzuknallen.

Further Directions:
Dialling codes and charges are shown in the booklet. Have money ready, but do not insert yet. Dial first — pay on answer. Lift receiver, listen for dialling tone, and dial carefully — then wait for a tone. When you hear dialling tone place your finger in the correct hole, rotate the dial firmly round to the stop and let it return by itself. Do this for each figure that you need to dial.

The standard tones and their meanings are:

Dialling tone *(a continuous purring)*	now start dialling.
Ringing tone *(a repeated burr-burr)*	the called number is being rung.
Engaged tone *(a repeated single note)*	the called number or lines are in use.
Number unobtainable tone *(a steady note)*	there is no service on the called number; check the code and/or number.
Pay tone *(rapid pips)*	heard when using a pay-on-answer coin-box. Ringing tone changes, when number answers to pay tone. You should now insert money. You cannot be heard until you do so. Press in coin.

Coin slots are shut until first pay tone. Insert more money on dialling calls at any time during conversation, or at once if pay tone recurs. Keep a message pad handy. Replace the receiver promptly and firmly on its rest. This stops the charging if you made the call, and avoids the possibility of your line being temporarily disconnected.

b) Teleprinter communication	*Fernschreibverkehr*
telex exchange	Telex-/Fernschreibvermittlung *f*
teleprinter network/installation	Fernschreibnetz *n*/-anlage *f*
teleprinter connection	Fernschreibanschluß *m*

teletype (message)	Fernschreiben *n*
telex subscriber	Fernschreibteilnehmer *m*
telex directory	Verzeichnis *n* der Fernschreibteilnehmer
telex charges *pl*	Fernschreibgebühren *f pl*
multiplex printer	Mehrfachdrucker *m*
teletypesetter	Fernsetzmaschine *f*
to teletype	fernschreiben
to operate a teleprinter	einen Fernschreiber bedienen
to type/to receive a teleprint message	ein Fernschreiben durchgeben/erhalten
by telex	durch Fernschreiben
telephotographic	bildtelegrafisch
manual	manuell/mit der Hand *(vermittelt)*
soundproof	schalldicht
graphic, *adv* graphically	anschaulich, lebendig, plastisch

Sätze und Redewendungen:

The United Kingdom telex service is fully automatic.	Der Fernschreibdienst in England ist vollautomatisiert.
Calls may be made direct between the telex users.	Die Fernschreibteilnehmer können unmittelbar miteinander Verbindung aufnehmen.
The subscriber types his message on the keyboard of his teleprinter.	Der Teilnehmer schreibt seine Mitteilung auf der Tastatur seines Fernschreibers.
For call charging purposes Britain is divided into 50 charging areas.	Für die Gebührenberechnung ist England in 50 Gebührenzonen aufgeteilt.
International subscriber dialling between London and Paris was inaugurated in March 1963.	Der internationale Fernschreiber-Selbstwählverkehr zwischen London und Paris wurde im März 1963 aufgenommen.
Skilled typists operate the teletype machines.	Geübte Maschinenschreiber(innen) bedienen die Fernschreiber.
Newspapers have teletype service.	Zeitungen sind an das Fernschreibnetz angeschlossen.

c) Telegram service — *Telegrafendienst*

telegram reception/office	Telegrammannahme *f*/-schalter *m*
telegram form	Telegrammformular *n*
sender/addressee of a telegram	Absender *m*/Empfänger *m* eines Telegramms
telegraphic/cable address	Telegrammadresse *f*/Drahtanschrift *f*

Communications

cablegram	Kabeldepesche f/-nachricht f
wording of a telegram	Wortlaut m eines Telegramms
handing in a telegram	Aufgabe f eines Telegramms
reply-paid telegram	Telegramm n mit vorausbezahlter Antwort, RP-Telegramm n
cash-on-delivery telegram	Telegramm n zu Lasten des Empfängers
telegraphic code/key	Telegrammschlüssel m
registered address	vereinbarte Telegrammkurzanschrift f
fast/greetings telegram	Blitz-/Glückwunschtelegramm n
letter telegram, LT, lettergram, telegram delivered by mail	Brieftelegramm n
inland/overseas telegram	Inlands-/Übersee-, Auslandstelegramm n
cipher/code telegram	verschlüsseltes Telegramm n
telegram to follow	nachzusendendes Telegramm n
forwarded telegram	nachgesandtes Telegramm n
urgent/deferred telegram	dringendes/gewöhnliches Telegramm n
telephoned telegram, telegram by telephone, phonogram	zugesprochenes Telegramm n
telegraphic answer	Drahtantwort f
telegraphic message	telegrafische Mitteilung f
telegraph messenger	Telegramm-, Depeschenbote m
telegraph acceptance	Drahtakzept n
telegraphic transfer	telegrafische Überweisung f
money order telegram	Überweisungs-/Postanweisungstelegramm n
telegraph pole/Am post	Telegrafenstange f
telegraph line	Telegrafenlinie f
telephoto	Bildtelegramm n, Funkbild n
telephotography	Bildtelegrafie f
ticker (telegraph)	automatischer Schreib-/Börsentelegraf m
to telegraph, to wire	ein Telegramm absenden, telegrafieren
to send off/to deliver a telegram	ein Telegramm aufgeben/zustellen
to dispatch a telegram	ein Telegramm befördern
to write a message in cipher	eine Nachricht chiffrieren

Sätze und Redewendungen:

He telegraphed the news.	Er gab die Nachricht telegrafisch durch.
We will let you know by telegram/wire/cable.	Wir werden Sie telegrafisch verständigen.
His father cabled money.	Sein Vater überwies telegrafisch Geld.

Telegraph services to overseas countries are operated from Electra House in London.	Der Telegrammverkehr nach Übersee wird von der Zentrale Electra House in London durchgeführt.
He sent a telegram to/he telegraphed his sister in New York.	Er schickte seiner Schwester in New York ein Telegramm.

d) Broadcasting — *Rundfunk/-übertragung*

broadcast	Rundfunk *m*/-sendung *f*/Rundfunk-, Fernsehprogramm *n*
broadcasting station	Rundfunksender *m*
studio	Studio *n*, Aufnahme-/Senderaum *m*, (Film-) Atelier *n*
transmitting station, transmitter	Sender *m*
receiving/sending station	Empfangs-/Sendestation *f*
transmitting aerial	Sendeantenne *f*
radio installation/tower	Funkanlage *f*/-turm *m*
radio/broadcast announcement	Rundfunkdurchsage *f*
broadcaster	Rundfunksprecher *m*
radio newsreel	Wochenübersicht *f (im Rundfunk)*
newscast *Am*	Nachrichtensendung *f*
news bulletin, *Am* news flash	Kurznachrichten *f pl*
newsreader, *Am* newscaster	Nachrichtensprecher *m*
broadcast/radio listener	Rundfunkhörer *m*
broadcast receiving licence	Rundfunkgenehmigung *f*
outside broadcasts *pl*	nicht im Studio aufgenommene Sendungen *f pl*
live broadcast	Direktübertragung *f*
time signal	Zeitzeichen *n*
light entertainment	leichte Unterhaltung *f*
radio/broadcast advertising	Rundfunkwerbung *f*
commercial broadcasting	Werbefunk *m*
to listen in to a concert	im Radio ein Konzert hören
to hear s.th. on/over the radio	etw im Radio hören
to speak over the radio	im Radio sprechen
to turn off/on the radio	das Radio aus-/einschalten
to speak into a microphone	in ein Mikrofon sprechen
on the radio	im Rundfunk

Sätze und Redewendungen:

Many people listen to the radio every day.	Viele Leute hören täglich Radio.
You can hear hourly news broadcasts.	Man kann im Radio stündlich Nachrichten hören.

222 Communications

The radio programme is broadcast from a studio.	Das Radioprogramm wird von einem Senderaum/Studio aus gesendet.
Radio studios are soundproof.	Rundfunkstudios sind schalldicht.
The programme must be carefully timed before being put on the air.	Das Programm muß zeitlich sorgfältig abgestimmt sein, ehe es ausgestrahlt wird.
News events, market quotations, and sport scores are brought to the world almost immediately.	Die neuesten Ereignisse, Börsennotierungen und Sportergebnisse werden beinahe direkt der Öffentlichkeit vermittelt.
Radio and television broadcasting has become a new tool for education.	Radio und Fernsehen sind neue Bildungsmittel geworden.
The means of communication provide the information necessary for decisions.	Die Kommunikationsmittel liefern die Informationen, die für Entscheidungen erforderlich sind.

e) Television (broadcasting) — Fernsehen

television station/tower	Fernsehstation *f*/-turm *m*
colour television	Farbfernsehen *n*
television camera/transmitter	Fernsehkamera *f*/-sender *m*
television set/receiver	Fernsehapparat *m*/-empfänger *m*
telecast, television broadcast	Fernsehsendung *f*
channel	Kanal *m*
television news	Fernsehnachrichten *f pl*
television screen	Bildschirm *m*
television announcer	Fernsehansager *m*
weather chart	Wetterkarte *f*
television coverage	Fernsehberichterstattung *f*
(tele)viewer	Fernsehteilnehmer *m*
television advertising	Fernsehwerbung *f*
commercial television	Werbefernsehen *n*
educational television	Schulfernsehen *n*
advertising time	Werbezeit *f*
telerecordings *pl*	Fernsehaufzeichnungen *f pl*
video-taped material	auf Band aufgenommene Fernsehsendungen *f pl*
video-recorder	Aufnahmegerät *n* für Fernsehsendungen, Videorecorder *m*
vision link	Kette *f* von Fernsehstationen
television wire broadcasting, pay television by wire	(gebührenpflichtiges) Kabelfernsehen *n*
to teleview *Am*	*itr* fernsehen, *tr* sich etw im Fernsehen ansehen
to broadcast on television	im Fernsehen übertragen

Nachrichtenverkehr

to switch the television on/off	den Fernsehapparat ein-/ausschalten
to appear on television	im Fernsehen erscheinen
to watch a television program(me)	ein Fernsehprogramm ansehen
to turn the dials of a receiver	einen Empfänger einstellen
to get through messages of warning	Warnmeldungen durchgeben
to sponsor a radio/television program(me)	ein Rundfunk-/Fernsehprogramm finanzieren
on television	im Fernsehen
televisual	Fernseh-
telegenic	telegen, bildwirksam

Sätze und Redewendungen:

Televiewers are well-informed about current affairs.	Fernsehteilnehmer sind über die Tagesereignisse gut informiert.
Two programmes are now being transmitted.	Zwei Programme werden zur Zeit ausgestrahlt.
Advertisements should be recognizably separate from the programme.	Werbesendungen sollten deutlich vom Programm abgesetzt sein.
The regional studio centres contribute programmes to the national network.	Die regionalen (Fernseh-, Rundfunk-) Studios erstellen Programme für das Sendernetz des Landes.
Black-and-white television gives less information than colour television.	Schwarzweiß-Fernsehen vermittelt weniger Informationen als Farbfernsehen.

f) Cinematography — Film-/Lichtspielwesen

cinema, *fam* pictures *pl*, *Am* movies *pl*	Kino *n*, Filmtheater *n*
cinema-/*Am* movie-goer	Kinobesucher *m*
admission price/fee	Eintrittspreis *m*
admission ticket	Eintrittskarte *f*
motion-picture company/industry	Filmgesellschaft *f*/-industrie *f*
producer	Filmproduzent *m*
screen rights *pl*	Filmrechte *n pl*
shooting	Dreharbeit *f*, (Film-) Aufnahme *f*
motion-picture camera/projector	Filmkamera *f*/-projektor *m*
release of a film	Filmfreigabe *f* für den Verleih
colour motion picture	Farbfilm *m*
silent/sound film	Stumm-/Tonfilm *m*
feature (picture)	Spiel-/Hauptfilm *m*
studio shot	Atelieraufnahme *f*

Communications

newsreel	Wochenschau f *(im Kino)*
synchronized sound film	synchronisierter (Ton-) Film m
sound recording	Tonaufnahme f
magnetic sound track	Tonspur f
educational/documentary film	Lehr-/Dokumentarfilm m
animated cartoon	Zeichentrickfilm m
cartoonist, animator	Trickfilmzeichner m
editing	Filmmontage f
cutting	Filmschnitt m
film studio/library	Filmatelier n/-archiv n
trailer	Filmvorschau f/-voranzeige f
credit titles *pl*	(Film-) Vorspann m
film/moving picture advertising	Filmreklame f
cinema advertising	Diapositivwerbung f *(im Kino)*
to go to the movies *Am*	ins Kino gehen
to shoot a film	einen Film drehen
to produce a film	einen Film herausbringen
to exhibit pictures	Filme vorführen
to film, to reel, to shoot	filmen
to microfilm	mikrofilmen
animated	lebend, sich bewegend
filmic	filmisch, Film-

Sätze und Redewendungen:

Cinema attendance has been steadily declining.	Die Zahl der Kinobesucher ist immer mehr zurückgegangen.
Newsreel cameramen operate under great difficulties.	Kameraleute, die die Wochenschau drehen, haben mit großen Schwierigkeiten zu kämpfen.
Newsreels are a vital form of communicating news to the world today.	Wochenschauen stellen heutzutage eine äußerst wichtige Art der Nachrichtenübermittlung dar.
By editing, the news of the day can be distorted.	Durch das Schneiden der Tagesschau können die Nachrichten verfälscht werden.
Documentary films can call attention to important problems.	Dokumentarfilme können die Aufmerksamkeit auf wichtige Probleme lenken.
People and their daily lives form ideal material for educational films.	Menschen und ihr Alltagsleben sind ausgezeichnet für Lehrfilme geeignet.
Home movie cameras use film that is either 8 mm. or 16 mm. wide.	Für Heimfilmkameras werden Filme verwendet, die 8 bzw. 16 mm breit sind.

The amateur film-maker must pay a great deal of attention to the lighting.	Der Filmamateur muß ganz besonders auf die Beleuchtung achten.
Great amounts of money are needed to produce a motion picture.	Die Herstellung eines Films ist sehr kostspielig.
This motion picture is a flop.	Dieser Film ist ein Reinfall/eine Niete.
Cinemas usually show films continuously during the greater part of the day.	Kinos führen Filme in der Regel durchgehend während des größten Teils des Tages vor.
The rental for a film is based upon a percentage of the box-office receipts.	Der Filmverleih ist mit einem Prozentsatz der Kasseneinnahmen gekoppelt.

g) Records — *Tonaufnahmen, Aufnahmegeräte*

tape-recorder	Tonbandgerät *n*
tape-recording	Tonbandaufnahme *f*
record	(Band-) Aufnahme *f*, Aufzeichnung *f;* Schallplatte *f*
record-changer	Plattenwechsler *m*
record library	Diskothek *f*
record-player, gramophone, *Am* **phonograph**	Plattenspieler *m*, Grammophon *n*
graph, diagram, chart	graphische Darstellung *f*, Schaubild *n*, Diagramm *n*
to videotape	*(eine Fernsehsendung)* auf Band aufnehmen
magnetic	magnetisch
educational	erzieherisch

Englisches Register zum Aufbauwortschatz

A. A. R. 161
abandoned 211
 ~ parcel 210
abolish 124
abolition 165
absence of postage 209
absorb 197
accelerate 138, 175
accept 147
 ~ a bill 153
 ~ (a) deposit(s) 143, 149
 ~ full liability 147
 ~ an offer 131
 ~ an order 131
acceptance 154, 213
 ~ credit 153
 ~ house 144
 documentary ~ credit 135
 telegraph ~ 220
 trade ~ 153
acceptor 152
accessory 205
accident 182
 ~ insurance 162
 motor ~ 171
accommodate 182
accommodation bill 153
accompanying: ~ documents 130, 210
 ~ letter 130
account 136, 148, 149, 163, 212, 213
 ~ day 156
 ~ holder 143
 ~ number 143
 ~ sales 124
 ~ turnover 143
 annual ~ 194
 bank ~ 149
 blocked ~ 143
 busy ~ 151
 clearing ~ 143
 credit ~ 143
 current ~ 148
 deposit ~ 143
 frozen ~ 143
 loan ~ 143
 overdrawn ~ 143
 post-office savings ~ 149
 profit and loss ~ 194
 savings ~ 143
 time deposit ~ 143
 transfer ~ 212
accountability 192
accountable 197
acknowledgement 210
 ~ of order 131
acting director 195
active partner 192
actuarial theory 160
actuary 160
ad valorem tariff 165
to address 131
address: ~ card 209
 abbreviated ~ 208
 business ~ 208
 cable ~ 219
 home ~ 208
 incomplete ~ 208
 incorrect ~ 208
 mailing ~ 208
 post-office ~ 208
 private ~ 208
 registered ~ 220
 telegraphic ~ 219
addressee 208, 219
addressing machine 208
addressograph 208
adhesive tape 138
adjust 141
adjustment 140
administration: customs ~ 164
admission: ~ fee 223
 ~ price 223
 ~ to quotation 156
 ~ ticket 223
admit 157
to advance 143
advance 148
advantage: price ~s 122
advertise 204
advertisement: classified ~ 202
 display ~ 203
 full-page ~ 203
advertiser 202
advertising 122, 200
 ~ agency 200
 ~ appeal 201
 ~ campaign 200, 204
 ~ consultant 200
 ~ department 200
 ~ drive 200
 ~ expenditures 200
 ~ manager 200
 ~ material 200
 ~ media 200
 ~ message 200
 ~ pamphlet 202
 ~ purposes 205
 ~ reply card 202
 ~ research 200
 ~ slogan 203
 ~ space 203
 ~ time 222
 broadcast ~ 221
 cinema ~ 224
 cooperative ~ 201
 direct ~ 201
 direct mail ~ 201
 film ~ 224
 institutional ~ 201
 mail-order ~ 201
 mass ~ 201
 moving picture ~ 224
 opportunity ~ 201
 outdoor ~ 201
 point-of-sale ~ 201
 press ~ 202
 radio ~ 203
 retail ~ 201
 screen ~ 203
 slide ~ 203
 supplementary ~ 201
 television ~ 203, 222
 tie-up ~ 201
 transport(ation) ~ 201
advice: ~ of delivery 210
 ~ of dispatch 131, 169
 ~ of duration and charge 216
 ~ of entry 212
 ~ of loading 210
 ~ of payment 213
 ~ of shipment 210
 ~ of transfer 212
 shipping ~ 187
adviser: investment ~ 144
aerobus 178
aerial: transmitting ~ 221
affiliation: enterprise ~ 192
agency: advertising ~ 200
agent: export ~ 125
 forwarding ~ 138
 import ~ 124
 import commission ~ 124

sales ~ 126
shipping ~ 184
travel ~ 180
aggrieved party 160
agreement 121
  conditional ~ 120
  hire-purchase ~ 120
  by mutual ~ 133
  partnership ~ 192
  price ~ 195
  tariff ~ 165
agricultural fair 129
air 181
  ~ brake 175
  ~ bridge 178
  ~ bump 181
  ~ cargo 181
  ~-cargo shipment 181
  ~ carriage 178
  ~ carrier 181
  ~ charter 178
  ~ coach 178
  ~-conditioned 172
  ~-conditioning 120
  ~ consignment note 181
  ~-cool 182
  ~ corridor 179
  ~ express 181
  ~ express tariff 181
  ~ flight ticket 180
  ~ freight 181
  ~-freight charges 181
  ~-freight forwarder 181
  ~-freight service 181
  ~-freight space 181
  ~-freight tariff 181
  ~-ground 182
  ~-hole 181
  ~-hostess 180
  ~ lane 179
  ~ letter 181
  ~-mechanic 180
  ~-minded 182
  ~ parcel 181
  ~-pocket 181
  ~ raft 178
  ~ route 179
  ~ screw 178
  ~-seal 182
  ~ service 178
  ~ shed 180
  ~ space 178
  ~ speed indicator 178
  ~ surcharge 209

~ taxi 178
~ terminal 179
~ tickets 182
~ ticket office 180
~ traffic control 178
~ traffic controller 179
~ transport 178
~ travel 178
~ –void 182
~ waybill 181
airborne 182
aircraft: ~passenger
  insurance 181
  all-cargo ~ 178
  feeder-service ~ 178
  vertical take-off ~ 178
aircrew 180
airdrome 179
airdrop 182
airfield 179
  ~ lighting 179
airfoil 179
airfreighter 178
airlift 181
airline 178
  charter ~ 178
  polar ~ 179
airliner 178
airmail 211
  ~ correspondence 209
  ~ item 209
  ~ letter 181
  ~ rate 181
  ~ service 181
  ~ stamp 181
airman 180
airpark 179
airplane 178
  propeller-driven ~ 178
  supersonic ~ 178
airport 179, 180
  ~ charge 179
  ~ customs office 180
  ~ of destination 179
  ~ of dispatch 179
  ~ of entry 179
  ~ restaurant 180
  commercial ~ 179
airproof 182
airsick 182
airstrip 179
airtight 182
airway 179
airworthiness 180
airworthy 182
airy 182

alarm call 216
all-cargo aircraft 178
allot 197
allow 135, 136
allowable 177
allowance 141
alteration 132
alternative question 201
altitude 179
amalgamate 197
amalgamation 195
ambulance 172
  motor ~ 172
amount 135, 151
  invoice ~ 134
analysis: market ~ 128
  sales ~ 200
anchor 188
anchorage (dues) 187
animated 224
  ~ cartoon 224
animator 224
annotation: authorized ~ 210
announcement 200
  ~ campaign 200
  broadcast ~ 221
  preliminary ~ 130
  radio ~ 203, 221
annual: ~ account 194
  ~ balance-sheet 194
  ~ general meeting 194
  ~ sales 116
  ~ statement 194
annuity 162
to answer the telephone 216
answer: telegraphic ~ 220
apologize 141
apology 140
appeal: advertising ~ 201
  sales ~ 204
applicant for insurance 160
application for transfer 212
appoint a representative 126
aqueduct 188
A. R. 210
area: ~ congestion 171
  ~ sample 201
  circulation ~ 200
  customs ~ 164
  marketing ~ 126
  sales ~ 120, 126
  type ~ 203
arrange 126
arrangement 131

arrears 213
  to be in ~ with s.th. 135
arrival 182
arrive by air 182
article 207
  ~s of association 193, 197
  ~s of incorporation 193
  imported ~ 124
  ship's ~s 184
articulated 176
A/S 124
assemble 176
assessment: ~ of credit-worthiness 192
  ~ of damage 160
assets: corporate ~ 193
  current ~ 196
  fixed ~ 196
  partnership ~ 192
assistant driver 171
association: purchasing ~ 116
assortment 117
assurance: life ~ 161
atop 176
attach 182
attend: ~ to the customs formalities 166
  ~ a fair 129
attention: ~-getter 117
  ~-gaining device 117
attestation 210
attractive 204
auction sale 155
audience 200
  ~ analysis 200
  ~ research 201
authenticity 212
authority: ~ to pay 213
  to have legal ~ 213
  port ~ 187
authorities: customs ~ 164
  fair ~ 128
automatic: ~ answering set 216
  ~ exchange 215
  ~ vending machine 120
automobile car 175
automotive industry 171
available 140
average: ~ circulation 202
  ~ price 135
aviation 178
avoid 182
axle load 175

baby bonds 157
to back a car 172
back: ~ of a bill 153
  ~ of a cheque 151
  ~ loads 168
backwardation 156
to bag 139
bag 207
  carrier ~ 137
  collective ~ 207
  paper ~ 137
  plastic ~ 137
baggage 180, 182
  ~ car 175
  ~ check 180
  ~ in excess 180
  checked ~ 180
  excess ~ 180
  free-~ allowance 180
bail goods to s.o. 120
bakery 117
balance: ~ of account 148
  ~-sheet 194
  bank ~ 142
  credit ~ 212
  debit ~ 213
Baltic Exchange 156
band: ~ conveyer 188
  conveyer ~ 191
to bank 145
bank 143, 147, 154
  ~ account 149
  ~ balance 142
  ~ bill 147
  ~ charges 142
  ~ cheque 151
  ~ connections 142
  ~ customer 142
  ~ deposits 148
  ~ giro 148
  ~ loan 142
  ~ manager 142
  ~ of England 145
  ~ operations 142
  ~ rate 143
  ~ return 145
  ~ safe 143
  ~ stamp 149
  clearing ~ 147
  commercial ~ 142
  Federal Reserve ~ 145
  issuing ~ 144
  joint-stock ~ 142
  merchant ~ 144
  overseas ~ 125
  post-office savings ~ 149

transferring ~ 213
banker: discount ~ 153
banking 142
  ~ functions 144
  ~ syndicate 195
  ~ transaction 212
  branch ~ 142
  deposit ~ 148
bankrupt 198
barber 118
barbershop 118
bargain 155
  ~ book 155, 157
  ~ sale 202
barge 185
to barrel 139
barrel 137
base 126
basic charge 208
basin 187
basket 137
batter down 204
B/E 152
beacon 188
beam 189
bear 156
  ~ market 155
bearer: ~ bonds 157
  ~ share 157, 194
bearish 158
behaviour: buying ~ 201
  client ~ 201
  consumer ~ 201
belt: ~ conveyer 188
  conveyer ~ 191
beneficiary 160, 213
benefit 198
  disability ~s 162
  sickness ~s 162
  unemployment ~s 162
to berth 189
berth 187
bi-monthly 205
bi-weekly 205
bid: ~ price 155
  take-over ~ 155
bilge 186
bill 147, 153, 154, 202, 212
  ~-broking 147
  ~ of credit 153
  ~ after date 153
  ~ of entry 165
  ~ of exchange 152, 153, 154
  ~ of health 185

~ of lading 186
~s payable 152
~s in portfolio 152
~s receivable 152
~ after sight 153
~ at sight 153
~ at usance 153
accommodation ~ 153
bank ~ 147
clean ~ 153
commercial ~ 153
discount ~ 147
documentary ~ 153
domestic ~ 153
external ~ 153
finance ~ 153
foreign ~ 153
foreign currency ~ 147
freight ~ 187
inland ~ 153
long ~ 153
parcel ~ 210
shipping ~ 186, 187
short ~ 153
sight ~ 153
trade ~ 147, 153
Treasury ~ 147
usance ~ 153
billboard 202
billing: ~department 134
  ~ machine 134
Bills of Exchange Act 153
black: ~market 127
  ~ marketeer 127
block 175
  ~ of shares 194
  ~ signal 175
  copy ~ 130
blocked account 143
blow up 203
blue chips 157
to board a plane 182
board 189
  ~ of directors 196
  ~ of managers 197
  shipping ~ 184
boarding card 181
boat 185
  ~ train 174
bond 147, 166
  ~ issue 196
  ~ market 155
  baby ~s 157
  bearer ~s 157
  convertible ~s 156, 196
  debenture ~s 196

industrial ~s 157
irredeemable ~ 156
mortgage ~ 156
premium ~ 156
redeemable ~ 156
registered ~s 157
Treasury ~ 157
bonded: ~debt 196
  ~ goods 165
  ~ warehouse 124
bondholder 196
bonding 165
bonus: ~issue 157
  ~ share 194
to book: ~a call 216
  ~ freight space 189
  ~ an order 131
book: ~loss 197
  ~ profit 197
  ~ of stamps 117
  ~ value 197
bargain ~ 155, 157
cheque ~ 149, 150
deposit ~ 142
savings ~ 142, 213
booking office 180
booklet 130, 202
  instruction ~ 130
to boom 204
boom market 155
boost 204
booth 126
borrow 147
borrowed: ~capital 192
  ~ funds 197
borrowing: ~cost 197
  ~ requirement 197
to bottle 139
bottle: shatterproof ~ 137
  unbreakable ~ 137
bottleneck 171
bottom 186
Bottom 138
bound for 189
bounty 126
  export ~ 125
bow 186, 189
to box 139
box 137
  ~ car 174
  ~ collection 207
  ~ number 203
  call ~ 215
  cash ~ 117
  plywood ~ 137
  wooden ~ 137

bracket 117
to brake 176
brake 176
  air ~ 175
braking capacity 175
branch: ~banking 142
  ~ line 174
  ~ office 143
brand: ~image 201
  ~ loyalty 201
  ~ preference 201
  private ~ 116
breach of contract 133
break: ~a contract 133
  ~ a train down 176
breakwater 188
bridge: air ~ 178
brigade: fire ~ 161
brisk 158
British: ~Industries Fair 129
  ~ week 126
to broadcast 222
broadcast 221
  ~ advertising 221
  ~ announcement 221
  ~ listener 221
  ~ receiving licence 221
  live ~ 221
  outside ~s 221
  television ~ 222
broadcaster 221
broadcasting 221
  ~ station 221
  commercial ~ 221
  spot ~ 203
broadside 202
brochure 130
broker: discount ~ 147
  export ~ 125
  import ~ 124
  insurance ~ 161
  ship ~ 184
brokerage: ship ~ 184
budget 120
bulk 211
  ~ advice of items 207
  ~ billing of items 207
  ~ cargo 187
  ~ carrier 185
  ~ entry of items 207
  ~ haulage 170
  ~ posting 207
  ~ supplies 122
bulkhead 186
bulky parcel 210

bull 156
 ~ market 155
bulletin: ~ of verification 210
 news ~ 221
 transit ~ 210
bullish 158
buoy 188
buoyant 158
burglary insurance 162
bus: ~ driver 171
 ~ operator 171
 ~ service to the airport 180
 trolley ~ 191
 urban ~ service 171
business 197
 ~ address 208
 ~ capital 193
 ~ card 209
 ~ combinations 195
 ~ enterprise 191
 ~ hours 117
 ~ manager 195
 ~ premises 161
 ~ relations 131
 ~ report 194
 ~ share 192
 ~ undertaking 191
 export ~ 125
 insurance ~ 160
 investment ~ 143
 shipping ~ 184
busy: ~ account 151
 ~ signal 215
buy 124, 157, 204
 ~ retail 118
 ~ wholesale 122
buyer 141
 ~ 's resistance 201
 overseas ~ 126
 prospective ~s 204
buying: ~ behaviour 201
 ~ conditions 130
 ~ habits 201
 ~ mission 126
 ~ motivation 201
 ~ motive 201
 ~ public 116
by(e)laws 193

cab 171
cabin: ~ personnel 180
 passenger ~ 179
cable 131
 ~ address 219
 ~ railway 191
cablegram 220
caboose 175
cage: elevator ~ 191
calculation of probabilities 160
to call at a port 189
call 216
 ~ box 215
 ~ number 215
 ~ option 156
 ~ signal 215
 ~ unit 216
 alarm ~ 216
 conference ~ 215
 emergency ~ 215
 local ~ number 215
 long-distance ~ 215
 personal ~ 215
 reversed charge ~ 215
 toll ~ 215
 trunk ~ 215
caller 215
camera: television ~ 222
campaign: advertising ~ 200, 204
 announcement ~ 200
 initial ~ 200
 test ~ 200
canal 188, 189
 ~ lock 188
 ~ traffic 188
 ship ~ 188
cancel 182
 ~ a contract 133
cancellation 131, 209, 213
canvas 137
capacity: market ~ 128
capital: ~ gains 192
 ~ stock 193
 borrowed ~ 192
 business ~ 193
 equity ~ 192
 fixed ~ 157
 minimum ~ 193
 partnership ~ 192
 proprietory ~ 192
 share ~ 193
 trading ~ 193
capitalization 197
capitalized value 197
capstan 186
captain 184
 flight ~ 180
caption 203

car 176, 206
 ~ card 202
 ~ dealer 171
 ~ ferry 185
 ~ hiring service 171
 ~ park 171
 ~ rental 171
 automobile ~ 175
 baggage ~ 175
 box ~ 174
 chair ~ 174
 club ~ 174
 container ~ 175
 dining ~ 174
 dome ~ 174
 elevator ~ 191
 freight ~ 174
 gondola ~ 174
 hopper ~ 175
 lounge ~ 174
 mail ~ 174, 206
 mail storage ~ 206
 multi-stor(e)y ~ park 171
 observation ~ 174
 passenger ~ 174
 platform ~ 175
 rack ~ 175
 railroad ~ 174
 refrigerator ~ 174
 rented ~ 171
 side-stanchion ~ 175
 sleeping ~ 174
 stock ~ 175
 tank ~ 175
 underground ~ park 171
 used ~ 171
carboy 137
card: ~ money order 213
 address ~ 209
 boarding ~ 181
 business ~ 209
 car ~ 202
 cheque ~ 151
 credit ~ 143
 letter ~ 208
 punched ~ 210
cardboard 137
 corrugated ~ 137
 crinkled ~ 137
care of 211
cargo 187
 ~ capacity 185
 ~ carrier 185
 ~ hatch 186
 ~ insurance 161

231

~ office 181
~ pit 181
~ space 186
~ steamer 185
~ tonnage 187
~ vessel 185
air ~ 181
air-~ shipment 181
bulk ~ 187
deck ~ 187
dry ~ 187
transit ~ 168
carload lot 174
carriage 168, 169, 174
  ~ forward 140
  ~ of mail 181
  ~ paid 140
  air ~ 178
  inland ~ 168
  intercity ~ 170
  local ~170
  passenger ~ 170
  property ~ 170
  railway ~ 174
carrier 186
  ~ bag 137
  ~'s charges 168
  ~'s route 207
  bulk ~ 185
  cargo ~ 185
  common ~ 168
  inland water ~ 188
  motor ~ 171
carry: ~loads 176
  ~ over 158
cartel 195
cartoon: ~film 203
  animated ~ 224
cartoonist 224
to case 139
case 140
  glass ~ 117
  wooden ~ 137
cash 148, 151, 157
~-and-carry supermarket 122
~-and-carry warehouse 122
  ~ box 117
  ~ on delivery 210
  ~ deposit 148
  ~ desk 118, 120
  ~ discount 135
  ~ dispenser 143
  ~ with order 134
  ~ price 120
  ~ sale 133

~ subscription 193
~ transaction 156
net ~ 134
cashier 149
~'s cheque 151
~'s initials 149
cask 137
cast anchor 188
catalogue: ~price 135
  exhibition ~ 129
  mail-order ~ 202
cater 118
cattle truck 175
caution marks 138
ceiling 179
central clearing bank 211
certificate: ~of guarantee 130
  ~ of inspection 130
  insurance ~ 161
  share ~ 156, 194
  stock ~ 156
c.& f. 139
chain: ~store 120
  ~ wholesaling 122
chair car 174
chairman 196
chamber: lock ~ 188
chandler: ship ~ 184
change: ~of address 208, 211
  ~s in demand 133
  ~s to tickets 180
  small ~213
changeover 171
channel 189, 222
  ~ freight 188
  navigation ~ 188
to charge 139, 163
charge(s) 207, 213
  airport ~ 179
  bank ~s 142
  basic ~ 208
  COD ~ 213
  customs ~s 164
  discount ~s 147
  loading ~s 187
  port ~s 187
  shipping ~s 184
  telephone ~s 215
  telex ~s 219
  transshipment ~ 171
  warehousing ~ 209
charity postage stamp 208
chart 225
  route ~ 171

to charter 189
charter: ~airline 178
  ~ party 186
to check: ~imports 124
  ~ samples 131
  ~ a slip 149
check: ~-in time 180
  ~-out point 120
  baggage ~ 180
  postal ~212
  spot ~ 207
chemicals 157
cheque 149, 151, 212
  ~ book 149, 150
  ~ card 151
  ~ — not to order 151
  ~ number 151
  bank ~ 151
  cashier's ~ 151
  confirmed ~ 151
  crossed ~ 151
  dishonoured ~ 151
  order ~ 151
  post-dated ~ 151
  postal ~212
chips: blue ~ 157
c.i.f. 139
c.i.f.c. 139
c.i.f.c. & i. 139
cinema 223
  ~ advertising 224
  ~-goer 223
cinematography 223
cipher 220
  ~ telegram 220
circular 202
circulation 200, 207
  ~ area 200
  average ~ 202
city terminal 179
claim 140, 163
  ~ letter 140
  deficiency ~ 140
  mortgage ~ 196
claimant 160
class: ~magazine 202
  economy ~ 180
  tourist ~ 180
classification: tariff ~ 165
classify 176
clear: ~a block 176
  ~ port 189
  ~ through the customs 166
clearance 180
  ~ inwards 187

~ outwards 187
~ price 135
clearing: ~ account 143
~ bank 212
~ house 145
~ transactions 212
clerk: shipping ~ 184
client behaviour 201
close: ~ company 193
~ corporation 193
closing 212
~ date 202
~ time 117
mail ~ time 207
club car 174
cluster 118
c/o 211
coach 174
air ~ 178
coal freighter 185
coastal waterways 188
coaster 185
coasting vessel 185
cockpit 179
COD: ~ charge 213
~ item 210
~ money order 213
~ parcel 210
code: ~ mark 207
~ sign 207
~ telegram 220
telegraphic ~ 220
codification 207
coding 207
coin 213
~-box telephone 215
cold front 181
collateral: ~ credit 142
~ security 142
collect 151, 166, 176
~ on delivery 210
collection 213
~ letter 135
~ money order 213
~ of (outstanding) amounts 135, 213
~ sequence 135
box ~ 207
collective: ~ bag 207
~ envelope 208
~ sack 207
collier 185
colour: ~ motion picture 223
~ television 222
column 203

combination 195
business ~s 195
corporate ~ 195
price ~ 195
combine 195
interlocking ~ 195
purchasing ~ 195
come to anchor 188
command the market 128
commemorative postage stamp 208
commence at death 163
commercial 203
~ airport 179
~ bank 142
~ basis 198
~ bill 153
~ broadcasting 221
~ fair 129
~ guide 130
~ invoice 134
~ letter of credit 135
~ motor vehicle 170
~ papers 209
~ partnership 192
~ practice 130
~ television 203, 222
commission 189
~ agent 124
export ~ house 126
export ~ merchant 126
insurance ~ 160
commodity 204
~ exchange 155
~ group 116
bulk ~ 187
imported ~ 124
common carrier 168
communication(s) 206
~ centre 206
~ engineering 206
~ satellite 206
~ service 206
teleprinter ~ 218
company 145, 158, 162, 193, 195, 197
~ law 193
~ name 193
~ records 194
close ~ 193
holding ~ 195
incorporated ~ 193
joint-stock ~ 193
motion-picture ~ 223

nationalized ~ 191
non-profit-making ~ 193
parent ~ 195
private (limited) ~ 193
public (limited) ~ 193
registered ~ 193
shipping ~ 184
steamship ~ 184
stock ~ 193
compartment: postal ~ 206
compensation 163
~ for damage 210
competition 197
price ~ 204
competitive 124, 126, 132
competitor: overseas ~s 126
complain 141
complaint 140, 141
complete: ~ a cheque 151
~ an order 131
complimentary copy 203
compulsory 198
~ insurance 160
~ liquidation 198
concealment: fraudulent ~ 140
concentration point 171
concern 195
concert 221
concessions: tariff ~ 165
conclude a contract 133
condition: ~s of carriage 181
~s of a contract 133
buying ~s 130
meteorological ~s 181
selling ~s 130
weather ~s 181
conditional agreement 120
conduct 197
conference call 215
confirm 182
confirmation 131
confirmed 136
~ cheque 151
confiscated 211
confiscation 166
congest the market 128
congestion: area ~ 171
connection: railway ~ 174
telephone ~ 215
teleprinter ~ 218
conquer the market 128

consignment 176
  ~ note 174
  air ~ note 181
consistent 204
consolidate shipments 169
consols 157
constitute 197
consular invoice 134
consultant: advertising ~ 200
  investment ~ 143
consulting: management ~ 195
consumer 120
  ~ behaviour 201
  ~ survey 201
consumption: final ~ 116
  petrol ~ 171
to contact 131
container 172, 176
  ~ car 175
  ~ ship 185
containerized 169
contango 156
contest 202
to contract 133, 143, 169
contract 133
  ~ of affreightment 186
  ~ of carriage 168
  ~ of indemnity 160
  ~ rates 187
  export ~ 125
  insurance ~ 160
  sales ~ 133
  savings ~ 213
  supply ~ 133
contracting parties 133
contractual 133, 198
contributions of the partners 192
control: ~ tower 179
  exchange ~ 145
  export ~ 125
convenience goods 117
convention: customs ~ 164
conversion: ~ of currency 213
  ~ table 213
convertible bonds 156, 196
convey 169
conveyance: ~ of goods 168
  public (means of) ~ 168
conveyer: ~ band 191
  ~ belt 191
  band ~ 188

belt ~ 188
convincing 204
co-operate 197
cooperative: ~ advertising 201
  ~ buying association 122
  ~ marketing association 122
  ~ selling association 122
  ~ store 120
  wholesale ~ (society) 122
cope 131
co-pilot 180
copy 200
  ~ block 130
  ~ date 202
  ~ deadline 202
  ~ department 200
  ~ point 203
  ~ writer 200
  complimentary ~ 203
  specimen ~ 203
  voucher ~ 203
copying ink pencil 210
corner shop 116
corporate: ~ assets 193
  ~ combination 195
  ~ debts 194
  ~ earnings 194
  ~ form 192
  ~ liabilities 194
  ~ name 193
  ~ profits 194
  ~ purpose 193
  ~ tax 194
corporation 193
  ~ stock 147
  close ~ 193
correction of address 208
correspondence 208
  airmail ~ 209
  business ~ 130
  official ~ 208
  unpaid ~ 209
corridor: ~ train 174
  air ~ 179
corrugated cardboard 137
cost: ~ conscious 121
  ~ price 139
  additional ~s 213
  borrowing ~ 197
  distribution ~s 122
  marketing ~s 128
  transport ~s 168

counter 207
  ~ banking transaction 212
  ~-offer 131
  ~ operation 207
  ~ transaction 207
  deposit ~ 143
  exchange ~ 143
  post office ~ 207
  teller's ~ 143
countries: overseas ~ 125
coupon 180
  interest ~ 195
to cover a cheque 151
cover 139, 163
  ~ note 161
  fully comprehensive ~ 162, 163
coverage 200
  television ~ 222
covered wag(g)on 174
covering: ~ letter 130
  ~ purchase 155
C.P. 140
craft 185
crane: floating ~ 188
  jib ~ 188
  pillar ~ 188
  travelling ~ 188
crash: ~ landing 179
  plane ~ 179
crate 137, 139
creamery 117
create: ~ bank money 149
  ~ demand 204
  ~ a fund 146
  ~ purchasing power 143
to credit 213
credit 136
  ~ account 143
  ~ balance 212
  ~ card 143
  ~ in current account 148
  ~ expansion 142
  ~ limit 142
  ~ policy 142
  ~ restriction 142
  ~ sale 133
  ~-sale agreement 120
  ~ slip 149
  ~ squeeze 142
  ~ titles 224
  collateral ~ 142
  discount ~ 147
  documentary ~ 135
  export ~ 125

import ~ 124
creditor: mortgage ~ 196
creditworthy 143
crew 184
crinkled cardboard 137
cross a cheque 151
crossing: grade ~ 175
    level ~ 175
cross-tie 175
crude oil 191
cruising speed 179
cumbersome parcel 210
cum-div 158
currency: ~ fluctuations 144
    ~ regulations 180
current: ~ account 149, 150
    ~ ~ balance 148
    ~ ~ credit 148
    ~ ~ customer 148
    ~ ~ money 149
    ~ assets 196
    ~ liabilities 196
    ~ postal account 212
    ~ savings account 213
curvature 175
curve in track 175
custody: safe ~ 143
customer 118, 119, 136, 143, 149
    bank ~ 152
    overseas ~s 126
    prospective ~ 201
    retail ~ 116
customhouse 164
customs 164, 166
    ~ administration 164
    ~ area 164
    ~ authorities 164
    ~ bill of clearance 165
    ~ bond note 165
    ~ charges 164
    ~ clearance fee 208
    ~ cleared 166
    ~ convention 164
    ~ debenture 165
    ~ declaration 165
    ~ documents 165, 166
    ~ drawback 166
    ~ duty 164, 166
    ~ entry 165
    ~ examination 165, 210
    ~ facilities 165
    ~ formalities 165, 166
    ~ invoice 165
    ~ offence 165

~ office 164, 166
~ penalty 165
~ rate 165
~ receipt(s) 165
~ reduction 165
~ regulations 164
~ revenue 165
~ seal 165
~ shed 165
~ store 165
~ tariff 165
~ territory 164
~ union 126, 165
~ warrant 165
airport ~ office 180
cut 126
    tariff ~ 165
cutting 224
C.W.O. 134

D/A 135
daily list 155
dairy 117
dam 188
to damage 169
damage(s) 160, 163
    ship ~ 186
date 138, 151, 154
    ~ of delivery 168
    ~ of dispatch 168
    ~ of invoice 134
    ~ of issue 153
    ~ plan 200
    ~ of shipment 139
    ~-stamp 209
    ~-stamp impression 209
    ~-stamping 209
    closing ~ 202
    copy ~ 202
    delivery ~ 139
    due ~ 212
    publication ~ 203
    release ~ 202
    shipping ~ 187
days: ~ after sight 136
    ~ of grace 153
    30 ~ net 134
deadline: copy ~ 202
deadweight tonnage 186
to deal 156, 197
dealer 156, 204
    car ~ 171
debar 182
debark 182
debenture(s) 144, 156, 196

~ bonds 196
~ conditions 196
~ holder 196
~ stock 196
~ to bearer 196
customs ~ 165
fixed ~ 156
mortgage ~ 156
naked ~ 156
simple ~ 156
to debit 213
debit: ~ balance 213
    ~ slip 149
debt 148
    bonded ~ 196
    corporate ~s 194
    mortgage ~ 196
    partnership ~s 192
decartelization 195
deceased 211
decelerate 175
deceptive 166, 205
deck cargo 187
declaration: ~ of value 209
    customs ~ 165
declare a dividend 197
to decrease 166
decrease 194
    ~ in exports 125
deduct 135
deductible 162
deed: partnership ~ 192
deep freezer 117
defaulting 158, 211
defect 140
    ~ in material 140
    ~ in workmanship 140
    hidden ~ 140
    latent ~ 140
defective packing 137
deferred: ~ share 194
    ~ stock 194
deficiency claim 140
deficit 176
delay 207
    ~ in delivery 139
deliver 138, 176, 220
deliverable 140
deliverer 139
delivery 138, 140, 141, 209
    ~ alongside the vessel 187
    ~ date(s) 138, 139
    ~ free of charges 208
    ~ instructions 139
    ~ on call 139

~ service 169
~ times 207
mail ~ 207
part(ial) ~ 139
postal ~ 207
special ~ 211
wrong ~ 141
demand 133, 151, 154, 157, 186
  ~ deposit 142, 148
  ~ note 135
  seasonal ~ 181
demarcation of markets 195
demonstration 204
demurrage 187
density 201
department: ~ store 120
  advertising ~ 200
  billing ~ 134
  copy ~ 200
  dispatch ~ 139
  export ~ 125
  foreign exchange ~ 143
  invoice ~ 134
  issue ~ 145
  loan ~ 143
  savings ~ 143
  securities ~ 143
  shipping ~ 139
  transfer ~ 212
dependability 174
to deposit 149, 212
deposit 149, 212
  ~ account 148
  ~ banking 148
  ~ book 142
  ~ counter 143
  ~s on current account 148
  ~ money 149
  ~ at notice 149
  bank ~s 148
  cash ~ 148
  demand ~ 142, 148
  long-term ~ 142
  medium-term ~ 142
  private ~s 142
  public ~s 142
  savings ~ 148
  short-term ~ 142
  time ~ 142
depositor 142, 149
depreciation 163
  ~ in value 160
derrick 186
description 130

desk: cash ~ 118, 120
destination 169
details 130
determination of responsibility 210
detour 176
develop 126
diagram 225
dial 223
  ~-a-disc 216
  ~ telephone 215
dial(ling): ~ tone 215
  long-distance ~ 215
Diesel: ~ engine 171
  ~ locomotive 175
  ~ powered 176
dieselization 175
diner 174
dining car 174
direct: ~ advertising 201
  ~ debiting 149
  ~ importation 123
  ~ mail advertising 201
  ~ subscription 209
director: acting ~ 195
  managing ~ 195
directory 206
  exhibition ~ 129
  telephone ~ 215
  telex ~ 219
disability benefits 162
disablement: permanent total ~ 181
to discharge 189
discharge 187, 211
disconnect 176
to discount 147, 154
discount 134, 158, 198
  ~ banker 153
  ~ bill 147
  ~ of a bill 147
  ~ broker 147
  ~ charges 147
  ~ credit 147
  ~ house 147
  ~ market 147
  ~ rate 147
  ~ terms 147
  cash ~ 135
  quantity ~ 134
  retail ~ 116
  series ~ 203
  trade ~ 134
discountable 148
discounting 153
discriminatory 205

dishonour a bill 154
dishonoured cheque 151
to dispatch 138
dispatch 211, 220
  ~ department 139
  ~ of mail 207
  ~ note 210
dispatcher: flight ~ 180
dispatching 207
disperse 118
dispersion 200
displacement 185
to display 122, 129
display 118, 129
  ~ advertisement 203
  ~ material 117
  ~ space 118
  window ~ 117
disposal 141
dispose 124
dissolution 192, 198
dissolve 198
distance 179
distribute: ~ a dividend 197
  ~ goods 138
distributing office 206
distribution 122
  ~ costs 122
  ~ expenses 122
  ~ network 122
  ~ point 171
  ~ of profits 194
dividend 158
  ~ warrant 195
division of profits 194
Do not store in damp place 138
dock 188
  ~ gate 188
  dry ~ 188
  floating ~ 188
docker 185
docks 187
dockworker 185
dockyard 188
documentary: ~ acceptance credit 135
  ~ bill of exchange 134
  ~ credit 135
  ~ draft 134
  ~ film 224
documents 133, 161, 197
  ~ against acceptance 135
  ~ against payment 135
  accompanying ~ 130, 210
  customs ~ 165, 166

dome car 174
domestic 198
　~ bill 153
　~ market 128
　~ premises 161
domicile: free ~ 139
door to door 169
doorstep sales 120
dormant partner 192
down payment 135
D/P 135
DPB 142
draft 133, 153, 185
　~ agreement 133
　documentary ~ 134, 153
drain 145
draught 185
draughtsman 200
draw: ~ in a loan 143
　~ samples 131
　~ up 133, 197
drawee 152, 153
drawer 150, 152, 153, 212
drawing 149
　line ~ 203
　retail ~ 117
dredge 189
dress a ship 189
dressing: window ~ 117
drive: advertising ~ 200
driver: ~-accompanied
　vehicle 171
　assistant ~ 171
　bus ~ 171
　engine ~ 175
to drop anchor 188
drop in share prices 194
drugstore 117
dry: ~ cargo 187
　~ dock 188
d/s 136
due: ~ date 154
　be ~ 154
　fall ~ 151
dues: port ~ 187
dull 158
dummy 117
dump 124
dunning letter 135
duplex telephony 215
duplicate 149
　~ invoice 134
duration: ~ of contract 133
　~ of a fair 129
　~ of flight 179
dust cart 172

dutiable 166
duty 166
　~-free shop 180
　~-paid 140, 166
　customs ~ 166
　export ~ 125
　preferential ~ 165
　protective ~ 165
　revenue ~ 165
　stamp ~ 153, 155

E. & O.E. 134
early train 174
earn: ~ 6 per cent 157
　~ a profit 118, 197
earphone 216
earpiece 216
economic situation 146
economy class 180
editing 224
editorial 205
educational 225
　~ film 224
　~ television 222
to effect 162
　~ delivery 138
effective 204
electric locomotive 175
elevated: ~ hump 175
　~ railway 174
elevator 191
　~ cage 191
　~ car 191
　~ shaft 191
　freight ~ 191
eligible for discount 154
embankment 188
embark 182
embedded in ballast 177
embezzle 151
embossing stamp 209
emergency call 215
employ 126
employee: postal ~ 207
enclosure: printed ~ 209
encourage 126
endorse 147, 151, 154
endorsee 153
endorsement 153
　~ in blank 151
endorser 153
endowment insurance 162
engaged signal 215
engine: ~ driver 175
　Diesel ~ 171
　gas ~ 171

petrol ~ 171
engineer 175
　flight ~ 180
engineering: communication ~ 206
　management ~ 196
engineman 175
enlargement 203
enquiry 210
　~ form 210
ensure 124, 182
enter 126, 166
　~ into an agreement 133
　~ an order 131
　~ a port 189
enterprise 197
　~ affiliation 192
　~ liability 192
　business ~ 191
　free ~ economy 191
　large-scale ~ 192
　market-dominating ~ 127
　monopoly ~ 195
　municipal ~ 191
　privately-owned ~ 191
　small-scale ~ 116
　sole-trader ~ 191
　state-owned ~ 191
entertainment 221
entitled to a dividend 198
entrance: port ~ 187
entrepreneur's profit 192
entrepôt trade 165, 166
envelope 208
equities 157, 194
equity: ~ capital 192
　~ share 157, 194
errand-boy 116
error in the invoice 141
escalator 191
establish a company 197
establishment: postal ~ 206
　retail ~ 116
estimate 131
evasion of customs 166
even up 158
event of damage or loss 160
ex-div 158
ex factory 138
ex ship 189
ex works 135, 138
examination: customs ~ 165, 210
examine: ~ passenger's baggage 182

~ samples 131
exceptional offer 131
to exchange 141
exchange: ~ control 145
   ~ counter 143
   ~ rate 155, 211
   ~ regulations 155
   automatic ~ 215
   commodity ~ 155
   foreign ~ 126
   foreign ~ department 143
   foreign ~ market 144
   manual ~ 215
   stock ~ 155, 157
   telephone ~ 215
   telex ~ 218
   trunk ~ 215
execute an order 131
exempt from charges 211
exhibit 129, 224
exhibition 127, 128
   ~ building 129
   ~ catalogue 129
   ~ directory 129
   ~ regulations 129
   ~ space 129
expand credit 143
expansion: credit ~ 142
expectation: ~ of life 161
   ~ of loss 160
expedite 176
expenditures: advertising ~ 200
expense 136
   distribution ~s 122
   hospital ~ 162
   shipping ~s 184
expiration of contract 133
export 125
   ~ agent 125
   ~ bounty 125
   ~ broker 125
   ~ business 125
   ~ commission agent 126
   ~ commission house 126
   ~ commission merchant 126
   ~ contract 125
   ~ control 125
   ~ credit 125
   ~ department 125
   ~ duty 125
   ~ earnings 125
   ~ figures 125
   ~ financing 125
   ~ firm 125
   ~ goods 125
   ~ house 125
   ~ incentives 125
   ~ increase 125
   ~ licence 125
   ~ manager 125
   ~ market 125, 126
   ~ merchant 125
   ~ order 125
   ~ packing 137
   ~ promotion 125
   ~ quota 125
   ~ regulations 125
   ~ sales 126
   ~ shipments 125
   ~ tariff 165
   ~ trade 123, 125
   ~ volume 125
exportable 126
exportation 125
exporter 125
exporting country 125
exports 125, 126
   total ~ 125
exposition 128
express 211
   ~ item 209
   ~ train 174
   air ~ 181
   air ~ tariff 181
extend a contract 133
extension 135
   telephone ~ 215
external: ~ bill 153
   ~ tariff 165
extract of account 212
extrashop 120

face: ~ of a bill 153
   ~ value 208
   type ~ 203
facilities: customs ~ 165
factory price 135
factual information 120
fair 127, 128, 129
   ~ authorities 128
   ~ management 128
   ~ market price 128
   ~ pass 129
   agricultural ~ 129
   British Industries ~ 129
   commercial ~ 129
   electrical goods ~ 129
   furs ~ 129
   industrial ~ 129
   leather goods ~ 129
   postage stamps ~ 129
   sample ~ 129
   specialized ~ 129
   textile goods ~ 129
   toy ~ 129
   trade ~ 129
   world ~ 129
fairgoer 128
fairground 128
fairsite 128
fall: ~ in share prices 194
   ~ in value 128
   sharp ~ 155
family-fare plan 180
f.a.q. 139
fare: reduced return ~ 180
   round-trip excursion ~ 180
farmers' marketing cooperative 122
f.a.s. 139
fashionable 119
fast: ~ freight 176
   ~ seller 117
   ~ telegram 220
   ~ train 174
fault 140
faulty packing 137
favour: in ~ of 136
to feature 204
feature (picture) 223
Federal Reserve Bank 145
fee: admission ~ 223
   insurance ~ 210
feeder: ~ line 170
   ~-service aircraft 178
ferry: car ~ 185
   train ~ 185
fibre-glass 137
fiduciary 146
   ~ issue 145
filler 137
filling: ~ material 137
   ~ station 171
to film 224
film 224
   ~ advertising 224
   ~ library 224
   ~ studio 224
   cartoon ~ 203
   documentary ~ 224
   educational ~ 224
   silent ~ 223
   sound ~ 223
   synchronized sound ~ 224
filmic 224

final consumption 116
to finance 126
finance 145
 ~ bill 153
financial year 193
Financial Times index and business 216
financing 196
  export ~ 125
  interim ~ 196
  preliminary ~ 196
  self-~ 196
fire 161, 162
  ~ brigade 161
  ~ insurance 161
  ~ loss 161
  ~ office 161
  ~ protection 161
firm 136, 158, 197
  ~ name 193
  ~ offer 130, 131
  ~ price 135
  export ~ 125
  mail-order ~ 122
fiscal year 193
fishmonger 117
fit out a ship 189
fix 197
fixed: ~ assets 196
  ~ capital 157
  ~ debenture 156
  ~ installations 175
  ~ interest bearing 158
  ~ interest securities 156
  ~ liabilities 196
  ~ price 135, 157
flash: news ~ 221
flat-bed truck 172
flatcar 175
flaw in printing 209
fleet 172
  ~ of vehicles 122
  merchant ~ 184
flight 181, 182
  ~ captain 180
  ~ dispatcher 180
  ~ engineer 180
  ~ schedule 179
  ~-test 182
  ~ timetable 179
  non-stop ~ 179
  regular ~ 179
  scheduled ~ 179
  scheduled overnight cargo ~ 181
float an issue 158

floating: ~ crane 188
  ~ dock 188
  ~ policy 161
floor space 120
florist 118
  ~'s shop 118
flower shop 118
fluctuations: currency ~ 144
  price ~ 128, 135
fluid 191
fly 182
  ~ a flag 189
flying: ~ experience 180
  ~ hours 180
  ~ personnel 180
  ~ range 179
  ~ safety 179
  ~ speed 179
  instrument ~ 179
fly-tag 210
foam 137
  ~-rubber 137
f.o.b. 139
folder 202
follow-up: ~ letter 202
  ~ order 131
food: ~ retailing 117
  frozen ~ 120
f.o.r. 139
forecast 146
forecastle 186
foreign: ~ bill 153
  ~ currency bill 147
  ~ exchange 126
forfeit 118
forfeiture 166
forgery 151
for-hire transportation 171
to form 197
form 210
  corporate ~ 192
  enquiry ~ 210
  invoice ~ 134
  proposal ~ 162
  telegram ~ 219
formalities: customs ~ 165, 166
fortuitous 211
to forward 175, 210
forward: ~ seller 156
  ~ transaction 156
forwarded telegram 220
forwarder: freight ~ 171
forwarding 207
  ~ agent 138
  ~ of mail 207

~ route 171
f.o.t. 139
found 197
founder('s) share 157, 194
four-door 172
four-wheeled 172
F.P.A. 161
fraction: sampling ~ 201
franco house 139
franking machine 209
free: ~ alongside quay 139
  ~ alongside ship 139
  ~-baggage allowance 139
  ~ on board 139
  ~ of charge 149
  ~ customer's warehouse 139
  ~ domicile 139
  ~ enterprise economy 191
  ~ gift 202
  ~ house 139
  ~ port 166
  ~ postage 208
  ~ on rail 139
  ~ sample 202
  ~ trade 124
  ~ trade area 126
  ~ on truck 139
freephone 216
freezer: ~ centre 120
  deep ~ 117
freight: ~ bill 187
  ~ car 174
  ~ elevator 191
  ~ forwarder 171
  ~ forwarding agent 126
  ~ insurance 161
  ~ list 169
  ~ note 187
  ~ space 186
  ~ train 174
  ~ yard 175
  air ~ 181
  channel ~ 188
  fast ~ 176
  ship's ~ 186
  slow ~ 176
freighter 185
  ~ services 181
  coal ~ 185
freightliner train 174
front: ~ page 203
  cold ~ 181
  warm ~ 181

frozen: ~ account 143
  ~ food 120
fuel 171
fulfilment of contract 133
full-page advertisement 203
fully: ~ comprehensive
  cover 162, 163
  ~ liable 198
fund: investment ~ 143
funds 143, 148, 151, 192
  borrowed ~ 197
funicular railway 191
furnish 138, 166
furniture 133
  ~ van 172
furs fair 129
fuselage 179
fusion 195
future transaction 156

G.A. 161
gang-board 186
gang-plank 186
gangway 186
gap: market ~ 127
garbage truck 172
gas: ~ engine 171
  ~ station 171
  natural ~ 191
gate: dock ~ 188
G.A.T.T. 164
ga(u)ge: narrow ~ 175
  standard ~ 175
general: ~ average 161
  ~ average adjuster 161
  ~ delivery item 208
  ~ meeting 197
  ~ partner 192
  ~ partnership 192
  ~-purpose truck 172
  ~ wholesaler 122
General Post Office 206
gift: free ~ 202
gilt-edged: ~ market 145
  ~ securities 146
gimmick 117
glass: ~-bottle 137
  ~ case 117
  ~-enclosed 176
  ~ padding 137
  fibre-~ 137
Glass! Handle with care 138
glass-wool 137
glut the market 128
gold: ~ and silver bullions 144

~ reserves 145
~ standard 145
gondola car 174
gone away 211
goods 118, 120, 121, 122,
  124, 125, 129, 138, 141, 144,
  169, 174, 176, 189
  ~ in bond 165
  ~ lift 191
  ~ shelf 117
  ~ station 175
  ~ train 176
  ~ wag(g)on 174
  ~ yard 175
  bonded ~ 165
  convenience ~ 117
  export ~ 125
  luxury ~ 117
  undeclared ~ 166
goodwill 118
G.P.O. 206
to grade 122
grade 176
  ~ crossing 175
gramophone 225
grant 126, 135
graph 225
graphic 219
graphically 219
greengrocery 117
greetings telegram 220
grey market 127
grocery 117
gross: ~ price 135
  ~ tonnage 186
  ~ weight 137
ground personnel 180
to group freight 169
group: ~ life insurance 162
  commodity ~ 116
  income ~ 201
grouped packet 210
guard: railway ~ 173
guide: commercial ~ 130
  railway ~ 174
gummed seal 209

hail insurance 162
hairdresser 118
  ~'s shop 118
hand-luggage 180
handbill 202
Handle with care 138
handling 176
  rough ~ 141
hangar 180

harbo(u)r 187
  ~ master 187
  ~ police 187
  ~ regulations 187
  ~ tug 188
  inland ~ 188
  river ~ 187
hatch: cargo ~ 186
  loading ~ 186
to haul 169
haulage: ~ firm 168
  bulk ~ 170
  road ~ 168, 176
haulier 168
hauling: long-distance ~ 168
  piggyback ~ 170
hauls: long ~ 170
  short ~ 170
head: ~ office 193
  ~ of household 201
head(ing) 203
headline 203
headphone 216
health regulations 180
hear 221
to hedge 144, 158
helicopter 178
heliport 178
high-price merchandise 117
high-speed 176
  ~ streamliner 174
hijacking 179
hire 121
  ~-purchase agreement 120
  ~-purchase finance company 120
  ~-purchaser 120
to hold 157
hold 186, 197
holder 157, 212, 213
  account ~ 143
  debenture ~ 196
  policy ~ 160
holding 129
  ~ company 195
holdings: security ~ 196
home: ~ address 208
  ~-produced 125
  ~-service agent 161
honour: ~ a bill 154
  ~ a cheque 151
  ~ delivery dates 138
hopper car 175
horizontal integration 195

hospital expense 162
hot money 145
house organ 202
household and personal effects insurance 162
hovercraft 185
H.P. price 120
hull 186
  ~ insurance 161
hypermarket 120

ice box 117
icebreaker 185
idle shipping 184
illegitimate 141
illiquid 143
image: brand ~ 201
  product ~ 200
impact 200
import: ~ agent 124
  ~ broker 124
  ~ commission agent 124
  ~ credit 124
  ~ list 124
  ~ merchant 124
  ~ quota 124
  ~ regulations 124
  ~ restrictions 124
  ~ tariff 165
  ~ trade 123
importation 124
  ~ in bond 124
  direct ~ 123
imported: ~ article 124
  ~ commodities 124
importer 124
importing: ~ country 124
  ~ firm 124
imports: invisible ~ 123
  principal ~ 123
  total ~ 123
impose duty on s.th. 166
impression in relief for the blind 209
improper packing 137
Inc. 198
incentives: export ~ 125
incidence of loss 160
income group 201
incoming 177, 189
incorporate 197
incorporated 198
  ~ company 193
Incoterms 139
to increase 166, 204
increase 147, 193, 194

~ of customs 165
~ in exports 125
~ in prices 135
~ in sales 116
export ~ 125
incur liability 163
indebtedness: net ~ 145
indelible pencil 210
indemnify 162, 213
indemnity 160
  ~ for damage 210
  ~ sum 160
independents 116
indication: service ~ 207
induce 119, 204
industrial: ~ bonds 157
  ~ fair 129
industry: automotive ~ 171
  motion-picture ~ 223
  motor ~ 171
  shipbuilding ~ 186
  transport ~ 168
inflammable 138
inflate 198
inform 216
information 204
  factual ~ 120
  tariff ~ 165
informative literature 126
initial campaign 200
initiate 131
inland: ~ bill 153
  ~ carriage 168
  ~ harbour 188
  ~ marine insurance 188
  ~ navigation 188
  ~ port 188
  ~ telegram 220
  ~ water carrier 188
  ~ water transport 188
  ~ waters 188
  ~ waterways 188
inner port 187
inquiry 130, 131
  further ~ 130
insert 203, 204
insertion 203
  ~ order 202
inset 203
insolvency 198
  ~ proceedings 192
insolvent 143, 198
instalments 120, 121
installation: radio ~ 221
  teleprinter ~ 218
institute 198

institutional: ~ advertising 156
  ~ investors 156
instruction(s): ~ booklet 130
  ~ for use 130
  according to ~s 131
  delivery ~s 139
  marking ~s 138
  packing ~s 137
  service ~ 207
instrument(s) 212
  ~ flying 179
  ~ landing 179
  negotiable ~ 153
insufficient 211
insurable 163
insurance 160, 163
  ~ broker 161
  ~ business 160
  ~ certificate 161
  ~ commission 160
  ~ contract 160
  ~ fee 210
  ~ against fire 161
  ~ market 144
  ~ policy 126
  accident ~ 162
  aircraft passenger ~ 181
  aviation ~ 162
  burglary ~ 162
  cargo ~ 161
  compulsory ~ 160
  credit ~ 162
  employers' liability ~ 162
  endowment ~ 162
  fidelity guarantee ~ 162
  fire ~ 161
  freight ~ 161
  group life ~ 162
  hail ~ 162
  household and personal effects ~ 162
  hull ~ 161
  inland marine ~ 188
  liability ~ 162
  life ~ 161
  life ~ company 161
  marine ~ 161
  motor vehicle ~ 162
  National ~ 162
  personal ~ 160
  products' liability ~ 162
  property ~ 160
  rain ~ 162

ship's ~ 186
third-party ~ 162
transport ~ 168
whole life ~ 162
windstorm ~ 162
insure 162
insured 160, 163
   ~ item 209
   ~ letter 210
   ~ parcel 210
insurer 160
integration 195
   horizontal ~ 195
   vertical ~ 195
intelligence: shipping ~ 184
intercity: ~ carriage 170
   ~ transportation 168
Inter-City train 174
intercontinental network 178
to interest 204
interest 118, 143, 147, 212
   ~ coupon 195
   ~ rate 147, 148
   mortgage ~ 196
   partnership ~ 192
   rate of ~ 147
interim financing 196
interior waters 188
interlocking combine 195
intermediary 122
internal tariff 165
International Commercial Terms 139
international: ~ carriage by air 178
   ~ service 207
interval 176
interviewer 201
introduce 204
introductory price 202
to invest 192
investment 147
   ~ adviser 144
   ~ business 143
   ~ consultant 143
   ~ fund 143
   ~ management 143
   ~ portfolio 143
   ~ shares 157, 194
   ~ stocks 143
   stock ~ 147
investor 198
inviolability 207
invisible imports 123

invite 197
   ~ offers 131
to invoice 135
invoice 134, 135, 136
   ~ amount 134
   ~ department 134
   ~ form 134
   ~ item 134
   ~ number 134
   ~ total 134
   ~ value 134
   commercial ~ 134
   consular ~ 134
   customs ~ 134
   duplicate ~ 134
invoicing 134
I.O.U. 153
ipsophone 216
ironmongery 118
irredeemable 158
   ~ bond 156
irrevocable 136, 154
to issue 147, 149, 182, 197
issue: ~ department 145
   ~ market 144
   ~ of a loan 144
   ~ of notes 145
   ~ of postage stamps 207
   ~ of a postal/money order 213
   ~ of securities 144
   ~ of shares 157
   ~ price 144
   bond ~ 196
   bonus ~ 157
   fiduciary ~ 145
issuer 144, 150, 152
issuing: ~ bank 144
   ~ house 144
item 118, 207, 208, 209
   airmail ~ 209
   COD ~ 210
   express ~ 209
   insured ~ 209
   invoice ~ 134
   ordinary ~ 209
   registered ~ 209
   undeliverable ~ 209
   unenclosed ~ 209
itemization 130

jet 178
   ~ propulsion unit 178
jetty 188, 189
jewellery store 118
jib crane 188

jobber 156
   ~'s turn 156
joint: ~ liability 192
   ~-stock bank 142
   ~-stock company 193
   ~ venture 192
journey: train ~ 173
jumbo jet 178
junction: railway ~ 174
junior partner 192
justified 141

keel 186, 189
keep: ~ an account 213
   ~ delivery dates 138
Keep dry 138
keg 137
key: ~ number 203
   telegraphic ~ 220
kiosk: self-service ~ 206
knock-down price 202
knot 186

label 210
   tie-on ~ 210
ladies' wear 118
laid-up shipping 184
lake 189
to land 182
landing: ~ gear 179
   ~ speed 179
   crash ~ 179
   instrument ~ 179
lane: air ~ 179
   ocean ~ 184
large-scale 126
   ~ enterprise 192
   ~ trading 120
   ~ transportation 169
lash 185
launch: ~ an issue 158
   ~ a ship 188
law: company ~ 193
laydays 187
layout: newspaper ~ 203
L/C 135
leading 143
   ~ question 201
leaflet 130, 202
leather goods fair 129
leave: ~ port 189
   ~ a profit 118
   ~ the ship 189
leaving 189
leeward 189
legislation: tariff ~ 165

legitimate 141
lend 143, 147
lending policy 142
letter: ~ card 208
  ~ of acknowledgement 130
  ~ post 208
  ~ sheet 130
  ~ telegram 220
  accompanying ~ 130
  air ~ 181
  airmail ~ 181
  claim ~ 140
  collection ~ 135
  covering ~ 130
  dunning ~ 135
  follow-up ~ 202
  insured ~ 210
  purchase ~ 130
  reference ~ 130
  returned ~ 209
  sales ~ 202
lettergram 220
level crossing 175
levy 166
liability 147
  ~ insurance 162
  ~ of the carrier 168
  ~ of the partners 192
  corporate ~ 194
  current ~ 196
  enterprise ~ 192
  fixed ~ 196
  joint ~ 192
liable 163
  fully ~ 198
  personally ~ 198
licence: broadcast receiving ~ 221
lie at anchor 188
lien 121
life: ~ assurance 161
  ~ insurance 162
  ~ ~ company 161
  ~ office 161
lift: passenger ~ 191
Lift Here 138
lighterage 187
lighthouse 188
lighting: window ~ 117
lightweight 176
limit: credit ~ 142
limited 198
  ~ partner 192
  ~ partner's share 192
  ~ partnership 192

line: ~ drawing 203
  ~ of goods 117
  branch ~ 174
  main ~ 174
  party ~ 215
  railway ~ 173
  shipping ~ 184, 189
  suburban ~ 174
  telegraph ~ 220
  telephone ~ 215
liner: passenger ~ 185
liquidate 198
liquidation: compulsory ~ 198
  voluntary ~ 198
liquidity 146
Liquids - do not tilt - keep in cool place 138
liquor store 117
list 132
  ~ of customers 130
  ~ of products 130
  ~ of suppliers 130
  ~ price 135
  address ~ 201
  freight ~ 169
  import ~ 124
  mailing ~ 201
  packing ~ 137
  stock ~ 155
listen 221
listener: ~ research 203
  broadcast ~ 221
  radio ~ 221
literature: informative ~ 126
live broadcast 203
lively 158
Lloyd's (Corporation) 124, 160
  ~ register 184
  ~ underwriters 160
to load 189
load 172
  axle ~ 175
  back ~s 168
  plane ~ 181
  ship's ~ 186
  wag(g)on ~ 174
loading: ~ charges 187
  ~ gear 186
  ~ hatch 186
  ~ platform 175
  ~ ramp 175
  ~ tackle 186
loan 143, 155

~ account 143
~ department 143
bank ~ 142
local 143
  ~ call number 215
  ~ carriage 170
  ~ delivery area 206
  ~ delivery zone 206
  ~ postal service 206
  ~ wholesaler 122
lock: ~ chamber 188
  ~-charges 188
  canal ~ 188
lockage 188
locomotive: Diesel ~ 175
  electric ~ 175
  steam ~ 175
  switching ~ 175
lodge: ~ a complaint 141
  ~ with the Registrar 197
London Tea Auctions 156
London Yellow Pages Classified 215
long-distance: ~ call 215
  ~ dial(l)ing 215
  ~ hauling 168
  ~ lorry 172
  ~ operator 215
longshore man 185
long-term: ~ credit 126
  ~ deposit 142
loose 211
  ~-leaf statement 143
lorry: long-distance ~ 172
loss 118, 163
  book ~ 197
  fire ~ 161
  transport ~ 168
lot: carload ~ 174
lounge car 174
lower 147, 166
loyalty: brand ~ 201
LT 220
luggage van 175
luxury goods 117

machine: addressing ~ 208
  automatic vending ~ 120
  billing ~ 134
  franking ~ 209
  sorting ~ 207
magazine 202
  class ~ 202

professional ~202
magnetic 225
 ~ sound track 224
mail 207, 210, 220
 ~ car 206
 ~ closing time 207
 ~ delivery 207
 ~-order advertising 201
 ~-~ catalogue 202
 ~-~ firm 122
 ~-~ wholesaler 122
 ~-out 202
 ~ storage car 206
 ~ ~ compartment 209
 ~ ~ van 206
 ~ van 174, 206
 surface ~ 207
mailing: ~ address 208
 ~ list 201
 ~ time 207
main line 174
majority 157
make-up 203, 207
making-up: ~ day 156
 ~ price 156
mammoth oil-tanker 185
manage 197
management 195
 ~ consulting 195
 ~ engineering 196
 ~ planning 196
 ~ policy 196
 fair ~ 128
 investment ~ 143
manager: advertising ~ 200
 bank ~ 142
 business ~ 195
 export ~ 125
managerial: ~ capacity 198
 ~ functions 196
 ~ position 196
 ~ staff 195
managing 198
 ~ director 195
 ~ partner 192
manual 219
 ~ exchange 215
manufacturer 131
manufacturing cost 197
margin: profit ~ 126
marine: ~ insurance 161
 mercantile ~ 184
 merchant ~ 184
mariner 184
to mark 140, 182

mark: code ~ 207
to market 122, 128
market(s) 119, 122, 124, 127, 147
 ~ analysis 128
 ~ capacity 128
 ~ condition 128
 ~ day 127
 ~-dominating enterprise 127
 ~ gap 127
 ~ place 127
 ~ price 128, 136, 155
 ~ regulations 127
 ~ structure 200
 ~ town 127
 ~ value 128, 155
 bear ~ 155
 black ~ 127
 bond ~ 155
 boom ~ 155
 bull ~ 155
 buyer's ~ 128
 covered ~ 127
 discount ~ 147
 domestic ~ 128
 export ~ 125, 126
 foreign exchange ~ 144
 gilt-edged ~ 145
 grey ~ 127
 insurance ~ 144
 issue ~ 144
 open-air ~ 127
 overseas ~(s) 126
 producer ~ 128
 seafood ~ 117
 security ~ 196
 seller's ~ 128
 share ~ 155
 slump ~ 155
 stock ~ 155
marketable 128, 158
marketeer: black ~ 127
marketing 128
 ~ area 126
 ~ costs 128
 ~ organization 128
marking: ~ instructions 138
 ~ of cases 138
 ~ requirements 138
marks: caution ~ 138
 shipping ~ 138
markup 116, 122
marshalling yard 175
mass: ~ advertising 201

~ communication media 215
master (mariner) 184
 harbour ~ 187
material: advertising ~ 200
 display ~ 117
 filling ~ 137
 packing ~ 137, 139
 video-taped ~ 222
maturity 143
maximize 119
maximum 126
 ~ price 135
means: ~ of conveyance 168
 ~ of payment 134
 ~ of transport 168, 191
measures: preventive ~ 179
 security ~ 179
mechanic 171
media: ~ research 200
 advertising ~ 200
medium-term deposit 142
meet: ~ the cost of s.th. 139
 ~ price competition 204
meeting 198
 ~ of the partners 192
 first ~ 193
 general ~ 197
memorandum 120
 ~ of association 193
men's wear 118
mercantile 189
 ~ marine 184
 ~ partnership 192
merchandise 118, 119, 204
 ~ offerings 116
 high-price ~ 117
merchant: ~ bank 144
 ~ fleet 184
 ~ marine 184
 ~ service 184
 ~ ship 184
 export ~ 125
 import ~ 124
merchantman 184
merge 197
merger 195
message 216, 219, 220
 ~ of warning 223
 advertising ~ 200
 telegraphic ~ 220
 teleprint ~ 219
meteorological: ~ conditions 181

~ observation 181
~ services 181
method: ~ of address 208
~ of payment 134
microfilm 224
microphone 221
middleman 122
mile: nautical ~ 186
minimize 163
minimum: ~ capital 193
~ prices 197
mining share 194
misleading 166, 205
missend 211
mission: buying ~ 126
mock 117
mode: ~ of payment 134
~ of transportation 168
mole 188
monetary 124
~ subscription 193
money 120, 143, 151
~ at call 142
~ at short notice 142
~ order 134, 213
~ ~ telegram 220
card ~ ~ 213
COD ~ ~ 213
collection ~ ~ 213
deposit ~ 149
hot ~ 145
short-term ~ 147
surplus ~ 147
monopoly enterprise 195
monorail 191
months after sight 136
moor 188
mooring pier 188
morning train 174
mortgage(s): ~ bond 156
~ claim 196
~ creditor 196
~ debenture 156
~ debt 196
~ interest 196
~ payable 196
~ receivable 196
most-favoured-nation clause 165
motion 175
motion-picture: ~ company 223
~ camera 223
~ industry 223
~ projector 223
colour ~ 223

motivation: buying ~ 201
motive 176
~ power 175
buying ~ 201
motor: ~ accident 171
~ ambulance 172
~ carrier 171
~-cycle 171
~-driven 172
~ fitter 171
~ freight train 172
~ industry 171
~ pool 171
~(-)scooter 171
~ ship 185
~ show 171
~ transport 170
~ vehicle 170
~ ~ insurance 162
~ ~ user 170
~ vessel 185
Motorail 174
motorcyclist 171
motoring 216
~ office 171
motorist 171
motorize 172
motorless 172
motorman 175, 191
movable 169
move consignments 172
moved 211
movie-goer 223
movies 223, 224
moving: ~ staircase 191
~ van 172
m/s 136
M.S. 185
multiple shop 120
multiples 120
multiplex printer 219
multi-stor(e)y car park 171
municipal enterprise 191
mutual: ~ benefit society 162
~ life offices 162
M.V. 185

to narrow 126
narrow ga(u)ge 175
National Insurance 162
natural gas 191
nautical mile 186
navigable 189
~ rivers 188
navigation 184

~ channel 188
inland ~ 188
navigator 180, 184
negotiable 151, 154
~ instrument 153
negotiate 133, 154
negotiation 153
tariff ~s 165
neon sign 203
net 134
~ cash 134
~ indebtedness 145
~ invoice value 134
~ price 135
~ tonnage 186
~ weight 137
network: distribution ~ 122
railway ~ 173
teleprinter ~ 218
news: ~ bulletin 221
~ flash 221
~ summary 216
newscast 221
newscaster 221
newspaper: ~ layout 203
~ space 203
newsprint 202
newsreader 221
news-reel 203, 224
radio ~ 221
nomenclature: tariff ~ 165
nominal 198
~ partner 192
~ value 155
non-acceptance 153
non-agreement 140
non-conformity 141
non-contractual 141
non-dutiable 166
non-fulfilment of contract 133
non-insurable 163
non-negotiable 154
non-payment 153
non-profit-making company 193
non-stop flight 179
note: ~s in circulation 145
consignment ~ 174
demand ~ 135
dispatch ~ 210
freight ~ 187
worn ~s 146
notice 132, 149
~ of entry 212
~ of loading 210

~ of non-acceptance 154
~ of payment 213
~ of savings deposit 213
~ of shipment 210
~ of transfer 212
at long ~ 150
at short ~ 150
noting 153
novelty 202
number: account ~ 143
    box ~ 203
    call ~ 215
    cheque ~ 151
    code(d) ~ 149, 203
    invoice ~ 134
    key ~ 203
    telephone ~ 215

objection 213
observation: ~ car 174
    meteorological ~ 181
ocean-going 189
    ~ vessel 185
ocean lane 184
off-season 204
offence: customs ~ 165
    motoring ~ 171
to offer 122, 131, 144, 163
offer 131, 140
    ~ without engagement 130
    counter-~ 131
    detailed ~ 131
    exceptional ~ 131
    firm ~ 130, 131
    oral ~ 130
    previous ~ 130
    special ~ 130
    suitable ~ 130
    written ~ 130
office: ~ of mailing 206
    ~ of origin 206
    ~ of posting 206
    ~ of redispatch 206
    ~ of reforwarding 206
    air ticket ~ 180
    booking ~ 180
    branch ~ 143
    cargo ~ 181
    customs ~ 164, 166
    distributing ~ 206
    fire ~ 161
    head ~ 193
    home service ~s 162
    life ~ 162

principal ~ 193
registered ~ 193
sorting ~ 206
telegram ~ 219
ticket sales ~ 180
official: ~ correspondence 208
    ~ quotation 155
offsetting 213
oil: ~ cloth 137
    ~ paper 137
    crude ~ 191
old-age pension 162
on-board bill of lading 186
open 149
    ~-air market 127
    ~ a credit 136
    ~ a fair 129
    ~ a letter of credit 138
    ~ policy 161
    ~ wag(g)on 174
    ~-water port 187
Open Here 138
operate 118, 122, 176, 197, 219
operation: ~s research 196
    counter ~ 207
operator: bus ~ 171
    long-distance ~ 215
opportunity advertising 201
optimum size 195
option: ~ dealing 156
    ~ on new shares 157
    call ~ 156
    put ~ 156
to order 118, 119, 131
order 118, 126, 131
    ~s on hand 131
    export ~ 131
    follow-up ~ 131
    insertion ~ 202
    money ~ 134, 213
    payment ~ 149
    postal ~ 213
    repeat ~ 131
    shipbuilding ~ 186
    shipping ~ 187
    to ~ 151, 212
    unconditional ~ 152
ordering 132
    ~ firm 131
ordinary: ~ item 209
    ~ parcel 210
    ~ partnership 192
    ~ shares 157
organization 129

marketing ~ 128
organize 129
original packing 137
o/s 140
out of stock 140
outdoor advertising 201
outgoing 189, 198
outlet 129
    retail ~ 116
outside broadcasts 221
overdraft: to run an ~ 143
overdrawn account 143
overdue payments 212
overhead 177
    ~ railway 174
overland transportation 168
overprint: postage stamp ~ 209
overseas: ~ bank 125
    ~ buyer 126
    ~ competitors 125
    ~ countries 125
    ~ customers 126
    ~ market(s) 126
    ~ shipment 184
    ~ telegram 220
    ~ trade 126
oversubscribe an issue 158
oversubscription 195
over-the-counter store 116
own 197
ownership: security ~ 196

P.A. 161
pack 139
package 210
packet: grouped ~ 210
packing 137
    ~ insert 202
    ~ instructions 137
    ~ list 137
    ~ material 137, 139
    ~ note 137
    bad ~ 137
    careful ~ 137
    careless ~ 137
    customary ~ 137
    defective ~ 137
    export ~ 137
    faulty ~ 137
    improper ~ 137
    original ~ 137
    proper ~ 137
    seaworthy ~ 137
    special ~ 137

waterproof ~ 137
page: double ~ spread 203
   front ~ 203
   title ~ 203
paid-in surplus 196
pamphlet 202
   advertising ~ 202
panel 202
paper: ~ bag 137
   ~ securities 147
   ~ shavings 137
   commercial ~ s 209
   oil ~ 137
   stamped ~ 210
   tissue ~ 137
   wax ~ 137
   wrapping ~ 137
par 157, 198
   ~ value 155
parachute 191
parcel: ~ bill 210
   ~ post 208
   ~ of shares 194
   abandoned ~ 210
   air ~ 181
   bulky ~ 210
   COD ~ 210
   cumbersome ~ 210
   insured ~ 210
   ordinary ~ 210
   postal ~ 210
parent company 195
pari: under ~ 158
park: car ~ 171
   pram ~ 120
parking space 120
part(ial) delivery 139
partial shipment 187
participate 129
participating share 194
particular average 161
particulars 130
partner 192, 197
   active ~ 192
   dormant ~ 192
   general ~ 192
   junior ~ 192
   limited ~ 192
   limited ~'s share 192
   managing ~ 192
   nominal ~ 192
   senior ~ 192
   silent ~ 192
partnership 192

~ agreement 192
~ assets 192
~ capital 192
~ debts 192
~ deed 192
~ interest 192
~ property 192
~ share 192
commercial ~ 192
general ~ 192
limited ~ 192
mercantile ~ 192
ordinary ~ 192
trading ~ 192
part-pay 197
party: ~ line 215
   aggrieved ~ 160
   charter ~ 186
to pass 166, 172
   ~ on a cheque 151
pass: fair ~ 129
passbook 142
passed for press 211
passenger 172, 182
   ~ arrival 180
   ~ cabin 179
   ~ car 174
   ~-cargo ship 185
   ~ carriage 170
   ~ lift 191
   ~ liner 185
   ~ plane 178
   ~ ship 185
   ~ train 174, 176
passport regulations 180
pasteboard 137
patchy 158
patronize 118
pay 118, 120, 126, 135, 147, 151, 163, 166, 197, 213
   ~ load 181
   ~-~ capacity 181
   ~ station 215
payable 132, 151, 163, 212
payee 150, 152
payer 150
paying-in book 149
   ~-~ slip 149
payment 134, 135, 136, 143, 144, 154, 209, 213
   ~ of accounts 134
   ~ on account 134
   ~ in advance 134
   ~ by bill of exchange 134
   ~ by cheque 134, 151

~ in full 195
~ by instalments 135
~ of invoices 134
~ obligations 135
~ order 149
~ of postage 208
down ~ 135
first ~ 135
overdue ~s 212
peak: ~ buying time 120
   ~ days 181
penalty: customs ~ 165
pencil: copying-ink ~ 210
   indelible ~ 210
pension: old-age ~ 162
perforation 209
perform 144
period: ~ of contract 133
   ~ of delivery 139
   ~ of retention 209
   ~ of validity 209
   high ~ 158
   low ~ 158
   prescribed ~ 212
   subscription ~ 209
periodical 202
perishable(s) 117, 119
permanent: ~ poster 202
   ~ total disablement 181
permission 156
permit 165
persistent 204
personal: ~ call 215
   ~ insurance 160
   ~ share 194
personally liable 198
personnel: cabin ~ 180
   flying ~ 180
   ground ~ 180
persuade 204
pertinent 204
petrol: ~ consumption 171
   ~ engine 171
   ~ station 171
petty average 161
phonogram 220
phonograph 225
phonopost 208
to pick up 172
pickup service 170
pictures 223, 224
pier 188
   mooring ~ 188
pigeonhole 207
piggyback hauling 170

247

pillar crane 188
to pilot 182
pilot 185
pilotage 185
pipeline 191
   ~ transportation 191
pit: cargo ~ 181
pitch up 176
to place: ~ advertisements 204
   ~ an issue 158, 197
   ~ (an) order(s) 118
place: ~of destination 140, 168
   ~ of dispatch 168
   ~ of issue 153
   market ~ 127
placing 155
plane: ~crash 179
   ~ load 181
   passenger ~ 178
   transport ~ 178
planning 129
   management ~ 196
plastic bag 137
platform: ~car 175
   loading ~ 175
plausible 205
ply 189
plywood box 137
P/N 153
P.O.B. 207
point: ~of sale 116
   ~-of-sale advertising 201
   concentration ~ 171
   copy ~ 203
   distribution ~ 171
   transshipment ~ 171
polar airline 179
policy: ~holder 160
   comprehensive ~ 161
   floating ~ 161
   insurance ~ 126
   lending ~ 142
   management ~ 196
   open ~ 161
   reinsurance ~ 161
   standard ~ 161
   tariff ~ 165
   transport ~ 169
pool 195
   motor ~ 171
pooled shipment 187
port 186, 187
   ~ authority 187
   ~ of call 187
   ~ charges 187
   ~ of delivery 187
   ~ of departure 187
   ~ of destination 187
   ~ of discharge 187
   ~ of distress 187
   ~ dues 187
   ~ entrance 187
   ~ of entry 187
   ~ of exportation 187
   ~ of importation 187
   ~ of registry 187
   ~ regulations 187
   ~ of shipment 187
   ~ of trans(s)hipment 187
   free ~ 187
   inland ~ 188
   inner ~ 187
   open-water ~ 187
   shipping ~ 187
portfolio 146, 147
   investment ~ 143
   security ~ 147
porthole 186
position: managerial ~196
post: ~-dated cheque 151
   ~ office 149, 206
   ~ ~ address 208
   ~ ~ counter 207
   ~ ~ money order 149
   ~ ~ savings account 149
   ~ ~ savings bank 149
   letter ~ 208
   parcel ~ 208
   railway ~ office 206
   telegraph ~ 220
   travelling ~ office 206
postage: ~free 211
   ~ meter 209
   ~-paid imprint 209
   ~ stamp(s) 207, 208, 209
   ~ stamps fair 129
   ~ stamp overprint 209
   charity ~ stamp 208
   commemorative ~ stamp 208
   free ~ 208
   insufficient ~ 209
   invalidated ~ stamp 209
   unstuck ~ stamp 209
postal: ~check 212
   ~ ~ account 149
   ~ ~ office 212
   ~ cheque 212
   ~ ~ office 212
   ~ compartment 206
   ~ delivery 207
   ~ employee 207
   ~ establishment 206
   ~ franking impression 209
   ~ giro account 149
   ~ giro central office 149
   ~ giro office 149
   ~ giro service 149
   ~ identity card 210
   ~ item 207
   ~ money order 149
   ~ order 213
   ~ parcel 210
   ~ savings bank book 213
   ~ savings deposit 149
   ~ secrecy 207
   ~ service 206
   ~ subscription 209
   ~ transport 206
   ~ truck 206
   ~ van 206
current ~ account 212
internal ~ service 206
international ~ service 206
local ~ service 206
rural ~ service 206
urban ~ service 206
postcard: reply ~ 208
   reply-paid ~ 208
poste restante 208
   ~ ~ item 208
poster 202
   ~ hoarding 202
   ~ pillar 202
   permanent ~ 202
   station ~ 202
posting: ~time 207
   bulk ~ 207
postman's walk 207
postmarking of items 209
postpone a purchase 120
pram park 120
preference: ~share 157, 194
   brand ~ 201
   tariff ~s 165
preferential: ~duty 165
   ~ tariff 165
preferred stock 157
preliminary: ~announcement 130
   ~ financing 196

premises: business ~ 161
  domestic ~ 161
premium 157, 163
  ~ bond 156
  ~ income 160
  ~ rate 160
  at a ~ 138
pre-pack 122
prepaid 211
prepayment: ~ in cash 208
  ~ in money 208
  ~ of postage 208
pre-plan 118, 182
prescribed period 212
present 149, 204, 213
presentation 151, 154
presenter 150
preserve 128
to press in bales 139
press 204
  ~ advertising 202
  ~ clippings 203
  ~ cuttings 203
preventive measures 179
price 124, 132, 135, 157
  ~ advantages 122
  ~ agreement 195
  ~ combination 195
  ~ competition 204
  ~ conscious 121
  ~ ex works 135
  ~ fluctutations 128, 135
  ~-list 130
  admission ~ 223
  average ~ 135
  bid ~ 155
  cash ~ 120
  catalogue ~ 135
  clearance ~ 135
  closest ~ 135
  cost ~ 135
  excessive ~s 135
  factory ~ 135
  fair-market ~ 128
  favourable ~ 135
  firm ~ 135
  fixed ~ 135, 157
  gross ~ 135
  H.P. ~ 120
  introductory ~ 202
  issue ~ 144
  knock-down ~ 202
  list ~ 135
  market ~ 128, 136, 155
  maximum ~ 135
  minimum ~s 197

net ~ 135
reasonable ~ 135, 198
recommended ~ 135
reduced ~ 141
retail ceiling ~ 116
retail (selling) ~ 116
sales ~ 135
seasonal ~ 135
selling ~ 135
shipping ~s 187
stock ~s 155, 194
total ~ 135
principal: ~ imports 123
  ~ office 193
printed: ~ enclosure 209
  ~ insert 209
  ~ matter 208
  ~ papers 208
printer: multiplex ~ 219
printing 211
private: ~ address 208
  ~ brand 116
  ~ deposits 142
  ~ letter-box 207
  ~ (limited) company 193
privately-owned enterprise 191
to proceed 182
proceedings 198
proceeds 153
produce 224
producer 122, 223
  ~ market 128
product 204
  ~ image 200
  ~ test 200
  ~ testing 117
professional magazine 202
profit 118, 124, 157
  ~ margin 126
  ~ and loss account 194
  ~ sharing 192
  book ~ 197
  corporate ~s 194
program(me): radio ~ 223
  television ~ 223
prolongation 153
promissory note 153
promote 124, 126
promotion: export ~ 125
  sales ~ 200
propaganda 204
  ~ slogan 209
propeller-driven airplane 178
proper packing 137

property: ~ carriage 170
  ~ insurance 160
  ~ of a company 193
  partnership ~ 192
proposal form 161
proposer of a contract 160
proprietorship: sole ~ 191
proprietory capital 192
prospect(s) 201, 204
prospective: ~ buyers 204
  ~ customer 201
prospectus 195
protect 120, 189
protection: fire ~ 161
  tariff ~ 165
protective duty 165
to protest 154
protest 153
provide 138, 163, 169, 213
provision 147, 194
public 118, 122, 197, 210
  ~ deposits 142
  ~ (limited) company 193
  ~ (means of) conveyance 168
  ~ telephone 215
  ~ transport 169
  buying ~ 116
publication 195
  ~ date 203
publicity: ~ slogan 209
  ~ value 201
publish 204
pull 175
pumping station 191
punched card 210
purchase 120
  ~ letter 130
  share ~ 194
purchasing: ~ association 116
  ~ combine 195
put: ~ into bags 210
  ~ a call through 216
  ~ in dock 188
  ~ option 156
  ~ into sacks 210
  ~ to sea 189
  ~ in a tender 157

quality 138, 204
  inferior ~ 141
  poor ~ 141
  standard ~ 128
quantity: ~ discount 134
  ~ of available traffic 168

quarantine 185
quarter 189
quay 188, 189
question: alternative ~ 201
  leading ~ 201
questionnaire 201
quorum 197
quota: export ~ 125
  import ~ 124
  tariff ~ 165
quotation 158
  official ~ 155
quote 132

rack car 175
radio 221
  ~ advertising 203, 221
  ~ announcement 203, 221
  ~ installation 221
  ~ listener 221
  ~ newsreel 221
  ~ program(me) 223
  ~ telephony 216
  ~ tower 221
raft: air ~ 178
rail 174, 175, 176, 186
  ~-highway bridge 175
  ~ service 174
  ~ traffic 174
  ~ transport(ation) 174
railroad: ~ car 174
  ~ yard 175
rails 175
railway: ~ carriage 174
  ~ connection 174
  ~ guard 173
  ~ guide 174
  ~ junction 174
  ~ line 173
  ~ network 173
  ~ post office 206
  ~ rates 174
  ~ switch tracks 188
  ~ traffic 174
  cable ~ 191
  elevated ~ 174
  funicular ~ 191
  overhead ~ 174
  underground ~ 191
rain insurance 162
raise 163
  ~ a charge 211
  ~ customs 166
  ~ money 148
ramp: loading ~ 175

range: ~ of samples 130
  flying ~ 179
rate 163
  ~ fixing 207
  ~ of customs 165
  ~ of duty 165
  ~ of interest 147
  ~ of issue 195
  ~ of postage 208
  airmail ~ 181
  bank ~ 143
  contract ~s 187
  customs ~ 165
  discount ~ 147
  exchange ~ 155, 211
  interest ~ 147, 148
  premium ~ 160
  railway ~s 174
  subscription ~ 209
  tariff ~s 187
  telephone ~s 215
  transport ~s 168
raw materials 124
ready: ~ for shipment 189
  ~ for shipping 189
  ~ money down 134
reap profits 197
recall 215
receipt 135, 210, 211
  ~ of goods 134
  ~ of order 131, 138
  customs ~ 165
  return ~ 210
receive 219
received-for-shipment bill of lading 186
receiver 223
  telephone ~ 215
  television ~ 222
receiving station 221
reception: telegram ~ 219
recipe service 216
recommended price 135
to record 149
record(s) 211, 225
  ~-changer 225
  ~ library 225
  ~-player 225
  company ~ 194
recorded daily cooking service 216
recorder: tape- ~ 225
  telephone ~ 216
recording: sound ~ 224
  tape- ~ 225
recoup a loss 198

recourse 153, 154
recoverable 163
recovery 213
redeemable 158
  ~ bond 156
redemption: share ~ 195
  stock ~ 195
reduce 124, 126
reduced price 141
reduction 213
  ~ of freight 187
  customs ~ 165
to reel 224
reference: ~ letter 130
  ~ slip 210
refrigerate 176
refrigerator 117
  ~ car 174
  ~ ship 185
  ~ truck 172
refund 163
refusal 131
refused 211
to register 146
Register of Business Names 193
register: ~ of the shareholders 193
  Lloyd's ~ 184
registered: ~ address 220
  ~ bonds 157
  ~ company 193
  ~ item 209
  ~ office 193
  ~ share 157, 194
  ~ tonnage 186
Registrar of Companies 193
registration 193
regular flight 179
regulation(s): according to ~ 133
  contrary to ~ 133
  currency ~ 180
  customs ~ 180
  detailed ~ 207
  exchange ~ 155
  exhibition ~ 129
  export ~ 125
  harbour ~ 187
  health ~ 180
  import ~ 124
  market ~ 127
  passport ~ 180
  port ~ 187
  service ~ 207
  visa ~ 180

reinsurance policy 161
reject an offer 131
to release 122, 126, 204
release: ~ of a film 223
 ~ date 202
relieve 197, 211
reminder 211
remit 135
remittance 134
remove 124
renew a contract 133
renewal 153
 ~ of contract 133
rent a car 172
rental: car ~ 171
rented car 171
re-open 143
reorder 118
repay 148
repeat (ad) 203
 ~ order 131
repercussions 146
replacement 141
replenish 131
reply: ~ coupon 131, 208
 ~-paid postcard 208
 ~-paid telegram 220
 ~ postcard 208
 advertising ~ card 202
report: business ~ 134
representative: wholesale
 ~ 122
request 130
 on ~ 131
requirement 211
 borrowing ~ 197
 marking ~s 138
rerouting 207
research: advertising ~ 200
 listener ~ 203
 media ~ 200
 operations ~ 196
reservation of title 133
to reserve seats 182
reserve(s) 145, 194
 gold ~s 145
 statutory ~s 194
resistance: sales ~ 201, 204
responsibility 211
restaurant: airport ~ 180
restore 198
restrain 197
restricted in supply 140
restriction: credit ~ 142
 import ~s 124
 traffic ~s 179

resume: ~ payments 135
 ~ speed 176
to retail 118
retail: ~ advertising 201
 ~ business 116
 ~ ceiling price 116
 ~ customer 116
 ~ discount 116
 ~ drawing 117
 ~ establishment 116
 ~ outlet 116
 ~ sale 116
 ~ sales 116
 ~ (selling) price 116
 ~ shop 116
 ~ store 116
 ~ survey 201
 ~ trade 116
 ~ trader 116
 ~ trading 116
 ~ turnover 116
 by ~ 119
retailer 116, 118, 122
retire 198
 ~ from a partnership
 197
retirement 160, 163
retractable 179
to return 141
return: ~ fare 180
 ~ receipt 210
 bank ~ 145
returned letter 209
revenue 181
 ~ duty 165
 customs ~ 165
reversed charge call 215
revocable 154
revoke a contract 133
ride at anchor 188
right: ~ of appeal 210
 ~ of cancellation 120
 ~ to information 198
 ~ to object 195
 ~ to protest 195
 ~ to receive a dividend
 194
 ~ of recourse 210
 ~ to vote 195
 subscription ~ 157, 194
ring s.o. up 216
rise: moderate ~ 155
 sharp ~ 155
risk 126
 ~ of conveyance 168
 ~ of non-payment 126

 ~ of theft 126
 at our ~ and expense
 141
 economic ~s 163
river 189
 ~ harbour 187
 navigable ~s 188
R.M.D. 134
road 172
 ~ haulage 168, 176
 ~ train 172
 ~ transport 170
 ~ transport industry 170
roadbed 175
roadworthiness 171
R.O.G. 134
roll of postage stamps 208
rolling stock 174
roll-on, roll-off ferry 171
roomette 174
round-trip excursion fare
 180
to route 172
route 182
 ~ chart 171
 ~ of dispatching 207
 ~ of forwarding 207
 air ~ 179
 en ~ 172
 forwarding ~ 171
 shipping ~ 184
 traffic ~s 174
 transport ~ 168
 trunk ~ 174
routing 171
 ~ of mail 207
rudder 186
rules of procedure 193
run: ~ at frequent intervals
 176
 ~ at regular times 176
runway 180
rural postal service 206
rush of orders 131

to sack 139
sack: collective ~ 207
safe: ~ custody 143
 ~-deposit box 143
 bank ~ 143
safety: flying ~ 179
sailor 184
sale 131, 204, 208
 ~ by sample 133
 ~ in the open market
 128

~ on approval 133
~ or return 133, 141
auction ~ 155
bargain ~ 202
cash ~ 133
credit ~ 133
retail ~ 116
sales 126, 133
~ agent 126
~ analysis 200
~ appeals 204
~ area 120, 126
~ contract 133
~ efforts 119
~ force 120
~ letter 202
~ price 135
~ promotion 200
~ resistance 201, 204
~ volume 116
account ~ 124
annual ~ 116
doorstep ~ 120
export ~ 126
to sample 131
sample 131, 141, 201
~ fair 129
~ of merchandise 208
~ of no value 130
area ~ 201
free ~ 202
sampling 201, 207
~ fraction 201
~-technique 201
satellite: communication ~ 206
saturation 128
savings: ~ account 213
~ book 142, 213
~ contract 213
~ department 143
~ deposit 148
~ ~ note 213
scale: ~ of postal charges 207
~ of postal rates 207
scarcity of tonnage 184
schedule: ~ of deliveries 207
~ reliability 182
flight ~ 179
time ~ 200
screen: ~ advertising 203
~ rights 223
television ~ 222
screw: air ~ 178
scrutinize 158

sea 189
seabee 185
seaborne: ~ trade 184
~ traffic 184
seafood market 117
seafreight 186
sea-going vessel 185
seal: ~ of approval 116
customs ~ 165
gummed ~ 209
seaman 184
seaplane 178
search s.o. 182
seasonal: ~ demand 181
~ swings 119
seating capacity 180
seaworthiness 185
seaworthy packing 137
secure 126, 144, 148
security: ~ holdings 196
~ market 196
~ measures 179
~ ownership 196
~ portfolio 147
~ precautions 182
~ underwriter 196
collateral ~ 142
securities 157
~ department 143
~ payment counter 143
fixed-interest-bearing ~ 158
gilt-edged ~ 147
paper ~ 147
see-through pack 120
selection of samples 130
selective 205
self-service kiosk 206
sell 118, 157
~ overseas 126
~ by/at retail 118
~ short 157
~ wholesale 122
seller 141
fast ~ 117
forward ~ 156
short ~ 156
slow ~ 117, 204
selling: ~ conditions 130
~ points 204
~ price 198
send 129, 131, 138, 210, 220
sender 210, 219
sending 207
~ station 221
senior partner 192

sequence: collection ~ 135
series discount 203
to service a loan 158
service(s) 122, 176, 211, 213
~ indication 207
~ instruction 207
~ regulation 207
~ station 118
air ~ 178
airmail ~ 181
bus ~ 180
communication ~ 206
cooking ~ 216
delivery ~ 170
domestic ~ 206
emergency dialling ~ 217
internal ~ 206
international ~ 207
merchant ~ 184
meteorological ~s 181
pickup ~ 170
postal ~ 206
rail ~ 174
recipe ~ 216
shared ~ 215
telegram ~ 219
telephone (information/call) ~ 216, 217
teletourist ~ 216
time ~ 216
through pallet ~ 181
weather (forecast) ~ 181, 216
set: television ~ 222
settle: ~ with cash 122
~ with the sender 213
settlement: ~ day 156
~ of a claim 160
~ of accounts 213
shaft: elevator ~ 191
to share 163
share(s) 144, 157, 158, 194, 197
~ capital 193
~ certificate 156, 194
~ at current quotation 195
~ in a company 193
~ market 155
~ of profits 192
~ prices 157, 194
~ purchase 194
~ redemption 195
bearer ~ 157, 194
bonus ~ 194

business ~ 192
cumulative preference
  ~ 194
deferred ~ 194
equity ~ 157, 194
founder('s) ~ 157, 194
fresh ~ 194
investment ~ 157, 194
limited partner's ~ 192
mining ~ 194
new ~ 194
ordinary ~ 157, 194
participating ~ 194
participating preference
  ~ 194
partnership ~ 192
personal ~194
preference ~ 157, 194
registered ~ 157, 194
shipping ~s 184
voting ~ 194
shareholder 193
  ~'s preemptive right
  194
shareholding 194
shed: air ~ 180
  customs ~ 165
shift 169
to ship 138, 189
ship 189
  ~'s articles 184
  ~ broker 184
  ~ brokerage 184
  ~ canal 188
  ~ chandler 184
  ~'s company 184
  ~ damage 186
  ~'s day 187
  ~'s freight 186
  ~'s insurance 186
  ~'s load 186
  ~'s protest 186
  container ~ 185
  full ~ 185
  merchant ~ 184
  motor ~ 185
  nuclear-powered ~ 185
  passenger ~ 185
  passenger-cargo ~ 185
  refrigerator ~ 185
  trading ~ 184
  transport ~ 185
shipboard 189
shipbuilder 186
shipbuilding: ~industry 186
  ~ order 186

shipment 189
  ~ of goods 184
  export ~s 125
  overseas ~ 184
  partial ~ 187
  pooled ~ 187
shipowner 184
shipper 171, 186
  ~'s manifest 187
  ~'s memorandum 186
  ~'s order 187
  ~'s papers 187
  ~'s representative 187
shipping(s) 184, 189
  ~ agent 184
  ~ advice 187
  ~ bill 186, 187
  ~ board 184
  ~ business 184
  ~ charges 184
  ~ clerk 184
  ~ company 184
  ~ date 187
  ~ department 139
  ~ expenses 184
  ~ intelligence 184
  ~ line 184, 189
  ~ marks 138
  ~ master 184
  ~ news 184
  ~ order 187
  ~ port 187
  ~ prices 187
  ~ route 184
  ~ shares 184
  ~ space 186
  ~ trade 184
  idle ~ 184
  laid-up ~ 184
shipway 188
shipwrecked 189
shipwright's wharf 186
shipyard 186, 188
shoot 224
shooting 223
shop: ~ hours 117
  ~-soiled 119
  ~-worn 119
  baker's ~ 117
  butcher's ~ 117
  corner ~ 116
  delicatessen ~ 117
  duty-free ~ 180
  florist's ~ 118
  flower ~ 118
  greengrocer's ~ 117

grocer's ~ 117
hairdresser's ~ 118
milk ~ 117
multiple ~ 120
retail ~116
speciality ~ 116
stationer's ~ 118
tobacconist's ~ 117
unit ~116
shoplifting 117
shopper 116
shopping: ~basket 117
  ~ behaviour 201
shore 189
  ~ leave 184
shoreward 189
short: ~seller 156
  ~-term 147
  ~-~ deposit 142
  ~-~ money 147
shortage 148
show-card 202
show-case 117
shunting yard 175
sickness 160
  ~ benefits 162
side: This ~ up 138
side-stanchion car 175
sidetrack 175
siding 175
to sign 120
  ~ a cheque 151
sign: code ~ 207
  neon ~ 203
signal: ~box 175
  block ~ 175
  busy ~ 215
  call ~215
  engaged ~ 215
  stop ~ 176
  time ~ 221
signature 212
  specimen ~ 151
silent: ~film 223
  ~ partner 192
single-axle 172
single line store 116
size 207
  optimum~ 195
skipper 184
slack 177
sleeper 174, 175
sleeping car 174
slide advertising 203
sliding scale 203, 207
sliding-scale tariff 165

slip: credit ~ 149
  debit ~ 149
  reference ~ 210
slogan: advertising ~ 209
  propaganda ~ 209
  publicity ~ 209
slow: ~freight 176
  ~ seller 117, 204
  ~ train 174
sluggish 158
slump market 155
small: ~change 213
  ~ coins 213
  ~-scale enterprise 116
smuggle 166
society: mutual benefit ~ 162
sole: ~proprietorship 191
  ~ trader 116, 191
  ~-trader enterprise 191
solicit: ~offers 131
  ~ orders 118
sorting: ~machine 207
  ~ office 206
sound: ~film 223
  ~ recording 224
  ~ track 224
soundproof 219
space: air ~ 178
  cargo ~ 186
  display ~ 118
  exhibition ~ 129
  floor ~ 120
  freight ~ 186
  newspaper ~ 203
  parking ~ 120
  shipping ~ 186
speak 221
speaking clock 216
special 131
  ~ delivery 211
  ~ offer 130
  ~ packing 137
specialist: ~periodical 202
  ~ wholesaler 122
speciality shop 116
specialize 122, 154
specialized: ~fair 129
  ~ trade 116
  ~ vehicles 172
specific 205
  ~ tariff 165
specification 130
specimen: ~copy 203
  ~ signature 151
spectacular 203

speculative: ~operation 156
  ~ transaction 156
to speed 138, 204
speed 169, 177
  ~ restrictions 176
  air ~ indicator 178
  cruising ~ 179
  flying ~ 179
  landing ~ 179
  supersonic ~ 179
  train ~ 174
sponsor 203, 223
sporting goods store 118
spot: ~(announcement) 203
  ~ broadcasting 203
  ~ cash 134
  ~ check 207
  ~ transaction 156
squeeze: credit ~ 142
s.s. 185
S.S. 185
stack 139, 172
staff: managerial ~ 195
  train ~ 173
stag 156
stainless 176
stamp: ~-cancelling machine 209
  ~ duty 153, 155
  airmail ~181
  bank ~ 149
  embossing ~ 209
  postage ~ 207, 208, 209
stamped: ~paper 210
  ~ wrapper 208
stamping 209
stand 127
standard: ~ga(u)ge 175
  ~ policy 161
  ~ quality 128
  gold ~ 145
standardized 176
staple goods 118
starboard 186
start a business 197
starting 177
state-owned enterprise 191
statement 163
  ~ of account 212
  annual ~ 194
  loose-leaf ~ 143
station: ~poster 202
  ~-wag(g)on 172

broadcasting ~ 221
filling ~ 171
gas ~ 171
goods ~ 175
pay ~ 215
petrol ~171
pumping ~ 191
receiving ~ 221
sending ~ 221
service ~ 118
television ~ 222
terminal ~175
transmitting ~ 221
stationer's shop 118
stationery store 118
statistical records 160
statistician 160
statutory reserves 194
STD 215
  ~ code 215
steam locomotive 175
steamboat 185
steamer 185
  cargo ~ 185
  turbine ~ 185
steamship 185
  ~ company 184
steel strapping 138
steels 157
stern 186
stevedore 185
sticker 210
stifle 197
stimulate 118, 129
stipulate 133, 135
to stock 118
stock(s) 122, 131, 138, 146
  ~ car 175
  ~ company 193
  ~ certificate 156
  ~ exchange 155, 157
  ~ ~ agent 156
  ~ ~ operator 156
  ~ ~ speculator 156
  ~ investment 147
  ~ list 155
  ~ market 155
  ~ prices 155, 194
  ~ redemption 195
  ~ warrant 194
  ~ yields 155
capital ~193
corporation ~ 147
debenture ~ 196
deferred ~ 194
investment ~s 143

out of ~ 119
preferred ~ 194
profit sharing ~ 194
rolling ~ 174
stockholder 193
stop 175
 ~ signal 176
stop-over 179
stopping train 174
storage 139
 ~ tanks 191
store 118, 204
 chain ~ 120
 clothing ~ 118
 cooperative ~ 120
 customs ~ 165
 department ~ 120
 electrical supply ~ 118
 hardware ~ 118
 household supply ~ 118
 jewellery ~ 118
 liquor ~ 117
 retail ~116
 single line ~ 116
 sporting goods ~ 118
 stationery ~ 118
 tobacco ~ 117
stow 189
streamer 202
streamlined 176
streamliner: high-speed ~ 174
streetcar 191
string 137
strong-room 143
structure: market ~ 200
 tariff ~ 207
stub 149
studio 221
 ~ shot 223
 film ~ 224
subject: ~ to alteration 132
 ~ to duty 166
 ~ to goods being unsold 132
 ~ to prior sale 132
submit: ~ an offer 131
 ~ customs documents 166
subrogation 160
to subscribe: ~ an issue 158
 ~ for shares 197
subscriber: ~'s telephone 215
 ~ trunk dial(l)ing 215
 called ~ 215

telephone ~ 215
telex ~ 219
subscription: ~ period 209
 ~ rate 209
 ~ right 157, 194
 ~ to shares 194
cash ~ 193
direct ~ 209
monetary ~ 193
postal ~ 209
subsidiary (company) 195
substantiate 163
suburban line 174
subway 191
sue for damages 141
suffer a loss 162
sum(s) due 213
summary: news ~ 216
summon 197
superette 120
supermarket: cash-and-carry ~ 122
supersonic airplane 178
supplement 140
supplementary advertising 201
supplier 138
supply 122, 124, 126, 138
 ~ contract 133
support 133
surcharge: air ~ 209
surcharged 211
surface: ~ mail 207
 ~ transport(ation) 168
surplus 196
 ~ money 147
 earned ~ 196
 paid-in ~ 196
survey: ~ report 161
 consumer ~ 201
 retail ~201
surveyor 161
susceptible to insurance 163
suspend payments 135
to switch 223
switch 175
switchboard: telephone ~ 215
switching locomotive 175
switchtower monitor 175
syndicate 195
 banking ~ 195

tackle: loading ~ 186
take: ~ action 204
 ~ out insurance 162
 ~ off 182
 ~ on passengers 175
 ~ in shares 158
 ~ ship 189
 ~ the wheel 172
take-off 179
 ~ bid 155
tank: ~ car 175
 ~ truck 172
tanker 172
 mammoth oil-~ 185
tanktrailer 172
tape: ~-recorder 225
 ~-recording 225
 adhesive ~ 138
tare 137
tariff(s) 164
 ~ agreement 165
 ~ classification 165
 ~ concessions 165
 ~ cut 165
 ~ heading 165
 ~ information 165
 ~ legislation 165
 ~ negotiations 165
 ~ nomenclature 165
 ~ policy 165
 ~ preferences 165
 ~ protection 165
 ~ quota 165
 ~ rates 187
 ~ structure 207
 ~ union 165
 ~ walls 165
 ad valorem ~ 165
 air express ~ 181
 customs ~ 165
 export ~ 165
 external ~ 165
 import ~ 165
 internal ~165
 preferential ~165
 sliding-scale ~ 165
 specific ~ 165
tax: corporate ~ 194
 transfer ~ 155
 vehicle ~ 171
taxation: vehicle ~ 171
to taxi 182
taxi 171
taxiway 180
technical handouts 126

technique: sampling- ~ 201
telecast 222
telegenic 223
telegram 131, 219, 220
~ to follow 220
~ form 219
~ office 219
~ reception 219
~ service 219
~ by telephone 220
cash-on-delivery ~ 220
cipher ~ 220
code ~ 220
deferred ~ 220
fast ~ 220
forwarded ~ 220
greetings ~ 220
inland ~ 220
letter ~ 220
money order ~ 220
overseas ~ 220
reply-paid ~ 220
telephoned ~ 220
urgent ~ 220
to telegraph 220
telegraph: ~ acceptance 220
~ line 220
~ messenger 220
~ pole 220
~ post 220
telegraphic: ~ address 219
~ answer 220
~ code 220
~ key 220
~ message 220
~ transfer 220
to telephone 216
telephone 131, 216
~ answering service 215
~ bill 215
~ booth 215
~ call 215
~ ~ service 217
~ charges 215
~ circuit 215
~ connection 215
~ directory 215
~ exchange 215
~ extension 215
~ information service 216
~ line 215
~ number 215
~ rates 215
~ receiver 215
~ recorder 216
~ service 215, 216
~ subscriber 215
~ switchboard 215
~ traffic 215
coin-box ~ 215
dial ~ 215
public ~ 215
subscriber's ~ 215
telephonic 216
telephony: duplex ~ 215
radio ~ 216
telephoto 220
telephotographic 219
telephotography 220
teleprint message 131, 219
teleprinter 219
~ communication 218
~ connection 218
~ network 218
~ installation 218
telerecordings 222
teleregister 180
teletourist service 216
to teletype 219
teletype 219
~ message 219
teletypesetter 219
teleview 222
(tele)viewer 222
television 222, 223
~ advertising 203, 222
~ announcer 222
~ broadcast(ing) 222
~ camera 222
~ coverage 222
~ news 222
~ program(me) 223
~ receiver 222
~ screen 222
~ set 222
~ station 222
~ tower 222
~ transmitter 222
~ wire broadcasting 222
colour ~ 222
commercial ~ 203, 222
educational ~ 222
pay ~ 203
pay ~ by wire 222
televisual 223
telex 219
~ charges 219
~ directory 219
~ exchange 218
~ subscriber 219
teller's counter 143
to tender 146
tender 157
terminal: ~ station 175
air ~ 179
terminate 121
terminus 175
terms: ~ of contract 133
discount ~ 147
territory: customs ~ 164
to test 118
test: ~ campaign 200
~ matches 216
product ~ 200
testing: ~ of products 117
product ~ 117
text: running ~ 203
textile goods fair 129
textiles 157
theft 162
third-party 162
~ insurance 162
thread 137
ticker (telegraph) 220
ticket 182
~-day 156
~ sales office 180
admission ~ 223
air ~s 182
tie-on label 210
tie-up advertising 201
till 117
TIM 216
time: ~ deposit 142
~ ~ account 143
~ of delivery 139
~ of maturity 153
~ of payment 153
~ schedule 200
~ service 216
~ signal 221
timely 205
timetable 174
flight ~ 179
tin: ~ can 137
~-case 137
tip-in 203
tissue paper 137
title: ~ page 203
credit ~s 224
T.L.O. 161
tobacco store 117
tobacconist's shop 117
toll call 215
tonnage 184

cargo ~ 187
deadweight ~ 186
gross ~ 186
net ~ 186
registered ~ 186
Top 138
total 212
   ~ exports 125
   ~ imports 123
   ~ price 135
   ~ transports 168
   invoice ~ 134
touch bottom 189
tourist class 180
tow 189
tower: control ~ 179
   radio ~ 221
   television ~ 222
towing vessel 188
toy fair 129
track 177
   double-~ 177
   single-~ 177
   sound ~ 224
tractor 172
   ~ truck 172
to trade 124, 157
trade: ~acceptance 153
   ~ barriers 124
   ~ bill 147, 153
   ~ discount 134
   ~ expansion 124
   ~ fair 129
   ~ gap 126
   ~-mark 204
   entrepôt ~ 165
   export ~ 123, 125
   free ~ 124
   import ~ 123
   overseas ~ 126
   retail ~ 116
   seaborne ~ 184
   shipping ~ 184
   specialized ~ 116
   transport ~ 168
   wholesale ~ 116, 122
trader: sole ~ 116, 191
trading: ~capital 193
   ~ partnership 192
   ~ ship 184
   large-scale ~ 120
   retail ~ 116
traffic: ~density 174
   ~ restrictions 179
   ~ routes 174
   air ~ control 178

canal ~ 188
rail ~ 174
railway ~ 174
seaborne ~ 184
telephone ~ 215
transcontinental ~ 168
transit ~ 168
water-borne ~ 184
trailer 172, 224
   ~-tractor unit 172
   semi-~ 172
   truck ~ 172
train 175
   ~ ferry 185
   ~ journey 173
   ~ speed 174
   ~ staff 173
   boat ~ 174
   corridor ~ 174
   early ~ 174
   express ~ 174
   fast ~ 174
   freight ~ 174
   freightliner ~ 174
   goods ~ 174
   Inter-City ~ 174
   local ~ 176
   morning ~ 174
   motor freight ~ 172
   passenger ~ 174, 176
   road ~ 172
   slow ~ 174
   stopping ~ 174
   vestibule ~ 174
   way ~ 174
tramp (steamer) 185
tram 191
transaction: banking ~ 212
   cash ~ 156
   clearing ~s 212
   counter ~ 207
   forward ~ 156
   future ~ 156
   speculative ~ 156
   spot ~ 156
transcontinental traffic 168
to transfer 135, 176
transfer 146
   ~ account 212
   ~ department 212
   ~ of risk 133
   ~ of title 133
   ~ tax 155
   telegraphic ~ 220
transferee 150
transferor 150

transferring bank 213
transire 165
transit 168, 169
   ~ bulletin 210
   ~ cargo 168
   ~ goods 168
   ~ traffic 168
transmission 207
transmitter 221
television ~ 222
transmitting: ~aerial 221
   ~ station 221
to transport 169, 181
transport 168, 169
   ~ advertising 201
   ~ costs 168
   ~ of goods by road 170
   ~ industry 168
   ~ insurance 168
   ~ loss 168
   ~ plane 178
   ~ planning 169
   ~ policy 169
   ~ rates 168
   ~ route 168
   ~ ship 185
   ~ trade 168
   ~ vessel 185
   air ~ 178
   inland water ~ 188
   motor ~ 170
   postal ~ 206
   public ~ 169
   rail ~ 173, 174
   road ~ 170
   road ~ industry 170
   total ~s 168
   water ~ 184
transportable 169
transportation 168, 169, 182
   ~ speed 168
   for-hire ~ 171
   intercity ~ 168
   large-scale ~ 169
   low-cost ~ 169
   overland ~ 168
   pipeline ~ 191
   surface ~ 168
transporter 168
transship 166, 189
transshipment 166, 171
   ~ charge 171
   ~ point 171
to travel 182
travel: ~agency 180, 182

~ agent 180
air ~ 178
travelling: ~crane 188
~ post-office 206
treasury: ~bond 157
~ bill 146
treatment: rough ~ 141
trend of the market 155
trolley bus 191
truck 172, 174, 206
~ fleet 171
~ tractor 172
~ trailer 172
cattle ~ 175
flat-bed ~ 172
garbage ~ 172
general-purpose ~ 172
postal ~ 206
refrigerator ~ 172
tank ~ 172
tractor ~ 172
trucker 171
trunk: ~call 215
~ exchange 215
~ route 174
trust 195
tube 137, 191
tug(-boat) 185
harbour ~ 188
turbine steamer 185
turnover 118
retail ~ 116
twine 137
two-axle 172
two-door 172
two-wheeled 172
to type a message 219
type: ~area 203
~ face 203

ultimate consumer 116
unavailable 140
unbusinesslike 198
unclaimed 211
unclean 186
unconditional order 152
unconfirmed letter of credit 135
undeclared goods 166
undeliverable 140
~ item 209
undercarriage 179
underground: ~car park 171

~ railway 191
underpayment 209
underwrite a risk 163
underwriter 156, 160
individual ~ 160
Lloyd's ~s 160
security ~ 196
undesirable 198
unemployment benefits 162
unenclosed item 209
unfounded 141
union: customs ~ 126, 165
unit: ~ shop 116
call ~ 216
Universal Postal Union 206
unjustified 141
unknown 211
unlimited 198
unpack 139
unpaid 211
unrestricted in supply 140
unsorted 211
unsurcharged 211
unwrap 139
UPU 206
UPU-Congress 206
urban: ~bus service 171
~ postal service 206
usance bill 153
used car 171
user of the post 208

validity to tickets 180
value: ~of stock 195
book ~ 197
capitalized ~ 197
face ~ 208
invoice ~ 134
market ~ 128, 155
nominal ~155
par ~ 155
publicity ~ 201
van 174, 206
furniture ~ 172
luggage ~ 175
mail ~ 174, 206
mail storage ~ 206
moving ~ 172
postal ~206
vault 143
vehicle: ~tax 171
~ taxation 171
motor ~ 170
specialized ~s 172
venture: joint ~s 192
verification: ~note 210

verify an account 149
vertical: ~integration 195
~ take-off aircraft 178
vessel 185
cargo ~ 185
coasting ~ 185
motor ~ 185
ocean-going ~ 185
passenger-cargo ~ 185
sea-going ~ 185
towing ~ 188
transport ~ 185
vestibule train 174
video-recorder 222
videotape 225
video-taped material 222
visa regulations 180
vision link 222
visitor to a fair 128
visualiser 200
voidable 163
volume: ~of imports 124
export ~ 125
sales ~ 116
voluntary 198
~ liquidation 198
vote: plural ~195
single ~ 195
voting share 194
voucher copy 203
voyage distance 168
vulnerable to recession 198

wag(g)on 176
~ load 174
covered ~ 174
goods ~ 174
open ~ 174
waiting: ~list 180, 182
~ room 182
waive charges 151
waiver 210
waiving of claim 210
walkie-talkie 216
walkway 180
wall sign 202
want ads 203
warehouse 166
~ to ~ 161
bonded ~ 124, 188
cash-and-carry ~ 122
warehousing charge 209
warm front 181
to warrant 163
warrant: customs ~ 165
dividend ~ 195

stock ~ 194
water: ~ transport 184
　~-borne traffic 184
　inland ~s 188
　interior ~s 188
watermark 209
waterproof packing 137
waterway: coastal ~s 188
　inland ~s 188
wax paper 137
way train 174
waybill 174
　air ~ 181
wear: ladies' ~ 118
　men's ~ 118
weather 182
　~ bureau 181
　~ chart 181, 222
　~ conditions 181
　~ forecast 181
　~ forecast service 216
　~ information and forecast 216
　~ map 181
　~ report 181
　~ service 181
weekly (paper) 202
weigh anchor 188
weight: gross ~ 137
　net ~ 137
well-founded 141

wharf 188
wheel 172
wheelless 176
whole life insurance 162
to wholesale 122
wholesale: ~ business 122
　~ cooperative (society) 122
　~ price index 122
　~ representative 122
　~ trade 116, 122
wholesaler 118
　general ~ 122
　local ~ 122
　mail-order ~ 122
　specialist ~ 122
wholesaling: chain ~ 122
winch 186
wind up 198
windlass 186
window: ~ envelope 208
　~ display 117
　~ dressing 117
　~ lettering 202
　~ lighting 117
windstorm insurance 162
wing 179
to wire 220
wire: ~ strapping 138
　~ tapping 216
　~ tying 138

withdraw 146
　~ money 149
　~ from a partnership 197
withdrawal 131, 207
women's outfitter 118
wood shavings 137
wooden: ~ box 137
　~ case 137
wording 220
world: ~ fair 129
　~ prices 128
worn notes 146
W.P.A. 161
wrap 139
wrapper 208
　stamped ~ 208
wrapping 137
　~ paper 137
writer: copy ~ 200
written offer 130
wrong delivery 141

yard: goods ~ 175
　freight ~ 175
　marshalling ~ 175
　railroad ~ 175
　shunting ~ 175
yield: ~ to redemption 157
　stock ~s 155

Deutsches Register zum Aufbauwortschatz

abbauen 124
abbremsen 176
abfertigen 166
Abfertigung 180
Abfertigungsbeamter 180
Abfertigungsflughafen 179
abfüllen 139
abgabenfrei 208
Abgangshafen 187
abgehend 189
abgeholt 211
abgereist 211
Abgrenzung 195
abhalten 197
abheben 149
Abhebung 149
Abholdienst 170
abholen 176
Abholgroßmarkt 122
Abholung 207
abkuppeln 176
Ablader 186
Ablaufberg 175
ablehnen 131
Ablehnung 131
abliefern 176
Abnehmerkartell 195
Abonnementsdauer 209
Abrechnungskurs 156
Abrechnungsstelle 145
Abruf 139
abrufen 189
Absatz 128
Absatzförderung 200
Absatzgebiet 126
Absatzgenossenschaft 122
Absatzkosten 128
Absatzorganisation 128
Abschlagszahlung 134
abschließen 126, 133, 162, 169
Abschluß 155
Abschwächung 194
absenden 131, 138
Absender 210, 213, 219
absetzbar 128
absetzen 124, 126, 128
absichern 144, 158
Abstellgleis 175
Abstellplatz für Kinderwagen 120
abwerfen 182
abziehen 135
Achsdruck 175

Achse 170
Adresse 208
Adressenänderung 208
Adressenliste 201
Adressiermaschine 208
Affiche 202
AG 193
Air Terminal 173
Airbus 178
Akkreditiv 135
Akontozahlung 134
Aktie 157, 194, 195, 197
Aktienarten 194
Aktienbank 142
Aktienbesitz 147, 194
Aktienbezugsschein 194
Aktienemission 157
Aktiengesellschaft 193
Aktienkapital 193
Aktienkauf 194
Aktienkurse 194
Aktienmarkt 155
Aktienmehrheit 157
Aktienpaket 194
Aktienurkunde 194
Aktienzeichnung 194
Aktienzertifikat 156, 194
Aktionär 193
aktuell 205
Akzept 135
Akzeptbank 144
akzeptieren 147
Akzeptkredit 153
Alleinbesitz 191
Allgemeines Zoll- und Handelsabkommen 164
Alternativfrage 201
Altersrente 162
amtlich 155
Amtszeichen 215
anbieten 131, 144
Anerkennung 213
Anfahrt 177
anfechtbar 163
Anforderung 130
Anfrage 130, 131
Angaben 130
angeben 132
Angebot 130, 140
angemessen 135
angeschmutzt 119
anhaltend 204
Anhängeadresse 210

Anhänger 172
Anker 188
Ankerplatz 187
Ankerwinde 186
anknüpfen 131
ankommen 182
Ankündigung 200
Anlage(n) 175
Anlageberater 143, 144
Anlagegeschäft 143
Anlagekapital 157
anlaufen 189
Anlaufhafen 187
anlegen 157, 189
Anlegestelle 188
Anleihe 144, 155
Anleiheschuld 196
anmelden 216
Annahme 153
annehmen 131, 153
annoncieren 204
Annullierung 120
Anreize 125
Anruf 215, 216
Anrufbeantworter 216
anrufen 215
Anrufer 215
anschaulich 219
Anschlagsäule 202
Anschlagtafel 202
Anschlagzaun 202
Anschlußauftrag 131
Anschrift 153, 208
ansehen 223
anstellen 126
Anteilschein 156
Antrag 212
Antragsteller 160
Antriebskraft 175
Antwort 220
Antwortkarte 208
Antwortpostkarte 208
Antwortschein 131, 208
Anweisung 152
Anwendungsbereich 204
Anzahlung 135
Anzapfen 216
Anzeige 202, 203
Anzeigenauftrag 202
Anzeigenausschnitte 203
Anzeigenschluß 202
Anzeigenwerbung 202
Apotheke 117

Apparat 216
Aquädukt 188
arbeiten 176
Arbeitgeber 162
Arbeitslosenunterstützung 162
arglistiges Verschweigen 140
Artikelserie 117
Atelier 221
Atelieraufnahme 223
Atomkraft 185
Attrappe 117
aufbringen 148, 189
aufeinanderstapeln 172
auffüllen 131
Aufgabe 220
Aufgabepostamt 206
Aufgabestelle 206
Aufgabezeit 207
aufgeben 180, 220
Aufhebung 212
Auflage 202
auflaufen 189
auflegen 158, 197
auflösen 176
Auflösung 192
Aufnahme 223, 225
Aufnahmefähigkeit 128
Aufnahmegerät 222, 225
Aufnahmeraum 221
aufnehmen 225
Aufrechnung 213
aufstapeln 139
Aufstellplakat 202
Aufstellung 130
Auftrag 118
Auftragsbestand 131
Auftragsbestätigung 131
Auftragseingang 131
Auftragserteilung 134
Auftragspostanweisung 213
aufweisen 126
Aufzeichnung 225
Aufzugkabine 191
Aufzugschacht 191
Ausfuhr 125
Ausfuhrabgabe 125
Ausfuhrbestimmungen 125
Ausfuhrdeklaration 187
Ausfuhrerlöse 125
Ausfuhrgenehmigung 125
Ausfuhrhafen 187
Ausfuhrhandel 123, 125
Ausfuhrkommissionär 126

Ausfuhrkontingent 125
Ausfuhrkontrolle 125
Ausfuhrland 125
Ausfuhrlenkung 125
Ausfuhrprämie 125
Ausfuhrrückgang 125
Ausfuhrsteigerung 125
Ausfuhrzoll 125, 165
ausfüllen 151
Ausgabe 157, 207
Ausgabeabteilung 145
Ausgabebedingungen 196
Ausgabekurs 144, 195
ausgeben 147, 197
ausgehend 189
ausgestellt 129
Ausgleich 136
ausgleichen 198
aushandeln 133
Aushändigung 208
Ausklarierung 187
Auskunft 204
Auslagen 213
Auslandsabsatz 125
Auslandsmarkt 125
Auslandstelegramm 220
Auslandsverkehr 207
Auslandswechsel 153
Auslassungen vorbehalten 134
auslaufen 188
Auslegerkran 188
ausleihen 143, 147
ausliefern 138
auspacken 139
ausreichend 163
ausrüsten 138
ausschalten 221, 223
ausscheiden(d) 198
ausschließen 182
ausschütten 197
Außenstände 135
Außenwerbung 201
Außenzoll 165
Aussichtswagen 174
ausstatten 138
ausstellen 129, 135, 149, 182
Aussteller 144, 150, 153
Ausstellung 127, 128, 213
Ausstellungsdatum 153
Ausstellungsdauer 129
Ausstellungsgebäude 129
Ausstellungsgelände 128
Ausstellungskatalog 129
Ausstellungsort 153
Ausstellungsraum 118

Ausstellungsstück 129
Ausverkaufspreis 135
Auswahlmustersendung 130
Auswahlverfahren 201
ausweiten 143
Auswirkungen 146
auszahlen 147, 149, 163
Auszahlungsbestätigung 213
Auszahlungsschein 213
Autobusbahnhof 171
Autobusbetrieb 171
Autofähre 185
Autofahrer 171
Autohändler 171
Autohof 171
Autoindustrie 171
automatisch 215, 220
Automobilausstellung 171
Autopark 171
Autoreisezug-Service 174
Autoschlosser 171
Autounfall 171
Autovermietung 171

Backbord 186, 189
Bäckerei 117
Bäckerladen 117
Bahn 174
Bahnanschluß(gleise) 188
Bahnfahrt 173
Bahnhofsplakat 202
Bahnkörper 175
Bahnpost 206
Bahnpostwagen 206
Baisse 155
Baissespekulant 156
Baissier 156
Bake 188
Band 222, 225
Bandaufnahme 225
Bank 153
Bank von England 145
Bankausweis 145
Bankdarlehen 142
Bankdirektor 142
Bankeinlagen 148
Bankenkonsortium 195
Bankgeschäfte 142
Bankguthaben 142, 148
Bankkonto 149
Bankkredit 142
Bankkunde 142
Banknotenausgabe 145
Banknotenumlauf 145

bankrott 198
Bankscheck 151
Bankspesen 142
Banktresor 143
Bankverbindungen 142
Bankwechsel 147
Bankwesen 142
bar 134
Bareinlage 148
Barfrankierung 208
Barfreimachung 208
Bargeld 157
Bargeldausgeber 143
Barken 185
Barpreis 120
Barverkauf 133
Barzahlung 134
Beanstandung 140
beantragen 158
Bedarf 117, 128, 181
Bedarfsdeckungsgüter 117
bedienen 219
Bedienungsanleitung 130
befahren 174
beflaggen 189
befördern 169, 172, 220
Beförderung 178, 185, 191
Beförderungsbedingungen 181
Beförderungsweg 171
Befrachter 186
Befrager 201
Befragter 201
befreien 211
befriedigen 118
befürchten 133
begebbar 153, 154
begeben 182
Begebung 144, 153
begleichen 139
Begleichung 134
Begleitadresse 210
Begleitbrief 130
Begleitpapiere 210
begründet 141
Begünstigter 160
behalten 141
Behälterwagen 175
Behandlung 141
Behelfsflugplatz 179
beherrschen 128
beibehalten 145
Beifahrer 171
beigeben 182
Beilage 203
beklagen 141

Bekleidungsgeschäft 118
belasten 213
beleben 129
belegen 211
Belegexemplar 203
beliefern 138
bemustern 131
benachrichtigen 216
benötigen 148
Benzinmotor 171
Benzinverbrauch 171
beraten 145
berechnen 135
berechtigt 141
Bereinigung 140
Bergwerksaktie 194
Berichtigung 208
berücksichtigen 163
Berufsspekulant 156
beschädigt 119
Beschädigung 161
beschaffen 126, 169
Beschaffenheit 207
Bescheinigung 210
beschicken 129
Beschlagnahme 166
beschlagnahmt 211
beschleunigen 175
beschlußfähig 197
beschränken 197
beschränkt 193, 198
beschriften 139
Beschriftung 138
Beschwerde 140, 141
Beschwerdebrief 140
beschweren 141
beseitigen 124
Beseitigung 165
Besetztzeichen 215
besitzen 197
Bestand 146
bestätigt 136, 151
Bestätigungsschreiben 130
Bestellungseingang 131
bestellen 118, 131
Bestellfirma 131
Bestellschreiben 130
Bestellung 131
bestimmt 205
Bestimmungsflughafen 179
Bestimmungshafen 187
Bestimmungsort 168, 169
bestreiten 158
besuchen 129
beteiligen 129
Beteiligung 194

Betrag 151, 213
betreiben 189
Betriebsführung 195
Betriebsleitung 195
Betriebstechnik 196
Bevorzugung 201
bewegen 224
beweglich 169
Bewegung 175
bewerben 129
bezahlen 135
Bezahlung 134
Bezogene(r) 150, 153
Bezugspreis 209
Bezugsrecht 157, 194
Bezugsschreiben 130
Bildschirm 222
Bildtelegrafie 220
bildtelegrafisch 219
Bildtelegramm 220
Bildunterschrift 203
bildwirksam 223
Bindfaden 137
Binnengewässer 188
Binnenhafen 188
Binnenmarkt 128
Binnenschiffahrt(sverkehr) 188
Binnenschiffahrtsunternehmen 188
Binnentransportversicherung 188
Binnenverkehr 168
Binnenwasserstraßen 188
binnenwirtschaftlich 198
Binnenzoll 165
Blankoindossament 151
Blechdose 137
Blechkiste 137
Blickfang 117
Blindenschriftsendung 209
Blindflug 179
Blitztelegramm 220
Blocksignal 175
Blockstrecke 175
bloßgehend 209
Blumenhändler 118
Blumenhandlung 118
Bodenpersonal 180
Bö 181
Boje 188
Boot 185
Bord-Boden-... 182
Bordkante 181
Bordkonnossement 186
Bordmechaniker 180

borgen 147
Börse 155
Börsenabrechnungstag 156
Börsenabschluß 155
Börsenbericht 155
börsenfähig 158
Börsenkurs 155, 194, 216
Börsenordnung 155
Börsentelegraf 220
Börsentendenz 155
Börsenumsatzsteuer 155
Börsenvertreter 156
Börsenzettel 155
Börsenzulassung 156
Branchenverzeichnis 130
Brandkasse 161
Brandschaden 161
Brandschadenversicherung 161
brechen 133
Breite 188
Bremsleistung 175
Briefbogen 130
Briefgeheimnis 207
Briefkarte 208
Briefmarke 209
Briefmarkenmesse 129
Briefmarkenrolle 208
Briefpost 208
Briefsendung(en) 208, 209
Brieftelegramm 220
Britische Industriemesse 129
Britische Woche 126
Broschüre 126, 130
Bruchlandung 179
bruchsicher 137
Bruttogewicht 137
Bruttopreis 135
Bruttoregistertonnage 186
buchen 131, 189
Buchgeld 149
Buchgewinn 197
Buchungsstelle 180
Buchverlust 197
Buchwert 197
Bug 186
Bullauge 186
Bummelzug 174
Busfahrer 171
Busverbindung 180

Charterfluggesellschaft 178
Charterflugverkehr 178
chartern 189

Charterpartie 186
Chartervertrag 186
Chemiewerte 157
Chiffrenummer 203
chiffrieren 220
City Terminal 179
Clearingbank 147
Code-Nummer 149
Container 169
Containerschiff 185
Container-Zug 174

Dachgesellschaft 195
Damenbekleidungsgeschäft 118
Damm 188
Dampfer 185
Dampflokomotive 175
Darlehenskonto 143
Darstellung 225
Datowechsel 153
Datumsstempel 209
Datumsstempelabdruck 209
Dauerplakat 202
decken 88
Deckladung 187
Deckung 151
Deckungsbestätigung 161
Deckungskauf 155
Defekt 140
degressiv 207
Deich 188
Depeschenbote 220
Deportgeschäft 156
Depositenbuch 142
Depositengeschäft 148
Depositeninhaber 142, 149
Depositenkonto 143, 148
Detailgeschäft 116
Detailhandel 116
Devisenabteilung 143
Devisenbewirtschaftung 145
Devisenkurse 216
Devisenmarkt 144
Diagramm 225
Diapositivwerbung 203, 224
Dichte 201
Diebstahlsrisiko 126
Dienst 189
Diensterfordernisse 211
Dienstleistungen 122
Dienstschreiben 208
Dienstvermerk 207
Dienstvorschrift 207

Dienstwagen 175
Dieselbetrieb 175
Diesellokomotive 175
Dieselmotor 171
direkt 123
Direktor 195
Direktübertragung 203, 221
Direktwerbung 201
dirigieren 172
Diskontbank 147, 153
Diskontbedingungen 147
Diskonterhöhung 147
Diskonterlös 153
diskontfähig 148, 154
Diskontgeschäft 147
diskontierbar 147
diskontieren 147, 153, 154
Diskontkredit 147
Diskontmarkt 147
Diskontsatz 143
Diskontsenkung 147
Diskontspesen 147
Diskontwechsel 147
Diskothek 225
diskriminierend 205
Dispacheur 161
Dividendenanspruch 194
Dividendenausschüttung 158
dividendenberechtigt 198
Dividendenpapiere 157, 194
Dividendenschein 195
Dock 188
Dokumentarfilm 224
Dokumente 135, 153, 161
Dokumentenakkreditiv 135
Dokumententratte 134, 153
Domizil 139
domiziliert 212
doppelseitig 203
Drahtakzept 220
Drahtanschrift 219
Drahtantwort 220
drahtlos 216
Drahtseilbahn 191
Drahtverschnürung 138
Dreharbeit 223
drehen 224
dringend 220
Drogerie 117
Drogerie 117
Drogstore 117
Duplikat 134
durchführen 182, 198
Durchfuhr 168

Durchgangszettel 210
durchgeben 219, 223
durchschnittlich 202
Durchschnittspreis 135
Düsenflugzeug 178
Düsentriebwerk 178
D-Zug 174

Echtheit 212
Economy-Klasse 180
Effekten 147
Effektenabteilung 143
Effektenarten 156
Effektenberater 144
Effektenemission 144, 156
Effektenhändler 156
Effektenportefeuille 143
Effektenverwaltung 143
Effektivverzinsung 157
Eigenfinanzierung 196
Eigenkapital 192
Eigentümer 197
Eigentumsübertragung 133
Eigentumsvorbehalt 120, 133, 187
Eigenwechsel 153, 212
Eilboten 211
Eilgut 176
Eilsendung 209
einachsig 172
einberufen 197
einbezahlen 197
einbringen 157
Einbruchdiebstahlversicherung 162
Eindeichung 188
einfahrend 177
einfliegen 182
Einflugschneise 179
Einfuhr 124
Einfuhrbeschränkungen 124
Einfuhrbestimmungen 124
einführen 204
Einfuhrhafen 187
Einfuhrhandel 123
Einfuhrkommissionär 124
Einfuhrkontingent 124
Einfuhrland 124
Einfuhrliste 124
Einführungskampagne 200
Einführungspreis 202
Einfuhrvolumen 124
Einfuhrwaren 124
Einfuhrzoll 165
eingefroren 143

eingetragen 193
eingleisig 177
einheimsen 197
einheitlich 204
einholen 131
einhüllen 139
einkaufen 128
Einkaufsbedingungen 130
Einkaufsdelegation 126
Einkaufsgenossenschaft 116, 122
Einkaufskorb 117
Einkaufsspitze 120
Einklarierung 187
Einkommensgruppe 201
Einlage 142, 149
Einlagekonto 148
Einlaufhafen 187
einleiten 198
einleuchtend 205
einlösen 151, 154
Einmannbetrieb 116
Einmannunternehmen 191
Einnahmen 181
einplanen 120
einräumen 126, 135
einreichen 157, 197
einsacken 210
einschalten 221, 223
Einschaltung 203
Einschätzung 192
Einschienenbahn 191
Einschreibsendung 209
einsetzen 126
Einspruchsrecht 195
einstecken 197
einstellen 135, 198, 223
eintragen 131, 151, 197
Eintragung 193
eintreibbar 119
eintreten 197
Eintrittskarte 223
Eintrittspreis 223
Einverständnis 133
einwickeln 139
einzahlen 149, 151
Einzahler 142
Einzahlung 149
Einzahlungsbeleg 149
Einzahlungsbuch 149
Einzahlungsschalter 143
Einzelhandel 116, 120
Einzelhandelsgeschäft 116
Einzelhandelskunde 116
Einzelhandelspreis 116
Einzelhandelsrabatt 116

Einzelhandelsumsatz 116
Einzelhandelsunternehmen 116
Einzelhandelswerbung 201
Einzelhändler 116, 122
Einzelhändlerbefragung 201
Einzelkaufmann 191
Einzelunternehmen 191
Einzelunternehmer 116
Einzelversicherer 160
einziehbar 163
einziehen 213
Einziehung 166, 213
Einzug 135
Einzugsauftragspostanweisung 213
Eisbrecher 185
Eisenbahn 175
Eisenbahnanschluß 174
Eisenbahnbetrieb 174
Eisenbahnbrücke 175
Eisenbahngütertransport 174
Eisenbahnknotenpunkt 174
Eisenbahnnetz 173
Eisenbahnschwelle 175
Eisenbahnstrecke 173
Eisenbahntarif 173
Eisenbahnverkehr 173
Eisenbahnwagen 174
Eisenwarenhandlung 118
elegant 119
elektrisch 175
elektronisch 180
Elektrowarengeschäft 118
Elektrowarenmesse 129
Emission 196
Emissionsabteilung 145
Emissionsbank 144
Emissionshaus 196
Emissionskurs 195
Emissionsmarkt 144
Emittent 144
Empfänger 208, 219, 220, 223
Empfangsbestätigung 210
Empfangshafen 139
Empfangsschein 210
Empfangsstation 221
en detail 119
en gros 122
Endbahnhof 175
Endbetrag 212
Endstation 179
Endverbrauch 116

Endverbraucher 116
entgegenkommen 136
entgegennehmen 143, 149
entgleisen 177
Entladetag 187
entlasten 211
entnehmen 131
entschädigen 213
Entschädigung 160
Entschädigungsbetrag 160
entschuldigen 141
Entschuldigung 140
Entwertung 209
erbringen 163
Erdgas 191
erfordern 176
Ergänzung 210
Ergänzungswerbung 201
erhalten 219
erhältlich 140
erheben 141, 151, 166
erhöhen 163, 166, 198
Erhöhung 193
erklären 198
Erlebensfallversicherung 162
erledigen 128, 131, 166
Erledigung 140
erleiden 163, 182, 189
ermäßigt 180
erneuern 133
erobern 128
eröffnen 129, 138, 149
erreichbar 216
errichten 126
erscheinen 223
Erscheinungsdatum 203
erschließen 126, 128
Erträge 155
Ertragswert 197
erwarten 157
Erzeugermarkt 128
erzieherisch 225
erzielen 197
Expedient 184
Export 125
Exportabteilung 125
Exportauftrag 125, 131
Exporteur 125
Exportfinanzierung 125
Exportfirma 125
Exportförderung 125
Exportgeschäft 125
Exportgüter 125
Exporthändler 125

Exportkaufmann 125
Exportkredit 125
Exportlieferung 125
Exportmakler 125
Exportverpackung 137
Exportvertrag 125
Exportvertreter 125
Exportvolumen 125
Exportziffern 125

Fabrikationsfehler 140
Fabrikpreis 135
Fachblatt 202
Fachgeschäft 116
Fachgroßhändler 122
Fachhandel 116
Fachmesse 129
Fachzeitschrift 202
Faden 137
Fahrbahn 171
Fahrbereitschaft 171
fahren 172, 176, 189
Fahrgastschiff 185
Fahrkilometer 168
Fahrplan 174
fahrplanmäßig 169
Fahrrinne 188
Fahrtmesser 178
Fahrwasser 188
Fahrwerk 179
Fahrzeug 170, 171, 185
Fakturiermaschine 134
Fakturierung 134
Fallbodenwagen 175
fällig 142, 213
Fälligkeit 143, 153, 154
Fallreep 186
Fallschirm 191
falsch 137
Falschlieferung 141
Faltprospekt 202
Familienbetrieb 116
Familientarif 180
Farbfernsehen 222
Farbfilm 223
Faß 137
Fäßchen 137
Fehldruck 209
Fehler 140
fehlerhaft 208
fehlleiten 211
Fehllieferung 141
Feinkostgeschäft 117
Feinkosthandlung 117
Fensterbriefumschlag 208
Fernamt 215

Ferngespräch 215, 216
Fernlaster 172
Fernlastfahrer 171
Fernlastverkehr 168
Fernmeldestelle 206
Fernmeldetechnik 206
fernmündlich 215, 216
Fernschreibanlage 218
Fernschreibanschluß 218
fernschreiben 219
Fernschreiben 219
Fernschreiber 219
Fernschreibgebühren 219
Fernschreibnetz 218
Fernschreibteilnehmer 219
Fernschreibverkehr 218
Fernschreibvermittlung 218
Fernseh- 225
Fernsehansager 222
Fernsehapparat 222, 223
Fernsehaufzeichnungen 222
Fernsehberichterstattung 222
Fernsehempfänger 222
fernsehen 222
Fernsehen 222, 223
Fernsehkamera 222
Fernsehnachrichten 222
Fernsehprogramm 221, 223
Fernsehsender 222
Fernsehsendung 222
Fernsehstation 222
Fernsehteilnehmer 222
Fernsehturm 222
Fernsehwerbung 203, 222
Fernsetzmaschine 219
Fernsprechansagedienst 216
Fernsprechanschluß 215
Fernsprechauftragsdienst 215, 217
Fernsprechbuch 215
Fernsprecher 216
Fernsprechgebühren 215
Fernsprechhörer 215
Fernsprechnachrichtendienst 216
Fernsprechnebenanschluß 215
Fernsprechnebenstelle 215
Fernsprechnummer 215
Fernsprechstelle 215
Fernsprechteilnehmer 215
Fernsprechverbindung 215

Fernsprechzelle 215
Fernverkehr 170
fertigstellen 131
fertig werden 131
fest 130, 158
Festgeldkonto 143
festhalten 128
festlegen 133, 197
Festlegung 171
festmachen 189
Festpreis 135
festsetzen 197
Feststellung 210
festverzinslich 155, 156, 158, 196
feuergefährlich 138
Feuerschutz 161
Feuerversicherung 161
Feuerwehr 161
fiduziarisch 146
Filialbanksystem 142
Film 224
Filmarchiv 224
Filmatelier 224
Filmaufnahme 223
filmen 224
Filmfreigabe 223
Filmgesellschaft 223
Filmindustrie 223
filmisch 224
Filmkamera 223
Filmmontage 224
Filmproduzent 223
Filmprojektor 223
Filmrechte 223
Filmreklame 224
Filmschnitt 224
Filmtheater 223
Filmvoranzeige 224
Filmvorschau 224
Filmvorspann 224
Filmwerbung 203
Filmwesen 223
finanzieren 223
Finanzierung 196
Finanzwechsel 153
Finanzzoll 165
finden 128
Firmenwerbung 201
Fischhändler 117
Fischhandlung 117
fixen 157
Flächenstichprobe 201
Flachwagen 175
Flasche 137
Fleischerladen 117

fliegen 180, 181, 182
Flieger 180
Fließband 191
Fluchtgeld 145
Flug 179
flugbegeistert 182
Flugbereich 179
Flugblatt 202
Flugdauer 179
Flügel 179
Flugerfahrung 180
Fluggast 180
Fluggastkabine 179
Fluggastraum 180
Fluggastversicherung 181
Fluggepäckabschnitt 180
Fluggeschwindigkeit 179
Flughafen 179, 180
Flughafenabfertigungsdienst 179
Flughafengebühr 179
Flughafenrestaurant 180
Flughafenzollamt 180
Flughöhe 179
Flugkapitän 180
Flugkarte 180
Fluglinie 178
Fluglotse 179
Flugplan 179
flugplanmäßig 182
Flugplatz 179
Flugplatzbefeuerung 179
Flugreise 178
Flugschein 180
Flugscheingültigkeit 180
Flugscheinverkaufsstelle 180
Flugschneise 179
Flugsicherheit 179
Flugsicherung 178
Flugstrecke 179
Flugstunden 180
Flugverkehr 178
Flugzeug 180, 181
Flugzeugabsturz 179
Flugzeugbesatzung 180
Flugzeugentführung 179
Flugzeughalle 180
Flugzeugladung 181
Flugzeugrumpf 179
Flüsse 188
flüssig 143
Flüssigkeit 138, 191
Flußmündung 187
Flutbrecher 188
Förderband 188, 191

fördern 124, 126
Forderungsabtretung 160
Forderungsberechtigte(r) 160
Forderungsübergang 160
Formblätter 210
Formulare 210
Fracht 139
Frachtbrief 174
Frachtdampfer 185
Frachtendienste 181
Frachter 185
Frachtermäßigung 187
Frachtflugverkehr 181
Frachtflugzeug 178
frachtfrei 140
Frachtführer 168
Frachtgut 176
Frachtkarte 210
Frachtkosten 140
Frachtraum 181, 186
Frachtrechnung 187
Frachtschiff 185
Frachtversicherung 161
Frachtvertrag 186
Fragebogen 201
Frankatur 209
Frankieraufdruck 209
Frankiermaschine 209
Frankierung 208
frei 139, 161
freigeben 126
Freigepäck 180
Freigepäckgrenze 180
Freihafen 166, 187
Freihandel 124
Freihandelszone 126
freihändig 128
freimachen 209, 211
Freimachung 208, 209
Freimachungsaufdruck 209
Freistempelmaschine 209
freiwillig 198
Fremdkapital 192
Fremdmittel 197
Fremdwährungswechsel 147
Friseur 118
Friseursalon 118
Frühzug 174
führen(d) 143, 213
Fuhrpark 171
füllen 139, 172
Füllmaterial 137
Fundgegenstand 207
Funkanlage 221

Funkbild 220
Funksprechgerät 216
Funkturm 221
Fusion 195
fusionieren 197

Ganzinvalidität 181
ganzseitig 203
Garant 156
Garantieschein 130
Garantievertrag 160
GATT 164
Gebrauchsanweisung 130
Gebrauchtwagen 171
Gebühr 208, 211
Gebührenansage 216
gebührenfrei 208, 211
Gebührenfreiheit 208
Gebührenstufen 207
Gebührensystem 207
gedeckt 163
Gedenkmarke 208
geeignet 126
Gefälligkeitstratte 153
gefragt 157
Gegenangebot 131
Gegensprechverkehr 215
gehen 166, 182, 189, 216, 224
gelangen 133
Geld 142, 145, 147
Geldeinlage 193
Geldgeber 203
Geldinstitut 120
Geldkurs 155
Geldüberhang 147
Geldumtauschschalter 143
Gelegenheitsgesellschaft 192
Gelegenheitswerbung 201
Gelenk 176
gelenkig 176
gemeinnützig 193
Gemeinschaftsunternehmen 192
Gemeinschaftswerbung 201
Gemischtwarenhandlung 117
Generalpolice 161
genormt 176
Gepäck 180
Gepäckwagen 175
gerechtfertigt 141
Gesamtausfuhr 125
Gesamtbetrag 134
Gesamteinfuhr 123

Gesamtpreis 135
gesamtschuldnerisch 192
Gesamtzuladungsgewicht 186
Geschädigte(r) 160
Geschäft 197
Geschäftsadresse 208
Geschäftsanteil 192
Geschäftsbank 142
Geschäftsbericht 194
geschäftsführend 192, 195, 198
Geschäftsführer 195
Geschäftsführung 195
Geschäftsjahr 193
Geschäftskarte 209
Geschäftsleitung 195
geschäftsmäßig 198
Geschäftsordnung 193
Geschäftspapiere 209
Geschäftsstunden 117
gescheitert 189
geschützt 189
Geschwindigkeit 169, 177
Gesellschaft 191, 192, 193, 197, 198
Gesellschafter 192, 193, 197
Gesellschafterversammlung 192, 194
Gesellschaftsanteil 192, 193
Gesellschaftseigentum 193
Gesellschaftseinlagen 192
Gesellschaftsform 192
Gesellschaftsgewinne 194
Gesellschaftskapital 193
Gesellschaftsname 193
Gesellschaftsrecht 193
Gesellschaftsregister 193
Gesellschaftsschulden 194
Gesellschaftssitz 193
Gesellschaftsstatuten 193
Gesellschaftssteuer 194
Gesellschaftsunterlagen 194
Gesellschaftsverbindlichkeiten 194
Gesellschaftsvermögen 192
Gesellschaftsvertrag 192
Gesellschaftsziel 193
Gesellschaftszweck 193
gesetzlich 194
gesperrt 143
Gespräch 216
Gesprächseinheit 216
Gestalter 200
gestorben 211

Gesundheitsvorschriften 180
Gesundheitszeugnis 185
Getreidemarkt 156
gewähren 141, 162, 163
Gewahrsam 143
gewerblich 171
Gewinn 156, 196, 197
Gewinnanteil 192
Gewinnausschüttung 194
gewinnberechtigt 194
Gewinnbeteiligung 192, 194
gewinnen 115
Gewinn- und Verlustrechnung 194
Gewinnverteilung 194
gewöhnlich 220
gezielt 205
gezwungen sein 148
Gipfelhöhe 179
Giralgeld 149
girieren 151
Giroabteilung 212
Girobank 147
Giroeinlagen 212
Girokonto 148
Giroverkehr 212
Girozentrale 212
Glasflasche 137
Glaswolle 137
glattstellen 158
Gläubigerwechsel 160
gleichmäßig 189
Gleise 175
Gleiskrümmung 175
Gleitzoll 165
Glückwunschtelegramm 220
GmbH 193
Goldreserven 145
Goldstandard 145
Gold- und Silberbarren 144
Goldwährung 145
Grammophon 225
graphisch 225
Gratisaktie 157, 194
Grenze 163
großangelegt 126
Großanzeige 203
Größe 195
Großeinkaufsgenossenschaft 122
großformatig 203
Großhandel 116, 122
Großhandelskette 122
Großhandelspreisindex 122

Großhandelsvertreter 122
Großhändler 122
Großunternehmen 192
gründen 197
Gründeraktie 157, 194
Grundgebühr 208
Grundlage 198
Grundschuld 196
Gründungsurkunde 193
Gründungsversammlung 193
Gruppe 202
Gruppenversicherung 162
Gültigkeitsdauer 209
günstig 135
Güter 125
Güterbahnhof 175
Güterbeförderung 184
Güterfernverkehr 168
Güterkraftverkehr 168
Gütermenge 171, 187
Güterspediteur 126, 171
Gütertransport 168, 174
Güterverkehr 170
Güterwagen 174
Güterzug 174
Gütesiegel 116
Guthaben 142
Guthabenübertragung 212
gutschreiben 213
Gutschriftanzeige 212
Gutschriftzettel 149, 212

Habensaldo 212
Hafen 187, 189
Hafenanlagen 187
Hafenarbeiter 185
Hafenbecken 187
Hafenbehörde 187
Hafendamm 188
Hafeneinfahrt 187
Hafengebühren 187
Hafenmeister 187
Hafenordnung 187
Hafenpolizei 187
Hafenschlepper 188
haften 198
Haftpflicht 192
Haftpflichtversicherung 162
Haftung 192, 198, 210
Hagelversicherung 162
Hand 219
Handel 124
handeln 157, 197
Handelsflotte 184
handelsgerichtlich 198

Handelsgesellschaft 192, 193
Handelskapitän 184
Handelskorrespondenz 130
Handelsmarine 184
Handelsmarke 204
Handelsmesse 129
Handelsrechnung 134
Handelsschiff 184
Handelsschiffahrt 184
Handelsspanne 116
handelsüblich 137
Handelsvertreter 126
Handelswechsel 147, 153
handeltreibend 189
Händen 211
Handgepäck 180
Handvermittlung 215
Handzettel 130
Haupteinfuhrwaren 123
Hauptfilm 223
Hauptpost(amt) 206
Hauptstrecke 174
Hauptversammlung 194
Haus zu Haus 161, 169
Hausbriefkasten 207
Haushaltsvorstand 201
Hausmarke 116
Hausratversicherung 162
Hausse 155
Haussespekulant 156
Haussier 156
haussierend 158
Haus- und Geschäftsräume 161
Haus- und Küchengeräte 118
Hauszeitschrift 202
Havarie 161, 186
Havarieerklärung 186
Havariekommissar 161
Heck 186
Heimathafen 187
Helling 188
Herabsetzung 213
herausbringen 224
Herrenbekleidungsgeschäft 118
herstellen 216
Heuervertrag 184
Hier anheben 138
Hier öffnen 138
hinauftreiben 147
hineinfahren 172
hinten 150
Hinterleger 142

Hinweiszettel 210
hoch notierend 158
Hochbahn 174
Hochseedampfer 185
hochseetüchtig 189
Höchstpreis 135
Holzkiste 137
Holzverschlag 137
Holzwolle 137
hören 221
Hörerforschung 201, 203
Hörmuschel 216
Hubschrauber 178
Hubschrauberlandeplatz 178
Huckepacksystem 185
Huckepackverkehr 170
hypothekarisch 156
Hypothekenforderung 196
Hypothekengläubiger 196
Hypothekenschulden 196
Hypothekenzinsen 196

illiquide 143
Importartikel 124
Importeur 124
Importfirma 124
Importhändler 124
Importkredit 124
Importmakler 124
Importvertreter 124
Inanspruchnahme 145
Incoterms 139
Indossament 153
Indossant 150, 153
Indossatar 150, 153
indossieren 151
Indossierung 153
Industriemesse 129
Industrieobligationen 157
Informationsmaterial 126
Inhaber 196, 213
Inhaberaktie 157, 194
Inhaberobligationen 157
Inhaberschuldverschreibungen 196
Inhaltserklärung 165
Inland 125
inländisch 198
Inlandsmarkt 128
Inlandspostdienst 206
Inlandstelegramm 220
Inlandsverkehr 206
Inlandswechsel 153
Innenhafen 187
Insassenversicherung 162

Inserent 202
inserieren 204
Insertionsauftrag 202
Instrumentenlandung 179
Intercity-Zug 174
Interessent 201
interessieren 204
interkontinental 178
international 195
Interviewer 201
Invalidenrente 162
Investmentanteile 157, 194
Investmentfonds 143
Investmentpapiere 143
irreführend 166, 205
Irrtümer vorbehalten 134

Jahresabschluß 194
Jahresbilanz 194
Jahresüberschüsse 196
Jumbo-Jet 178
juristisch 198
Juweliergeschäft 118

Kabeldepesche 220
Kabelfernsehen 222
Kabelnachricht 220
Kabine 191
Kahn 185
Kai 188
Kajütenbett 187
Kalkulationsaufschlag 116
kalkulieren 135
Kaltfront 181
Kanal 188, 222
Kanalfracht 188
Kanalschleuse 188
Kanalverkehr 188
Kanzel 179
Kapital 192
Kapitalanlagen 143
Kapitalanteilschein 156
Kapitalbeschaffung 196
Kapitalgesellschaft 193
Kapitalgewinne 192
Kapitalisierung 197
Kapitalsammelstellen 156
Kapitalzuführung 196
Kargoversicherung 161
Kartell 195
Kartenanweisung 213
Kartenbrief 208
Kartenschluß 207, 209
Kartierung 207
Karton 137
Kaskoversicherung 161

Kassa 134
Kassageschäft 156
Kasse 120
Kassenschalter 143
kassieren 151
Kassierstelle 120
Kastenleerung 207
Katalogpreis 135
Kauf 133
kaufen 118, 120, 157
Käufer 116, 118, 120
Käufermarkt 128
Kaufgewohnheiten 201
Kaufhemmung 201
Kaufmotiv 201
Kaufunlust 201
Kaufverhalten 201
Kaufvertrag 120, 133
Kautionsversicherung 162
Kennzeichen 207
Kennziffer 203
Kesselwagen 175
Kette 222
Kettenladen 120
KFZ-Besteuerung 171
KFZ-Steuer 171
KG 192
Kiel 186
Kielraum 186
Kino 223, 224
Kinobesucher 223
Kisten 138
Klage 141
klagen 141
Klappenschrank 215
Klarsichtpackung 120
Klebestreifen 138
Klebezettel 210
Kleinflughafen 179
Kleingeld 213
Kleinhandelsgeschäft 116
Kleinhandelsunternehmen 116
Kleinhändler 116
Kleinlebensversicherung 161, 162
Kleinobligationen 156
Klimatisierung 120
Knoten 186
Knüller 117
Kochrezept 216
Kodierung 207
Kohlendampfer 185
Kollektion 117
Kombiwagen 172
Kommanditanteil 192

Kommanditgesellschaft 192
Kommanditist 192
Kommunalwerte 147
Komplementär 192
Konferenzgespräch 215
Konkurrenten 125
Konkurs 198
Konnossement 186
konsequent 204
Konservendose 137
Konsortium 195
Konsulatsfaktura 134
Konsumenten 116, 122
Konsumentenbefragung 201
Konsumgeschäft 120
Konto 143, 148, 151, 212, 213
Kontoauszug 143, 212
Kontoguthaben 212
Kontoinhaber 142, 143, 149, 212
Kontokorrent 150
Kontokorrenteinlagen 148
Kontokorrentguthaben 148
Kontokorrentkonto 148
Kontokorrentkredit 148
Kontokorrentkreditzinsen 148
Kontokorrentkunde 148
Kontonummer 143
Kontostand 148
Kontoumsatz 143
Kontraktfrachten 187
Kontrollabschnitt 149
Kontrollturm 179
Konzern 195
Konzernentflechtung 195
Konzerngesellschaft 195
Konzernverflechtung 195
Konzernzusammenschluß 195
Konzert 221
Konzertzeichner 156
Kopfbahnhof 175
Kopfhörer 216
Kopie 186
Kopilot 180
Korb 137
Korbflasche 137
Kosten 139
kostenbewußt 121
kostenlos 149
Kostenvoranschlag 131
Kraftfahrzeugbenutzer 170
Kraftfahrzeugverkehr 170

Kraftfahrzeugversiche-
rung 162
Kraftstoff 171
Krankengeld 162
Krankenhauskosten 162
Krankenwagen 172
Krankheit 160
Kredit 143
Kreditabteilung 143
Kreditausweitung 142
Kreditbedarf 197
Kreditbrief 153
Krediteinschränkung 142
kreditfähig 143
Kreditfähigkeit 192
Kreditkarte 143
Kreditkaufvertrag 120
Kreditknappheit 142
Kreditkonto 143
Kreditkosten 197
Kreditpolitik 142
Kreditrahmen 142
Kreditverkauf 133
Kreditversicherung 162
kreditwürdig 143
kreuzen 151
Küchenrezepte 216
Kühlbereich 120
kühlen 182
Kühlschiff 185
Kühlschrank 117
Kühlwagen 172, 174
kumulativ 194
kündbar 142, 158
Kunde(n) 126, 139, 201
Kundenliste 130
Kundenverhalten 201
Kundenwechsel 147
kündigen 121, 143, 149
Kündigungsfrist 149
Kurs 155
Kursabschwächung 194
Kursanstieg 155, 194
Kursbuch 174
Kursrückgang 194
Kurswert 155, 195
Kurve 175
Kurzanschrift 208
kurzfristig 142, 147, 150, 196
Kurznachrichten 221
Kurzwerbung 203
Küstendampfer 185
Küstennähe 140
Küstenschiffahrtswege 188
küstenwärts 189
Kux 194

Ladebaum 186
Ladefähigkeit 181, 185
Ladegeschirr 186
Ladeluke 186
Laden 116
Ladendiebstahl 117
Ladenhüter 117
Ladenkasse 117
Ladenpreis 116
Ladenregal 117
Ladenschluß 117
Ladenverkauf 116
Laderaum 186
Ladewinde 186
Lager 139, 188
Lagerfrist 209
Lagergebühr 209
Lagerhaus 188
lagern(d) 209
Land 125, 126, 189
Landebahn 180
Landebrücke 188
Landegeschwindigkeit 179
landen 182
Länderspiele 216
Landpostdienst 206
Landstraße 172
Landtransport 168
Landungssteg 186
Landurlaub 184
Landwirtschaftsausstellung 129
langfristig 142, 150, 196
Längsseitlieferung 187
Lash-Schiff 185
Lasten 220
Lastenaufzug 191
Lastschriftzettel 149
Lastzug 172
Lattenkiste 137
Laufbursche 116
Laufgang 180
Laufkran 188
Laufplanke 186
Laufzeit 153
Laufzettelformular 210
lebend 224
lebendig 219
Lebenserwartung 161
Lebensmittel 117, 120
Lebensmittelgeschäft 117
Lebensversicherung 161
Lebensversicherungsanstalt 161

Lebensversicherungs-
verein 162
lebhaft 158
Lederwarenmesse 129
Leerverkäufer 156
leewärts 189
legen 188
Lehrfilm 224
Leibesvisitation 182
leicht 176
Leichter 185
Leichtergebühr 187
leisten 149
leiten(d) 196, 198
Leiter 125
Leitkarte 171
Leitung 207
Leitweg 207
Leseranalyse 200
Leserforschung 201
Leserschaft 200
Letztverbraucher 116
Leuchtturm 188
Leuchtwerbung 203
lichten 188
Lichtspielwesen 223
Lieferant 184
Lieferantenliste 130
Lieferanweisungen 139
lieferbar 140
lieferbereit 140
Lieferfrist 139
liefern 118, 138
Liefertag 139
Liefertermin 139, 168
Lieferung 137, 139, 141
Liefervertrag 133
Lieferverzug 139
Liegegebühren 187
liegen 157, 188
Liegeplatz 187
Liegetage 187
Liquidationskurs 156
Liquidationstag 156
Listenpreis 135
Litfaßsäule 202
LKW 170
LKW-Anhänger 172
LKW-Fracht 171
LKW-Transportunternehmer 171
Lloyds 160
Lloyds Schiffsregister 184
Lochkarte 210
Logis 186
Lok(omotiv)führer 175

Lokomotive 175
Lombardkredit 142
Londoner Teemarkt 156
löschen 189
Löschen 187
Löschhafen 187
Löschung 212
lose 177, 209
Lotse 185
Lotsengebühr 185
Luft 182
Luftbrücke 178
luftdicht 182
Luftdruckbremse 175
Luftexpressfracht 181
Luftexpresstarif 181
Luftfahrt 178
Luftfahrtversicherung 162
Luftfracht 181
Luftfrachtbrief 181
Luftfrachtbüro 181
Luftfrachtführer 181
Luftfrachtkosten 181
Luftfrachtraum 181
Luftfrachtsendung 181
Luftfrachttarif 181
luftig 182
Luftkissenboot 185
Luftkorridor 179
luftkrank 182
luftleer 182
Luftloch 181
Luftpost 211
Luftpostbeförderung 181
Luftpostbrief 181
Luftpostbriefsendung 209
Luftpostdienst 181
Luftpostleichtbrief 181
Luftpostmarke 181
Luftpostpaket 181
Luftpostsendung 209
Luftposttarif 181
Luftpostzuschlag 209
Luftraum 178
Luftschraube 178
Luftstewardess 180
Lufttaxi 178
lufttüchtig 182
Lufttüchtigkeit 180
Luftverkehr 178
Luftverkehrsdienst 178
Luftverkehrsgesellschaft 178
Luftweg 178, 181
lustlos 158
Luxusgüter 117

magnetisch 225
Mahnbrief 135
Mahnschreiben 135
Makler 122
Mangel 140
mangelhaft 137
Mängelrüge 140
Mannschaft 184
manuell 219
Marke 201
Markenbild 201
Markenprofil 201
Markentreue 201
Markierung 138
Markierungsanweisungen 138
Markierungsvorschriften 138
Markierungszeichen 138
Markt 127, 128, 145, 147, 155
Marktanalyse 128
marktbeherrschend 127, 195
Marktbude 127
Marktflecken 127
marktgängig 128
marktgerecht 128
Markthalle 127
Marktlage 128
Marktlücke 127
Marktordnung 127
Marktplatz 127
Marktpreis 136
Marktstand 127
Marktstruktur 200
Markttag 127
Marktwert 128
Marktwirtschaft 191
Maße 207
Massenaufgabe 207
Masseneinlieferung 207
Massengüter 185, 187
Massengüterverkehr 170
Massengutladung 187
Massenkommunikationsmittel 215
Maßnahme 179
Material 174
Materialfehler 140
Matrose 184
maximieren 119
Meer 187
Mehrfachdrucker 219
Mehrzweckwagen 172
Meistbegünstigungsklausel 165

Meldeschluß 180
Mengenrabatt 134
Merchantbank 144
Messe 127, 128, 129
Messeausweis 129
Messebesucher 128
Messegebäude 129
Messegelände 128
Messeleitung 128
Messeordnung 129
Metzgerladen 117
mieten 172
Mietwagen 171
mikrofilmen 224
Mikrofon 221
Milchgeschäft 117
Milchladen 117
minderwertig 141
Mindestkapital 193
Mischsendung 210
mitarbeiten 146
mitnehmen 172
Mitteilung 216, 220
mittelfristig 142
Mittelsmann 122
Mittelsperson 122
Möbelwagen 172
modisch 119
Mole 188
Monat 136
Morgenzug 174
Motor 172
Motorantrieb 172
motorisieren 172
motorlos 172
Motorrad 171
Motorradfahrer 171
Motorroller 171
Motorschiff 185
Müllabfuhrwagen 172
mündelsicher 145, 147
mündlich 130
Münzfernsprecher 215
Muster 130, 133, 141
Musterkollektion 130
Mustermesse 129
Muttergesellschaft 195

nachbestellen 118
Nachbestellung 131
Nachforschungen 210
Nachfrage 186
Nachfrageformblatt 210
Nachfrageformular 210
Nachfrist 153
nachhaltig 204

nachkommen 135
nachlässig 137
Nachnahme 140
Nachnahmebetrag 213
Nachnahmepaket 210
Nachnahmepostanweisung 213
Nachnahmesendung 210
Nachricht(en) 200, 216, 220
Nachrichtendienst 206
Nachrichtensatellit 206
Nachrichtensendung 221
Nachrichtensprecher 221
Nachrichtensystem 206
Nachrichtenverkehr 206
nachsenden 210, 220
Nachsichtwechsel 153
Nacht-Frachtflug 181
Nachzugsaktie 194
nachzugsberechtigt 194
Nahverkehr 170
Name 153
Namensaktie 157, 194
Namensobligationen 157
Navigation 184
Navigator 180
Nebengleis 175
Nebenkosten 213
Nebenstrecke 174
nehmen 118
Nennbetrag 196
Nennwert 155, 158, 198, 208
Neon-Leuchtwerbung 203
netto 134
Nettofakturenwert 134
Nettogewicht 137
Nettopreis 135
Nettoregistertonnage 186
Nettoverschuldung 145
Nichterfüllung 133
Nichtübereinstimmung 140, 141
Nominalwert 155
nominell 198
Normalpolice 161
Normalspur 175
Normalzeit 216
Notenausgabe 145
Nothafen 187
notierend 158
Notierung 155
Notizblock 130
Notruf 215
Nutzfläche 120
Nutzlast 181

Oben 138
oben 177
oberirdisch 177
Oberleitungsbus 191
Obligationen 156, 196
Obligationeninhaber 196
Obligationsschuld 196
obligatorisch 198
Obst- und Gemüsehandlung 117
Obus 191
öffentlich 142, 168, 169
Öffnungszeiten 117
OHG 192
Ölleitung 191
Ölpapier 137
Omnibusplakat 202
Order 151
Orderscheck 151, 212
ordnungsgemäß 211
Organisation 129
Originalverpackung 137
örtlich 143
ortsfest 175
Ortspostdienst 206
Ortsverkehr 170
Ortszustellbereich 206
Ortung 184

Packliste 137
Packpapier 137
Packschein 137
Packungsbeilage 202
Packwagen 206
Paket 210
Paketinhaltserklärung 165
Paketkarte 210
Paketpost 208
palletiert 181
Papier 153, 212
Papierabfälle 137
Papiersack 137
Papierwerte 147
Pappe 137
pari 158, 198
Parkfläche 120
Parkhochhaus 171
Parkplatz 171
Parteien 133
Passagierflugzeug 178
Passagierkabine 179
Passagierschiff 185
Paßvorschriften 180
Pauschalpolice 161
Person 198

Personal 180
Personenaufzug 191
Personenfahrstuhl 191
Personengesellschaft 192
Personenkreis 200
Personenverkehr 170
Personenversicherung 160
Personenwagen 174
Personenzug 174
persönlich 198
Pfandbriefinhaber 196
Pfandbriefmarkt 155
Phonopostsendung 208
Pier 188
Pipeline 191
Piste 180
Plakat 202
planen 182
planmäßig 181
Planung 129
Plastiksack 137
plastisch 219
Plattenspieler 225
Plattenwechsler 225
Plattformwagen 175
Platz 182
Platzbelegung 180
Plazierung 155
Polarroute 179
Portefeuille 147
portofrei 211
Portofreiheit 208
Postabonnement 209
Postabteil 206
Postamt 206
Postanschrift 208
Postanweisung 134, 149, 213
Postanweisungstelegramm 220
Postauftrag 213
Postauftragspapiere 213
Postausweiskarte 210
Postbeamter 207
Postbediensteter 207
Postbeförderung 206
Postbenutzer 208, 210
Postbezug 209
Postdienst 206
Postdienststelle 206
Postfachabholung 207
Postgeheimnis 207
Postkarte 208
postlagernd 208
Postpaket 210
Postschalter 207

Postscheck 212
Postscheckamt 149, 212
Postscheckkonto 149, 212
Postscheckzentrale 149
Postschluß 207
Postsendung 207, 210
Postsparbuch 213
Postsparkasse 149
Postsparkassenguthaben 149
Postsparkonto 149
Postverkehr 149
Postversandwerbung 201
Postwagen 174, 206
Postwertzeichen 207, 208, 209
Postzustellung 207
Präferenzzoll 165
Prämienanleihe 156
Prämieneingang 160
Prämiensatz 160
Preis 120, 128, 135, 198, 202
Preisabsprache 195
Preisanstieg 135
Preisauftrieb 135
Preisausschreiben 202
preisbewußt 121
Preisentwicklung 135
Preiserhöhung 135
preisgegeben 210, 211
Preiskartell 195
Preiskonkurrenz 204
Preisliste 130
Preisschwankungen 128, 135
Preissteigerung 135
pressen 139
privat 142
Privatanschrift 208
Privatunternehmen 191
Probe 133
Probeexemplar 203
Probenummer 203
probieren 131
Produktimage 200
Produkttest 200
Produktversicherung 162
Prolongation 153
prolongieren 158
Propellerflugzeug 178
Prospekt 195, 202
Protest 153
Provision 139
Prüfbescheinigung 130
prüfen 131, 149, 158
Publikum 200
Pumpstation 191

Qualität 141
Quarantäne 185
quittieren 211

Rabattmarkenheft 117
Rabattstaffel 203
Räder 176
Radio 221
Rangierbahnhof 175
Rangierlokomotive 175
Rate(n) 121
Ratenkauf 120
Ratenkaufvertrag 120
Ratenzahlung 120, 135
Ratenzahlungsvertrag 120
Rauchwarenmesse 129
Rechnung 134, 213
Rechnungsabteilung 134
Rechnungsausgleich 213
Rechnungsbetrag 134
Rechnungsdatum 134
Rechnungseinzug 149
Rechnungsfehler 141
Rechnungsformular 134
Rechnungslegungspflicht 192
Rechnungsnummer 134
Rechnungsposten 134
Recht 120
rechtsfähig 193
Rechtskraft 213
Rechtspersönlichkeit 193
rechtzeitig 205
redaktionell 205
Reederei 184, 189
Reedereibetrieb 184
regeln 141
Regenversicherung 162
Registerbeamter 193
Registertonnen 186
registrieren 146
Regreß 153
reichen 132
Reihe 135
Reingewinn 196
Reiseagentur 180
Reisebüro 180
Reisegeschwindigkeit 179
Reisende(r) 126
Reklamation 140
Reklame 200
Reklamedrucksache 202
Reklamefeldzug 204
Reklamepreis 202
Reklamerundschreiben 202
Reklameverkauf 202

Reklamezettel 202
Rektascheck 151
Reling 186
Remboursbank 144
Rembourskredit 135
Remittent 152
Renner 117
Rente 162
Rentenmarkt 155
Reportgeschäft 156
Reserven 145
Respekttage 153
Retourtarif 180
Rettungsfloß 178
rezessionsempfindlich 198
R-Gespräch 215
Richtpreis 135
Riesendüsenflugzeug 178
Riesenöltanker 185
Risiko 126
Risikoübergang 133
Rohgewinnaufschlag 116
Rohöl 191
Rohrleitung 191
Rollbahn 180
rollen(d) 174, 182
Rolltreppe 191
Ro-Ro-Fähre 171
rostend 176
RP-Telegramm 220
Rückfracht 168
Rückfrage 130
Rückgaberecht 133
Rückgang 155
Rückgriff 153
Rückgriffsrecht 210
Rücklage(n) 194, 196
Rückmeldung 210
Rückprämiengeschäft 156
Rückruf 215
Rückschein 165, 210
Rückseite 153
Rückstand 135
Rückstände 213
Rückstellung 194
Rückversicherungspolice 161
Rufnummer 215
Rufzeichen 215
Ruhestand 160
Rundfunk 221
Rundfunkdurchsage 221
Rundfunkgenehmigung 221
Rundfunkhörer 221
Rundfunkprogramm 221, 223

Rundfunkreklame 203
Rundfunksender 221
Rundfunksendung 221
Rundfunksprecher 221
Rundfunkübertragung 221
Rundfunkwerbung 203, 221
Rundreisetarif 180
Rungenwagen 175

sachdienlich 204
sachgemäß 137
Sachinformation 120
Sachschaden 160
Sachversicherung 160
Säcke 207
saisonbedingt 181
Saisonpreis 135
Salonwagen 174
Sammelanschluß 215
Sammelladung 187
Sammelsack 207
Sammelpunkt 171
Sammelumschlag 208
Sattelschlepper 172
Sattelzugmaschine 172
Sättigung 128
Satz 163
Satzspiegel 203
Satzung 193
säumig 158, 211
Schachtel 137
Schaden 140
schadenersatzpflichtig 163
Schaden(s)ersatz 141, 160, 210
Schadenshäufigkeit 160
Schadenserwartung 160
Schadensfall 160
Schadensfeststellung 160
Schadensregulierung 160
Schadensversicherung 160
Schadenszertifikat 161
schaffen 143, 146
schalldicht 219
Schallplatte 216, 225
Schalter 207
Schalterdienst(verrichtung) 207, 212
Schaltschrank 215
Schatzanweisung 147
schätzen 133
Schatzwechsel 147, 157
Schaubild 225
Schauermann 185
Schaufensterbeleuchtung 117

Schaufensterbeschriftung 202
Schaufensterdekoration 117
Schaufensterständer 117
Schaumgummi 137
Schaumstoff 137
Scheck 134, 151
Scheckfälschung 151
Scheckkarte 151
Schecknummer 151
Scheckzahlung 151
Scheingesellschafter 192
schicken 131
schienengleich 175
Schienenverkehr 174
Schiff 185, 188, 189
Schiffahrt 184
Schiffahrtsaktien 184
Schiffahrtsbehörde 184
Schiffahrtsgesellschaft 184
Schiffahrtslinie 184
Schiffahrtsnachrichten 184
Schiffahrtsstraße 184
Schiffahrtsverkehr 184
Schiffahrtsweg 184
schiffbar 188, 189
Schiffbauer 186
Schiffbauindustrie 186
Schiffbauauftrag 186
Schiffbruch 189
schiffbrüchig 189
Schiffsanschluß 174
Schiffsbedarf 184
Schiffsbesatzung 184
Schiffsbestand 184
Schiffsboden 186
Schiffseigner 184
Schiffsfracht 186
Schiffskapitän 184
Schiffsladung 186
Schiffsmakler 184
Schiffsmaklergeschäft 184
Schiffsmannschaft 184
Schiffsplatz 187
Schiffsraum 186
Schiffsraummangel 184
Schiffsregister 184
Schiffsrumpf 186
Schiffsschaden 186
Schiffstonnage 184
Schiffsverkehr 184
Schiffsversicherung 186
schlaff 177
Schlafwagen 174
Schlafwagenkabine 174

Schlauchboot 178
Schleppdampfer 185
Schlepper 185, 188
Schleppkahn 185
Schleppschiff 188
Schlepptau 189
Schleusengeld 188
Schleusenkammer 188
Schleusentor 188
schließen 133, 143
Schließfach 143
Schlußnotenregister 155
schmälern 126
Schmalspur 175
schmuggeln 166
schnellaufend 176
Schnellzug 174
Schnur 137
schöpfen 149
Schott 186
Schotterbettung 177
Schreibtelegraph 220
Schreibwarenhandlung 118
Schriftart 203
schriftlich 130
Schulden 192
Schuldsaldo 213
Schuldschein 153
Schuldverschreibung 156, 196
Schulfernsehen 222
schützen 120, 189
Schutzzoll 165
Schwankungen 1 81
Schwarzhändler 127
Schwarzmarkt 127
Schwimmdock 188
Schwimmkran 188
See 189
Seefahrt 184
Seefahrzeug 185
Seefracht 186
Seefrachtvertrag 186
Seehandel 184
Seekanal 188
seemäßig 137
Seemeile 186
Seeschiffahrt 186
Seetüchtigkeit 185
Seeversicherung 161
Segeltuch 137
Seidenpapier 137
Selbstbehalt 162
Selbstkostenpreis 135
Selbstwählfernverkehr 215

Selbstwählfelefon 215
Sendeantenne 221
senden 138
Sender 221
Senderaum 221
Sendestation 221
Sendung 207, 208, 209, 211, 221
senken 166, 197
Senkrechtstarter 178
Service 181
setzen 135, 182
Sicherheit 142
Sicherheitsvorkehrungen 179
sicherstellen 124, 144
Sicht 151, 154
Sichteinlage 142
Sichtwechsel 153
Siegelmarke 209
sitzen 176
Sitzplätze 180
Sitzungen 198
Skonto 134
Solawechsel 153
Sonderangebot 130
sorgen 182
sorgfältig 137
Sortierfach 207
Sortiermaschine 207
Sortiment 117
Sortimenter 122
Sozialversicherung 162
Spalte 203
Sparabteilung 143
Sparbuch 142, 213
Spareinlage 148
Spareinzahlungsschein 213
Sparkonto 143, 213
Sparvertrag 213
Spediteur 168, 184, 187
Spedition 184
Speditionsagent 187
Speditionsgebühren 168
Speditionsgeschäft 184
Speicher 188
Speisewagen 174
Spekulationsgeschäft 156
Sperren 213
Sperrholzkiste 137
sperrig 210
Spesen 136
spesenfrei 149
Spezialfahrzeuge 172
spezialisieren 154
Spezialshop 120

Spezialverpackung 137
speziell 205
spezifisch 165, 205
Spielfilm 223
Spielwarenmesse 129
Spirituosenhandlung 117
Spitzenpapiere 157
Spitzenwerte 157
Sponsor 203
Sportartikelgeschäft 118
Spot 203
Sprechbrief 208
sprechen 221
staatlich 191
Staatsanleihen 157
Stadtanleihe 147
Städtezug 174
städtisch 171, 191
Stadtpostdienst 206
Stahlbandumreifung 138
Stahlwerte 157
Stammaktie 157, 194
Stammkapital 193
Stammkunde 118
Standardqualität 128
Stapel 188
Start 179
Startbahn 180
starten 182
Statistiker 160
statistisch 160
Statuten 193
Stauer 185
Stauraum 209
steigend 158
steigern 126
Steigungen 176
Stellung 196, 198
stellvertretend 195
Stellwerk 175
Stempelmaschine 209
Stempeln 209
Stempelpapier 210
Sterblichkeit 160
Steuer 172
Steuerbord 186
Steuermann 184
steuern 182
Steuerruder 186
Stichprobe 201, 207
Stichprobenanteil 201
Stichprobenverfahren 201
Stimmrecht 195
Stimmrechtsaktie 194
stornieren 133
Stornierung 120, 131

Stoßkraft 200
Straßenbahn 191
Straßenbahnplakat 202
Straßenbrücke 175
Straßentransport 170
Straßenverkehrsgewerbe 170
Straßenzustandsbericht 216
Strecken 174
Streckenkarte 171
Streckennetz 178
streichen 182
Streichung 213
Streifband 208
Streifenanzeige 202
Streuung 200
Strichzeichnung 203
stromlinienförmig 176
Stromlinienzug 174
Stückauszeichnung 117
stückweise 119
Studio 221
Stummfilm 223
Sturmversicherung 162
Suchanzeige 203
suchen 124
Suggestivfrage 201
summarisch 207
Supermarkt 120
Supermarktkette 120
synchronisiert 224

Tabakwarenhandlung 117
Tage 134, 136
Tankstelle 118, 171
Tankwagen 172
Tara 137
Tarif 207
Tariffrachten 187
Tarifierung 165
Tarifposition 165
tätig sein 118
Taxe 171
teilen 163
Teilhaber 192
Teilhafter 192
Teilkaskoversicherung 162
Teilladung 186
Teillieferung 139
Teilnehmer 215
Teilzahlung 120
Teilzahlungsvertrag 120
Telefon 216
Telefonbeantworter 216
Telefonbuch 215

Telefondienst 215
Telefonie 216
telefonisch 216
Telefonleitung 215, 216
Telefonrechnung 215
Telefonverkehr 215
Telefonzentrale 215
telegen 223
Telegrafendienst 219
Telegrafenlinie 220
Telegrafenstange 220
telegrafieren 220
telegrafisch 220
Telegramm 219, 220
Telegrammadresse 219
Telegrammannahme 219
Telegrammbote 220
Telegrammformular 219
Telegrammkurzanschrift 220
Telegrammschalter 219
Telegrammschlüssel 220
Telexvermittlung 218
Termineinlage 142
Termingeschäft 156
Terminplan 200
Terminverkäufer 156
testen 118
Text 200, 203
Textabteilung 200
Texter 200
Textilmesse 129
Textilwerte 157
Tiefe 188
Tiefgang 185
Tiefgarage 171
Tiefkühlanlage 120
tiefkühlen 175
Tiefkühlschrank 117
Tiefkühltruhe 117
Tieflader 172
tilgbar 156, 158
Tintenstift 210
Titelseite 203
Tochtergesellschaft 195
Todesfall 163
Todesfallversicherung 162
Tonaufnahme(n) 224, 225
Tonbandaufnahme 225
Tonbandgerät 225
Tonfilm 223, 224
Tonnage 184
Tonspur 224
Totalverlust 161
Touristen 216
Touristenklasse 178, 180

tragbar 216
Tragfläche 179
Tragtasche 137
Trampschiff 185
Transit 168
Transithandel 165
Transitladung 168
Transitverkehr 168
Transitwaren 168
transkontinental 168
Transport 169, 170, 184
Transportart 168
Transportband 188, 191
Transportfahrzeug 168
Transportflugzeug 178
Transportgefahr 168
Transportgeschwindigkeit 168
Transportgewerbe 168
Transporthaftung 168
transportierbar 169
transportieren 169
Transportkosten 168
Transportmakler 184
Transportmittel 168
Transportschaden 168
Transportschiff 185
Transporttarif 168
Transportunternehmen 168, 171
Transportunternehmer 168
Transportversicherung 168
Transportvertrag 168
Transportvolumen 168
Transportweg 168, 171
Transportwesen 168
Trassant 150, 152
Trassat 152
Tratte 153
treffen 131
Treibstoff 171
Tresorraum 143
treuhänderisch 146
Trickfilmzeichner 224
Trocken lagern 138
Trockendock 188
Trockenfracht 187
Trockenstempel 209
Truppentransporter 185
Trust 195
Tube 137
Turbinendampfer 185
Turmkran 188

Überbringer 139
Überdruck 209
übereinstimmend 204
Übereinstimmung 132
Übergang 175
übergeben 120
Übergepäck 180
überhöht 135
Überlandverkehr 168, 170
Überliegegeld 187
Übermittlung 207
Übernahmeangebot 155
Übernahmekonnossement 186
übernehmen 144, 146, 147, 163
überprüfen 149
Überschallflugzeug 178
Überschallgeschwindigkeit 179
Überschrift 203
überschwemmen 128
Übersee 189
Überseebank 125
überseeisch 125, 126
Überseemärkte 126
Überseetelegramm 220
Überseetransport 184
übertragbar 151
übertragen 222
überweisen 135
Überweisung 220
Überweisungsscheck 151
Überweisungstelegramm 220
überzeichnen 158
überzeugen(d) 204
überziehen 143
Überziehung 195
Uferstraße 188
Umbruch 203
umfahren 172
umfangreich 126
umgeben 176
umgruppieren 176
Umhüllung 137
Umladegebühr 171
umladen 166, 189
Umladen 171
Umladung 166
Umlauf 207
Umlaufvermögen 196
Umleitamt 206
umleiten 176
Umleitung 207
Umrechnungskurs 211
Umrechnungstabelle 213
Umsatz 151
Umsatzsteigerung 116

Umsatzvolumen 116
Umschlag 166
Umschlagamt 206
umschlagen 166
Umschlagen 171
Umschlaghafen 187
Umschlagplatz 171
Umschreibungen 180
umstellen 118
Umstellung 175
umtauschen 141
unanbringlich 209
unbedingt 152
unbegründet 141
unbekannt 211
unberechtigt 141
unbeschränkt 198
unbestätigt 135
uneinbringlich 119
uneinheitlich 158
unentgeltlich 149
unerwünscht 198
Unfallversicherung 162
Unfallwagen 172
unfrankiert 209, 211
ungedeckt 145
ungenügend 209, 211
ungeordnet 211
ungerechtfertigt 141
ungesichert 156
ungültig 209
unkaufmännisch 198
unkündbar 158
unsachgemäß 137, 141
unsichtbar 123
Unten 138
unter 136
unterbringen 158, 197
Unterbringung 155
Untergrundbahn 191
unterhalten 143
Unterhaltung 221
Unterlagen 160
Unternehmen 127, 191, 195
Unternehmensberatung 195
Unternehmensforschung 196
Unternehmenshaftung 192
Unternehmensplanung 196
Unternehmenspolitik 196
Unternehmensverflechtung 192
Unternehmenszusammenschluß 195
Unternehmerfunktionen 196

Unternehmergewinn 192
unterschlagen 151
unterschreiben 151
Unterschrift 212
Unterschriftsproben 151
untersuchen 182
unterwegs 169, 172
Unterzeichner 212
untilgbar 156, 158
unverbindlich 130, 135
Unverletzlichkeit 207
unvorhergesehen 211
unwiderruflich 136, 154
unzerbrechlich 137
unzustellbar 140, 209
Ursprungssparkasse 213
Usowechsel 153

Valutenkurse 216
veranlassen 119
veranstalten 129
Veranstaltung 129
verantwortlich 197
Verantwortung 210
verbindlich 130
Verbindlichkeiten 134, 196
Verbindung 131
Verbraucher 120
Verbraucherhöchstpreis 116
Verbraucherverhalten 201
Verbrauchsgüter 117
Verbreitung 200
Verbreitungsgebiet 200
verbuchen 149
verderblich 119
vereinbar 207, 220
Verfalltag 212
Verfrachter 186
Verfrachtung 184
verfügbar 180
Vergleichsverfahren 192
Vergrößerung 203
Verjährungsfrist 212
Verkauf 117, 120, 128, 202, 208
verkaufen 128
Verkäufermarkt 128
Verkaufsabrechnung 124
Verkaufsanalyse 200
Verkaufsappell 204
Verkaufsargumente 204
Verkaufsbedingungen 130
Verkaufsfläche 120
Verkaufsförderung 200
Verkaufsförderungsmaterial 117

Verkaufsgebiete 195
Verkaufsgenossenschaft 122
Verkaufsort 201
Verkaufspersonal 120
Verkaufspreis 135
Verkaufsstelle 116
Verkehr 168
Verkehrsaufkommen 168
Verkehrsdelikt 171
Verkehrsdichte 174
Verkehrseinschränkungen 179
Verkehrsflugzeug 178
Verkehrsmittel 168, 169, 201
Verkehrsmittelwerbung 201
Verkehrsplanung 169
Verkehrspolitik 169
Verkehrsspitze 181
Verkehrsstau 171
Verkehrstauglichkeit 171
Verladegebühr 187
Verladekosten 184
verladen 189
Verladepapiere 187
Verladepreise 187
Verladerampe 175
Verladung 189
verlagern 169
Verlagsstück 209
Verlangen 154
verlängern 133
verlangsamen 175
Verleih 223
Verlust- und Gewinnrechnung 194
vermeiden 182
Vermerk 211
Vermittler 122
Vermittlung 215
Veröffentlichung 195
Veröffentlichungstermin 202
verpacken 169
Verpackung 137
Verpackungsmaterial 137
Verpackungsvorschriften 137
Verrechnung 151
Verrechnungskonto 143
Verrechnungsscheck 151
verringern 126
Versand 184, 207
Versandabteilung 139

Versandamt 206
Versandanzeige 169, 187
Versandauftrag 187
Versandbahnhof 139
versandbereit 189
Versanddatum 139, 168
Versandgroßhändler 122
Versandhafen 139, 187
Versandhaus 122
Versandhauswerbung 201
Versandkatalog 202
Versandkosten 184
Versandliste 169
Versandmarkierung 138
Versandort 168
Versandtag 187
verschaffen 148
verschicken 131
Verschiebebahnhof 175
verschieben 169
verschiffen 138
Verschiffung 184
Verschiffungsbescheinigung 210
Verschiffungshafen 187
Verschiffungskosten 184
verschließen 182
verschlüsselt 220
Verschmelzung 195
Verschweigen 140
versehen 140, 172, 182
versenden 138
Versender 186
versicherbar 163
Versicherer 160
versichern 162, 163
Versicherte(r) 160
Versicherung 139, 162, 163
Versicherungsantrag 161, 162
Versicherungsarten 161
versicherungsfähig 163
Versicherungsgebühr 210
Versicherungsgeschäft 160
Versicherungsmakler 161
Versicherungsmarkt 144
Versicherungsmathematik 160
Versicherungsmathematiker 160
Versicherungsnehmer 160
Versicherungspolice 160
Versicherungsprovision 160
Versicherungsträger 160
Versicherungsverein 162

Versicherungsvertrag 160
Versicherungswesen 160
Versicherungszertifikat 161
Versorgung 147
verstaatlicht 191
verstauen 189
Versteigerung 155
Versuchskampagne 200
verteilen 138, 154
Verteilerpunkt 171
Verteilfach 207
Vertrag 133
vertraglich 133, 198
Vertragsablauf 133
Vertragsbedingungen 133
Vertragsbruch 133
vertragschließend 133
Vertragsdauer 133
Vertragsentwurf 133
Vertragserfüllung 133
Vertragserneuerung 133
vertragsgemäß 141
Vertragsurkunde 120
vertrauenerweckend 205
Vertreter 161
Vertriebskosten 122
Vertriebsnetz 122
Vertriebsorganisation 128
Verwaltung 143
Verwaltungsrat 196
verweigert 211
Verzeichnis 206, 219
Verzicht 210
verzichten 151
verzogen 211
Verzögerung 207
verzollen 166
verzollt 140, 166
Verzollungsgebühr 208
Verzug 158
Verzugszinsen 212
Videorecorder 222
Viehwagen 175
vierrädrig 172
viertürig 172
vierzehntäglich 205
Vignette 210
Visavorschriften 180
Vitrine 117
Vollhafter 192
Vollkaskoversicherung 161, 162
Vollzahlung 195
Vollzugsordnung 207
von Haus zu Haus 161, 169
Vor Nässe schützen 138

Vorankündigung 130
Voranmeldung 215
Voranzeige 130
vorausbezahlt 210, 220
vorausplanen 118
Vorauszahlung 134
vorbehalten 132
vordatiert 151
Vorderdeck 186
Vorderseite 153
Vorfinanzierung 196
vorführen 224
Vorführung 204
Vorlage 151
vorlegen 149, 166
Vorliebe 201
vormerken 131
vornehmen 139, 143, 157
Vorortbahn 174
Vorprämiengeschäft 156
Vorrat 140
vorrätig 119
Vorratsbehälter 191
Vorratstank 191
vorschießen 143
vorschriftsmäßig 133
vorschriftswidrig 133
Vorsicht 138
Vorsichtsmarkierungen 138
Vorsitzender 196
Vorspann 224
Vorwahl 215
Vorzeiger 150
Vorzugsaktie 157, 194
Vorzugszoll 165

Wachspapier 137
Wachstuch 137
Wagenführer 191
Wagenmiete 171
Waggon 139
Waggonladung 174
Wahrscheinlichkeitsrechnung 160
Währungsumrechnung 213
Währungsvorschriften 180
Wandelanleihe 156
Wandelschuldverschreibungen 196
Wandzeichen 202
Waren 117
Warenakkreditiv 135
Warenangebot 116
Warenautomat 120
Warenbegleitschein 133
Warenbezeichnung 130

Warenbörse 155
Warengruppe 116
Warenhaus 120
Warenmuster 208
Warenprobe 208
Warenrechnung 134
Warensortiment 117
Warentest 117
Warenumschlag 118
Warenversand 184
Warenverzeichnis 130
Warenwechsel 147, 153
Warmfront 181
Warnmeldungen 223
Warteliste 180
Wasser 184
wasserdicht 137
Wasserfahrzeug 185
Wasserflugzeug 178
Wasserverdrängung 185
Wasserzeichen 209
Wechsel 134, 147, 152, 153, 154
Wechselarten 153
Wechselaussteller 152
Wechselbank 147
Wechselbestand 147, 152
Wechselbezogener 152
Wechseldiskont 147
Wechseldiskontierung 153
Wechselforderungen 152
Wechselgeber 152
Wechselhandel 147
Wechselmakler 147
Wechselmarke 153
Wechselprotest 153
Wechselrecht 153
Wechselschulden 152
Weckdienst 216
Weiche 175
Weitergabe 153
weitergeben 151
Wellenbrecher 188
Wellpappe 137
Weltausstellung 129
Weltpostkongress 206
Weltpostverein 206
Werbeabteilung 200
Werbeagentur 200
Werbeaktion 201
Werbeantwortkarte 202
Werbeargument 203
Werbeaussage 200
Werbeberater 200
Werbeblatt 130
Werbebotschaft 200

Werbebrief 202
Werbebroschüre 130, 202
Werbedirektor 200
Werbedurchsage 203
Werbefeldzug 200, 204
Werbefernsehen 203, 222
Werbefläche 203
Werbeflagge 209
Werbeforschung 200
Werbefunk 221
Werbegeschenk 202
Werbegeschenkartikel 202
Werbekampagne 200
Werbekosten 200
Werbekraft 201
Werbeleiter 200
Werbematerial 200
Werbemuster 202
Werbenummer 203
Werbepreis 202
Werbeslogan 203
Werbestempel 209
Werbetafel 202
Werbeträger 200
Werbeträgerforschung 200
Werbetrommel 204
Werbewesen 200
werbewirksam 204
Werbezeit 222
Werbezwecke 205
Werbung 200, 201
werfen 128
Werft 186, 188
Werk 135
Wertangabe 209
Wertbrief 210
Wertgebühr 210
Wertminderung 160
Wertpaket 210
Wertpapier(e) 145, 147, 155, 156, 196, 212
Wertpapierbesitz 196
Wertpapierbestand 143, 196
Wertpapierbörse 155
Wertpapierinhaber 196
Wertpapiermarkt 196
Wertpapierportefeuille 147
Wertpapierschalter 143
Wertsendung 209
Wertverlust 128
Wertzoll 165
Wettbewerb 202
Wetteramt 181
Wetterbedingungen 181
Wetterbeobachtung 181

Wetterbericht 181
Wetterdienst 181, 216
Wetterkarte 181, 222
Wettervorhersage 181, 216
Widerruf 131
widerrufen 133
widerruflich 154
wiedereröffnen 143
Wiederholungsanzeige 203
Wiederholungsrabatt 203
Wiederverkäuferrabatt 134
windig 182
Wirksamkeit 200
Wochenmarkt 127
Wochenschau 203, 224
Wochenübersicht 221
Wochenzeitung 202
Wohltätigkeitsmarke 208
Wohnwagen 172
Wolkenuntergrenze 179
Wortlaut 208, 220
WPV 206
wünschenswert 198

XP-Gespräch 215

zahlbar 132, 151, 163, 212
Zahlbarstellung 212
zahlen 118, 120
Zahlkarte 149
Zahlung 134, 135, 153, 213
Zahlungsanweisung 213
Zahlungsaufschub 135
Zahlungsdienst 212
Zahlungsempfänger 150, 152, 213
Zahlungsermächtigung 213
Zahlungsfrist 153
Zahlungsmittel 134
zahlungsunfähig 143, 158, 198
Zahlungsverweigerung 126
Zahlungsweise 134
Zähnung 209
Zeichentrickfilm 203, 224
zeichnen 158, 197
Zeit 169
Zeitschrift 202
Zeitungsanzeigenteil 203
Zeitungsbeilage 207
Zeitungspapier 202
Zeitzeichen 221
Zentralbank 145
ziehen 131, 146, 176
Zinsen 139
Zinsschein 195

Zivilflughafen 179
Zoll 166
Zollabfertigung 210
Zollabfertigungsschein 165
Zollabkommen 164, 165
Zollamt 164
zollamtlich 166
Zollauskunft 165
Zollauslieferungsschein 165
Zollbegleitschein 165
Zollbehörde 164
Zollbestimmungen 164
Zolldokumente 166
Zolldurchlaßschein 165
Zölle 164, 166
Zolleinfuhrschein 165
Zolleinlagerung 165
Zolleinnahmen 165
Zollerhöhung 165
Zollerleichterungen 165
Zollfaktura 134, 165
Zollflughafen 179
Zollformalitäten 165, 166
Zollfreiladen 180
Zollfreischein 165
Zollgebiet 164
Zollgebühren 164
Zollgesetzgebung 165
Zollhinterziehung 166
Zollinhaltserklärung 165
Zollkontingent 165
Zollpapiere 165
zollpflichtig 166
Zollplombe 165
Zollpolitik 165
Zollpräferenzen 165
Zollquittung 165

Zollrevision 165
Zollrückvergütung 166
Zollsatz 165
Zollschranken 165
Zollschuppen 165
Zollschutz 165
Zollsenkung 165
Zollspeicher 124, 165, 188
Zollstrafe 165
Zolltarif 165
Zolltarifschema 165
Zollunion 126, 165
Zollvergehen 165
Zollverhandlungen 165
Zollverschluß 124, 165, 166
Zollverwaltung 164
Zollvorschriften 180
Zollwesen 164
Zollzugeständnisse 165
Zubringerdienst 170, 179
Zubringerflugzeug 178
Zug 174
Zugabe 202
zugelassen 210
zugesprochen 220
Zugfähre 185
Zuggeschwindigkeit 174
Zugkraft 175
zugkräftig 204
Zugmaschine 172
Zugpersonal 173
Zugschaffner 173
zugunsten 136
zulässig 177
Zurückbehaltungsrecht 121
zurückerstatten 163
zurückgewinnen 198

zurücknehmen 141
zurückschicken 141
zurückstoßen 172
zurückzahlbar 158
zurückzahlen 148
zusammenarbeiten 197
Zusammenfassung 216
zusammenschließen 197
Zusammenschluß 195
zusammenstellen 147, 169, 176
zusätzlich 205
Zuschauerforschung 201
zuschlagfrei 211
zuschlagpflichtig 211
zusenden 131
zusteigen lassen 175
zustellbar 140
Zustelldienst 169
zustellen 220
Zustellgang 207
Zustellzeiten 207
Zuverlässigkeit 174
Zwangsversicherung 160
zweckdienlich 204
zweiachsig 172
zweigleisig 177
zweimonatlich 205
zweirädrig 172
zweitürig 172
zweiwöchentlich 205
Zwischenaufenthalt 179
Zwischenfinanzierung 196
Zwischenhändler 122
Zwischenlandung 179
Zwischentitel 203
Zwischenverkauf 131

Band I
Englisch-Deutsch
Balacron-Einband
Klettbuch 5181

Band II
Deutsch-Englisch
Balacron-Einband
Klettbuch 5182

Schöffler-Weis erschließt in zwei Bänden einen Wortschatz von etwa 180 000 Wörtern. Er bietet ein Höchstmaß dessen, was sich in einem Taschenwörterbuch überhaupt unterbringen läßt. Auch die Technik und Wirtschaft, der Sport und das Nachrichtenwesen werden in großem Umfang darin berücksichtigt.

Schöffler-Weis ist für jeden, der englische oder amerikanische Zeitungen oder eine Lektüre aus der englischen und amerikanischen Literatur lesen will, ein praktisches und zuverlässiges Hilfsmittel.